INTO THE
DANGER
ZONE

INTO THE DANGER ZONE

SEA CROSSINGS OF THE FIRST WORLD WAR

TAD FITCH AND MICHAEL POIRIER

The
History
Press

To the memory of all who fought and died in the Great War,
and to all of those affected by it, in commemoration of a
century's passing. You are not forgotten.

First published 2014

The History Press
The Mill, Brimscombe Port
Stroud, Gloucestershire, GL5 2QG
www.thehistorypress.co.uk

British Library Cataloguing in Publication Data.
A catalogue record for this book is available from the British Library.

ISBN 978 0 7524 9711 2

Typesetting and origination by The History Press
Printed in Great Britain

Contents

Foreword

By Hugh Brewster

'The "state of war" begins, in fact, at the pier,' wrote American passenger Will Irwin of his crossing on the *Lusitania* in early February 1915. Irwin's eyewitness account, just one of many included in this comprehensive history of the great liners during the Great War, seems tinged with naïvety in hindsight. The war had been under way for just over six months but daily life in the United States had not been much affected by it. For Irwin, the wartime precautions taken by the Cunard liner add a frisson of danger to an otherwise routine voyage. He describes the British naval cruisers that pass as 'monotonously waiting for something to happen'. Winter gales make it a rough crossing but Irwin believes the liner rolls so heavily because of 'certain mysterious and very heavy contraptions of steel she was not meant to carry'. And he suspects that some of the 'mysterious' passengers on board are engaged in 'pretty little spy games'. When they reach the Irish Channel, he records that 'tomorrow morning, escorted by a guide cruiser, we shall zig-zag through the mine fields into port'. Then, 'the least imaginative among us will realize that we are entering a world at war'.

Even the most imaginative of Irwin's fellow travellers, however, would likely not have envisaged a German U-boat dispatching the famous luxury liner to the bottom in eighteen minutes. Yet this would be the *Lusitania*'s fate only three months later. The shocking loss of 1,198 lives during the 7 May 1915 sinking caused outrage in Britain and America. With it came the realisation that the same industrial progress that allowed the creation of modern marvels like *Lusitania* and her sister *Mauretania*, ships that could convey passengers across the Atlantic in elegant comfort in just seven days, had also led to the horrors of modern industrial war. Two weeks before the *Lusitania* was torpedoed, poison gas had been released on the Western Front outside Ypres. Clearly, this was a war unlike any the world had seen before.

After the loss of the *Lusitania*, one might think there would be very few civilian passengers willing to venture aboard ships in wartime. Yet the first-person accounts so carefully selected by authors Poirier and Fitch relate stories of escape from a remarkably long roster of torpedoed ships – the *Arabic*, the *Hesperian*, the *Persia*, the *Sussex* and many others. The loss of the *Titanic*'s sister ship, the

Britannic, sunk by a mine while serving as a hospital ship in 1916, is detailed here, as is the torpedoing of the *Carpathia*, the liner that rescued the *Titanic*'s survivors. (Ironically, the *Californian*, the ship that stood by while the *Titanic* went down, also met with the same end.) In all, the authors inform us, there were over 5,000 ships sunk by U-boats during the four years of war and 15,000 people died as a result. Over one-third of all the men who served on the U-boats, nearly 5,000 in total, also perished. Yet, as the authors point out, the world had seen the potential of submarine warfare and German U-boats would be put to even more deadly effect during the Second World War.

An impressive array of photographs are displayed here, complementing the text and illuminating this outstanding chronicle of one of the lesser-known chapters in Great War history. For liner enthusiasts, naval history buffs and anyone interested in the First World War, here is an invaluable addition to their reference shelf.

Hugh Brewster
Toronto

Hugh Brewster is the author of fifteen books for adults and young readers. He has written several books about the *Titanic*, including *Gilded Lives, Fatal Voyage: The Titanic's First Class Passengers and Their World* (2012). Two of his books are about the Canadians in the First World War: *At Vimy Ridge* (2006) and *From Vimy to Victory*, which will be published in 2014.

Acknowledgements

Tad Fitch would like to thank: my co-author Mike for his hard work and for making the experience of working on this book a very positive and smooth one. Also, my wife Jackie for her patience, never-ending support, and editorial assistance as I spent many hours in virtual isolation while working on this book. Thank you to my father Jerry and brother Jason for sharing their interest and passion for history with me, and to my cat Gracie for her constant companionship and strong 'moral support' as I was working on this project. I also appreciate the support and enthusiasm that my family, friends and co-workers have shown for my work over the years. It means the world to me.

Mike Poirier would like to thank: first, my co-author Tad for taking on an idea and turning it into a reality with his vision, amazing organisation and research skills, and determination. Shelley Dziedzic for introducing me to the world of ocean liners, and Jim Kalafus for teaching me how to research history. Finally, thank you to my family and friends for their support – Cheryl Grayko, Brittany Bailey, Dylan Germano, Ken Tasho, Austen Bourassa, Mike Tullie, Bob Gordon & family, Eric Robichaud, Nick Maione, Mary Thompson, Frank Gaschen, Trish Verria-Mignella, Bob Bracken, Mike Findlay, Jack Eaton, Lori Grenier, Leighton H. Coleman III, Shawn Simmons, Doug Reed, Dan Hatton, Cliff Barry, Ann Jarosz, Paul Kloiber, Hal Corley, Karen Lewis, Paul Latimer, Brian Cordeiro, Eric Cimochowski, Jean Timmermeister, Bruce Drapeau, Phil Lebeouf, Joe Vuolo, John Wesley Shipp, Phil Hind, Anthony Cunningham and the Woodcock family. Also, the Johnson, Poirier, Bourassa, Wardyga, Bucka, Grayko, Simons, Sanquedolce & Nobrega families and my beloved Tina Bradbury.

Both authors thank the following individuals for their help and assistance, which proved invaluable to this volume: special thanks are owed to Steve Hall, without whose help and support this book may never have been published; Hugh Brewster for his assistance and for writing the wonderful foreword – we very much appreciate it; J. Kent Layton and Mark Chirnside for taking time out of their busy schedules to review our manuscript and share their frank thoughts and observations regarding it; Amy Rigg and the entire team at The History Press for your assistance and support, and for being willing to publish our work; Trevor Powell for generously allowing the authors to use items from his personal collection in this work; Demetrio 'Dimi' Baffa Trasci Amalfitani di Crucoli and his family for allowing us to publish the letters written by Angela Countess Bakeev, and Jill Capaldi for translating them from Italian; Neil Fotheringham for the use of Jacob Fotheringham's private account; the Lincolnshire Archives for allowing us to quote Harold Beechey's account; and Eddy Lambrecht for generously allowing us to use rare photographs from his outstanding private collection.

Many others supplied us with accounts or photographs for use, or support in general, and their help is greatly appreciated. These include (in alphabetical order): Mark Astbury, George Behe, Gavin Bell, William Brower, The Columbia Basin Institute of Regional History, Ioannis Georgiou, Martin and Jan Gombert, Charles Haas, Sam Halpern, Brian Hawley, Peter Kelly, Mandy Lenanton, Don Lynch, Kit Abbott Mead, Jenya Nesmeyanov, Phyllis Ryerse, Eric Sauder, Pierette Simpson, Tarn Stephanos, Craig Stringer, Kalman Tanito, Rich Turnwald, Geoff Whitfield, Russ Willoughby, Bill Wormstedt and Cary Young. Thank you to Gudmundur Helgason and the team at uboat.net for maintaining such a wonderful website and invaluable tool for researchers. Also, thank you to the Titanic Historical and Titanic International Societies.

If you contributed to this volume, and somehow your name slipped through the cracks and does not appear in the acknowledgements, we apologise. If you inform us of the omission, we will make sure that this is corrected in future editions.

Finally, despite all of the hours that we spent researching, writing and proofreading this manuscript, it is possible that some mistakes have managed to slip through. These mistakes are ours alone, and should not be attributed to anyone else.

Authors' Note: A Century Separates Us

As the end of the Edwardian Era loomed, shipping companies such as the White Star Line and Cunard Line were locked in a fierce competition for the transatlantic passenger trade, which was then at its peak. The competition for customers between shipping companies spurred the development of ever larger, faster and more luxurious passenger liners, the like of which had never been seen. Passengers were able to quickly travel between Europe and America in peace and high luxury. Optimism for the future and confidence in technology were at an all-time high.

The maritime industry experienced a great setback in 1912, in the aftermath of the tragic sinking of the *Titanic*. It did not take long, however, before new safety features and regulations, along with new innovations in technology and shipbuilding designs, led to restored levels of confidence amongst the public, and increased optimism for the future.

Few noticed the ominous clouds of discontent that were hanging over Europe, and those who did were often cast as alarmists. Tensions amongst the great nations such as Italy and France, as well as the empires of Germany, Britain, Austria–Hungary and Russia – all of which had been simmering since the balance of power in Europe shifted in the late 1800s, began to reach a boiling point. Militarism, imperialism, over-inflated senses of nationalism, and a series of ill-conceived alliances made Europe a virtual powder keg, waiting to be ignited. On 28 June 1914, the proverbial match was at last tossed on to this pyre. It happened when the Archduke Franz Ferdinand and his wife were assassinated by a member of the Black Hand.

This event started a chain reaction, giving Austria–Hungary a pretext to invade Serbia, leading directly to the outbreak of what was called the Great War. Aptly named, this unprecedented holocaust ended the lives of over 16 million people, and raged for over four years. As conflict engulfed Europe, Americans who were abroad began fleeing back to their homeland, trying to avoid the growing

Archduke Franz Ferdinand with his wife Sophie and children. (*Illustrated London News*, 1914/Authors' Collection)

dangers of war. Simultaneously, many Europeans, those who were willing and able to do so, attempted to relocate to safer locales. Because of this, the number of passengers on westbound journeys across the Atlantic swelled, while the number of passengers making the eastbound voyage to Europe shrank considerably.

As the scale and enormity of the conflict spread, many civilian resources and modes of transportation, including a significant number of transatlantic passenger liners, were withdrawn from commercial service, and conscripted into the war effort. The mighty luxury liners were quickly adapted to cope with the constant dangers of war: paint schemes were changed, portholes were blocked or painted over, and deck lights were blacked out to make vessels both less visible and, if spotted, to confuse the enemy. Decks designed for a leisurely stroll by passengers and public rooms designed for comfort saw astonishing transformations. They quickly grew cluttered with war materials and paraphernalia – and frequently with weapons – which the ships' designers had rarely envisioned or made proper provision for. In some cases, deck guns and defensive measures were installed to protect the ships against surface raiders or other enemy vessels. Aesthetics were cast aside in favour of practical uses of space.

In fact, on some voyages, the liners were more heavily laden with troops, weapons and supplies than they were with civilian passengers. At the same time, many ships that were under construction, and which had been intended for civilian use, were requisitioned by the military. Immediately upon delivery from the shipyards, they were put into service as troop transports, hospital ships and the like. Some were sunk before the war's end, and they never had a chance to fulfil their intended purpose. They were never fitted out with their luxurious fittings and appointments, and no passengers ever had the pleasure of journeying aboard them in peace.

The coming of the war also brought a new technological terror with it: the 'unterseeboot', or U-boat. The most advanced form of submarine yet developed, these craft would prove a very effective weapon for Germany, both from a practical and a psychological standpoint. In an attempt to blockade and cut off supplies to the Allied nations, Germany soon adopted a strategy of sinking any civilian and merchant vessels that were carrying troops or supplies in aid of the Allied war effort. At first, the German government observed what were known as prize rules, aka cruiser rules, a long-held maritime code of honour. Under this system, the submarines would first surface and warn crewmembers aboard merchant vessels of their intent to capture and search their ship; an inspection of the ship's cargo would follow, and if contraband was found, time would be given for the passengers and crew to evacuate. Only then would the U-boat sink the vessel.

Such a quaint set of rules quickly proved less than effective in such a fiendish era of warfare. Thus, on 4 February 1915, Kaiser Wilhelm II declared the waters around the British Isles a 'war zone', making any merchant vessels crossing through potentially liable to attack without warning. No longer would Allied vessels be subject to the pleasantries of prize rules. The sinking of neutral vessels and the deaths of American citizens on the *Lusitania* and other ships, along with the sinking of the *Sussex*, led to the still-neutral United States protesting and threatening to sever diplomatic ties. Germany, afraid of America's entry into the war, soon reimposed restrictions on submarine activity.

As the war and stalemate in Europe continued, the situation grew more and more desperate for Germany and the rest of the Central Powers. The Allied nations also began adopting more deceptive and effective submarine countermeasures. In response, and in an attempt to attain victory or force a favourable peace agreement, Germany declared wholly unrestricted submarine

Kaiser Wilhelm II.
(*Collier's*, 1917/
Authors' Collection)

warfare against her enemies and against neutral shipping in 1917, regardless of the consequences, or whether it would anger the United States. Under this unflinching new campaign, no ship plying the North Atlantic, whether belonging to Allied or neutral nations, would be safe from attack. All of this inevitably led to additional tragedies. Not only were the vessels sunk, but many civilian lives were lost as well. By war's end, fewer than 375 operational U-boats had managed to sink over 5,000 merchant ships, with a loss of over 15,000 lives. Even this astounding record of success – and its terrible cost in both lives and resources – proved too little to win the war for Germany.

A century now separates us from the opening volleys in the Great War, which later became know as the First World War. Yet the ramifications of the conflict shaped the remainder of the twentieth century, and continue to affect us a century later. In recognition of the centennial of the war's outbreak, it is the aim of the present authors to recount what it was like for both military members and civilians alike to experience voyages and crossings in a time of war and uncertainty. During those years, one's vessel was constantly in harm's way from any number of dangers, including not only U-boats but also mines, bad weather and enemy surface vessels. Attacks were frequent, and tragedy all too common.

While much has been written about the naval and maritime aspects of this war, this perspective of those events is a fascinating and little-explored chapter in the history of the First World War. We hope that the vivid first-hand accounts and narrative included in this oral history help the reader to step into the shoes of those who experienced the events. In doing so, we aim to properly honour all of those involved, and keep their memory alive.

Tad Fitch & Mike Poirier

1

The Dawning of the Great War, 1914

July–August 1914

It had been less than a month since the brutal assassination of the Austro-Hungarian Empire's Archduke Franz Ferdinand and his wife Sophie, during a visit to Sarajevo on 28 June 1914. Tensions in Europe were already high, and Serbian nationalist Gavrilo Princip's actions in the streets of that city would soon touch off a chain reaction that would lead to the First World War. Immediately following the tragic events, public opinion and sympathy was largely for the Austro-Hungarians.

The assassination began a month of frantic diplomatic efforts between the Austro-Hungarians, German Empire, Russian Empire, France and Britain, which was called the July Crisis. Following their own secret inquiry into the killings, the Austro-Hungarian Government, wanting to end the Kingdom of Serbia's interference in Bosnia, issued an ultimatum to them on 23 July, with compliance demanded within forty-eight hours. This ultimatum included a series of ten severe demands, with the intention of provoking war with Serbia.[1] Great Britain and Russia understood and sympathised with many of the Austro-Hungarians' positions but disagreed with their imposition of such a short timescale. Despite this, they advised that Serbia comply with the demands in order to avoid war.

The following day, Foreign Secretary Sir Edward Grey, speaking on behalf of the British Government, asked that France, Italy, Great Britain and Germany 'who had no direct interests in Serbia, should act together for the sake of peace simultaneously'.[2] On 25 July, Serbia agreed to eight of the ten demands in the ultimatum, rejecting two that they viewed as a threat to their ability to survive as an independent nation. This led to Austria–Hungary severing diplomatic ties with Serbia, causing the latter to begin the mobilisation of its military. The Russian Empire, not wanting its influence in the Balkans reduced, also began preparations for war.

Failing to accept Serbia's partial acceptance of their demands, Austria–Hungary declared war on 28 July. This set off a cascade of declarations of war, mandated by the complicated web of alliances between nations allied to each other, to support one another in times of conflict. On 1 August, Germany declared war on Russia, and on 3 August, they declared war on France, shortly after the French government refused a demand to remain neutral. On 4 August, following Germany's invasion of neutral Belgium for the purposes of using it to cross into France, Great Britain declared war on Germany. Continuing the chain reaction, Austria–Hungary declared war on Russia on 6 August, and Serbia declared war on Germany that same day.

The first battle of the war, the Battle of Liège, began in Belgium on 5 August. By that time, all of Europe was well on its way to what would become the most devastating conflict that the world had yet seen. Despite this, and unbelievably in hindsight, the outbreak of war was greeted with enthusiasm and excitement by many in Europe. Each nation thought that their respective forces would quickly defeat the enemy, and lead their homeland to greater glory and prominence. Nobody expected that the war would last long.

On the other side of the Atlantic, most in the United States supported remaining neutral at the start of the war, even though there was a natural Anglophile element inclined to support the British. Despite this, there was an aspect of sympathy in the American press and amongst the public for the Austro-Hungarians and Germans initially, although public opinion began to shift against them since they had attacked Belgium, a neutral nation. Opinion shifted further following allegations and accounts of atrocities committed in Belgium in summer 1914. Still, most strongly supported neutrality, and did not want to get involved in a 'European problem'. President Woodrow Wilson's administration pushed for a peaceful settlement to the conflict, while insisting that the United States remain 'neutral in thought and deed'.[3] Most Americans had no idea that war was imminent in the spring of 1914, and thousands of tourists and those travelling overseas were caught completely off guard when the conflict erupted.

This lack of concern is illustrated by a letter from an American passenger named Nellie, who was travelling home aboard the new liner RMS *Aquitania* during the last week of June and first week of July 1914. Writing to a friend named Rilla on 4 July, just six days after the assassination of Archduke Ferdinand, she made no mention of this event, or the rising tensions in Europe:

Dear Rilla just a few lines to tell you that we are having a fine time. I was a little sea sick but I am feeling fine now we had a fine dance on Friday evening so I feel kind of tired today but I am enjoying myself while I can. There are about 5,000 people on board with the news we had a storm Thursday night but we did not feel very much of it on this boat one would think we were in some

An example of a shipboard advertisement for a grand concert on board another Cunard liner, the RMS *Carmania*. Grand concerts were frequently used to raise money for charities. (Authors' Collection)

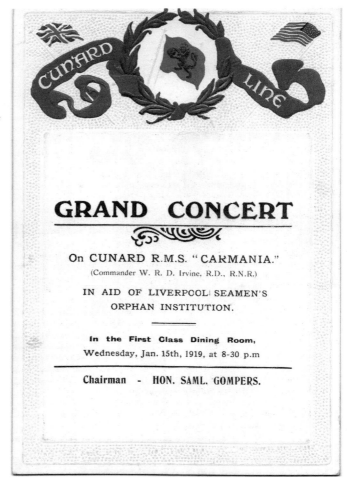

large hotel it is something grand. I would like you to see this ship it is worth a great deal to see we have lots of music every day we are going to have a grand concert tonight.

Saturday I wrote as soon as I got on board but was too late for the mail so I am just sending this short note will write you a long letter when I get home and settled down …[4]

Another American woman, travelling to Europe aboard the RMS *Oceanic* for a holiday, kept a diary of her travels. Jotting down quick entries between 4 July and her arrival in port in England on 11 July 1914, she also did not make any mention of the assassination or possibility of war in Europe. In fact, she appears to have been thoroughly enjoying her trip, and these concerns, if she had any, were in the back of her mind, as can be seen in the following excerpts from her diary:

An artistic representation of the famous White Star liner RMS *Oceanic* steaming along at night. (Authors' Collection)

July 4, 1914 (on board S.S. *Oceanic*)
A lovely day – a delightful send off – a most enjoyable trip so far …

July 5, 1914
Most gorgeous morning – had a fine bath – port hole open – it is so fine – enjoyed my breakfast a most enjoyable day … champagne was fine – port hole open all day & night.

July 6, 1914 (at sea)
Another beautiful day – thank God … very warm – no port holes open.

July 7
Clear – bright – less warm – had 2 mile walk before breakfast – sea was rough in afternoon – racks on tables – very high seas …

July 8
Clear in the morning – showers during day … sea still high … Saw smoke of a steamer on the horizon – in the afternoon … a brilliantly lighted steamer – signals passed between our vessels & the latter.

July 9

… sports on deck in afternoon … sea still high – port holes closed.

July 10

Last day at sea –Very sorry – winds high sea rough.

July 11

Steamer stopped in at Plymouth, Eng. 5.30a.m.

" " " Cherbourg – France 11.30" "

taken off by tender …

The next entry in her diary, dated 12 July, details her visit to Lisieux, France. Apparently busy, or distracted, she made no further entries until 4 August 1914, when at last, mention of the troubles in Europe found their way into her diary. Evidently caught off guard and frightened, she jotted down the following entry:

Aug. 4, 1914 (Paris, France)

Paris under martial law war between France, Germany, Russia, Serbia – people very anxious – provisions scarce.[5]

There were no further entries in her diary. It is these dire circumstances that passengers and crewmembers making the transatlantic crossing had to contend with. It was a great period of uncertainty. Nobody knew what was going to happen. Once war had been officially declared, the worries on travellers' minds were so palpable that they hung over their heads like a thick fog.

Accounts from some of the 'about 2,000' passengers who were travelling aboard the RMS *Mauretania* of the Cunard Line, following its departure from Liverpool, England on 1 August 1914, illustrate the mood and anxieties that travellers experienced after the outbreak of war.[6]

An American passenger who was aboard, apparently well-informed of the situation in Europe, expressed a good deal of apprehension about the trip home in a letter he wrote on 1 August:

We sailed, but! We do not know that we shall reach the states. War clouds are hovering over Europe. Germany and France have just recalled their big steamers: will England?

We are sailing on an English vessel, the largest [sic] and fastest of the English commercial fleet, an auxiliary cruiser. Will they call us in? Now here is the situation: England, France, and Russia form the 'Triple Entente'. Germany, Austria and Italy form the 'Triple Alliance'. Now Austria has attacked Serbia and Serbia is a friend of Russia. Russia will attack Austria, there we are! And of

RMS *Mauretania* prior to the war. (Authors' Collection)

course England will have to help out France and Russia. We are sailing in an English steamer, will they recall us for fear that she may be captured? Or for fear that they may need her?

The travelers all seem quiet enough but under the calm appearance does there not lurk a certain apprehension? Most of us have enough money to reach the States. Would it not be troublesome to have to go back to England? And if so what then?

I just heard a man talk, and he said 'they will not call us back. I have just had a chat with the Second Officer. We will get to the United States … '

Writing on 3 August, this same passenger had heard further news, which somewhat reassured him:

Just received news that war has been declared between Russia and Germany. England is still neutral. We are sailing out towards the States. For our comfort we can not but feel for the poor people who will have to go and fight. Our sympathy too goes out to all the travellers who … cannot get home as they had planned. Personally I am glad that I am among those who left …

We heard that President Wilson wishes to bring all shipping under the American flag. This would be a tremendous benefit to humanity. We all pray that this may done and that the commercial vessel may be allowed to proceed to land.[7]

Another passenger aboard *Mauretania* was Mildred Corson, an American from Hartford, Connecticut, who was travelling with Wallace Pierce, president of the import and grocer based S.S. Pierce Company in Boston, along with his son and daughter. She had sailed for England aboard the RMS *Caronia* on 14 July. During the latter part of July, Mildred and her party noted that there had been 'comparably little war excitement, the prevailing sentiment being that Great Britain would do well to avoid engaging in the struggle'.

The first four days of *Mauretania*'s voyage proceeded without incident. Until then, most aboard were ignorant of the fact that England had declared war on Germany during the voyage, and shipboard activities were maintained as if nothing was wrong. News was so scant, that some aboard speculated that the ship's crew was intentionally preventing anything that could be regarded as 'war news' from reaching passengers.[8] In fact, this was because the British Admiralty had taken over all land-based wireless stations, and had forbidden the transmission of any messages 'except those necessary in the mobilisation of the armies, movements of troops and assembling of warships'.[9]

This façade of normalcy began to crumble by Wednesday, 5 August. The passengers were dining quietly in the first-class dining saloon, when at 8.30 p.m., most of the lights were unexpectedly extinguished. Mildred reported that this gave rise to 'war rumours and conjectures of every description'.[10] Little did the passengers realise, but a half an hour earlier, the crew had received the following

HMS *Essex*. (Authors' Collection)

dire wireless message from the British cruiser HMS *Essex*, which was also in communication with the RMS *Cedric*, and ordered both ships to divert from their intended port of call in New York:[11]

> There are three German cruisers off the coast between Halifax and New York. Run into Halifax without delay.[12]

After receiving this message, Captain James Charles issued orders to show no lights, and the majority of lights on the vessel were either extinguished or veiled, and many of the portholes of the vessel were covered with canvas, or hastily painted black to block out light from the interior.[13]

Passengers, curious from the sudden change in circumstances aboard the ship, began leaving the dining saloon, only to find that the promenade deck was also closed in with canvas, and that the ship's bow and stern lights had been extinguished. When she heard of this, Mildred Corson initially believed that these actions were taken due to the fact that earlier, it had been raining, and there were heavy seas.

When she came out on deck at 10 p.m., Mildred found that the weather had cleared up somewhat, although there was a 'fog blanket'. A full moon occasionally broke through the layer of haze, illuminating the ocean. The *Mauretania* was sailing full speed ahead, and waves were washing over her forecastle. At several points, Mildred and others passengers believed that the ship was going to be swamped. The sea was so rough that water had sprayed as high as the boat deck, one of the topmost decks on the ship. Despite the haze, the vessel did not use her fog horn, which disconcerted some of the passengers, who feared that they would collide with another vessel, since the lights were also shut off. From 9 p.m. until *Mauretania* reached port on Thursday, the vessel reportedly maintained a top speed of 27.5 knots, higher than its guaranteed service speed of 24.5 knots.[14] This high rate of speed and seeming risk-taking gives an idea of how tense and dire the ship's crew viewed the situation with the outbreak of war.

Passenger George B. Winship, a survivor of the sinking of RMS *Republic* in 1909, gave a detailed description of the scene aboard as *Mauretania* abruptly turned course north towards Halifax, and raced through the rough seas. He also noted the vibration the ship was experiencing, a problem that both *Mauretania* and her sister ship *Lusitania* experienced at high speeds:

> The tremendous activity of the engines caused the ship to vibrate from center to circumference. It fairly leaped through the water, and for more than half an hour the sudden turn northward caused the great hulk to list to starboard side in a way very unpleasant to deck walkers. After the turn, however, she righted, and during the rest of the night, the good ship made rapid progress through a

choppy sea until this port [Halifax] was reached, when we learned for the first time that war had been declared against Germany by England. The cruiser *Essex* overhauled us early in the morning and escorted us to Halifax, as she later did the *Cedric* of the White Star Line.[15]

The American man who had written the letters expressing apprehension about the voyage and whether they would indeed reach the United States, wrote the following regarding the day's events:

What a night! At about 6 o'clock the sailors put up canvas all over the decks. No lights are permitted to shine. Everything is dim on deck you barely can see your way around. To the corners the passengers talk about the all absorbing topic of war …

A man standing on the 'A deck' of *Mauretania* takes in the ship's beauty. (Authors' Collection)

Writing later that night, he also commented on the vibration and rough seas:

> The *Mauretania* is racing as if possessed. We shake in our berths ... because
> of the excessive vibration. Everything trembles, long nerve racking oscillations
> adds itself to the vibrations. The sea has become rough but no one is sick ... I
> try to sleep but the effort seems hopeless.[16]

By 10.30 p.m. that night, those aboard heard that two German battlecruisers were
near, and possibly in pursuit of the *Mauretania*. Passengers reported hearing a
loud noise, and some believed that the cruisers had fired at them. This claim,
substantiated or not, was reported in the press in the following way:

> Those on board the ship knew somehow that two German battle cruisers
> were near, and at 10.30 o'clock a loud shot from one of them was heard.
> Another report was heard later in the evening. The names of the two German
> greyhounds who pursued the British steamship are not definitely known to
> any of the passengers, but they were undoubtedly two members of the trio
> which has been prowling about the coast of America for some months past, the
> *Dresden*, *Strassburg* and *Karlsruhe*. These are among the fleetest ships of the entire
> German navy, but they were evidently far outclassed by the English merchant
> steamer.[17]

Passenger William Neale, president of the Texas Cotton Palace Association, also
heard that *Mauretania* had been fired upon, although he did not see this for
himself:

> A report was current, and many passengers claimed they saw a flash of two shots
> fired at us from a German warship. This may or may not have been so; I did not
> see it, but it is entirely probable that it happened. Meanwhile, many of the ladies
> were extremely nervous, and a good many of the passenger list did not take off
> their clothes during the whole of Wednesday night.[18]

As the *Mauretania* arrived safely in Halifax at 10.30 a.m. Thursday morning, it
was greeted by a ferry boat crowded with cheering Canadians, and a brass band.
Mildred Corson described the scene as follows:

> It was the first time that a ship the size of the British leviathan had entered
> Halifax harbor, which is of splendid size for the reception of ocean-going
> giants. The band struck up 'God Save the King', and many of the passengers
> joined in singing the British anthem, thankful that the safety of their lives was
> assured ... At 5 p.m. the *Cedric* of the White Star line put in her appearance and

soon anchored beside the *Mauretania*. A few minutes later the *Essex* hove in with shouts of joy and prolonged cheering from all the seafarers on board the small boats in the harbor and the lusty throats of several thousand people who had gathered along the shore.[19]

The *Mauretania* was reported in the press as having completed its voyage across the Atlantic in four days and sixteen hours, which was allegedly its fastest crossing at the time. The crew bragged that the vessel would have completed the voyage 'fully six hours shorter if the steamer had kept right on toward New England and not headed for Halifax'.[20] In fact, the crossing had taken several hours longer than the reported time, far from breaking the ship's personal record. *Mauretania* had held the Blue Riband, the award for fastest transatlantic crossing speed, since 1907, and would hold the speed record for twenty-two years total before being usurped.

Passengers were kept aboard the *Mauretania* overnight following the arrival, a fact which did not sit well with them. Most were extremely anxious to head home or to their intended destinations, but the Cunard Line had to figure out how to transport the passengers there first, and what to do with the load of Royal Mail that they had been carrying. The company ultimately arranged for a special train service to New York, but some passengers had decided not to wait, chartering a tug boat to take them ashore that evening. Eventually, additional arrangements were made, and the passengers still aboard were sent on their way via train. It was reported in the papers that 'one Austrian and twenty-eight Germans' aboard were initially held as 'prisoners of war' following the arrival.[21] In reality, these passengers were simply interned until the Canadian Government could determine what to do with them. Thus ended the saga of *Mauretania*'s first wartime crossing.

Following this voyage, the British Admiralty informed Cunard that upon its return to Liverpool, the *Mauretania* would be requisitioned to serve as an armed merchant cruiser. They were also informed on 7 August 1914 that the RMS *Aquitania* was to serve in this capacity as well. *Aquitania* was quickly converted for its new role. Its luxurious fittings were removed and put in storage, and the vessel was armed and assigned to patrol the Western Approaches. However, this did not last long, as during its second patrol, the vessel was damaged in a collision with the Leyland liner *Canadian*. This, coupled with concerns about its high level of coal consumption led to the vessel being decommissioned and laid up until the following spring.

It was soon realised that very large passenger liners such as the *Mauretania* were totally unsuitable for use as auxiliary warships, owing to a lack of defensive armour needed to survive a sustained firefight, the massive expense of operating the vessels and need for frequent coaling, and their sheer size, which left them vulnerable to attack. This point was underscored by the sinking of two German passenger liners by the Royal Navy early in the war that had been similarly converted.[22]

Unlike the *Aquitania*, the Admiralty dropped their plans to convert *Mauretania* and returned the vessel to civilian service on 11 August. *Mauretania* made three round trip revenue-earning crossings between Liverpool and Halifax during the months of September and October 1914, but was soon taken out of service and laid up in Liverpool due to the declining number of passengers crossing the Atlantic, particularly on the eastbound portion of the voyages, due to the war. Its furnishings were removed and placed in storage while the Admiralty determined what the best use for it and the other large passenger liners not yet in service would be.[23]

At the start of the war, the Imperial German Navy kept its High Seas Fleet in safe harbours and out of direct conflict with the Royal Navy. While Germany had a modern fleet of warships, they did not have as many as the British, and wanted to avoid being lured into a direct surface battle between fleets. To compensate for this disadvantage in numbers, Germany attempted another tactic: on the same day Great Britain declared war, German ships were caught illegally laying mines just off the coast of England. Mines were also laid off the coast of Ireland and North Sea ports, to disrupt naval activities and shipping,

An Imperial German Navy sailor posing with a mine. (Authors' Collection)

and proved a deadly hazard.[24] Merchant vessels were quickly directed to stick solely to shipping lanes that had been swept for mines, which helped reduce the number of mine-related incidents.

From the quickness with which Germany began mining operations, it was gathered that they had dispatched their minelayers to sea even prior to Britain declaring war on them, anticipating that conflict between the empires was imminent. On the evening of 5 August 1914, the SS *Königin Luise*, a former steam ferry for the Hamburg America Line that had been specially fitted out as a minelayer, was spotted depositing its lethal cargo off the English coast by a fishing vessel. The crew reported what they had seen to the scout cruiser HMS *Amphion*, and soon, additional British vessels were heading to the location. The *Königin Luise* continued to lay mines, subsequently fleeing back toward neutral waters, and through one of its own minefields, hoping that its pursuers would hit them. The destroyers HMS *Lance* and HMS *Landrail* pursued the ship and were soon engaged in battle. The *Lance*'s guns fired the first British shots of the war. The destroyers were joined in their pursuit by HMS *Lark* and HMS *Linnet*.[25]

By this time, the *Königin Luise* had been badly damaged by extremely accurate gunfire from the Royal Navy vessels. Its speed reduced, and being unable to offer any further resistance, the German captain ordered his vessel scuttled, so that it wouldn't fall into enemy hands. As the crew were abandoning ship, the vessel rolled over to port and sank. It was the first German naval loss of the war. Forty-six of its crew of 100, many badly wounded, were subsequently rescued from the water.

The *Königin Luise*, which was fitted out as a minelayer during the war. (*The Illustrated War News*, 1914/Authors' Collection)

HMS *Amphion*. (Authors' Collection)

The *Königin Luise* sinking after its battle with Royal Navy vessels. (Painting by W.L. Wyllie/ Authors' Collection)

In a sad twist of fate, on 6 August, the *Amphion*, which had twenty-one of the rescued German sailors aboard, struck a mine that had been laid by the *Königin Luise*. The scout cruiser, ablaze, but afloat despite its back being broken, still carried some forward momentum, and veered back into a row of mines. The ensuing explosion detonated the *Amphion*'s forward magazine, and it sank in fifteen minutes. Debris sprayed the nearby vessels, injuring and killing some individuals, including a German survivor aboard one of the other ships. Approximately nineteen of the twenty-one rescued German sailors aboard died

British sailors, and German prisoners rescued from the *Königin Luise* were buried next to each other after being killed in the *Amphion* sinking. (*The Illustrated War News*, 1914/Authors' Collection)

at the hand of their own mines. In all, 148 British sailors were also killed. Just two days into Britain's involvement in the war, *Amphion* was their first naval loss, and the men who died aboard it were the empire's first casualties of the war.[26]

Meanwhile, in the absence of a current threat from the German High Seas Fleet itself, the British turned their attention to the German merchant vessels that were currently scattered at neutral ports overseas, or in various European ports. The British Admiralty feared that Germany was also planning on converting these ships into armed merchant cruisers. This would allow them to become commerce raiders, or at the very least, to move war supplies.

As a result, the Admiralty sent three *Monmouth*-class cruisers – the HMS *Berwick*, HMS *Lancaster* and HMS *Essex*, to sit outside the 3-mile limit marking America's territorial waters, near the entrances to neutral ports, including New York.[27] This is why the *Essex* had been on hand to escort the *Lusitania* and *Aquitania* into Halifax when they were told to divert from their course to New York. It was intended for the cruisers to blockade German merchant vessels in neutral ports, thus preventing them from leaving and being armed.

To assist with this quasi-blockade, the British Admiralty quickly requisitioned additional liners, such as Cunard's RMS *Carmania*, and converted them into armed merchant cruisers. Eight 4.7in deck guns were installed on *Carmania's* deck. It was redubbed the HMS *Carmania* and was put under the command of Royal Navy Captain Noel Grant. The British blockade proved somewhat ineffective, as on 3 August, the North German Lloyd passenger liner SS *Kronprinz*

Wilhelm, which had been in New York harbour, slipped out undetected. Its crew had blocked out the vessel's portholes and extinguished the lights, making it nearly invisible at night-time.[28]

The vessel, a former Blue Riband winner, sped away, and was commissioned into the Imperial German Navy. The crew then received orders to sail south toward the West Indies to rendezvous with the German light cruiser *Karlsruhe*.

Smoke billows from the funnels of the *Carmania*. (Authors' Collection)

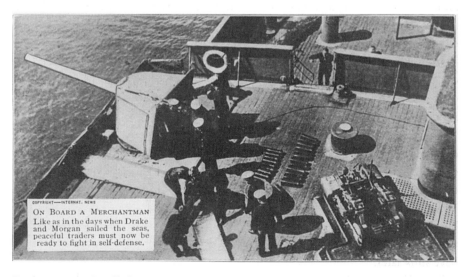

Deck guns were installed on many merchant ships during the war. (*Illustrated World Magazine*, 1915/Authors' Collection)

Karlsruhe. (Illustrated London News, 1914/Authors' Collection)

There, the ship would receive coal and be converted into an armed merchant cruiser. The *Karlsruhe* was already based in the Caribbean when war broke out, and proceeded to fit out the *Kronprinz Wilhelm* with two 88mm deck guns, a machine gun, thirty-six rifles and ammunition. *Karlsruhe*'s navigation officer, Lieutenant Commander Paul Thierfelder, was transferred aboard to serve as its commander. Several other crewmen were transferred aboard.

While Britain was dominating the action at sea, Germany was experiencing far more success on land. Under the Schlieffen Plan, which called for a quick and decisive defeat of France in the west, in order to avoid a two-front war, Germany was advancing through neutral Belgium. The goal was to quickly outflank the French Army. While the Belgians put up a spirited defence during the Battle of Liège, lasting from 5 August to 16 August 1914, buying time for the Allies to organise and prepare the defence of France, German forces continued pressing forward, and were soon pouring over France's border.

Back at sea, after a period of fitting out and training, the *Kronprinz Wilhelm* experienced a high degree of success as a commerce raider, proving the concerns of the British Admiralty correct. During the ship's 251 day voyage operating off the coast of South America, the crew managed to capture fifteen vessels: ten British, four French and one Norwegian. A Russian schooner was also stopped but subsequently released. Thirteen of the fifteen captured vessels were sunk by the *Kronprinz Wilhelm*, with a fourteenth vessel being rammed, and thought to have sunk later.

The *Kronprinz Wilhelm* overtook its victims using its speed and large size, ordered them to stop and then boarded them. The crew also lured in unsuspecting ships by pretending to be in distress, or a ship of a friendly nation. The vessels were usually caught off guard and, lacking adequate or any defensive measures, quickly surrendered. Once aboard, a boarding party would search the ship, and if nothing of value or military significance was found, they would be released. However, if the vessel held valuable cargo or contraband, the crew and passengers, who were treated with respect, would be transferred, along with their baggage, aboard the *Kronprinz Wilhelm*. The cargo and coal would then be confiscated, and the captured vessel sunk. The crew accumulated armament as their journey continued. Throughout its entire career as a surface raider, not a single life was lost.

Eventually, the *Kronprinz Wilhelm* was forced to make for the nearest neutral port in the United States, owing to dwindling coal supplies, and ill crewmembers. On 11 April 1915, the vessel pulled into port off Newport News, Virginia. Its crew was interned, and the vessel laid up in the Norfolk Naval Shipyard.[29] Upon arriving in the United States, First Lieutenant Alb Warneke conducted an interview with reporters, reflecting on the *Kronprinz Wilhelm*'s journey, and took the opportunity to sarcastically rub their successes in the face of Britain, and Foreign Secretary Sir Edward Grey in particular:

> We left New York Aug. 3 and put into the great big ocean … We were not a warship then, but three days out, in [sic] the Bermudas, we met the German cruiser *Karlsruhe*. We took from her two 3-inch guns which we mounted on the bow of the ship and took Lieut. Capt. Thierfelder, her navigating officer, to command our ship. We also took seventeen of the *Karlsruhe*'s junior officers and men, took on more coal and provisions and put to sea. We made for the South Atlantic and the first ship we encountered was a British ship *Indian Prince*,

The *Kronprinz Wilhelm* (right) alongside the *Prinz Eitel Friedrich* (left), in early 1917 while both vessels were interned by the United States. (Naval Historical Center Collection, NH 42416)

Sir Edward Grey. (*Collier's*, 1917/
Authors' Collection)

which we sank Sept. 4, 1914. From that time on we remained in the open, destroying the enemy where we might find her. I want to say that Sir Edward Grey, the British foreign secretary, has been kind to us and that if Great Britain had been organized as well as we were to patrol the South Atlantic we never could have remained alive these many months. Sir Edward Grey sent us those two big guns on our after deck. He sent them to us on the British *La Correntina* Oct. 7. When we got these four-inch guns we felt pretty safe. *La Correntina* couldn't use her guns because she didn't have any ammunition. We didn't give her battle because she was helpless, but after we took her guns and what of her cargo we wanted we put some bombs into her and down she went.

We made ammunition for her guns on board ship. Some of the merchant ships we sank with our own guns, some we blew up with bombs and in some cases we were compelled to ram the ships.

Sir Edward Grey was also kind to us in sending us coal, for we took on board from enemy ships during our voyage more than 20,000 tons.

We were a peculiar looking crowd until France came to our rescue with the uniforms we wear. We made the uniforms for all our merchant crew from cloth captured from the French steamship *Guadeloupe*, Feb. 23. The color is not exactly German, but the cloth is good. We wanted dark blue, but could find only this grey blue and so you see we are strange looking German sailor men today.

From the *Guadeloupe* we also got shoes, leather and thousands of dollars worth of things which were on their way for the French army. I tell you the sinking of the *Guadeloupe* was a bad stroke for the French.

When asked by a reporter about the German supply ship SS *Odenwald*, which was then interned by the United States in San Juan, Puerto Rico, First Lieutenant Warneke stated that it was 'the worst thing America had done … Why did you Americans not give clearance to the *Odenwald*? We heard all about it by our wireless. We had good wireless apparatus aboard all the time and Sir Edward Grey kindly sent us several new sets when we needed them'.[30] Warneke was referring to an incident early in 1915 where the *Odenwald* tried to break out of the harbour in order to resupply German U-boats, and American forces fired warning shots to get it to halt. Even though the United States was still neutral at the time, these were widely considered the first shots of the war fired by the nation's forces against any vessel of the Central Powers, and caused additional tension between the United States and Germany.[31]

Mines and commerce raiders aside, there were many other concerns and hazards for people trying to make transatlantic crossings in the early days of the war. Besides British passenger liners such as the *Mauretania*, which were making westbound journeys across the Atlantic when war was declared, there was the issue of passenger liners that were caught heading eastbound toward the war. One such vessel was the North German Lloyd liner SS *Kronprinzessin Cecilie*, which left New York on 28 July 1914, bound for Plymouth, England, Cherbourg, France and then on to Bremen, Germany.

Anxieties regarding the war were not exclusive to those aboard British liners. Being a German vessel, one which happened to be carrying over 10 million dollars worth of gold and silver in its cargo, Germany believed that the risk of the *Kronprinzessin Cecilie* being intercepted by British or French cruisers was significant, and on 31 July, ordered Captain Charles Polack to turn the vessel around, and head back to a neutral American harbour. The *Kronprinzessin Cecilie* was just 850 miles from Plymouth when this order was received, and immediately turned and headed west toward the United States. Crewmembers hurriedly painted the tops of the ship's four buff-coloured funnels black, hoping that from a distance, this colour scheme might lead to it being confused with the RMS *Olympic*, or another White Star Line vessel if all four funnels weren't visible.[32] Sewell Haggard, an associate editor for *Cosmopolitan Magazine*, happened to be a passenger on the liner, and later wrote an account of the voyage:

> The war scare was on, and naturally, the majority of her first cabin passengers being English and German, there was some speculation as to what would happen to the ship should war be declared … Persons familiar with Spanish-American war incidents recalled that ships leaving port after that war was declared were … released by prize courts. So speculation died down and the voyage became the usual uneventful trip across the Atlantic. There was a dance each night; English, French and German passengers fraternized in the smoking

room and expressed the hope to one another that a way out of the difficulty would yet be found. The weather was good …

There was a dance in progress on deck and there was the usual assembly in the smoking room. At a few minutes past ten some of the passengers were startled by signs that the ship was being turned around. They announced this discovery to others, only to be laughed at. At 10.20 Captain Polack entered the smoking room. He carried his huge bulk a little more erect; his face appeared to be a little more serious than usual.

'Gentlemen.' said he, 'I want your attention. I have an announcement to make. War has broken out between England, France, Russia and Germany and we are going back to America. We have plenty of coal and I think we will get back safely. I want the gentlemen to assist me in allaying the fears of the women'.

No one uttered a sound for what seemed to be a very long time. I was seated at a table with an Englishman, a Bavarian and a Greek. The Bavarian, a kindly-faced gentleman of perhaps fifty, was the first to break the silence. He arose – we all arose – he grasped each by the hand, the Englishman last, and as he grasped the Englishman's hand he said, very intensely, 'I am sorry, very sorry'.

Afterward, it was learned that he was Major General Kristof Kiefeber, retired, of the German Army. The Englishman makes a living selling war materials. After the captain left the smoking room an American approached him and asked if it were not possible to buy the ship, here and now, and sail under the American flag. The captain did not think this was possible, he said, and hurried toward the bridge. Before he reached there, he was hailed by an Englishman and asked if it were not possible to transfer the English passengers to the *Carmania* of the Cunard line, which was supposed to be near.

The captain thought this impossible also, and smiled and passed on. 'We'll keep as far away as possible from the *Carmania*' he shouted back. The captain had received his orders by wireless at 10 o'clock. They were brief, no waste of words. 'Turn back and make for an American port with all speed'. The decision as to a port was to await developments.

That the situation might become serious now began slowly to dawn upon the passengers. Did ever a greater prize sail the seas in time of war than the *Kronprinzessin Cecilie* with her $11,500,000 of gold and silver consigned to France and England? Were there any British and French warships near? Was it usual for British and French warships to sail up and down the American coast? If so, what were the chances of slipping by? And so it went.

No one could answer, but the questions were asked over and over again. But what of the bridge? What was going on there? The ship was 850 miles out of Plymouth when she turned back. She would have reached that port Sunday night or Monday morning. The problem confronting Captain Polack was to get his load of gold and human souls back to America without being overhauled by a French or English warship. There was no answer from England, it is true, but he did not know it.

He could not afford to send wireless messages because he would betray himself, but he could intercept. Every message … admonished him to be careful; they told him that French and English vessels were talking about that great prize, the *Kronprinzessin Cecilie* with her gold on board.

Friday night he considered himself reasonably safe. He steered far to the north out of the beaten path, but took no further precautions. Saturday the usual Marconi newspaper was omitted and at the lunch table each passenger found a printed notice that the electric lights would be turned out that night in order to conceal our identity from passing vessels, and that we must be content with oil lamps. In the afternoon the four smokestacks were painted black at the tops as a further measure of concealment. At dinner we found the windows in the saloon heavily curtained, also the smoking room. There were no deck lights. To make matters worse, from the standpoint of the passengers, Saturday brought a dense fog.

But the fog was to the liking of the captain. He sent the ship along at the best speed she could make through the thick weather and with the fog horn silent. There was small chance of him being seen through this black curtain.

Many passengers remained on deck all night and others retired fully clothed. They remembered the *Titanic* and they wanted to be prepared for emergencies. Sunday saw a great change in the ship's company. There was no hysteria, but something portentous could be even felt if it was not visible. Passengers tried to joke, but the attempt was feeble. They tried to discuss something other than that which most concerned them, only to return to the one topic.

Again Sunday night there was fog. The nerves of the passengers were on edge. A delegation ascended to the bridge and asked the captain to please blow the fog whistle and to carry the usual side and stay lights demanded by the laws of navigation. Otherwise, they declared, the women folk would not consent to go to their staterooms. Soon we heard the fog whistle sounding and when I made a round of inspection the lights were burning. Some passengers said the lights were out until they made their request. I cannot say whether or not that statement is accurate.

Meantime the captain was having other worries besides requests from passengers. The Marconi operator had intercepted messages from the French cruiser *Frient*, detailed to protect French fishing off the banks and from the British cruiser *Essex*. The enemy was somewhere in the neighborhood. The crew were showing the strain. The dining room stewards were abstracted and not as attentive as they were during the first days of the voyage, it was difficult to get a cabin steward, as they had other things to think about, it was not uncommon to see stewardesses in tears. They have brothers, sons, fathers, husbands and sweethearts who may be sacrificed in the war.

In the smoking room, there were no more cigars and cigarettes to be had and yet the voyage was only one day longer than the usual voyage across the Atlantic.

The men just seemed to smoke more. After the famine began those who had tobacco divided with those less fortunate. Two professional gamblers who were aboard were wiser than the rest. They scented the tobacco famine from afar and laid in supplies.

By Monday the attitude of some of the passengers bordered on indignation. They could not see why the lives of passengers should be subjected to such danger to save a merchant ship from an enemy, even if it did carry millions in gold. To them the peril to their lives was real. They could see that the fog was thick and they could tell that the vessel was making almost, if not her best speed. Was this safe seamanship?

A protest was written out and an attempt made to get the signatures of citizens of the United States. The first man approached replied that he would not sign it, and that if signatures were obtained he would start a movement for written endorsement of the captain, that he believed that the captain was doing his duty.

A canvass of the vessel showed that a majority of the Americans held the same opinion, and the protest was dropped. Some of the passengers, however, did take the matter up with the captain. His answer was that the passengers were his first consideration, that he would give up the ship rather than sacrifice them. But there was little or no danger, he declared. They were too far to the north, too far out of the course of shipping for a collision.

Monday night came and with it more fog. By this time the passengers were speculating as to what port we were headed for. The same question was being debated on the bridge. The wireless was telling the captain that vessels down around New York and Boston were trying to creep along the coast within the five-mile limit in order to be safe from seizure. This indicated to him that it would be unwise to attempt to make New York or Boston. He did not dare ask for specific information. He had to make up his mind on such fragments of information as he could grab from the air. Portland first came to his mind, but then he favored a less known port. He heard of Bar Harbor, of course, but he was not certain of the waters thereabouts. And here enters C. Ledyard Blair, of Blair Brothers, Bankers, New York. Mr. Blair's father, D. C. Blair, has a summer home at Bar Harbor and the sons had sailed the yacht, the *Eagle*, in these waters so often that he knows his way around there as well as he does in Wall street. Figuratively speaking, Mr. C. Ledyard took the helm, and Captain Polack was mighty glad to have him do it.

We were headed for Bar Harbor, but the information was confined to the bridge. We folk below were not even told to pack our luggage. Those who stayed awake could tell that something was in the wind. We were taking soundings every little while. Evidently we were running into some place that we were not quite sure of. The fog was thick, but we were not going fast, a most abnormal thing for the voyage. The fog horn was crying out every minute. Then daylight and the fog lifted.

Mrs. Howard Hinkle, of Cincinnati, and her daughter were awakened by the unusual doings. She got up and peered out of a port hole. She could see land. 'I do wish we would land at Bar Harbor' she said to her daughter. Mrs. Hinkle had a cottage at Bar Harbor. She took another look; the land round about seemed familiar. 'Why, it is Bar Harbor' she exclaimed. And so the treasure ship had found a safe port. The hour was 4.54 a.m. We had turned around at 10 o'clock on the Friday night previous and we had traveled 1,680 miles, fifty hours of it through fog. 'A thing which was of the greatest advantage to us', chuckled the captain.

Soon boats came out from Bar Harbor with newspapers and we read in them that we had been captured and were being conveyed to port, also that we were safe at Bremen. The German general – he of the smoking room incident – was leaning over the rail looking at the hills that seemed so inviting. 'Well, I am mighty glad to be here', he said, 'but I would rather have gone down with the ship than to have seen her captured'.

Later on, passengers caught sight of the captain on deck after one hour's sleep, all he had had in twenty-four hours. Of course they congratulated him, said many things that would sound funny in other circumstances. 'I thank you', he responded, 'and I, too, am glad to be home, but it could never have been done without the old man upstairs'.[33]

Having arrived safely in port, Captain Polack had the first opportunity to relax in several days. He released the following statement, commenting on the voyage:

The *Kronprinzessin Cecilie* after arriving safely in Bar harbour, Maine. (*The Independent*, 1914/ Authors' Collection)

We left New York on Tuesday, July 28, at 1 a.m. We were ordered back to America by wireless when about 850 miles off the English coast. The wireless was official from our company from Bremen … We immediately started back. I didn't know where to go, but caught a wireless from *Sayville*, L.L., and other ships telling that we were being watched by cruisers on account of the $11,500 on board consigned to England and France. Every cruiser from other countries was after this shipment.

We were at one time in communication with the French fishing cruiser *Frient* and the British cruiser *Essex*, but we managed to dodge them on account of the fog. We were able to send no news ourselves for fear of being located. We got news from the Long Island coast as far down as Norfolk that every ship was keeping within the three-mile limit and that we were being watched for, so we could not ask if the line to New York was clear for fear of betraying our position. We therefore come north. We did not want to go to Portland, as Bar Harbor was nearer and safer. At no time were we pursued by warships, as far as I know.[34]

After its valuable cargo and passengers were offloaded, the *Kronprinzessin Cecilie* remained in guard in Bar Harbour, Maine for six weeks, then was escorted to Boston, where it was to be interned indefinitely.

War paranoia was just as rampant in ports and harbours in the United States as it was aboard vessels at sea. There was much concern when the North German Lloyd passenger liner SS *Barbarossa* left New York Harbour unannounced from a pier near where the *Kronprinz Wilhelm* had slipped out on 3 August. The *Barbarossa* had been observed being coaled and provisioned that very same day, obviously in preparation for a quick departure. The vessel soon returned to the safety of the neutral United States, taking refuge in Hoboken, New Jersey, where it was interned. It was being widely reported in the press that German merchant vessels, concerned about British naval vessels lurking just offshore, were hugging the coast of the United States, hoping to stay within the nation's territorial waters.

A number of other vessels were still missing or unaccounted for. As a result, when the RMS *Olympic*, the sister ship of the ill-fated *Titanic*, arrived in port during the night of 5 August, from Southampton, England, it created quite a stir. The crew had been warned by the HMS *Essex* 'to look out for the enemy', and thus, the vessel raced into port ahead of schedule, with nearly all of its lights extinguished. Slipping past Fire Island in New York, witnesses could not distinguish which large passenger liner it was, which caused a momentary panic.[35]

One of the passengers aboard the *Olympic* was State Senator Henry Steele, of North Dakota, who was travelling with his wife Maude. He described the situation aboard the White Star liner as they rushed home from Europe:

The officers of the ship were plainly worried … as they had good cause to be, for it is a $12,000,000 boat. The passengers didn't relish the idea of being taken back to Germany, so there was little trouble about enforcing the order not to show any lights.

Every light in staterooms had to be hooded and the stewards went around constantly to see the curtains were drawn. When we were two days from New York we were met by a British cruiser, which I understand was *Essex*. It accompanied us the rest of the ways.

We went through Germany and saw nothing there to indicate war preparations, but heard a good deal off anti-English talk. Our way to England lay across the northern boundary of Belgium about twenty-five miles from Liège. In London we saw two train-loads of soldiers leaving for a practice camp, they said, but really mobilizing for war.[36]

Meanwhile, rumours circulated regarding a plot to blow up the Hamburg America liner SS *Vaterland*, which was then in port at Hoboken, New Jersey. The largest passenger liner in the world at the time of its launch in April 1913, the *Vaterland* had been in service for less than a year when war was declared. Not taking any chances, the rumours led officials to significantly increase security near the pier, which was reported in the press:

The German steamship agents here are taking every precaution, it was learned tonight, to prevent any hostile movement being carried out against their vessels in this port. The *Vaterland* of the Hamburg-American line is closely guarded by city police and private detectives at her Hoboken pier. It was admitted that the company's officials are adopting measures to frustrate any attempt to blow up the vessel. The German consul in New York today directed that all the French waiters on the *Vaterland* be discharged, and it is said this order will be extended to other German ships in port.

At the *Vaterland*'s pier tonight a powerful searchlight was turned upon every passing vessel in the Hudson, following it until it passed out of the vicinity of the company's docks. The *Vaterland* was being loaded with coal all day, but it was stated by the company that no move would be made to send the vessel to Germany, nor would the *Imperator*, now in Hamburg, leave that port.[37]

While the plot to destroy *Vaterland* never materialised, a safe return to Germany was rendered impossible by British naval superiority in the North Atlantic. Thus, the liner would remain interned in Hoboken for nearly three years. Its fellow Hamburg America liner *Imperator* was laid up in its home port of Hamburg to prevent it from being captured, or interned in a foreign port.

Back in New York, the Cunard liner RMS *Lusitania* was scheduled to depart at noon on Tuesday, 4 August 1914. Since the vessel would be sailing toward Europe, the number of passengers booked aboard it was greatly reduced, since most did not want to head toward a continent that had just erupted in conflict. Up until the last minute, there was a good deal of uncertainty and speculation as to whether the trip would be cancelled, and even if it wasn't, whether the ship would then be requisitioned by the British Admiralty and converted into an armed merchant cruiser.

At the scheduled departure time, Captain Daniel Dow had not yet received word on whether to proceed with the voyage, so he sent the chief officer ashore to the British Consulate to inquire about what they should do. Told to proceed as planned, Captain Dow ordered that all of the ship's lights be put out except for its navigation lights, and eventually, the *Lusitania* cast off. Just 200 passengers were aboard – far below average. Before departure, a large quantity of grey paint had been bought from New York vendors and brought aboard.[38]

One of *Lusitania*'s passengers described the late departure:

In utter darkness, save for a masthead and sidelight, we started on surely what must have been one of the most memorable sea trips of modern times. We passed the North-German Lloyd and Hamburg-Amerika docks, where the enormous *Vaterland* was lying, having been afraid to come out on August 1, when she was due to sail. She would, doubtless, have liked to inform the German cruisers that we had left port, but her wireless was controlled by American authorities. In the Narrows we passed the *Olympic* hurrying into port … All lights were now extinguished, even the masthead light, and the ship was in complete darkness.[39]

Another one of the small number of passengers aboard the ship was Richard Harding Davis, who was a journalist. He was very pleased to be travelling in a first-class suite:

We got off in a great rush, as the Cunard people received orders to sail so soon after the Government had told them to cancel all passengers, that no one expected to leave by her, and had secured passage on the *Lorraine* and *St Paul*.

They gave me a 'regal' suite which at other times costs $1,000 and it is so darned regal that I hate to leave it. I get sleepy walking from one end of it to the other; and we have open fires in each of the three rooms. Generally when one goes to war it is in a transport or a troop train and the person of the least importance is the correspondent. So, this way of going to war I like.[40]

Just minutes after leaving the pier, a very loud bang was heard below decks, causing a great deal of excitement. The noise came from one of the ship's four turbine engines, which had broken down. With only three turbines operating, the vessel's speed would be greatly reduced. This led to immediate speculation that the machinery had been damaged by a German saboteur, as illustrated by Herbert Corey, one of the passengers aboard, when he said 'Ten minutes away from the dock in New York, the low pressure turbine went to smash. Obviously it had been tampered with by some emissary of Germany while the boat lay at the pier'. Corey gave a dramatic account of this event:

> It was 1.15 in the morning when the *Lusitania* backed away from her pier in New York. To do so, steam was turned into the low-pressure turbine, which is used for reversing the propeller. 'Whang!' went the engine.
>
> There can be no doubt that it had been tampered with while the steamer lay at the pier. A screw the size of a five-cent piece once before played hob with this delicate engine. Someone had monkeyed with the steam ports this time. The evident plan was not to prevent the *Lusitania* from sailing, but to cripple her that she would prove easy prey for a faster vessel that might be lying in wait.[41]

The following day, Wednesday, 5 August, conditions were hazy, and the seas were rough. An unidentified vessel was sighted near *Lusitania,* and according to Herbert Corey, some aboard believed that this was the prophesied enemy vessel that the alleged saboteur had set them up to rendezvous with:

> That faster vessel – according to Captain Dow – was laying in wait. We were fifty miles off the coast … when she was sighted on Wednesday morning. Fortunately, she was at a distance estimated at six miles.
>
> 'I can only say that she was a destroyer, burning oil and that she chased us' said the officer on watch at the time. 'She did not run up a signal flag giving her nationality. She merely signaled to us "You are captured. Heave to!"'
>
> But we didn't heave to. Instead we ran as hard as a cripple chasing a pig. The sea was a bit tumbled, and in a minute a wraith of fog crept over the sea, shutting off a view of the presumed enemy. When it lifted, she was out of sight. Captain Dow had shifted his course, and eluded her.[42]

Another passenger described this same incident, but gave additional details:

> … we sighted a warship on our port quarter, and as we watched her intently, not knowing what her nationality was, we saw her swing round, and deliberately try to cut us off. At the same instant we changed our course and ran for it. She seemed to gain a little on us, but you could see the heavy seas breaking over her bows, and presently there was a puff of white smoke or steam, but we heard

nothing. Just then, the mist came on thicker, and we gradually lost her. We heard afterwards that the captain had wired to the *Essex* to come to us quick, and that the puff of smoke, which many of us had thought was a steam-whistle, was probably a gun fired. We also heard that she signalled to us to lay to, which order we declined to comply with.[43]

Everyone aboard was relieved once the unidentified vessel vanished over the horizon. Herbert Corey lampooned the efforts of the vessel to catch *Lusitania*, which was not able to travel at anything approaching her top speed due to the damaged turbine engine:

Captain Dow said she was a German destroyer. Everyone worried busily. By and by the destroyer was dropped by a steamer which could steam a scant nineteen knots in her one-legged form.[44]

On 6 August, the *Lusitania*'s crew finally utilised the grey paint that had been hurried aboard before the ship left port. Crewmembers painted the funnels and superstructure grey in an attempt to camouflage the ship. Richard Harding Davis described the scene:

We now are a cruiser and are slowly being painted grey, and as soon as they got word England was at war all lights were put out and to find your way you light matches. You can imagine the effect of this Ritz Carlton idea of a ship wrapped

Crewmembers hastily painting the *Lusitania*'s funnels grey. (*Illustrated London News*, 1914/Authors' Collection)

in darkness … I do not expect to be allowed to see anything but will try to join a French army. I will leave Bessie near London with Louise at some quiet place like Oxford or a village on the Thames. We can 'take' wireless, but not send it, so as no one is sending and as we don't care to expose our position, we get no news. We are running far North and it is bitterly cold.[45]

Davis gave another vivid account of the vessel's transformation, and the strange way in which the news of England and Germany being at war was broken to them:

When, on August 4, the *Lusitania*, with lights doused and air-ports sealed, slipped out of New York harbour the crime of the century was only a few days old. And for three days those on board the *Lusitania* of the march of the great events were ignorant. Whether or not between England and Germany the struggle for the supremacy of the sea had begun we could not learn.

But when, on the third day, we came on deck the news was written against the sky. Swinging from the funnels, sailors were painting out the scarlet-and-black colours of the Cunard line and substituting a mouse-like grey. Overnight we had passed into the hands of the Admiralty, and the *Lusitania* had emerged a cruiser. That to possible German war-ships she might not disclose her position, she sent no wireless messages. But she could receive them; and at breakfast in the ship's newspaper appeared those she had overnight snatched from the air. Among them, without a scare-head, in the most modest of type, we read: 'England and Germany have declared war'. Seldom has news so momentous been conveyed so simply or, by the Englishmen on board, more calmly accepted. For any exhibition they gave of excitement or concern, the news the radio brought them might have been the result of a by-election.

Later in the morning they gave us another exhibition of that repression of feeling, of that disdain of hysteria, that is a national characteristic, and is what Mr. Kipling meant when he wrote : 'But oh, beware my country, when my country grows polite!'[46]

Some of the messages received via wireless, combined with scuttlebutt aboard the vessel, proved to carry less than accurate information about the state of the war, instilling false hopes and concerns alike. Herbert Corey described some of the rumours, involving battles and victories that existed only in the minds of those who heard them:

The wireless news went perfectly crazy. We heard of a naval battle in the North Sea in which nineteen German ships and six British vessels went to the bottom. Captain Dow sent up a rocket from the bridge. In the midst of his gratulation he sounded a note of grief:

'Poor O'Callahan' he mourned. 'He went to the bottom in his flagship, the *Iron Duke*'.

Next day it developed that there had been no battle, no lost *Iron Duke*, no martyr O'Callahan. Therefore, the morning paper, which might have contained this cheering information did not appear. The … passengers … were left to play with their fears and surmises.

Upon the authority of the bridge the statement was made that some seafaring liar in New York had reported the *Lusitania* blown up and sunk with all hands. This was disquieting, to say the least. Not a man or woman on board but had friends in New York – and in London, where, according to bridge authority, the story had been reprinted – to which this fake meant the bitterness of death. But the use of the wireless was not permitted.

'We are under war orders' announced the bridge. 'Not a word may be sent by wireless'.

… We passed into the realm of the unreal. The moment that wireless news began to come in, we were treated to the wildest feats of surmise treated as fact the imagination can conceive. A battle was reported in which 30,000 Germans were killed – no wounded being reported – while 15,000 brave Frenchmen laid down their lives. Alsace and Lorraine had been regained. The Teuton hordes were in full retreat. England had sent an immense army to Belgium.

'If this is true' asked Frederick Roy Martin, manager of the Associated Press at New York, 'let me get in touch with my office. I can get the exact truth for you at once'.

'We are not permitted to use the wireless' was the reply. 'We can receive but not send'. [47]

The rest of the voyage, slowed by the difficulties with the engine, proceeded largely without incident. However, the atmosphere was far from normal, and it was impossible for passengers to ignore the fact that they were at war, as Corey described:

At night the steamer crept along without a light showing. Even her green and red lights were off duty. Her windows were curtained. Her interior halls were dark. One groped to find one's stateroom at night through gloomy passageways, colliding with shuddering stewards who spoke in whispers.

It was weird, an unusual experience. People who owned sensibilities began to feel them jerking. It brought home to them the fact that war is actually upon the seas – that after half a century of peace the privateer may again be regarded as a possibility, and that innocent people are exposed to the danger of capture as prisoners of war.

'Suppose we are captured?' asked Guy Standling [Standing], the actor, of the
British consul in New York, previous to embarking upon the *Lusitania*. 'In that
event, what will be my status as a British non-combatant?'

'Undoubtedly', said the consul, 'you will be exchanged – ultimately'.

… And so we sauntered along on the slowest voyage the *Lusitania* has ever
made – her log shows it – talking, worrying, whispering, lights out, dodging
every time a fishing smack's sail showed on the horizon, as nervous as a boarding
school girl at her first party. In the safe of the vessel was $6,000,000.00 in gold
(Note: That sum is vouched for by gossip only; no officer would confirm it!)
not to speak of thousands of dollars carried by individuals.[48]

Lusitania finally concluded her voyage on 11 August, arriving safely in Liverpool
at 10 p.m. The vessel had bypassed its usual stop at Fishguard, Wales. At first, none
of the passengers were allowed to disembark. Hours passed. The passengers'
tempers began to flare, and they demanded an explanation for the delay. The
response was simple: 'War!' Later, the official explanation given was that all of the
buoys in the River Mersey had been lifted, and since it was foggy, guiding the
Lusitania to the landing pier 'in absolute safety' was deemed impossible.[49]

Unlike her sister ship *Mauretania*, the *Lusitania* was not laid up. With most of
the other large passenger liners on the transatlantic route either requisitioned
for military use or stuck in neutral ports, *Lusitania* was the only elite liner left in
passenger service: The White Star Line's *Olympic*, due to plummeting passenger
bookings, would eventually be laid up due to costs and to prevent it from falling
victim to enemy action, the Hamburg America liner *Imperator* remained stuck in
its home port and the *Vaterland* was still interned in New Jersey.

With fewer passengers travelling the Atlantic due to the war, the Cunard Line,
with the backing of the British Admiralty, enacted cost-cutting measures, such
as shutting down the *Lusitania*'s No. 4 boiler room, to reduce coal consumption.
This effectively decreased the vessel's top speed by 4 knots to 21 knots, as it was
felt that the ship would be quite safe at that speed. The public was not informed
of this decision, which did not become widely known until well after the fact.

This seeming complacency in regards to the safety of the *Lusitania* was due
in part to the success of the Royal Navy in blockading the German fleet in
its home ports, and its effective measures against German armed auxiliary
cruisers. On account of this, the British Admiralty had declared the transatlantic
commercial routes 'safe' for passenger liners within ten days of the outbreak of
war, and *Lusitania* was allowed to resume its normal duties, so long as the number
of passenger bookings justified the costs of keeping it in operation.[50] Within a
month or two of the voyage that ended on 11 August, *Lusitania*'s funnels were
painted 'black', and by some point prior to 27 November, Cunard had dropped
her 'disguise', and the funnels were again painted 'red with black tops, the Cunard

colours', because it was felt that Germany no longer posed any serious threat to the ship.[51]

Unfortunately, these weren't the only instances of complacency on the part of the Admiralty, or indeed, amongst the command of the Allied nations. At the beginning of the war, few took the threat imposed by German U-boats seriously. While U-boats were the most advanced submarines yet designed, they were also susceptible to mechanical problems, and the Allied commanders viewed them as more of a danger to their own crews than they were to enemy vessels. Furthermore, the military worth of submarines had yet to be demonstrated on a large scale in war.

Since Germany's surface fleet was effectively blockaded by the British, it was perhaps inevitable that they would begin devising strategies for deploying their small number of U-boats against their enemies. At the beginning of the war, the Germany Navy had twenty-eight commissioned U-boats, plus sixteen under construction. Of those in active duty, *U-1* to *U-4* were not suitable for combat and were being utilised for training purposes, while an additional four were being refitted. This left a meagre twenty U-boats ready for action when war erupted.[52] This only reinforced the Allied view that U-boats posed little threat.

On 6 August, two days after Britain declared war on Germany, the latter sent a flotilla of ten U-boats north from their base in Heligoland to attack Royal Navy vessels in the North Sea. The primary targets were heavy and light cruisers. This first submarine war patrol in history was an utter failure. On 8 August, *U-9* had one of its engines break down and had to return to base. That same day, *U-15* spotted three British battleships on manoeuvres, and fired a torpedo at HMS *Monarch*, missing, and accomplishing nothing other than alerting the enemy to their presence.

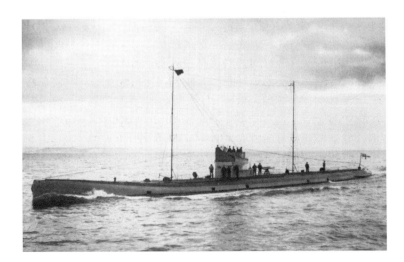

A U-boat heading out on patrol. (Authors' Collection)

The following morning, HMS *Birmingham* spotted *U-15* sitting on the surface, with no sign of lookouts on the conning tower or deck. The men on *Birmingham*'s bridge could hear what sounded like hammering coming from within the U-boat. Apparently, it had suffered a mechanical failure. The *Birmingham* altered its course, and as it bore down on the crippled U-boat, its target slowly got underway, but it was too late. The *Birmingham* rammed the submarine just aft of the conning tower, slicing it in two, and sinking it with all hands. A third U-boat from the flotilla, *U-13*, later turned up missing, and there was no clue as to its loss.[53]

On 12 August, the seven remaining U-boats returned to base, without having sunk a single Royal Navy vessel. Some were alarmed that the U-boats had demonstrated a range of operations much further than what was expected, leaving the safety of the Royal Navy fleet's unprotected anchorage at Scapa Flow, Scotland in question. Despite this, the ease with which *U-15* had been sunk reinforced the idea that U-boats were of little threat.[54] The fact that there had only been a single sinking by a submarine in the history of war up until that point – the CSS *H.L. Hunley* sank the USS *Housatonic* during the American Civil War on 17 February 1864 – likely contributed to this assessment of submarines as an ineffective weapon.

While the *Lusitania* had been completing her previous voyage to Europe, there remained many Americans abroad who were extremely eager to leave the war behind, and head back to their homes in the United States. One such individual was John E. Jacobson, a banker from Dazey, North Dakota. Jacobson was a member of a North Dakota commission that had participated in the presentation of a bust of Abraham Lincoln to Norway, as part of Fourth-of-July exercises being conducted in Kristiania.[55] He had travelled to Europe as a first-class passenger aboard *Olympic*. He was planning on touring Germany, and as fate would have it, narrowly avoided the outbreak of war by changing his plans at the last minute and returning to Norway. Jacobson was about to depart for Liverpool when he was informed that the *Aquitania*, aboard which he had booked his return passage to America, had been requisitioned by the British Admiralty to be converted into an armed merchant cruiser.

Jacobson altered his travel plans once more, heading to Bergen, Norway. However, this too changed when he learned that there were already 7,000 people at the port trying to gain passage to both England and the United States. He then learned that there was room left in steerage aboard the Scandinavian America Line's SS *United States*, which had arrived in Kristiania on 7 August 1914. Once word spread about these few existing spaces, there was a mad rush for the Scandinavian America Line's offices and pier. Jacobson stated that 'some Americans offered as high as $500 for steerage places, but without success … The company could have made a tremendous profit, but charged only the regular tariff rate'. It was reported that 900 passengers crowded into the steerage areas for the voyage.

Jacobson was one of the lucky few who was able to book passage aboard the *United States*, and soon was crammed below deck in the hold of the vessel for the eleven-day journey to the United States, a far cry from the comfortable trip home aboard *Aquitania* that he had been anticipating. Rough seas made matters worse:

> I was assigned to a place in the forward part of the bow ... The bow, I guess, is the most active part of a ship, for we were tossed up and down continuously for eleven days and the motion was awful hard on a man who has ridden nothing more rambunctious than an automobile on the North Dakota prairies for ten years.

Jacobson, although he described himself as 'the sickest banker in many days', was not about to complain. He was so thrilled when he finally arrived safely in the United States, that he said the conditions aboard the ship had been 'more than sufficient'.[56]

Another American who had been in Europe, Sister Carrie Bainbridge of Dodge City, Kansas, was also eager to leave the war zone. Bainbridge had been on a lengthy trip, passing through Ireland, Scotland, England, France and Belgium. She was in Paris when war broke out, and after heading back to England, booked passage on the Cunard liner RMS *Andania*. Like *Lusitania*, this vessel had been hastily painted grey in an attempt to camouflage it:

> We were in Paris when war was declared and the French people were wild with excitement. There were fights between the people wanting war and those who did not. We saw the French soldiers in their uniforms of bright red trousers, black coats trimmed in scarlet with white belts. As the French people refused

RMS *Andania*, as depicted on a pre-war postcard. (Authors' Collection)

to cash our travelers' cheques we had to hurry across the English Channel to
England, and a hard time we had getting out with the little French money we
had among us. It was due to Mr. Davidson's management that we did get out.

Going across the Channel we saw quite a number of gunboats moving
around. We had visited in Frosterly in the northern part of England but two days
when Johnny Bull [England] entered in the war game and then we thought of
home, but we didn't go until eight days later. We visited a sea resort, Bright[on]
Beach. Our booking on the big *Olympic* was for September 10, but the war
canceled this and we felt lucky to secure passage on the *Andania* on August 18.
Roy had to stand in line for a whole day before the steamship office to secure
these. Our booking was for the steerage, but Roy tipped the purser £2 (about
$10) and we were put in lovely staterooms above.

There was only one class over all the ship and the steerage had been furnished
up in first-class shape. Before the *Andania* sailed she was given a painting of gray
paint like that of battleships to make her invisible at sea. No lights were allowed
on the decks and heavy canvas curtains were used to keep the ship dark on the
outside. Two gunboats kept in sight for two days after leaving Liverpool. Our
course was far north and we sighted several icebergs on the trip home and some
heavy fog.

We landed at Montreal August 27 … [57]

Following its safe arrival in New York on 5 August, the RMS *Olympic* quickly
departed for Liverpool 'without passengers, mails or cargo'. Before leaving,
the vessel's formerly white superstructure had been painted grey, and her buff-
coloured funnels were painted a darker shade of grey. Additionally, all of the ship's
twenty-nine boilers were lit, including seven that were usually held in reserve,
allowing *Olympic* to achieve an average speed of 24 knots with the aid of the Gulf
Stream currents. [58] After arriving safely in England, the White Star Line, wanting to
maintain passenger service between Britain and America despite the war, arranged
for the vessel to depart from Liverpool rather than its typical port of Southampton.

Scheduled to depart for New York on 22 August, *Olympic* did not leave until
the following morning, due to a large troop ship blocking its egress. There were
at least 810 first-class passengers crowded on board, trying to escape the war,
the highest number the ship had ever carried. For comparison, on the return
voyage to Europe, there would be just eighty-seven first-class passengers. [59] One
passenger on the 23 August voyage to New York was Clare Benedict. Benedict
had heard rumours and stories of the supposed brutality and atrocities of the
German Army in Belgium, and took them with a healthy bit of skepticism:

At length the unhappy London days came to an end through the kindness of
our nearest male relatives, who, by a piece of good fortune which was almost

incredible, chanced to be in England for the first time in many years. They gave us one of their cabins on the *Olympic*, which was finally announced to sail on August 22d. We did not get off, however, until the morning of the 23d, owing to the sudden departure of a large troop ship, which had to have the right of way. It made us actually ill to look at the smart British soldiers and to think of what might be in store for them!

This was our last sight of that England which had been a second home to us for so many happy years, and, like our farewells to Austria and Germany, it cost us bitter pangs – pangs which the non-traveller cannot in the least understand.

The voyage, although devoid of alarming incidents, was, nevertheless, horribly uncanny. Everything was closed soon after four, blinds were drawn, iron shutters were pulled down, and even behind these, the electric lamps on deck were carefully darkened. Not a ray of light escaped from the great liner except what was absolutely necessary for navigation.

Meanwhile, behind the darkened portholes, most of the passengers indulged in their accustomed pleasures; they played cards, danced and flirted as if there had been no such thing as war either on land or at sea. The women arrayed themselves in costly dresses of the most extreme fashion, the men encouraged them in this, and went on betting on the run; together, they danced the tango in the saloons and even on deck; in short, they behaved, in our opinion, with revolting flippancy considering the tragic circumstances. And not only that – by persistently ignoring the agony of a whole continent, as well as our own actual danger, and by pursuing their petty pastimes in the face of these things, they missed an experience that could scarcely be duplicated …

… When we reached shore, our thankfulness was beyond all words, even the dock looked beautiful to us, and the custom house officers, instead of being enemies, became real friends. They treated us with the most sympathetic courtesy.

As we drove across the city and finally passed under the great Metropolitan tower, we drew a long breath of relief; humanly speaking, we were in safety at last after one whole month of continual anxiety … It had been one long agony, and now we were home again, far away from the terrible fighting, beyond the reach of hostile cruisers or airships, though not beyond the reach – alas! – of sickening heartache for all the suffering multitudes in stricken Europe!

In the course of the last month we had been forced to leap many difficult hurdles; the first was the making up our minds to leave Bayreuth, the second, our decision to abandon our luggage, the third, our reluctant, final departure from Germany, which involved breaking off all communication with many beloved friends. Hurdle after hurdle … confronted us in London – difficulties about money, serious problems in regard to necessary medicine from Paris, innumerable … complications in connection with our lost luggage – and over and above all these ... the dreadful hurdle of the English hatred against Germany. We surmounted these obstacles ... then came the voyage, which was one huge hurdle in itself.

Having leapt it, we drew, as I said a long breath − no more hurdles now, only rest and whatever peace we could hope for. But we were mistaken ... we beheld, looming up ominously in front of us, a cruel hurdle ... perhaps the worst of all. The American press had taken the English point of view, it vied with England, indeed, in vilifying Germany and the Germans. Receiving no direct news at first, except through English channels, it had, as a body, accepted the English version unconditionally. Germany and Germany only was blamed, all other belligerents were praised and believed in to the fullest extent. Belgians, Russians, French and Servians [Serbians] were brave and disinterested; Germans, on the other hand, were treacherous and brutal. Atrocities were reported as having been committed solely by the Germans, whereas the Allies were given a clean sheet in every respect. The Kaiser was responsible for all the bloodshed, the other European rulers were noble, peace-loving individuals.

Utterly exhausted and sick at heart, we gazed at this last hurdle − had we the strength to attempt it? A great wave of homesickness swept over us; for the first time, we seriously questioned our decision, had we remained in Germany we could at least have avoided this conflict, a conflict with friends, most of whom would inevitably follow the lead of the press ...

... we were surrounded by the same determined hostility, the same preconceived opinion was held almost universally ... In desperation, I seized my pen, one feeble protest I would make on Germany's behalf.

Americans are proverbially fair-minded, they do not follow the lead of any land − not even that of England − with blind confidence. Let them reflect upon Germany's record, her intellectual eminence, her splendid part in helping suffering humanity, her music ... her poetry ... her science and philosophy, her enlightened system of hygienics, her fine mercantile marine, which has carried so many of us safely across the ocean, her gallant army, which is not daunted by a whole world of enemies, her patient professors, who have laboured so unselfishly for the good of all mankind, her skilled and honest artisans ... her great artists in all lines, who have added so much to the joy of nations, finally, her princes, who from the Emperor to the obscurest ruler of the tiniest principality, are distinguished among European royalties for their culture, their devotion to duty, their clean lives. And now consider, are all these people scoundrels − are they liars and brutes, are they enemies of progress? Is it not conceivable that there may be another side?[60]

Ruth James, the wife of Kentucky Senator Ollie James, was aboard the *Olympic* during this same voyage. By happenstance, she had been in Berlin the day before

Ruth James. (United States National Archives and Records Administration/Authors' Collection)

war was declared, and was informed by American Ambassador James Gerard that 'she might do well to leave the country'. Soon they were aboard a train and were on the way to what Ruth believed was St Petersburg, Russia:

> Ambassador Gerard secured accommodations for us on the finest train leaving Berlin for the Russian frontier. We thought we were well on our way when the train suddenly pulled into Copenhagen. None of the passengers on board had been diverted. We never were told why it had been done. I remained in Copenhagen four days while awaiting a chance to cross to London. Finally I managed, with twenty-four other Americans, to get aboard a small freight steamer that drew but twelve feet of water. But even with that light draft the captain of the freighter was afraid to proceed at more than a snail's pace. He had been informed that mines had been strewn along the coast and through the English Channel. We managed to get through the mine fields without mishap, but everyone aboard the ship was extremely nervous.

Once in England, Ruth was able to book passage aboard the *Olympic*, arriving in New York on 29 August. Newspapers reported that there were '1,772' passengers aboard the ship, and that 'nearly all were Americans'.[61] On the return trip to Liverpool, there were just eighty-seven first-class passengers, holding the pattern of there being a larger number of passengers heading westbound away from the war aboard liners, and a very low number of passenger bookings on the eastbound crossings back to Europe. Despite the falling number of bookings, the *Olympic* remained in commercial service for a bit longer. During its last crossing on 21 October 1914, *Olympic* departed New York for Glasgow, Scotland, with just 153 passengers aboard.

On the sixth day of the voyage, 27 October, the *Olympic* was passing near Lough Swilly off the north coast of Ireland, and received a distress call from the British battleship HMS *Audacious*. The *Audacious* had struck a German mine off Tory Island, and was taking on water. Once the stricken battleship was sighted, *Olympic*'s captain, Herbert Haddock, ordered his vessel stopped and his crew to man the lifeboats.

In an organised fashion and without panic or hesitation, the *Olympic's* crewmembers, professional seamen, firemen and stewards alike, manned the boats, and rowed through the rough seas over to the *Audacious*, took off as many of her crew as they could safely manage and landed them aboard the *Olympic*. Two-hundred and fifty of the battleship's crewmembers were saved this way, with the rest being taken off by Royal Navy vessels. A small number remained aboard to try saving their ship. The *Olympic* joined in one of the three attempts at towing the *Audacious* to safety, but increasingly rough seas and darkening skies made this task near impossible. Soon, the ship's quarterdeck became awash. The remaining crewmen were evacuated, and just hours after *Olympic* departed for Lough Swilly, the *Audacious* capsized, the magazine detonated in a 'tremendous explosion', and the ship sank stern-first.

Due to the heroic efforts of the *Olympic's* crew, only one person died in the incident, a crewmember aboard the HMS *Liverpool*, who was killed by flying debris. Fearing that the sinking would harm morale, the British Government and Admiralty attempted to keep it a secret, the *Olympic* not being allowed to proceed to Belfast until 2 November, where her passengers eventually disembarked. Despite the British Government's best efforts, the details of the sinking leaked out.[62]

Following this voyage, the White Star Line withdrew *Olympic* from service, due to the reduced demand in bookings, and the threat posed by mines and submarines. The ship was then laid up in Belfast. Other White Star vessels such as RMS *Baltic* and *Adriatic* accommodated the reduced number of passenger crossings as the year drew to a close.[63]

RMS *Adriatic*. (Authors' Collection)

Passengers playing shuffleboard on the deck
of the *Adriatic* in 1914. (Authors' Collection)

September–December 1914

By September 1914, Britain was still maintaining its naval superiority over
Germany in the North Atlantic. This dominance was reinforced on 28 August
by their victory in the First Battle of Heligoland Bight, the first naval surface
battle of the war. The battle consisted of the Royal Navy dispatching a fleet of
destroyers, cruisers and submarines to ambush Imperial German Navy destroyers
during their regular daily patrols near the German coast. Catching their enemies
by surprise, three German light cruisers and one destroyer were sunk, with three
more light cruisers being damaged. German casualties consisted of 712 killed,
530 wounded, and 336 taken prisoner. No British vessels were sunk in the
action, although one light cruiser and three destroyers sustained damage. Overall,
British casualties consisted of just thirty-five men killed, and forty wounded. This
outcome led Kaiser Wilhelm II and the German Government to further restrict
the actions of the High Seas Fleet, ordering them to remain in port, and to avoid
any actions that may place them in harm's way from superior forces.[64]

While Germany's surface fleet could make little headway against the Royal
Navy, they were about to make the British regret their assessment that U-boats
were of little threat. On 5 September, *U-21*, commanded by Kapitänleutnant

Otto Hersing, spotted the HMS *Pathfinder*, a British scout cruiser patrolling off the coast of Scotland. A single torpedo was fired at the vessel. Lookouts aboard the *Pathfinder* spotted the torpedo wake heading toward their ship at a range of 2,000 yards and the officer on watch took evasive action, but to no avail.

The torpedo struck *Pathfinder* beneath its bridge and exploded, triggering a chain reaction that detonated the ship's magazine in a massive secondary explosion. The forward structure of the ship disintegrated. The ship sank in around five minutes, taking all but eighteen of the 277 crewmembers aboard with it.[65] The explosion was so massive that it was easily seen from land. One man on shore, Aldous Huxley, described the explosion in a letter to his father, sent on 14 September 1914:

> I dare say Julian told you that we actually saw the *Pathfinder* explosion – a great white cloud with its foot in sea. The St. Abbs' lifeboat came in with the most appalling accounts of the scene. There was not a piece of wood, they said, big enough to float a man – and over acres the sea was covered with fragments – human and otherwise. They brought back a sailor's cap with half a man's head inside it. The explosion must have been frightful.[66]

Kapitänlcutnant Hersing, the commander of *U-21*, recorded his thoughts on the sinking in his log, after his submarine became the first since the American Civil War to sink an enemy vessel. It also became the first to sink an enemy ship with a submarine-launched, self-propelled torpedo. His words were ominous, and accurately predicted the course that the war would take:

U-21 (left) and *U-22* (right) passing the coast of Laboe, Germany. (Authors' Collection)

I believe I have shed the first blood using submarines within this war ... My men are in great spirits because of our victory. I have spoken to many of them and they feel as if they are immortal ... Though High Command believes this will be a swift and honourable war, I think otherwise. The recent enemies that we have encountered show that it will be a bloody and deadly war.[67]

While the sinking of the *Pathfinder* was a wake-up call to the British Admiralty, an even more tragic incident a few weeks later would shatter all doubt that remained about the threat posed by U-boats.

Also early in the month, there was a mishap that would claim the first Allied passenger liner of the war. On 8 September, the HMS *Oceanic* was patrolling the waters around the Shetland Islands. The former 'pride of the White Star Line' had been requisitioned at the beginning of the war and converted into an armed merchant cruiser, complete with 4.7in deck guns and a compliment of Royal Marines. The ship was commissioned on 8 August and placed under the command of Royal Navy Captain William Slayter, who had orders to stop and search any merchant vessel suspected of carrying supplies for Germany or its allies, as part of the blockade of that nation. The vessel's merchant master, Captain Henry Smith, also remained aboard the *Oceanic*. Essentially, the ship had two captains, which appears to have caused some confusion.

The *Oceanic* was zigzagging to avoid any potential attacks from U-boats, and this manoeuvring made accurate navigation difficult. Unbeknownst to the crew, they were approximately 14 miles off-course, and were approaching the notorious Shaalds of Foula. This reef came within a few feet of the surface of the water, and was easily visible as a line of white water when there was significant wave action. However, on a flat calm day such as 8 September, no sign of its presence could be detected.

During the morning watch, Captain Smith was uneasy with the vessel's course, and altered its heading back out to sea. Captain Slayter felt the change in course and reappeared on the bridge, countermanding Smith's orders, manifesting the difficulties of the ship having two masters. It turned out to be an ill-informed decision, as within moments the ship grounded itself on the Shaalds with a sickening crunch, and was unable to be moved. Several vessels attempted to tow the *Oceanic* off the reef, to no avail.

With the *Oceanic* hopelessly stranded and its bottom torn out, the order to abandon ship was given. Over 600 men had to be evacuated, including a German prisoner 'who thought it all a great joke'. One of the *Oceanic*'s officers was Lieutenant Charles H. Lightoller, who had been second officer aboard RMS *Titanic*. For the third time in his career, he found himself loading and lowering lifeboats aboard a doomed ship. Lightoller, having served aboard *Oceanic* on more than one occasion before the war, had a special affinity for the ship, and was greatly saddened by its impending loss. Author Patrick Stenson aptly described this in his biography on Lightoller:

> … as he sat at the tiller of his bobbing lifeboat … Lightoller was … overcome by an urge to have just one more look around his old love … He had his men row back alongside the ship … It was a haunting experience to walk about the deserted, silent decks which had once buzzed with such life and activity … With a lump in his throat, Lightoller walked onto the bridge to stand … one last time where he had spent so many vigilant hours; hours brimming over with memories, some funny, others less funny such as in the depths of winter at the height of a raging North Atlantic gale; but then when it lifted, such a lark it was sliding on the wet rubber floor from one end of the bridge to the other, an art he developed to perfection until the day he crashed into Captain Cameron.
>
> He was going out through the chartroom when he caught sight of … that familiar old face he had scowled at with scorn as often as he had smiled upon it lovingly … it was still gazing down at him as ever with that customary two-faced grin, friendly but with an unmistakable hint of smugness – the ship's clock. He walked up to it … and then, gripped by a rush of blood to the head, clutched it in both hands and wretched it from its mountings. As he bore it away under his arm … what better memento could he have of his *Oceanic* years …

The *Oceanic* was so firmly planted atop the rocks, that for two weeks it stood there, like some sort of perverse monument. On 29 September, a heavy gale blew through the area, and the *Oceanic* disintegrated under the pressure of the wind and sea, its remains scattered underwater along the Shaalds. The war had claimed its first passenger liner, ironically lost to poor navigation and not enemy fire.

After the sinking, Captains Slaytor and Smith, along with Lieutenant David Blair, the ship's navigator, were court-martialled. Blair received a reprimand for stranding the ship, while both captains were absolved of any blame. This was particularly surprising since Blair had been under the supervision of the captains at the time of the accident. Blair had been the *Titanic's* original second officer before a last minute shake-up in officer assignments and ranks led to his departure prior to the maiden voyage. He was blamed for the lookouts not having access to binoculars in the crow's nest, a fact that has often been erroneously cited as a reason for the accident. Now, Blair shouldered the blame again. Following the *Oceanic's* loss, the British Admiralty changed their policy so that merchant ships would have their own captains, rather than two being in charge.[68]

Meanwhile, a German submarine was about to remove all doubts the British had as to the threat posed to surface ships by U-boats. On 22 September, *U-9*, commanded by Kapitänleutnant Otto Weddigen, spotted three obsolete British cruisers on patrol in the North Sea, HMS *Aboukir*, HMS *Hogue* and HMS *Cressy*.

U-9, which was somewhat obsolete itself, being powered by paraffin engines, rather than diesel engines like the newer class of U-boats, was able to catch the old cruisers. This is because they were not zigzagging to avoid submarines as the Admiralty had recommended, but were sailing straight ahead, and at less than the advised speed. Lookouts had been posted to search for periscopes, but could not prevent what was about to happen.

U-9, which sank three British cruisers in one day. (*Collier's*, 1917/Authors' Collection)

Kapitänleutnant Otto Weddigen. Sadly he would be killed in action just months after his triumph. (Authors' Collection)

An artistic representation of HMS *Cressy* sinking. Captain Robert W. Johnson was reportedly last seen standing atop the hull of the ship before it went under. (Authors' Collection)

Taking advantage of the situation, Weddigen moved to strike. The *Aboukir* was torpedoed first, and the captains of the *Hogue* and *Cressy*, believing that their fellow vessel had struck a mine, came to assist. The *Hogue* and *Cressy* were then attacked, with all three vessels quickly sinking. The action had lasted less than two hours, and a total of 1,459 crewmembers were killed.

Following the sinking of another cruiser, the HMS *Hawke*, on 15 October, Kapitänleutnant Weddigen was awarded the Iron Cross First Class for his actions, and the rest of the crewmembers of the *U-9* were awarded the Iron Cross Second Class.[69] The *Hawke* is well known for having collided with the RMS *Olympic* in September 1911, causing significant damage to both vessels.

The tragic sinkings on 22 September had far-reaching consequences. They negatively impacted British public opinion about the war, and made the Royal Navy look inept at the very time that some nations were still deciding which side of the conflict to support. It also awoke the British Admiralty and the rest of the Allied nations to the very real danger and lethality of the U-boat. No longer would submarines be considered little threat, a fact that was not lost on the German Navy, who began formulating plans to effectively deploy U-boats in the war effort. With Germany having about twenty operational U-boats at the start of the war, and twenty-nine in service and combat-ready by the end of 1914, additional submarines would be needed. Manufacturing was ramped up, and by the war's end, 375 U-boats would be churned out of just ten shipyards.[70]

Even before a U-boat had sunk a single British vessel, some in the British Admiralty had expressed concerns about the range that German submarines could travel, which threatened the security of the Royal Navy's anchorage in Scapa Flow. The sinking of the *Aboukir*, *Hogue* and *Cressy* inflamed these concerns even further, to the point where the British fleet was sent to other ports in Scotland or to Ireland until additional defensive measures could be installed at Scapa Flow. In essence, by destroying such a small number of vessels, Germany had forced the vaunted Royal Navy fleet to relocate from its home base.

While the war at sea was shifting away from being a completely one-sided affair in favour of the British, the war on land was yielding mixed results for both the Allied nations and Central Powers. Between 3 and 11 September 1914, the Russian Army had managed to defeat the Austro-Hungarians at the Battle of Rava Russka, which took place in what is now Ukraine. However, Russian forces experienced a significant defeat between 9 and 14 September in the First Battle of Masurian Lakes. Suffering massive casualties, they were forced to withdraw their troops from East Prussia entirely.

On the Western Front, after pressing through Belgium, German forces continued to advance through France, with the goal of taking Paris as quickly as possible, which would end the war. German troops got within 30 miles of the city, which was preparing a siege defence. The French Government had withdrawn to the safety of Bordeaux. However, the tide turned when Allied forces won a

German soldiers in the trenches. (Authors' Collection)

decisive victory in the First Battle of the Marne between 5 and 12 September. This unexpected and unlikely defeat effectively spelled the end of Germany's Schlieffen Plan and hopes for a quick end to the war. Combat on the Western Front would soon descend into a stalemate of bloody trench warfare, which would dominate the conflict in Europe for the remainder of the war.

At sea, a strange and unprecedented battle was about to take place. The Hamburg South American Line's *Cap Trafalgar*, a passenger vessel, had been requisitioned at the beginning of the war by the Imperial German Navy, outfitted with weaponry and charged with sinking British merchant shipping as it rounded Cape Horn. On 14 September, *Cap Trafalgar* put into harbour on the island of Trindade, 500 miles off the coast of Brazil, the site of a hidden German supply base.[71]

While the vessel was pulling into port, smoke from her funnels was spotted on the horizon by lookouts aboard the HMS *Carmania*. Having been converted into an armed merchant cruiser shortly after the war began, the *Carmania* arrived in Shell Bay, Bermuda near the end of August. The crew knew that *Cap Trafalgar* had been spotted in the area, but it was believed that it had headed south. Ironically, the *Cap Trafalgar* had disguised itself as the *Carmania*. One of its funnels was removed, and it was painted to resemble the other vessel. It was hoped that the altered profile would trick British merchant vessels, and allow the ship to get in close to them before striking.

When the two vessels finally met, a brutal surface battle erupted, the first time that two passenger liners had ever engaged each other in armed combat. A contemporary account detailed the encounter:

> ... *Carmania* was steaming under a cloudless sky of tropic blue towards the small jagged peaks of Trinidad [Trindade] ... It was a weird spot, long reputed to be the Treasure Island where the pirates of past history had buried ill-gotten gains ...
>
> On rounding Nine-Pin Peak, which rises 850 feet sheer out of the sea, the Cunard liner sighted a strange ship at anchor close under the lee of the land. Her crew seemed to be taking aboard coal at express speed, with two ships alongside and all derricks up. Though one funnel had been lifted out and some alterations had been made in her appearance, it was evident that the stranger was *Cap Trafalgar*, and the German captain, the moment he saw *Carmania* steaming towards him, cast off both his colliers, tripped his anchor, and steamed to the south-east at full speed. Perhaps he expected to find other ships in company coming round the far side of the island; some fleet, in fact, against which he had no chance in a pitched battle. It may be that the colliers which had gone ahead signalled to him that the coast was clear, for *Cap Trafalgar*'s helm was suddenly put hard-a-port, and she turned boldly to meet her oncoming foe. It was in

such manner that these ocean giants, so short a while ago peaceful competitors, faced each other as mortal enemies.

Carmania's first shot was fired across the bows of the German ship, which at once opened fire, concentrating all her guns on the bridge and upper deck of the British vessel, no doubt to disable her. *Carmania* retaliated by blazing shot on shot all along the enemy's waterline, so as to procure her immediate destruction. The range was 2,800 yards, and the two ships, in fierce action, crossed each other, *Cap Trafalgar* passing astern of *Carmania*, who soon edged away to keep out of range of a quick-firing machine-gun. She carried out this manoeuvre until the splashes showed these shells were all falling short.

Soon the concentrated German artillery caused a fire to break out on the bridge and charthouse – its primary object. The British guns, firing incessantly, became so hot that the crews could hardly work them; the helm of *Carmania* was put over to port to bring her fresh broadside into action. Besides this, the alteration, of course, brought the ship before the wind, giving the fire less draught and the crew a better chance to extinguish it. The German shells had cut the water mains, and until the latter were mended the firemen could do nothing. The captain had to abandon the bridge and con the ship from right aft, and soon the flames were shooting up high to the funnel-tops. Meanwhile the gunnery lieutenant had to concentrate all his attention on the repair of the water pipes, and though the battle raged as fiercely as ever, the fact that the ship had perforce to be kept right before the wind prevented any manoeuvring.

Meanwhile *Cap Trafalgar*, who was now running almost parallel to *Carmania*, began to make a bad list to starboard. Our fire had taken dead effect.

The German captain, as a last resource, turned his ship towards the island, possibly in the hope of beaching her. There remained no time for this. The water continued to pour into the ship, now steaming along on her side. It became evident that no power could save her, so she stopped, and a few of the starboard boats were lowered.

Cap Trafalgar, a little later, turned right on her beam ends, and as the sea dashed over her decks the great liner slowly righted herself. The masthead flags still flew in brave defiance, the eagle and iron cross fluttering for one brief moment among clouds of steam and black smoke belching upwards to the sky. Then the whole fabric sank, with the deadly sound of bursting hatches and rushing water. The survivors were afterwards picked up by one of the German colliers, for the crew of *Carmania* were still intent on putting out the fire on board their own ship. To save life or make prisoners might have meant her loss in the midst of her great victory.

It is not known what the enemy's losses were. The English had nine killed, five seriously wounded, and twenty-one slightly.

A depiction of the aftermath of the Battle of Trindade. In the foreground, the *Cap Trafalgar* settles on its side as men scramble to get into the lifeboats. In the background, the *Carmania's* bridge and superstructure are ablaze. (Painting by W.L. Wyllie/Authors' Collection)

Both crews fought most gallantly, and as armed liners were something quite new in naval warfare, the battle aroused a great deal of interest when the news became public. The Admiralty sent the following message to Captain Noel Grant:

'You have fought a fine action to a successful finish'.

Brief but eloquent praise![72]

The hour-and-a-half battle came to be known as the Battle of Trindade. The *Carmania* suffered severe damage in its victory. Seventy-three German shells had found their mark and exploded, with the fragments piercing 380 holes all over the ship. The bridge of the vessel was devastated, and the superstructure damaged by fire.[73] The *Carmania*, effectively knocked out of action, had to be escorted into port at Pernambuco, Brazil, and was later dry docked for lengthy repairs in Gibraltar.

Before *Cap Trafalgar* had sunk, her crew had managed to send out a distress call. Ironically, the *Kronprinz Wilhelm* received the message and later arrived on the scene, but did not realise the compromised position that the *Carmania* was in, and fearing an attack by British vessels, steamed away without firing a shot.[74] Had the crew realised the sorry state of the former Cunard liner, then the *Carmania* could

The *Carmania's* devastated bridge after the battle. *(The Illustrated War News*, 1914/ Authors' Collection)

have been finished off with relative ease. It was a missed opportunity. While the battle had proved to the Royal Navy that armed merchant cruisers could sink large surface vessels, the amount of damage *Carmania* sustained showed that passenger liners, without heavy armour or other defensive measures, simply could not absorb the type of damage that occurs in a pitched surface battle. This reinforced the British Admiralty's earlier decision not to deploy large passenger liners like *Mauretania* as armed merchant cruisers.

After the Admiralty had requisitioned the *Aquitania* at the outbreak of war, the Cunard Line was desperate to find another vessel to fulfil its role in the transatlantic passenger route. The candidate that they selected was the RMS *Campania*, an aging passenger liner recently chartered to the Anchor Line to complete crossings from Glasgow to New York. A former Blue Riband winner, the vessel had once been the largest and fastest passenger liner afloat, but had long since been eclipsed by more modern vessels. Between August and October 1914, *Campania* filled the *Aquitania's* role in the passenger service, but the vessel, launched in 1893, proved too old and run-down for this duty, and after three crossings was sold for scrap. During its brief return to its former glory, one of the passengers that travelled aboard *Campania* was a British journalist, Frederic Martyn, who was travelling from New York to Liverpool. His colourful account, illustrating the friendly rivalry between America and Britain, gives some insight into the goings-on during *Campania's* brief resurgence as a passenger liner:

> This latter ship (*Campania*) was built expressly to be the fastest ocean-going vessel afloat, and actually lowered the New York to Queenstown record to five days seventeen hours twenty-seven minutes in 1893; but before the war she had been laid aside by the Cunard Company as being no longer serviceable, though only twenty years old. On the outbreak of hostilities she was again

RMS *Campania* prior to the war. (Authors' Collection)

placed on the Atlantic service. Later she was requisitioned by the Government, and, I believe, did good service in the North Sea as a seaplane ship.

I crossed on the *Campania* from New York to Liverpool, and it seemed to me, and, apparently, to every other British passenger, to be a curious circumstance that the ship's band never once played 'God Save the King', or any other British patriotic air, although it was a British ship and we were in a state of war. In place of the national anthem at the end of a band performance, 'Tipperary' was always played. The general impression among the passengers of British nationality was that this omission was due to a weak-kneed desire to avoid wounding the susceptibilities of the Americans on board; but I hardly think so, because the air of the British national anthem is the same as that of 'My country, 'tis of thee', which is the real national anthem of the United States, and those Americans who would have resented the playing of the British national anthem could have claimed, more Americano, that the band was playing theirs.

A converse instance of this being done occurred after the finish of the final game in the International polo match in America, in which the British team beat the Americans. I saw that game in the company of half-a-dozen young New Yorkers, who won the game for America before it had even started, and frantically waved miniature specimens of 'Old Glory' every time one of the American champions made a hit. When the match was over the band played either 'America' or 'God Save the King', whichever way one took it. I chose to take it as 'God Save the King', and duly raised my hat.

'Come on, boys', said one of my Yankee friends, 'let's go out and buy some Union Jacks. We can't do less when this Britisher takes oft his roof to "My Country, 'tis of Thee."'

'But I didn't'. I protested. 'I don't see why I should uncover to "America" when you take no notice of it. I raised my hat because I thought they were playing "God Save the King" in honour of the British victory'.

The idea that an American band should play a foreign national anthem to celebrate an American defeat amused them very much, and they took some pains to convince me that there could be no possible doubt that the bandmaster had intended to play 'America' and nothing else.

'You may be right, boys', I retorted, 'but it doesn't signify. That tune is always "God Save the King" to me, even when all the rest of the people who hear it believe it to be "My Country, 'tis of Thee" or "Heil Dir im Siegerkranz"'.

But I have got side-tracked and must get back to the *Campania*. I often think of my British fellow-passengers on that trip. Almost without exception they had left good jobs or flourishing businesses in the United States and paid their own passages to England to join up in Kitchener's Army. Two of them had been my fellow-passengers on the *Aquitania* in the preceding May, and both of them had got comfortably settled down in the Far West when the war came along. I wonder how many of those good fellows are left, and whether those who are left will make their fresh start in the States or in the Old Country. It is to be hoped that they will elect to stay here now, as we can ill afford to lose those who have proved themselves to be true Britons.[75]

'Kitchener's Army' is a reference to Field Marshal Lord Horatio Kitchener, Britain's Secretary of State for War, who was one of the few to have foreseen the war potentially being a long, drawn-out conflict. He organised the build-up of the largest volunteer army in Britain's long history, and significantly expanded the production of materials and supplies needed to win the conflict.

Frederic Martyn was one of the last passengers who had the pleasure of journeying aboard *Campania* before it was taken out of service. However, while the ship was awaiting demolition, the old workhorse was given yet another lease on life. The British Admiralty bought it and converted it into an armed merchant cruiser capable of carrying seaplanes. It was commissioned as the HMS *Campania*. The goal was to use *Campania*'s airplanes to patrol for German vessels in the North Sea. During her sea trials, one of the Royal Navy officers serving aboard the ship was Charles Lightoller, survivor of the loss of the *Titanic* and *Oceanic*.[76]

Later, more radical alterations were made to *Campania*. The ship was the first to be modified to have a permanent flight deck, which was installed on the bow, and was the first to have an aeroplane take off from a deck of this kind. Aircraft had previously been launched from temporary flight decks on other vessels. This

HMT *Campania*. Note the
dramatic changes in appearance,
including the flight deck on
the forward portion of the ship.
(Imperial War Museum, SP114)

made the *Campania* a key step in the evolution of aircraft carriers.[77] When these modifications were made, the forward funnel was replaced with two narrower side-by-side funnels, giving it a total of three, and the aft deck was altered to allow the ship to serve as an observation balloon platform. The vessel's appearance was altered so radically that it scarcely looked like its former self. Sadly, *Campania's* colourful career ended when it sank on 5 November 1918, just six days before the armistice was signed, following a collision with two other Royal Navy vessels in a squall.

Meanwhile, while most Americans were fleeing Europe, one individual, Walter Austin, chanced an eastbound trip to Europe, hoping to witness some of the 'doings'. With a self-professed taste for adventure, Walter had attempted, unsuccessfully, to join the Massachusetts militia in order to fight in the Spanish-American War in 1898. He had happened to be in Japan during the Russo-Japanese War between 1904 and 1905, but had not witnessed much of the action. As such, he desired to visit the Western Front. On 14 October 1914, he set sail aboard the *Lusitania*, hoping to fulfil his dream of finally witnessing a war:

> … I sailed from New York on the *Lusitania* for Liverpool. I must confess that I had no better excuse for going abroad than sightseeing, but that seemed to me reason enough. The first general European war in ninety-nine years had burst upon an unsuspecting world, and I wanted to have a glimpse of those conditions that had long been talked of as possible, but that few, if any, Americans had expected would come in their day. Besides, I had wagered a box of cigars with a friend of mine that I could get to England, Germany, Belgium and France and return to New York before Christmas. Hence my determination to smell the smoke of Battle in order to puff the cheroot of Peace.
>
> We had a very smooth passage and sighted but one vessel during the entire trip. The steamer's transformation gave us our first intimation of warfare. It was painted gray throughout, and at night all lights were carefully covered. When we arrived off the Welsh coast at night we had a sterner omen of strife, for searchlights from the shore were constantly played on us. But there was no apparent anxiety among the passengers, since that was before the days of submarine 'frightfulness', and we docked safely.[78]

The 20 October brought another significant event in the course of the war: the first sinking of a merchant ship by a U-boat. Had Walter Austin known the true danger that U-boats would pose during the war, he may have thought twice about braving the Atlantic. The event in question occurred after the Salvesen, Christian & Company liner, SS *Glitra*, was stopped and searched 14 miles off the coast of Norway by *U-17*.[79]

During the incident, the German crewmembers observed prize rules, the customary maritime code between nations which held that crewmembers and passengers aboard merchant vessels must be allowed to evacuate and get to safety, before the ships could be sunk. The only exceptions to these rules were warships, which were considered fair game, and merchant vessels that posed a threat to their attacker. German U-boats largely adhered to prize rules early in the war. Pains were taken to ensure the safety of people aboard their targets. In some cases, survivors were actually taken aboard the submarines and dropped off at neutral ports, and in other instances, the U-boat crewmen gave provisions to the survivors in the lifeboats before departing the scene.

After the captors came aboard and searched the *Glitra*, they ordered all of the merchant vessel's crewmembers to board the lifeboats and evacuate. Once all of them were off the ship, crewmembers of the *U-17* opened the sea valves and scuttled the ship. No lives were lost, and the lifeboats were soon towed ashore by a Norwegian vessel, which observed but did not interfere with the events, since Norway was a neutral country.

The incident was a harbinger of things to come. Merchant vessels would fast become the prime targets of U-boats, in an attempt by Germany to blockade

A U-boat crew picking up survivors from a merchant ship that they sank. (Authors' Collection)

United States Secretary of State
William Jennings Bryan. (Library
of Congress, Prints & Photographs
Division)

Britain and cut off supplies that were being shipped to the Allied nations. Britain
had essentially erected an illegal long-range blockade of Germany by this time
using the Royal Navy. When neutral nations protested, Britain insisted that
this was necessary, as keeping their vessels at the 3-mile offshore limit allowed
for under international law would place them within range of German coastal
defences. Since November 1914, Britain had also declared the whole of the
North Sea a 'military area', and had begun laying mines to deter or cut off passage,
particularly between the coast of Belgium and Dover, to prevent U-boat access.
Neutral vessels were warned to enter at their own risk.

Additionally, instead of simply stopping and inspecting neutral ships bound for
Germany at sea, Britain began forcing these vessels into port, leisurely inspecting
them, impounding contraband, and at times, keeping useful non-contraband
cargo for themselves, although they typically paid compensation for it. They then
sent the vessels on their way with nothing that could be of use to Germany or her
allies. Neutral nations were understandably upset at this arrangement, and filed
complaints, to no avail. American President Woodrow Wilson's foreign policy
advisor, Edward House, commented on these tactics, saying 'The British have
gone as far as they possibly could in violating neutral rights, though they have
done it in a most courteous way'. Additionally, President Wilson and Secretary of
State William Jennings Bryan filed a protest with the British Government, saying
that they 'saw no need to starve Germans', to no avail.[80]

Britain continually expanded what constituted contraband, seizing not just war
materials and munitions but virtually any manufacturing materials. They even

declared grain contraband in March 1915, once the blockade forced Germany to take its grain supplies under government control. Britain argued that this move would mean that the grains would reach German soldiers before civilians, which was a dubious claim at best.[81]

These changes in policy affected the neutral United States and riled many, since America had been shipping war supplies, foodstuffs and general goods and materials to both the Allied Nations and Central Powers for profit. The Royal Navy seized or turned back American merchant vessels carrying these goods, drawing the ire of some. The British felt that the effectiveness of this blockade would take time, due to the large amount of farmland that Central Power nations possessed.

Because of Britain's actions, some German commanders hoped that their slowly growing U-boat fleet could retaliate in kind, strangling their enemy's economy, and that this counter-blockade would force Britain to surrender. The German public, which was already feeling some impact from the Royal Navy blockade, was strongly behind such a tactic. A counter-blockade necessarily shifted the focus of U-boats from Royal Navy vessels to merchant vessels, although they still did not possess enough operational submarines to effectively enact a full-scale counter-blockade. Germany was left with little choice, since its surface fleet was hemmed in its home port by the superior numbers of the Royal Navy.

Germany's Secretary of State of the Imperial Naval Office, Grand Admiral Alfred von Tirpitz, commented on the idea of a counter-blockade in an interview. 'England wants to starve us. We can play the same game. We can bottle her up and destroy every ship that endeavours to break the blockade'. When asked if Germany had enough U-boats to carry out this planned retaliation, Tirpitz defiantly answered 'Yes, we are superior to England in submarines of the larger types'.[82] However, privately, Tirpitz knew better, advocating for a U-boat blockade of the Thames estuary while Germany began to build submarines in larger numbers.[83] The war at sea was quickly morphing into a war of commerce rather than a war between opposing navies.

Unfortunately, the war at sea would not remain as civilised as it had when *U-17* scuttled the merchant vessel *Glitra*. Six days later, *U-17* torpedoed the French ferry SS *Admiral Ganteaume* in the English Channel.

Grand Admiral Alfred von Tirpitz. (*Collier's*, 1917/ Authors' Collection)

The incident sparked international outrage, not only because, in violation of prize rules, this was the first instance of a merchant vessel being attacked without warning but also because there were 2,000 Belgian refugees aboard at the time. Fortunately, the vessel did not sink, and was able to be towed to port. Forty people died in the attack.

The survivors of the attack were rescued by the South Eastern and Chatham Railway liner SS *The Queen*. One of the men aboard *The Queen*, Thomas McClune, described the rescue:

> I was sitting by the taffrail on the starboard side of the *Queen*, along with a few friends, when I saw a huge volume of smoke, and water rise around the *Admiral Ganteaume*, which at the moment would be about 360 yards ahead of us … the *Admiral Ganteaume* hoisted her signal of distress. Then we heard our captain pipe, 'All hands on deck', and we knew something serious had happened … Everyone at once said 'She has struck a mine'.
>
> Unable to get near enough on one side, Captain Carey, with superb seamanship, swung his boat right round. As the *Queen* made her way across the 'nose' of the *Ganteaume* the steward came to me and asked me if I were willing to help, as the *Ganteaume* had struck a mine. I replied, 'Yes', and saw an attempt to lower the *Queen*'s boats. The sea apparently was too heavy and Captain Carey drew his ship alongside the ill-fated vessel. As we did so, five Belgian soldiers dived from the *Ganteaume*. Four of them immediately sank and did not reappear. The other swam a short distance and then he sank.
>
> The *Ganteaume* lowered a boat full of people, but as soon as it touched the water it dived straight down and we saw no more of the occupants. The scenes on the French vessel were simply beyond description. Men and women were fighting; others climbing into the rigging and sliding down ropes into the water. As soon as we got close alongside her there was an immediate rush for the *Queen*. The sea was rather high, and the boats heaved to and fro and it was impossible to run a bridge across. The passengers from the *Ganteaume* had simply to jump from one boat to the other. Some of them missed their footing or failed to hold the taffrail and they either dropped into the water or were crushed between the boats.
>
> I took my stand with the steward and helped him to catch the babies as they were thrown from the *Ganteaume*. I had a terrible experience in this work. As the last child was thrown the boat heaved away, and I just touched the child's shawl. The little one fell short of the ship and was crushed between the two vessels as they came together again. A man who jumped from the other boat missed his foothold, and though he held the ropes his legs were crushed.
>
> The rescue work of Captain Carey and his crew was magnificent, and I do not think there would have been a life lost if there had been no panic. After the

terrified people had all got on board they shrank in horror to the opposite side of our boat with the result that it began to list very seriously. Accordingly they were instructed to distribute themselves more evenly but before they could be induced to do so they had to be dragged apart. They clung to each other in an ecstasy of terror. Then came the most pitiful scene of all. Children had been separated from their parents, husbands from their wives, and our first care was to restore the children to their parents. I shall never forget the spectacle as we conducted the little ones round the boat and one by one they were identified.

Nearly all the men, women and children had their faces and hands and clothes blackened by the flying soot from the *Ganteaume*. Nearly all were soaked with water. The scenes on arrival of the *Queen* at Folkestone were also indescribable. On all sides people shouted, 'Vive L'Angleterre'! [long live England]

Food was quickly provided for them but no-one who passed through the awful tragedy will ever forget their terrible tragedy.[84]

In the ensuing weeks and months after the attack, Germany was fiercely criticised because *U-17* had not warned the vessel prior to attacking, and was not flying the German flag during the action. Due to the backlash, Germany initially denied having attacked the *Admiral Ganteaume*, saying that it must have hit a 'rogue mine'. Even the survivors initially believed it was a mine hit. Eventually, a fragment of the torpedo, with German writing on it, was found in one of the *Admiral Ganteaume*'s lifeboats, revealing the truth. Newspaper reports labelled the sinking murder, saying that it was 'treacherously torpedoed', and 'cannot be excused by any strategical or military reason'.[85] The headlines failed to consider that the submarine commander had no way of knowing that there were such a high number of refugees aboard the vessel at the time, and that there was no feasible way for the crew to safely warn the vessel, since the English Channel was teeming with British warships.

Four days after *Admiral Ganteaume* had been attacked, there was yet another tragedy at sea. However, this time the incident had nothing to do with the actions of enemies. The event in question involved the HMHS (His Majesty's Hospital Ship) *Rohilla*. The vessel had begun its life in 1906 as the SS *Rohilla*, a steamship built in the Harland & Wolff shipyards for the British India Steam Navigation Company. In 1908, the vessel permanently entered military service, and at the onset of the First World War, it was requisitioned by the British Admiralty and converted into a hospital ship. Her passenger accommodations were converted into hospital wards, and two operating theatres were installed. In accord with Geneva Convention requirements, the vessel, which already was white, had a thick green band painted around the hull, and flew the red cross, to mark its purpose.

On Thursday, 29 October 1914, the same day that the Ottoman Empire entered the war on the side of Germany and the Central Powers, *Rohilla* was steaming down the eastern coast of England, heading for Dunkirk, France, to pick up wounded troops fresh from the front lines. The weather deteriorated throughout the day, and by nightfall gale force winds had picked up, with increasing wave action. Due to wartime conditions, lights on shore had been blacked out, which rendered landmarks hard to see, and navigating that much more difficult. At 4 a.m. on Friday, 30 October, *Rohilla* struck a reef at Saltwick Nab, just south of Whitby, England.

With the ship damaged, Captain David Neilson was forced to decide whether to leave the *Rohilla* atop the reef and hope that the terrible weather would not impede a rescue operation, or to attempt to ground the vessel, to prevent it from sinking before help could arrive. He chose the latter course of action, but the vessel collided with an underwater outcropping with such force that the hull fractured in two places. With *Rohilla's* back broken, it was just a matter of time before the heavy wave action would completely dismantle the ship, dragging sections of it into deeper water.

The vessel was only 500 yards from shore, but the heavy waves and gale force winds complicated the rescue efforts. The Rocket Brigade, a group of men devoted to the rescue of seafarers, was soon on the scene to start rescue operations.

The *Rohilla* breaking apart in the surf. (Authors' Collection)

Three rockets with ropes attached were fired from shore, but all missed. It was the rescuers' intention to fire the rockets over the *Rohilla*, so that those aboard could secure the lines to their vessel, and pass survivors ashore one at a time via a boson's chair.

The Whitby lifeboat could not be launched from the port due to the extremely rough seas, but with 229 people aboard the *Rohilla*, the rescuers would not be deterred. As a crowd of spectators grew on shore, they carried the boat by hand across land, launching it from the beach closest to the ship. Time was of the essence, because people had begun to be washed overboard by the waves, and it was feared they would drown, or be dashed on the rocks.

After five-and-a-half long hours, the lifeboat was able to rescue the first load of passengers off *Rohilla*, seventeen in all. Among them were all five women who were aboard, including Stewardess Mary Keziah Roberts, a *Titanic* survivor. A second attempt was made, in which eighteen additional survivors were rescued, although the Whitby lifeboat was so damaged that it could not continue to be used in the rescue efforts. With the gale continuing to rage, the rescue efforts were slowed, lasting fifty nightmarish hours in all, and requiring the use of six Royal National Lifeboat Institution lifeboats, including the Tynemouth motor lifeboat *Henry Vernon*.

The pounding surf caused *Rohilla*'s stern to break off and collapse into deeper water, dragging survivors with it. Some aboard the stricken liner leapt for it, and made a desperate attempt to reach shore through the waves. Some made it safely to land, while others drowned. Those left aboard had no heat, and little food and water for the entirety of the ordeal.

Finally, on Saturday, 31 October, after many on shore had given up all hope of more people being saved, a signal was received from the vessel, saying 'It's a long, long way to Tipperary', which was described as a 'cheery, yet tragic hint that they had waited long for aid'. Soon, the last of those aboard were pulled off the disintegrating wreck of the hospital ship. One sailor had refused to leave without his black cat, and carried his half-starved pet into the lifeboat. Captain Neilson was the last person to be rescued. When all was said and done, 144 of the 229 aboard survived.[86] The sinking would be used as propaganda, complete with the false claim that the ship had fallen victim to a German mine. Following his rescue, Captain Neilson gave a detailed account concerning the events to the press, which was published under the headline 'Was the *Rohilla* Mined?':

> Off St. Abbs Head the ship rolled badly. I altered the course to clear the mine fields, and believed that my course would bring me seven miles off Whitby and four miles off Flamborough Head.
>
> At four o'clock on Friday morning it was shown that the ship was closer to the shore than expected. When the ship struck … with a grating sound …

I thought I had struck a mine, and feel certain I struck a mine outside the rock. It would have been disastrous to run the ship off land after the first shock, which threw people off their feet, and threw me against the telegraph. It would have been suicide to put my ship to sea, as all hands would have drowned.

Early on Friday morning the ship was struck fore and aft by heavy seas. At daylight I fully expected her to break up.

Signals told me that the Whitby lifeboat was coming. Several lines from the rocket brigade fell on the ship, but could not be secured. The rocket brigade worked day and night splendidly, and we owe the members of the brigade a deep debt of gratitude.

The Whitby lifeboat was launched after being dragged over the rocks, and it rescued two parties.

The tide had risen somewhat, and the sea was running much higher when the lifeboat made its second trip about ten o'clock on Friday morning in great stress and difficulty. It rescued doctors and the sick berth stewards.

Another lifeboat next morning made several attempts at rescue, getting comparatively close to the ship, when eddies swirled her away. The Scarborough lifeboat arrived and stood by during the night.

In view of the serious position I suggested on Saturday afternoon that the swimmers might try to swim ashore. Many attempted to do so, and I watched the current and directed them. About thirty, I am told, reached shore alive.

On Friday afternoon, about high water, the after-part of the ship broke away, and those clinging on there were washed off and drowned.

On Saturday afternoon I was signalled back to shore. 'The ship is breaking rapidly. Look out for swimmers'.

I then called all hands on deck, and said I thought the ship could not hold out until daylight. I advised all officers and men to make rafts of doors or shutters, as they would stand little chance if the ship broke up at high water. The men agreed, and many went overboard, some being drowned.

I advised the fifty remaining to keep close together for warmth, and they huddled in the cabins below. They had no food or fire. A thimbleful each of water was obtained from somewhere on Saturday afternoon. We were rescued on Saturday morning by the Tyne motor-lifeboat, which used oil on the water.[87]

An inquiry was held after the sinking, and Captain Neilson was exonerated of any negligence or wrongdoing, although it was recommended that all passenger liners in the North Sea carry rockets capable of firing a line to shore, and that Whitby be provided with a motor lifeboat.

By the end of 1914, the war had been raging for five months, and the conflict was continuing to escalate, ushering in horrors that could scarcely have been imaginable in the years prior to the conflict. An example of this is the First Battle of Ypres, which began on 19 October, and ended in an Allied victory. Heavy losses were inflicted on both sides, and the battle marked the end of the 'race to the sea'. The war would thereafter be heavily dominated by trench warfare and a static Western Front.

The number of Royal Navy warships sunk by U-boats in 1914 totalled eight, while one Imperial Russian Navy armoured cruiser was sunk, three merchant vessels had been sent to the bottom, and one Albanian sailing vessel had been captured as a prize. This totalled 64,163 tons of shipping sunk or captured by U-boats for the year.[88] This came at the loss of five submarines, two of which were destroyed early in August when Germany sent out the first submarine war patrol in history.

U-boat production was not yet increased to the number that would be needed in order for Germany to make them a more effective weapon. Just fifteen U-boats were constructed in all of 1914.[89] The German Government realised that those numbers would have to improve, although there was still internal debate over how much emphasis to place on the submarine war. The best chance for an immediate boost in numbers came from the smaller UB and UC class U-boats, which were intended to be ready by March 1915. However, these new U-boats would still have to undergo testing and sea trials to prove they were ready to be deployed. Another issue facing U-boats was how long it took them to sail from existing submarine bases to enemy trade routes. As a result, the Imperial German Navy moved down into Flanders, Belgium, and set up U-boat bases at Zeebrugge, Bruges and Ostend.[90]

So far, U-boats had largely restricted their attacks to legitimate targets and adhered to prize rules. No matter how shocking the attacks were to Britain or the general public, they were not war crimes but tragic losses in the midst of a deadly conflict, where it was kill or be killed. Unfortunately, as the British naval blockade of Germany began to take its toll in 1915, the war at sea was not to remain as civil. As the Western Front devolved into the bloody stalemate of trench warfare, the losses at sea in 1914 would be eclipsed as the First Battle of the Atlantic turned even deadlier, and made transatlantic crossings even more perilous, for both sailor and civilian alike.

2

Escalation, 1915

January–February 1915

At the start of 1915, the war continued to escalate. The 19 January saw the first German Zeppelin bombing raid, and from that point until the end of the war, the German Navy and Army Air Services would mount over fifty bombing raids on the United Kingdom, an attempt at strategic bombing that became a frequent night-time occurrence, and terrorised civilians in London and elsewhere. There were twenty airship raids in 1915 alone. Elsewhere, between 26 January and 4 February, German and Ottoman forces were defeated by the British in the action known as the Raid on the Suez Canal. This marked the beginning of the Sinai and Palestine Campaign.

Back at sea, a significant loss was incurred by the Royal Navy on 1 January, when the 15,000 ton battleship HMS *Formidable* was attacked by *U-24*, while it was on patrol in the English Channel. Submarine activity had been reported in the area, but was not thought to be a threat due to rough seas and wind conditions. The *Formidable* was hit by two torpedoes, capsizing and sinking. Of the 780 men aboard, 547 lost their lives. U-boats began to step up their attacks on merchant shipping as well. In January alone, seven British merchant vessels were captured or sunk. With prize rules generally being observed, there were around twenty-one men killed, all of which occurred in the sinking of the SS *Oriole*, which apparently had not been warned and sank with all hands.[1]

In response to Germany's stepped-up targeting of merchant vessels, on 31 January and 10 February 1915, the British Admiralty issued secret orders instructing merchant captains on how to defend themselves from submarines, including painting over the names of their vessels and ports of call, flying the flags of neutral countries and altering their appearance to resemble neutral ships, not stopping if ordered by a U-boat but to immediately open fire, and if unarmed, to turn and attempt to ram U-boats when they were sighted. More advanced anti-submarine countermeasures had not yet been invented. They had also begun installing hidden deck guns on some merchant vessels. These could be sprung upon U-boats that surfaced alongside to warn the crews to evacuate, a necessary step Germany had to take in adhering to prize rules.

Once Germany, already distressed by Britain's blockade, found out that their enemy was disguising their ships by hiding behind the flags of neutral countries, they were infuriated. With Kaiser Wilhelm II's approval, a 'war zone decree', was issued on 4 February: The territorial waters around Great Britain and Ireland would officially be considered a war zone as of 18 February. Germany warned that they:

> ... will endeavor to destroy every enemy merchant ship that is found in this area of war without it always being possible to avert the peril, that thus threatens persons and cargoes. Neutrals are therefore warned against enemy ships that cannot always be avoided ... The German Government may expect that the neutral powers will show no less consideration for the vital interests of Germany than for those of England and will aid in keeping their citizens and the property of the latter from this area. This is more to be expected, as it must be in the interest of the neutral powers to see this destructive war end as soon as possible.[2]

Germany was clearly concerned that neutral vessels could be accidentally attacked, since British merchant vessels were flying false flags, hence they warned neutral vessels away.

The 'war zone decree' was perhaps given without due consideration to how the United States would react. On 10 February, President Wilson sharply denounced the move, warning against any 'overt acts' on Germany's part. He threatened that if 'an American vessel or the lives of American citizens' were lost as a result, America 'would be constrained to hold the Imperial German Government to a strict accountability'. This caused a temporary panic, as German officials suddenly realised that they might be risking drawing America into the war. Several neutral nations reacted poorly to this change in policy, as did Italy, which due to the Triple Alliance, was nominally an ally of Germany and Austria–Hungary, although hardly an enthusiastic one.[3]

While President Wilson and the American Government appeared to be coming down on Germany for their actions more harshly than they did on Britain, this was not without reason. While Britain's blockade of Germany and their handling of neutral shipping was considered illegal, no American lives were threatened by their actions, just delays and issues regarding revenue. Germany's new policy, however, could potentially cost lives, which Wilson stated would not be tolerated. The United States did protest to London about British vessels hiding behind American flags, as this misuse of neutral flags was cited as the sole reason that Germany's declaration of a war zone around the British Isles was a danger to American vessels. Reportedly, Germany officials were 'delighted' that America had protested against this practice, and were prepared 'to assert conditionally a guarantee that merchant ships sailing under American flags will not be attacked'.[4]

On Friday, 5 February, William D. Boyce, an American 'newspaper proprietor of Indianapolis and Chicago' was travelling to Europe aboard the RMS *Lusitania*. During the crossing, Captain Daniel Dow created quite a stir by swinging out the ship's lifeboats and hoisting a large American flag on the stern of the vessel, evidently worried about being attacked by U-boats. This was done not because Dow felt that this would disguise his ship as a neutral vessel, as that was impossible given the *Lusitania*'s size and profile, but that it would serve as notice that he was carrying passengers and mail of the neutral United States. Boyce described the events:

It was early Friday morning, as the liner stopped, when every one aboard had … been expecting sight of land. There was a sea as well as a mist and it was not plain for a few minutes why the vessel had been brought to a stop … we stopped for half an hour and … the officers told passengers the captain wanted to take soundings to find out exactly where we were.

Owing to the mist … there was quite a little excitement aboard when the crew swung out a couple of lifeboats and made ready others … the crew were seen making toward the stern of the ship with the Stars and Stripes, which were quickly run up on the flag mast. We then, divined the meaning of this action, although no word of German submarine activity in the Irish Sea had reached us during the voyage.

Once the vessel started again she crammed on all speed and made direct for Liverpool, where we landed early Saturday morning. I did not note whether the Stars and Stripes were still flying when we arrived in the Mersey.[5]

The flag-raising incident created quite a stir in the press given the political tensions that were being created by such actions. Captain Dow was unwilling to discuss the incident, although he admitted that he might take such action again if he felt it necessary.

Will Irwin, another passenger, gave a detailed account of the crossing. He mentioned Boyce in his account, but unlike him, hesitated to describe the actual flag-raising for fear of being censored. Irwin took note of alleged 'spy games' that took place aboard, and the 'mysterious' cargo that the *Lusitania* had been carrying:

Captain Daniel Dow. (Authors' Collection)

Will Irwin. (United States National Archives and Records Administration/Authors' Collection)

... the 'state of war' begins, in fact, at the pier. This was no common sailing of an Atlantic liner ... There was much excitement in the crowd ... Wives clung emotionally to their husbands; a few women, blinded by their tears, refused to wait to see us off, but ran away down the pier before the deckhands drew up the gangplank.

When, finally, the shores of America faded away in the mist, we came across our first sign of real war – the British cruisers which for four months have stood at anchor just outside the neutral zone, monotonously waiting for something to happen. We always bestow a little sympathy, in passing, on the crew of the *Essex*.

... This is a passenger list of old, experienced voyagers. It had been a rough passage ... but no winter trip on the Atlantic is very comfortable. Besides, the *Lusitania* is loaded with certain mysterious and very heavy contraptions of steel she was not meant to carry, and she rolled miserably in the winter gale.

Nevertheless, the dining-saloon and the smoking-rooms have been almost as well filled in the rough days as in the smooth. These are people who got over the habit of seasickness long ago. There is the regular delegation of American buyers, over to get the advance spring styles from Paris. Most of them will not cross the Channel this season; the Parisian dressmakers will move their stocks over to London and meet them halfway. There are at least a dozen gentlemen, American and foreign, concerned in supplying the allies with munitions and clothing. There is a delegation of young and adventurous Americans billeted to our hospital at Paris: they are going to drive motor ambulances from the front to the base hospitals ...

... Ex-Senator Lafe Young, of the *Des Moines Capital*, is going over at age 66 to be his own war correspondent. The other newspapermen aboard tell him that this business of sending cub reporters to a great war has got to stop. George Doran, the publisher, is on his way to see why British authors are not writing. Mark Sullivan, editor of *Collier's* is trying to inform himself first hand on the European situation ... Dr. Crozier, of Winnipeg, veteran of the Boer

War, finding himself too old for any more fighting, will go to the front as an army surgeon. W.D. Boyce, the Chicago newspaper publisher, is on his way to Petrograd, not so much because he wants to write about the war, as because he cannot stay away from trouble.

Senator Young remarked yesterday in the presence of Captain Dow, skipper of the *Lusitania*:

'It would be fun to make every one on board tell why he is going to Europe'.

'Hm' said Capt. Dow, 'I'm thinking you'd get some long passages of silence'.

For we have a few mysterious passengers, who seek no smoking-room acquaintances and try to make themselves as inconspicuous as possible. I cannot repeat some of the things I have heard, but there are two or three very pretty little spy games going on under the surface of life on the *Lusitania* … I suspect that as soon as we land in Liverpool, two or three of our passengers will disappear, not to be seen again until the war is over …

We have been going through the motions of a regular voyage … but we have little heart for the game. The auction pool was a failure; the smoking-room gave it up on the fourth night. But the ship's concert became a live issue. The men who went down on the *Cressy*, the *Aboukir* and the *Hogue* were naval reservists, and as such came under the benefits of the Seaman's Fund. The mariners of England must take care of their widows and orphans. Joe Coyne and Frank Belcher started to make this the greatest concert ever held on the high seas. Fate counted them out, however. The cold sea air gave Coyne neuralgia, and Belcher, on the night of the biggest gale, was pitched from his berth and strained his ankle. However, Seton-Thompson, introduced by Senator Young as the greatest animal authority since Noah, impersonated the beasts of the forest, Elsie Janis imitated stage people until she wore out her voice, and an English conjurer favored. The collectors got almost one hundred pounds.

Now we are rolling along the milky waves of the Irish Channel. These seas, in peace time so busy and frequented by crafts of all classes, are now as barren and deserted as the open Atlantic … We shall anchor in the Mersey tonight. Tomorrow morning, escorted by a guide cruiser, we shall zig-zag through the mine fields into port. Before that, the British authorities will have put us under formal arrest, that they may search the more readily for spies and secret agents. And the least imaginative among us will realize that we are entering a world at war.

Later: Now this, at the very threshold of war, illustrates the mystery which surrounds all things European in these days; perhaps it illustrates what a world of rumor this has become. This morning, just off the Irish headlands, we slacked up and hove to. The wireless crackled busily for a few minutes, the sailors made some changes in our appearance, which I shall not mention for fear of the censors, then we proceeded again. At 10 o'clock, the regular wireless news appeared on the bulletin board. It consisted merely of the official communiqués. A little later, however, the rumor grew that ten British merchantmen were torpedoed yesterday by submarines in the English Channel. The stewards, when they talk at all, maintain stoutly that it is true. The officers just as stoutly deny it. We shall not know until the pilot brings the newspapers.[6]

The rumours that Irwin had heard regarding ten British merchant vessels being sunk the day before the *Lusitania* arrived in Liverpool turned out to be false.

When the *Lusitania* next departed Liverpool for the United States on 13 February, the Cunard Line apparently felt there was enough of a threat to the ship that it should be camouflaged again. As soon as *Lusitania* left port, crewmen scrambled about, painting the funnels black.[7] One of the passengers aboard during this voyage was Arthur W. Highfield, president of the Webster Manufacturing Company, accompanied by his wife. Highfield was heading home after six weeks abroad on business. His account of the crossing mentions the uproar that Captain Dow caused by hoisting the American flag on the previous trip, as well as giving a description of his transatlantic crossing to England a month and a half earlier aboard the Cunard Line's RMS *Franconia*.

Highfield describes the strong sense of unity in wartime England, and how everyone was working towards the goal of victory. His description of the *Lusitania* crossing contained some ominous undertones, as the actions taken to protect the great liner make it clear that British officials were at least somewhat worried about the vessel's safety, although publicly, they seemed to show little concern in regards to U-boats and other threats. For its part, Cunard had actually lowered the price of second-class fares following the flag-raising incident, projecting an air of confidence.

Reinforcing this view were the recent statements of Sir Norman Hill, manager of the Liverpool and London War Risk Association, which insured vessels against war hazards, and had 'the right to veto any sailings which it considers involve too much risk'. He said that it had not been considered necessary to do so, and 'We don't consider that the presence of one or two German submarines in Liverpool Bay involves any unreasonable risk to the safety of our ships'. It was stated in the press that 'the big ships with high speed run comparatively little danger from submarines', and pointed out that the government war risk rate had not been altered, although the marine risk rates 'are generally doubled since *U-21* made her appearance in the Irish Sea.' It was also pointed out that the war risk rates were still much lower than they were 'while German commerce destroyers [i.e. the *Kronprinz Wilhelm*] were at large last August'.[8] Highfield's description of the escort out of Liverpool that *Lusitania* received suggests that perhaps not everyone shared this opinion regarding the safety of the large liners:

Our voyage on the *Lusitania* was interesting because of the furore [sic] Captain Dow had caused by flying the stars and stripes into port … We boarded the vessel at 7.30 in the evening and soon afterward dropped down the River Mersey to anchor. It was at this point that I first observed a British warship, in this case a torpedo boat destroyer. The destroyer left us as soon as we dropped anchor, and giving it a two-hours' start to see that the way was clear, we proceeded out of the river.

We passed into the channel at night nad [sic] soon lights from a distant vessel could be seen, barely discernible in the fog. Afterward I learned that the vessel was a British dreadnaught standing on guard to protect our ship, the 'sly grey fox of the sea', as the *Lusitania* is now known. Our pilot, James Durant, was not dropped this trip, but continued with us to New York. He said the *Lusitania* is the prize ship flying under British colors, and would be a great 'catch' for the opposing nations.

The entire trip to New York was made in record time. The British fleet guarded our path and kept the officers informed of any impending danger. In this way, with the passengers ignorant of the situation, the *Lusitania* actually flew to cover of American territory.

Our trip to England was equally as exciting as that on the *Lusitania*. Leaving New York on the Cunard liner *Fanconia* [*Franconia*] we awakened the next day to behold ourselves in Halifax, tied to a wharf instead of being hundreds of miles at sea. Not a passenger was allowed to leave the boat. Here the crews loaded the ship with ammunition, motor vehicles, food, and gold and silver bullion. Several high officials of the Canadian troops made the trip with us.

English people talk little of war, but think much more. They give no idle boasts, but with a grim determination are entering into the conflict 'for Old England's sake'.

Americans are royally welcomed by the English. It is particularly touching to step into a foreign land and be made to feel 'at home' when you know there is sorrow and grief on every side of you … The morning following our arrival in Liverpool a police officer came to our apartments in the Hotel Adelphi. Courteously he called me by name, chatted for half an hour and then asked me to drop around to headquarters at my leisure 'to register. England wants to protect Americans', the officer said.

I went to headquarters that afternoon and when I entered I met the highest officials. They laughed and talked with me, said they were glad to welcome an American. During this time, I almost told them my life history. In this way the welcome to English shores was typically democratic and made me think that I was in America.

Preparations for war in London move on a smooth, quiet, machine-like system. The parks, hotels, private residences and palaces are filled with soldiers.

There are 10,000 quartered in the Tower of London and 8,000 in the famous
Crystal palace. Nothing is too good for the English soldiers and at the expense
of the government they are given the best of accommodations. Recruits are
received daily. In the grist are youths in their teens and iron-gray, stern-faced
men … Soldiers, after six months' training, under cover of darkness, when all
London sleeps, board trains and 'cross'. Quite by accident I saw a train leave
early one morning. There is nothing said of the movement of troops, but a
person 'feels' the activities just the same. You know the men are leaving.[9]

Contrary to Highfield's beliefs, the *Lusitania*'s 13 February crossing was not 'made
in record time'. In fact, it had taken six days, ten hours and six minutes, a very
long crossing for the ship. This was due to the fact that Boiler Room No. 4 was
still not in use, owing to the desire to conserve coal. When the ship arrived safely
in New York, it was noted that for the first time, it was flying the red British
merchant marine flag, rather than the blue British Royal Naval Reserve flag. At
no point during this voyage was the American flag flown.[10]

It is interesting to note that when Highfield crossed to England aboard
Franconia, both munitions and Canadian troops were being transported aboard
the ship. Canada, as a dominion of the British Empire, had immediately and
unhesitatingly supported the declaration of war against Germany and its allies.
Canada's significant contributions and sacrifices during the conflict would
become an important part of its heritage, ultimately allowing it to become
more independent.

Another significant event in the war occurred on 19 February: British and
French naval forces bombarded Ottoman forts in the Dardanelles, after vessels
probing the straits were fired upon. A second attack was launched on 24 February.
These actions marked the beginning of the Gallipoli Campaign. During this ten-
month battle of attrition, the Allies aimed to secure the critical sea supply route
through the Straits of the Dardenelles to Russia between the Aegean Sea and
Black Sea, and to capture the Ottoman capital of Constantinople.

As February drew to a close, U-boats continued to attack merchant shipping,
although only one more vessel was sunk than in January. However, there was an
increase in the number that were torpedoed without warning. When questioned
about this, the German Government stated that since U-boats were vulnerable,
they dared not surface near, and warn, any merchant vessel that could potentially
be armed. It was frequently claimed in the press that submarine crews were cold-
blooded since they did not always rescue survivors of the sunken vessels. It was
explained by Germany that U-boats were so small that they could not take on
survivors in every instance.

For the month, nine vessels were sunk by U-boats, totalling 22,784 tons. Two
additional merchant vessels were damaged. This acceleration in the number

A ship shudders as it receives a torpedo hit from a German U-boat. (Authors' Collection)

of attacks on commerce would dramatically increase over the course of the following month.[11]

February 1915 also marked the start of construction on the Dover Barrage. The barrage would consist of a series of long, light steel indicator nets that were to be anchored to the sea floor at various depths, and were designed to entangle submarines. The indicator nets would be accompanied by layers of minefields, and would be patrolled by Royal Navy destroyers. The barrage was designed to cut off the passage of U-boats through the English Channel, thus reducing their ability to attack merchant shipping there, and forcing the submarines to sail around England and Scotland through the North Sea in order to be resupplied. Following *U-8* getting caught in an indicator net and being scuttled in March 1915, U-boats were ordered not to pass through the English Channel while new tactics were being considered.

Eventually, Germany discovered that the Dover Barrage could be penetrated, given the lack of reliability of the British mines, and a shortage of Royal Navy destroyers available to patrol the barrage. A unique solution to the difficulties of nets was the installation of serrated net cutters on the bows of some U-boats, designed to prevent entanglement in nets or mine cables. Eventually, U-boat commanders found that they could pass through gaps between the indicator nets, or simply surface and coast along the surface of the English Channel under cover of darkness. However, fear on the part of Imperial Germany Navy commanders had bought Britain a year, during which the channel was not utilised by German forces.[12]

A net cutter is plainly visible on the bow of this U-boat. (Authors' Collection)

March–April 1915

Back at sea, some passengers still had to brave the transatlantic crossing. Many did not feel that they were taking a great risk in doing so. One example was Jack Bolar of Bedale, England, who boarded the *Lusitania* at Liverpool on 20 March, headed for New York. By that point, Captain Daniel Dow was no longer in command of the ship. Following the crossing that concluded on 6 March, an exhausted Dow informed Cunard Chairman Alfred Booth that travelling through the waters of the declared 'war zone' around the British Isles did not bother him, but he disagreed with the ship carrying munitions and civilians. Cunard immediately gave him leave, explaining that Dow was 'tired and really ill'. Captain William T. Turner, who had previously been master of both the *Mauretania* and *Aquitania*, was given command of *Lusitania*, and would be completing his first voyage as her captain.[13] Despite these goings-on, passengers such as Jack Bolar did not seem concerned during the trip, as evidenced from the following letter that he wrote to his brothers and sisters from aboard the vessel:

Captain William Turner. (J. Kent Layton Collection/ Library of Congress, Prints & Photographs Division)

On our way to New York.

March 24th, 1915

My Dear Bros & sisters

Thanks so much for your very nice letter and wire. I was very sorry that I did not see you before I left England but I expect I shall be seeing all again before long God willing.

I have had a lovely trip up to now I have been sick once for about half an hour and we about 3 parts away to New York. I have had to leave this letter to go and look at 3 ice bergs two off [sic] them were a good size they were about 5 miles away and they looked quite as large as this boat and this is like a small town. It is about as far from Bedale Church down to your shop so that gives you an idea. When we left for Liverpool their [sic] was two destroyers took us out to see [sic] and we were well protected by our war ships and every one feels quite safe I expect you will think that it is quite a trieding [sic] ride but there is plenty of fun concert and skipping football and all kinds of games down stairs to take your time up. I will write you again in a few days so good by [sic] all for the preasent [sic].

Your loving bro

Jack Bolar xxxx[14]

An assistant purser on the same voyage, Len Sloane, wrote a brief letter to his mother once *Lusitania* was near the Ambrose Channel Light Vessel, just outside the port of New York and New Jersey. Like Bolar, he too described the crossing as uneventful. However, as they were getting close to port, he did note the presence of one of the Royal Navy cruisers, patrolling outside of the 3-mile limit of the United States' territorial waters:

Len Sloane posing in uniform. (Mark Astbury Collection)

Ambrose Ch L.V.
March 26th 1915

Dear Mother

Just a line to let you know I have arrived, expect to be in dock by 9 p.m. Have had a good passage & the weather is very good.

We have just passed one of our sea dogs outside the three mile limit. Hope all are well. Thanks for your letter at stage. Lehar Op:

Love to all,
Len[15]

Near the end of March, an event occurred that would draw the neutral United States to the very precipice of war. The event in question was the capture and sinking of the Elder, Dempster & Company liner RMS *Falaba* by *U-28*. This was the first passenger liner sunk by a U-boat in the war. The *Falaba* departed Liverpool on 27 March, with planned stops at several British colonies along the West Africa coast.

The vessel had 147 passengers and ninety-seven crewmembers aboard. It was also carrying 13 tons of contraband cartridges and gunpowder. On 28 March, the *Falaba* was making 13½ knots as it steamed south-west through the Irish Sea. Captain Frederick Davis expected the vessel to be off the Welsh coast, near an outcropping of rocks known as the Smalls. At 11.40 a.m. a trawler was spotted off the port side of the ship. Soon, crewmembers and passengers noticed that a submarine was sailing along in front of it.

RMS *Falaba*. (*The Illustrated War News*, 1915/Authors' Collection)

Captain Davis ordered the helmsman to change course to show the submarine *Falaba*'s stern and began steaming away, in case it was hostile. Passengers were not yet alarmed, watching with curiosity. After the submarine altered course and began pursuing *Falaba*, that changed and passengers began going below deck to get their lifebelts in case it became necessary to evacuate. Soon, the pursuer was close enough to be identified as a U-boat, flying the German ensign. In short order, the U-boat overhauled its prey, firing a rocket as a warning.

Captain Davis ordered the *Falaba*'s engines stopped, and the submarine, which was in fact *U-28*, pulled alongside. Meanwhile, the ship sent a wireless message saying that they had stopped, were likely to be torpedoed, and asked that a battleship be informed. At noon, the submarine's commander, Kapitänleutnant Georg-Günther von Forstner, hailed *Falaba* through a megaphone, saying 'take to the boats, as they were going to sink the ship in five minutes'. Confident that he could take his time in sinking the vessel, von Forstner allowed his crew to come on deck and watch the events.

Rough seas made it difficult for the crewmen to properly lower the lifeboats, and the evacuation was described as a 'scramble'. The scene was chaotic: falls slipped as the lifeboats were being lowered. Some got stuck on one side, sending the boats slamming down into the water, flooding them, and casting people into the frigid ocean. At 12.05 a.m., Kapitänleutnant von Forstner decided that *U-28* was at risk and could wait no longer. He fired a single torpedo at *Falaba*, striking the forward starboard end of the ship. The explosion detonated the munitions in the cargo, causing a large explosion that could be heard 16 miles away. The ship began listing to starboard and settling by its stern, sinking just five minutes later.

For a short time after this, *U-28* remained on the scene, giving false hope to those in the water that it might rescue them. Ultimately, the U-boat dove and did not surface again. Rescue came in the form of several small steam drifters, which had left Milford Haven that morning for fishing grounds, including the *Eileen Emma*. The destroyer HMS *Liffey* eventually took many of the survivors off the smaller vessels. Overall, 104 people were killed in the sinking.[16] One of the survivors, William McLelly of London, gave a detailed account of the attack:

> Everyone on board became excited when it became known that a submarine was near, and the passengers crowded on deck. The captain of the *Falaba* put on full steam, but very soon it became evident that we had no chance of getting away from the enemy three quarters of an hour after we sighted the submarine she was within hailing distance of us. She appeared to be one of the latest and biggest boats, and was carrying a good-sized gun, which was bearing on the *Falaba*.

The *U-28*, photographed from the *Falaba* during the attack. (*Daily Mirror*, 1915/Authors' Collection)

As soon as the submarine got near us the commander sent up a rocket. Then, coming nearer, he ordered our captain to get every passenger into the boats at once, saying in good English, 'I am going to sink the ship'.

Then followed a terrible scene. Some of the boats were swamped, and the occupants thrown into the sea, several being drowned almost immediately. One man whom I afterwards met was picked up after being in the water an hour.

Barely ten minutes after we received the order to leave the ship, and before the last boat was lowered, I heard a report, and saw our vessel heel over. The pirates had actually fired a torpedo at her at a range of 100 yards, when they could distinctly see a large number of passengers and crew, including the captain, the purser, and other officers still on board. It was a dastardly thing to do – nothing but murder in cold blood.

The *Falaba* soon went to the bottom. Without waiting to see how we fared in the boats, the submarine made off in the direction from which she had come.

After we had been in the boats about two hours we were picked up by a Lowestoft trawler and two other trawlers. Three hours later we were landed at Milford Haven.[17]

An officer who survived the sinking, speaking anonymously, gave the following account:

> It was murder, simply murder. We saw the submarine in the distance on our starboard side. It signalled us to stop, but we made a run for it, hoping we could outdistance the submarine. We failed to do this, as she was making 18 knots and we could only do 13.
>
> It was a large submarine, and looked to be one of the newest. We stopped at last. I was told she hailed, though I did not hear anything. There was a nasty sea running and some of the boats which we launched were immediately swamped.
>
> I noticed that one boat fell into the water as she was being lowered. Scores of persons were in the sea, for some other boats had been swamped as well. In fact, all the boats except three foundered.
>
> They gave us no time to get away. They torpedoed us while there were still many on board, and while one boat was actually being lowered. I tell you, it was a murderous game they played. They made no attempt to save anybody, although there was only one trawler in sight, and no destroyers or cruisers.[18]

Another surviving crewmember, Quartermaster R. Monteith also gave a vivid description of the events:

> … we sighted a submarine, whose number appeared to have been blotted out. We tried to avoid her by manoeuvring, but by means of signals, she ordered us to stop.
>
> Captain Davis, however, did not immediately obey the order, and the submarine, which was very fast, overhauled us and gave us ten minutes to leave our vessel. Lifebelts had already been distributed among the passengers and crew, and the boats were swung on the davits ready for lowering.
>
> … The crew proceeded to lower the boats, of which there were seven. The first dropped some distance into the water, and was smashed to pieces.
>
> Of the others, two were swamped by the heavy sea which was running, and the occupants thrown into the turbulent water. The other four boats were safely launched with about thirty occupants each.
>
> The women on the *Falaba* numbered nine, and of these six were saved in the boats. The other three, despite entreaties, refused to leave the ship, being afraid to get into the boats and be lowered into the stormy waves …
>
> When the torpedo was launched at the *Falaba* there would be about forty people aboard – most of them comprising the crew. The torpedo hit us abaft the engine-room: there was a tremendous explosion, the vessel heeled over, and went down in ten minutes.

In view of the terrible scene which ensued, it was marvellous how both passengers and crew behaved. The boats had been lowered with great difficulty, the crew working with magnificent pluck and skill.

When we were struck the forty people remaining on the *Falaba* had to do the best they could for themselves, as all the boats had gone. I jumped overboard, as did others, and managed to get hold of a piece of wreckage, which helped keep me afloat until I was picked up by one of the boats.

Captain Davis, when I saw him last, was taking a plunge from the sinking vessel. He was picked up afterwards, but died from exposure.

Among the women who were saved was one plucky lady passenger, who kept as cool as any of the men, and helped to bale out the water from the boat in which she was rescued.

From the time we saw the submarine until the sinking of the vessel, as far as I could guess, was about twenty-five minutes. There were some soldiers aboard on their way to the West Coast of Africa, and they gave all the assistance possible to the crew in the terrible circumstances.[19]

Arthur H. Killip, one of the musicians on board the *Falaba*, also survived the sinking. Following the rescue, he gave a detailed account of the disaster:

About a mile off, when getting our music ready for lunch, we saw a long grey thing in the water, but did not know what to make of it. It was lying behind a trawler … we could not discover what it was. Suddenly it began to draw near,

Falaba's passengers and crewmembers don lifebelts as they prepare to abandon ship. (*Daily Mirror*, 1915/Authors' Collection)

coming at the rate of about eighteen knots an hour. It came along towards the port side, and we were at first completely deceived.

The craft was then flying the British white ensign, and we thought we were all right. Almost immediately after we began to feel a little queer, for the German flag was hoisted next to the white ensign, and a few seconds later the vessel, which we now realised to be a German submarine, ran up a third flag, this time a 'Death's head and cross bones'. We knew then what we were in for yet nobody was terrified, though we naturally felt very anxious. The submarine went round swiftly to the port side of the *Falaba*, and exhibiting a blue flash ordered us to stop.

We stopped at once, and were ordered to get the boats out. I heard Captain Davis sing out the order to man the boats, and the passengers were directed to get into them. One of the boats unfortunately broke as it was being lowered, and some of the people struggling in the water below were hurt. The ladies displayed remarkable calmness throughout. Meantime I had secured a lifebelt, and I began to look round for a lifeboat into which I could get.

After finding two or three that were full, I saw one in which there was some room. When it had been lowered to the level of the second deck I jumped from the deck above and landed all right into the boat I was aiming for …

Survivors from the *Falaba* cling to a capsized lifeboat as one of the rescue vessels approaches. (*The Illustrated War News*, 1915/Authors' Collection)

The passengers helped eagerly to row the lifeboat I was in, which was No. 3, their help being necessary, as not many of the crew were available. They held back, greatly to their credit, to allow the passengers accommodations behaving very nobly indeed. We were in the lifeboat a couple of hours, when we were taken on board the *Eileen Emma*, a drifter, which happened to come up. It was at this time that I had my narrowest escape. My hands were tired with the unusual effort of rowing, and as we were being transferred the hand I put out to touch the drifter's rail was so numbed that I could not grasp it, and I fell into the water. I cannot swim, but I made an effort to keep myself on the surface, and succeeded in catching a rope, holding on till I was pulled on board.

When we were well away from the *Falaba* we could see the submarine, and we also heard a very loud explosion, which sent up a column of smoke and water, higher than the funnels … The *Falaba* went over on her side, and began gradually, yet unceasingly to sink by the stern. We were a good way off when she sank.

One of the first persons I noticed on board the trawler was Captain Davis. He was in a state of complete exhaustion, and died soon after being taken on board. He must have been, I think, greatly affected, and I was told by other survivors that he was hurt, probably by reason of being thrown against something. The whole disaster was over in about ten minutes.[20]

The attack sparked public outrage. Scrutiny in the press mounted, fuelled by biased claims of 'murder', 'jeering Germans' that lined the decks of *U-28*, mocking those in the water as their ship sank, etc. To make matters worse, one of the passengers that had been killed was Leon C. Thrasher, a mining engineer and American citizen who had been travelling as a second-class passenger. Once this was learned, pressure mounted on the United States to make an official response.

President Wilson, under the advice of Counselor to the State Department Robert Lansing, drafted a note condemning the attack and Germany's actions. Lansing advocated for a harder-line approach with Germany, i.e. the 'strict accountability' that on 10 February, President Wilson had declared would follow the loss of the lives of any American citizens as the result of Germany's submarine policy. Lansing contended that Thrasher's death had resulted from an illegal act by a German captain, and that law required that a naval commander ensured the safety of passengers before sinking a vessel as a prize.

Secretary of State William Jennings Bryan, disagreed fervently, believing that 'virtually no law, no moral principle, and no national interest were worth the risk of war'. He believed that Thrasher, being plainly aware of Germany's recent 'war zone decree', had voluntarily risked death. In his letter to the president, he wrote 'I cannot help feeling that it would be a sacrifice of the interests of all the people to allow one man, acting purely for himself and his

Robert Lansing. (*Collier's*, 1917/Authors' Collection)

own interests, and without consulting his government, to involve the entire nation in difficulty when he had ample warning of the risks which he assumed'.[21]

After persistent requests by Bryan, President Wilson hesitated for three weeks, consulting his cabinet and other advisors, although he was still in favour of issuing a 'solemn and emphatic protest against the whole thing'. During this diplomatic delay, Bryan obtained documents and eyewitness statements relating to the sinking of the *Falaba*. This information suggested that instead of immediately stopping and beginning the evacuation, the crew of the *Falaba* had used the allotted time to send distress signals to nearby Royal Navy patrol vessels, had sent up distress rockets to signal for help, and that the U-boat had only fired at the last minute as other vessels approached.[22]

Bryan suggested that instead of protesting the death of Thrasher, which could lead to war, the United States should speak on behalf of the 'tens of thousands who are dying daily in this causeless war', and that the president should make a public appeal for the acceptance of mediation. Wilson was moved by Bryan's words, and while rejecting his recommendation to appeal for peace, he decided 'Perhaps, it is not necessary to make formal representations … at all'.

The resolution of the whole affair, which became known as the 'Thrasher Incident' prevented the United States from being drawn into the war. However, on 28 April 1915, the day after Wilson backed down from a formal protest, a German plane bombed the SS *Cushing*, an American freighter, in the North Sea. On 1 May, *U-30* attacked the American tanker SS *Gulflight* without warning. Two American sailors drowned after leaping overboard, and the captain died of a heart attack during the incident. Neither ship sank, and the events were

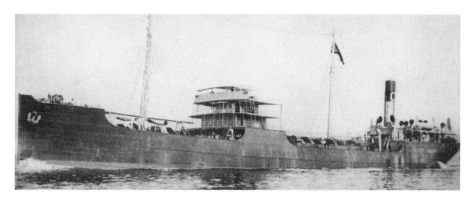

The SS *Gulflight*. (*Collier's*, 1917/Authors' Collection)

accidental, as American flags and markings had not been seen prior to the attacks. Germany apologised, but the incidents ignited further tensions between the two nations. Public opinion in the United States continued to shift against them, and some began referring to Germans as 'Huns', a term frequently used in Allied propaganda to emphasise the idea that all Germans were barbarians.[23]

Including the *Falaba*, the total number of merchant vessels sunk or damaged by U-boats during March 1915 dramatically increased. They had managed to sink or capture thirty-six vessels, for a total loss of 79,369 tons of shipping. Six vessels were damaged but did not sink.[24]

April 1915 would mark a significant development on the Western Front. The German Army employed chlorine gas during the Second Battle of Ypres, the first successful and large-scale use of gas as a weapon. The battle lasted from late April 1915 until late May 1915, with no clear victor.

At the beginning of April, the *Lusitania* was about to leave port on what would be its final complete New York to Liverpool crossing. The *Lusitania* was scheduled to depart on 3 April, but a late-season blizzard had hit the East Coast of the United States early that morning, dropping 10 inches of snow, and bringing wind gusts up to 75 miles per hour. It was reported that 'in the North River it was impossible to see from one shore to the other'. After all 830 passengers had boarded, Captain Turner decided that it would be ill-advised to leave port in driving snow, and attempt to blindly manoeuvre to open waters. Several other vessels had attempted to depart throughout the day, and none managed to make it past Sandy Hook due to the conditions.[25]

Owing to the weather, it would be 4 April, Easter Sunday, before *Lusitania* was able to depart, a considerable delay. One of the passengers aboard was Joseph Gallagher of Lima, Ohio. He noted that the crew was taking precautions against both submarines and spies:

The *Lusitania* in New York Harbour. (Authors' Collection)

… she was detained in New York nearly 24 hours by an unusually violent blizzard, and it is true that a couple of passengers, both American, alarmed by the talk about submarines in the smoking room, cancelled their passages and crossed by the American liner *St. Paul*. On the last night of the voyage, again, when we were tearing up St. George's Channel at top speed a few nervous women refused to sleep in their cabins and spent an uncomfortable night on sofas and cushions in the saloon.

With the exception of these isolated instances, however, there was as much joking and laughter on the subject of submarines as though they were nothing more than phantom *Flying Dutchmen* and it was quite a common jest, if we saw a fellow passenger gazing dreamily at the sea, to ask him if he had 'spotted a periscope' yet.

On the other hand, the official precautions that were actually taken against attack were very thorough. All through the voyage the ship was darkened at night, and when the Irish coast was neared, it was evident that Captain Turner, at least, had no illusions about the possibility of being torpedoed.

Every boat was swung out, ready to be launched at a moment's notice, deck lights were extinguished altogether, and the saloon lights were put out at an unusually early hour. Passengers, too, were requested to remain 'indoors'.

Right from New York the ship had been steaming at a comparatively slow pace, considering her real speed, 'til we got near Ireland … but on the Friday

The cover of the
passenger list for
Lusitania's scheduled
3 April 1915 voyage.
(Authors' Collection)

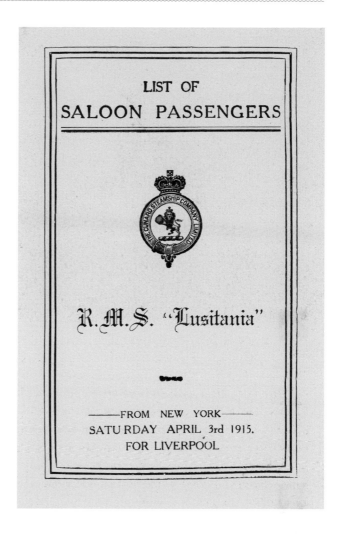

LIST OF
SALOON PASSENGERS

R.M.S. "Lusitania"

————FROM NEW YORK————
SATURDAY APRIL 3rd 1915.
FOR LIVERPOOL

before reaching Liverpool it was obvious to all of us that she was going full
steam ahead for the last lap.

The increased vibration alone was enough to show the veriest landlubber
that the race for safety had begun. And at noon the next day there was quite
a little crowd round the log-board to see if the ship had done anything in the
way of breaking record. To everybody's intense surprise the log showed only
450 miles; figures, if anything, slightly under the average daily run we had made
from New York. The mystery was explained (unofficially) later on when we
heard that the run was in actual mileage 580 miles, but that we had been 'zigzagging' out of our course for the express purpose of baffling any submarine
that might be lying in wait for us. I cannot vouch for the truth of this statement
but it is the only explanation that seems to fit the facts.

Another singular incident occurred on the same night. In spite of the warning to passengers to avoid the decks, one of the steerage passengers persisted in remaining on the lower deck. Presently he began striking matches with the apparent object of lighting his pipe. This he found a strangely difficult proceeding. Match after match was struck, flared up with uncommon brilliance in the intense darkness and then went out. His curious proceedings were not left unmarked, and before long one of the detectives on board – and there were few of us who even suspected the presence of these unobtrusive officials – went up to him, took him by the arm and led him away.

Whether, as the detective suspected, he was actually trying to signal the liner's whereabouts to some German pirate, or whether he was merely a fool who did not realize the criminality of his act I cannot say. But he was certainly locked up for the night and kept under close supervision until we reached Liverpool. Of his ultimate fate, I know nothing. He was not, by the way, the only suspect on board. At least three other individuals were detained at the landing stage as suspicious persons but here again I know nothing of how they fared eventually.

I have quoted these incidents to show, light hearted as the passengers were the Cunard company were fully alive to the submarine peril and took every precaution against the danger that common sense could suggest.

There was one precaution I think no one neglected to take, little though he may have thought of the danger. And that was to see that the lifebelts in his cabin were handy and to make sure, by experiment, that he could slip one on easily at a moment's notice. But, as I say, the dominant note that remains in my mind of the behavior of the whole ship's company on the … homeward trip was an unfailing lighthearted cheerfulness. Indeed … the precautions taken against submarine attack, so far from frightening the passengers actually added a pleasant touch of excitement and zest to the voyage.

It must be remembered, too, that nobody supposed for a moment that even a German submarine would attack without warning or that ample time would not be given all on board to escape. So that at the worst all we anticipated was a few hours in an open boat and plenty to talk about for the rest of our lives.

One began to sense the fact that a great war – a world war – is actually in progress.[26]

Another passenger aboard the same voyage was Charles Edward Russell, the noted socialist and co-founder of the National Association for the Advancement of Colored People (NAACP). Russell, contrary to Gallagher's claim, indicates that there was a high degree of tension and paranoia aboard during the crossing:

Charles Edward Russell. (*Review of Reviews and World's Work*, 1907/Authors' Collection)

Everybody watched the sailors. They are getting every lifeboat out of its bed and swinging it outboard all ready to launch. This looks like business: ordinarily the lifeboats rest on their beds from port to port and year to year.

Next, the stewards tack black paper over the windows, pull the shutters over the stateroom ports, screw down the deadeyes, blanket the sides in canvas and put out all the deck lights. That is the most shivery of all; you put your head out of the cabin door and seem to be stepping in to a bale of black wool. And through it the steamer is ripping, without showing a ray of light.

After these precautions, the careful male passenger takes down the life preserver from the top shelf of the closet and drills himself, and his womenkind if such there be, in its use.

Passengers are told if they go to bed that night, to have the life preserver and warm clothing handy. Open boats at night are colder than Greenland's icy.

Some of us improve on this sound advice by putting on the warm clothing, and the life preserver over that, and sitting up all night. I may observe here that at this stage of the voyage nobody talks about submarines, battleships nor sunken vessels.

By some secret psychology the whole subject is dropped. Also we bear ourselves with an elaborate unconcern. But one thing betrays us. At dinner there is some crash of machinery somewhere below, and half the company jump up breathless. Tension – we all feel it.

When we are shot fairly into the danger zone, 300 pairs of eyes sweep incessantly that dull gray stretch of water. No periscope the size of a man's hand could escape that scrutiny of the volunteer guard. The loom of a peaceful trawler in the mist brings out every pair of glasses in the two cabins.

And now, where are those convoys? We are right in the midst of the danger field. On this spot, the *Punxatawney* was sunk with all hands, and over there the *City of Shoreditch* was struck down. Where are the convoys? ... they are at least 500 miles ahead, and somewhere in the North Sea.

The afternoon grinds away in this feverish fashion ... there isn't any submarine, any visible convoy, any frowning battleship. We are not stopped, nor interfered with, nor observed, and so far as we can detect, if we were a German pirate we could sail right up the Mersey and shell Liverpool itself.

But when, with the lamps of the city ahead, the stewards turn on the deck lights and the boats are swung in again, you can tell what weight has been on the passengers' minds by the cheer they raise – a cheer and more than one huge sigh of relief.

But, how about those convoys anyway? Why, there weren't any. The British government didn't provide them. The ship is one of the nation's dearest possessions and cost a staggering sum, to which the government contributed, but the government didn't provide any guard for it, and it might have been sunk as easily as the *Falaba*, the *Wayfarer*, and the rest of the great fleet of recent merchantmen that now paves the Irish Sea.

When you are about to board a steamer for Liverpool and you read in the dispatches how all the waters thereabout are alive with submarines zealously sinking everything that floats, the news is not exhilarating. Here is an account of a steamer like yours torpedoed close by Liverpool lightship itself – the audacious undersea raider! It jolts you up a lot inside; there's no use denying it.

The most of us would fain die a dry death, if any, and anyway, to be spilled in the middle of the night from a warm berth into the icy waters of the Irish Sea is no way to treat a man of peace. It gives you gooseflesh to think about it ...

... Still, I shall always maintain that goose flesh is only in good form when roasted and brought to the table with apple sauce. It has no proper business to come bothering around when you lie in your berth and count up how many steamers have been torpedoed in St. George's channel towards which you are now flying. So, to cheer us up, they circulated that story about the convoy of British warships (which never came) to see us across.

But, everything has an end, and finally the great *Lusitania* tied up at the dock in Liverpool. We are going down the gangway from the steamer to the landing stage. But, who are all these clean shaven, furtive looking men that go snooping about, plainly watching the passengers?

Scotland Yard detectives, no less; a whole drove of them; and the business of landing is drawn out five hours, that they may scrutinize everybody. They pick out six of our passengers and have them detained by the police ... The spy mania! Because of the war, it is epidemic in England now ...[27]

Reverend W. Waldo Weller, Vice Consul of the United States at Glasgow, had been aboard the *Lusitania* during this voyage, along with his family. In his account, he mentioned a hitherto unmentioned incident in which a young man aboard passed away during the crossing, and since the ship lacked the facilities for storing the body, was buried at sea. Concerns about U-boats no doubt played a role in the fact that the vessel did not slow down during the memorial ceremony and burial. Weller also mentions the slow crossing speed, which was due to the one boiler room still being shut down:

> Outside the three-mile limit, we came across one of England's converted cruisers, in her gray paint, St. George's flag at the stern. There was nervousness on board and passengers were not entirely at ease, even on this sailing …
>
> … there were large numbers of children on board and a great many unaccompanied women, going home to meet their families or husbands abroad. The *Lusitania* presented then, as always, a very wonderful and impressive sight. To go aft, and high up on the Sun Deck, which is the highest deck, a view forward shows the rows of lifeboats on both sides of the ship – two deep. The great vessel rose and fell as easily and beautifully upon the long ocean swell as a living creature. Three of her monstrous funnels belched out black clouds of smoke. The fourth funnel was not in use.
>
> Yet the trip was hourly growing more gloomy as we approached England. Thursday night a young man died and Friday evening at 6 o'clock Captain Turner, who was in command on our voyage, as on the last one, with all the chief officers, came to the stern, and after a brief moment of service, without the slightest slowing in speed, that young man was buried at sea; the propellers churning the sea, the vessel heeling to one side as she sped along without a moment's pause. That afternoon the boats on both port and starboard side had been swung out on the davits, preparatory for any emergency. All of us passengers watched the performance with more curiosity than fear.
>
> But Friday night was to be a gloomy and disturbed one, for after midnight we would be off the Irish coast. Early in the evening all ports were closed, dead lights as well, and saloon windows curtained. The decks were plunged into total darkness. Down in the state room corridors a steward could be heard calling out 'Put those lights out; do you want an officer from the bridge down?' The emergency oil lamps glimmered there and there along the companion ways, and as night wore on only the deep rumble of the propellers could be heard. I took an English gentleman, who impresses the water mark on English paper currency, out upon the deck, and pointed the great funnels out to him. Now all four of them were in use; hitherto a series of boilers had not been used. They were smoking like volcanoes, the ship was traveling at a very great speed and increasing apparently every moment. There was a hiss as of escaping steam, the black water boiled with white patches of foam as we sped along. Night wore on. Soon everything was quiet; all were in bed. But as we lay in our berths we could hear the terrific churning of the propellers under the incredible speed. We were tossed from the one side to the other of our berths. Not only was the

ship going exceedingly fast, she was zigzagging as well, and it was a night of worry and fear for almost everybody. But the night passed, and the morning broke foggy, with rain falling. In the distance the Irish coast could be seen.

Our speed had availed us for we were past Kinsale Head … In fact, our speed of the night before had taken us well up the Irish Sea. The day was foggy and rain fell most of the morning. This was our exceeding good fortune. But here are two strange features of the case. The ship, although in a danger zone, was going quite slowly, and during the entire morning not a torpedo boat or cruiser or war vessel of any kind met us … All day Saturday we passed up the Irish Sea, and again at night all lights went out – then we came to the Mersey Bar. There was suspense, for right here a ship had been hit. Then we were on the bar, and minute more and all lights flashed on. We had passed the bar, no harm could befall us. A few hours and we were off Liverpool. The rumble of the propellers ceased – the anchors went down. It was the longest trip ever made in point of time of passage by the *Lusitania*. Now was an hour of rejoicing; then again all was quiet. Everyone slept roundly and well that night. Breakfast was to be served next morning at 6.30 and all were soon to land.

That was the last time this beautiful ship was to cast anchor in safety off Liverpool …[28]

After safely completing its crossing on 10 April, the *Lusitania* remained in port until departing for New York once again on 17 April. However, instead of heading for the open sea, the ship anchored in the River Mersey until nightfall. By doing so, Captain Turner was following an order given by the British Admiralty. The Admiralty had also issued a series of directives for vessels operating in the waters of the declared 'war zone'. The list of directives were as follows:

1. To avoid headlands, where U-boats typically hunted
2. To steer a mid-channel course
3. To operate at full speed off harbours
4. To preserve wireless silence within 100 miles of land, save for an emergency
5. To post extra lookouts
6. To maintain lifeboats ready for lowering and provisioned
7. To keep on the move outside ports and harbours
8. To steer a zigzag course

Captain Turner did not zigzag as *Lusitania* sailed through the 'war zone' waters, heading for America.[29]

On 25 April 1915, Allied forces landed at Gallipoli, in an attempt to secure the peninsula and capture Ottoman forts that were controlling access to the Straits of

An airplane flying over the *Lusitania* on 17 April 1915. (Authors' Collection)

the Dardenelles, and then capture Constantinople. After British and French naval forces had previously failed to secure the straits by sea, a land invasion became inevitable. The area where the Australian and New Zealand Army Corps (Anzac) troops landed became known as Anzac Cove. British and French forces landed that same day, several miles to the south-west at Cape Helles. Both landings were badly mismanaged, and became bloodbaths.

The Gallipoli Campaign would drag on until the Allied forces were evacuated on 9 January 1916. Few substantial gains would be made beyond the territory captured on the first day of the invasion. Estimates indicate that there were as many as 252,000 Allied casualties, and between 218,000 and 251,000 Ottoman casualties.[30] The campaign was considered a substantial victory for the Ottoman forces, and a devastating defeat for the Allies, who failed to take their objectives, despite the costs in blood and treasure.

The campaign was also the first major battle undertaken in the war by Australia and New Zealand. Despite being countries only since 1901 and 1907 respectively, and despite their heavy losses, both nations often mark the campaign as the birth of their national consciousness. The large amount of equipment and troops that were being moved through the Mediterranean, as well as the number of wounded being evacuated, would eventually press additional passenger vessels into military service to serve as transports and hospital ships.[31]

Another significant development in the war took place on 26 April, when Britain, France and Russia signed the London Pact, a secret agreement intended to gain the alliance of Italy. A nominal ally of Austria- Hungary and Germany, Italy was to declare war on them within a month, and in exchange, was promised territorial gains from the Allies following the war, if they were victorious.[32]

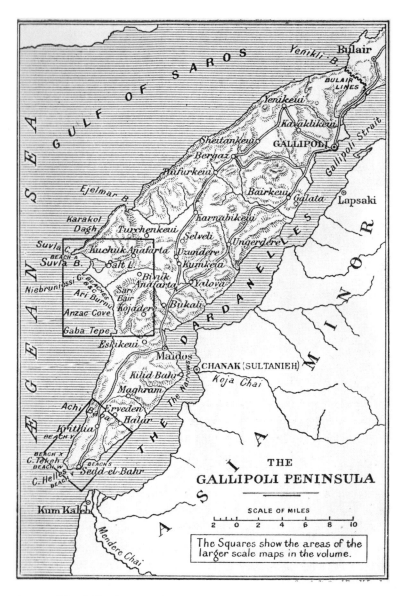

A map of the Gallipoli Peninsula. The Anzac Cove and Cape Helles landing sites are marked by boxes. (Authors' Collection)

After entering the war, Italy repeatedly launched attacks into Austria, making little progress and suffering significant casualties. Its army was then completely routed by an Austro-Hungarian counteroffensive in 1917, before making gains into their territory during the last weeks of the war in 1918. While the Italian contribution to the outcome of the war would prove to be minimal and Italy was ultimately denied many territories promised in the treaty, the London Pact was significant in that it eliminated another ally, albeit a weak one, from the Central Powers' column.

Meanwhile, April 1915 had proved to be another deadly month at sea. U-boats managed to sink or capture thirty-seven vessels for a grand total loss of 61,632 tons of shipping. Two vessels were damaged in encounters with submarines. More people were killed by U-boats than during the previous month, although fewer ships were sent to the bottom. However, 684 of these deaths came from the sinking of the French cruiser *Léon Gambetta* by the Austro-Hungarian submarine *U-5*, a significant incident in the bourgeoning Mediterranean U-boat campaign. Most U-boat attacks and sinkings up to that point had taken place in the Atlantic. The commander of *U-5* at the time was Georg Ritter von Trapp, who would later gain fame through the musical and movie that was based on his family, *The Sound of Music*.[33]

May–June 1915

As May 1915 began, several significant military actions were taking place on land. On the Eastern Front, the Gorlice-Tarnów Offensive was under way. The Western Front remained stuck in a bloody stalemate, but things were going much better for Germany on the Eastern Front. This offensive was intended as a minor operation to relieve the pressure that was being exerted on Austro-Hungarian troops by the Russians, but resulted in the Central Powers recapturing Galacia and the total collapse of the Russian lines in the area.

On the Gallipoli Peninsula between 6 and 8 May, Allied forces suffered yet another setback in the campaign at the Second Battle of Krithia, when they were defeated by the Turks. With the operations to capture the Dardanelles becoming a complete disaster, someone needed to take the blame. Winston Churchill, the First Lord of the Admiralty, was removed from his position on 25 May, because he was one of the foremost responsible for planning the Gallipoli Campaign. Churchill would remain in the Cabinet for several more months, and then rejoined the British Army, serving on the Western Front. The failure of the amphibious landings in Gallipoli stuck with Churchill. Nearly three decades later during the Second World War, as Prime Minister, he was initially reluctant to embrace Operation Overlord, the plan for the D-Day invasion. This may have been due in part to memories of the Gallipoli Campaign.

Meanwhile, back in New York, the RMS *Lusitania* was scheduled to depart for Liverpool on Saturday, 1 May. Dock workers and crewmembers were swarming over the pier, busy loading the ship's cargo. Amongst more mundane cargo such as foodstuffs, periodicals, furs, etc., there were items that the British themselves had classified as 'absolute contraband' earlier in the war: 4,200 cases of Remington rifle cartridges, 1,248 empty shrapnel shells and eighteen cases of non-explosive fuses.[34] The fact that munitions were being carried on a British merchant liner that was carrying British civilians and civilians from neutral countries such as the United States had disquieted the *Lusitania*'s former commander, Captain Dow, and was one factor that had led to his apparent breakdown and departure.

German spies on the New York waterfront had recently relayed information that was passed on to Berlin regarding the 'depressed mood' of the liner's crewmembers, and stated that some had hoped that the upcoming voyage would be 'the last Atlantic crossing during the war'.[35] While there is no evidence that Cunard or the British Admiralty were planning on pulling the *Lusitania* from passenger service, it does illustrate that the constant pressure and threat of attack from U-boats and other vessels, factors which had finally got to Captain Dow prior to his replacement by Captain Turner, were also wearing on the everyday crewmen aboard.

Compounding matters, the German Embassy in Washington DC purchased an advertisement that was published in all of the New York newspapers on the day of *Lusitania*'s departure:

NOTICE!

Travellers intending to embark on the Atlantic voyage are reminded that a state of war exists between Germany and her allies and Great Britain and her allies; that zone of war includes waters adjacent to the British Isles; that, in accordance with formal notice given by the Imperial German Government, vessels flying the flag of Great Britain, or of any of her allies, are liable to destruction in those waters and that travellers sailing in the war zone on ships of Great Britain or her allies do so at their own risk.

IMPERIAL GERMAN EMBASSY
Washington, D.C., 22 April, 1915[36]

The warning created a buzz amongst the New York press, and some travellers were alarmed by this new development. Although no specific ship was mentioned in the German Embassy's warning, it appeared to many to be aimed at the *Lusitania*. When German Ambassador Johann Heinrich von Bernstorff was asked about the statement, he replied that it was merely a friendly warning. However, Germany was fully aware that *Lusitania* and other merchant vessels had been carrying contraband cargo in the form of munitions and war stuffs. Since Germany's declaration of the 'war zone', this meant that the ship had essentially become a blockade-runner.[37]

Due to the alarm that the German Embassy had created, Charles P. Sumner, Cunard's general agent in New York, issued a statement to passengers gathering at Pier 54, hoping to calm their nerves:

The truth is that the *Lusitania* is the safest boat on the sea. She is too fast for any submarine. No German war vessel can get her or near her. She will reach Liverpool on schedule time and come back on schedule time just as long as we are able to run her in the transatlantic trade.

Continuing on, Sumner added that he had no fear of submarines whatsoever, pointing out that the British Navy was responsible for all British ships and 'especially for Cunarders'. He also stated the following:

The Germans have been trying to spoil our trade for some time. I anticipate that from this time on every German method that can be devised will be used to keep people from traveling on our ships.[38]

The press also descended upon Captain Turner, informing him about the warning in the papers. He laughed, saying 'I wonder what the Germans will do next. Well, it doesn't seem as if they had scared many people from going on the ship by the look of the pier and the passenger list'. Cunard Line agents denied that there were any cancellations due to the statement from the German Embassy, and also stated 'there was no truth in the printed reports that several prominent passengers had received anonymous telegrams warning them not to sail ... '.[39] It had been rumoured that some of the passengers had received 'warnings in the form of unsigned telegrams that it would be best for them to sail by some vessels other than the *Lusitania*, and that the *Lusitania* would be torpedoed when she neared or got into European waters'.[40]

One of the more prominent passengers who allegedly received one of the warnings was Alfred G. Vanderbilt I, who was travelling first class to see his stable in England and 'look over some property he had there'. The anonymous sender reportedly told him 'Have it on definite authority that the *Lusitania* is to be torpedoed. You had better cancel passage immediately'. Nobody, including Vanderbilt, seemed to take the warnings seriously.[41]

Boarding the vessel was slow, due to additional security and fear of sabotage. There had been a fire on board the French Line vessel SS *La Touraine* in March 1915, which some feared had been set by a German national. This led to other shipping companies stepping up their already tight wartime security measures. Passengers had to line up in single file, as Cunard clerks and detectives scrutinised each individual and their ticket, and searched their baggage and carry-on luggage.[42]

Shortly before its 10.00 a.m. departure time, the *Lusitania* was unexpectedly delayed because the British Admiralty had requisitioned the Anchor Line vessel SS *Cameronia*, and forty-one passengers from that ship were being transferred aboard. These passengers were 'enormously pleased', as the *Lusitania* was far larger and faster. The ship finally departed at 12.30 p.m., with 1,959 people on board.

The first few days of the voyage proceeded without any incident. One of the foremost things on Captain Turner's mind was to comply with the British Admiralty's directive to 'keep on the move outside ports and harbours', by arriving at the Mersey Bar off Liverpool as the tide was coming in. This would prevent the *Lusitania* from having to sit outside the harbour entrance where U-boats typically lurked, while waiting for the pilot to board the ship and take charge of navigating her safely up the channel. He ran calculations to determine the proper speed and course to ensure his vessel would arrive with, and not before or after, the tide. Turner also made the decision to stay awake and remain on the bridge all day and night Friday, and all the way through until the vessel had safely arrived in Liverpool.

In the early morning of 6 May, Captain Turner began preparing his ship for passing through the waters of the 'war zone decree'. In what must have surely disturbed unseasoned travellers, the crew began removing the canvas covers from the lifeboats and swinging them out over the water. Turner did not have the boats lowered level with the deck, nor did he have the ship's collapsible boats prepared for use, evidently thinking he had done enough to comply with the Admiralty's instructions to 'maintain lifeboats ready for lowering'. Turner doubled the number of crewmen posted on lookout duty, ensured that the ship's lights would be blacked-out that night, and that all watertight doors unessential to the operation of the ship were closed. The captain also made sure that the engines were ready for a burst of speed in case it was needed. That afternoon, passengers were disappointed when the distance of the daily run was posted in the public rooms, because they had expected that the ship would 'show a burst of top speed' as they neared the 'war zone' waters, and that had not yet happened.

Meanwhile on land, submarine activity off the southern coast of Ireland led to increasing concerns for *Lusitania*'s safety. One U-boat in the region was *U-20*, under the command of Kapitänleutnant Walther Schwieger, who already had six kills credited to him. Schwieger was not known for adhering to prize rules: on his vessels, his crew's safety came first. *U-20* had just sunk three ships in quick succession; on 5 May, the merchant schooner *Earl of Latham* off the Old Head of Kinsale, where prize rules were observed, and then on 6 May, the SS *Candidate* and its sister ship SS *Centurion*, which were both torpedoed without warning. Fortunately, no crewmembers died in the incidents. Schwieger had also tried, unsuccessfully, to attack the White Star Line's SS *Arabic*. *U-20* remained in the Irish Channel following the attacks.

On the evening of Thursday, 6 May, and the morning of Friday, 7 May, numerous wireless messages were sent out by the Admiralty, cautioning merchant vessels that there had been increased submarine activity in the waters ahead. The warnings repeated the previous directives that had been given to avoid headlands and steer a mid-channel course while maintaining full speed. On Saturday morning, one of the last warnings *Lusitania* received had been initiated at the request of Cunard Line Chairman Alfred Booth himself, who wanted to ensure that everything possible was being done to protect his vessel. An important coded message was sent by the Admiralty, with the specific instructions 'Make certain *Lusitania* gets this'. More than any of the other warnings, this message should have alerted Captain Turner to the danger lying ahead:

> Submarines active in southern part of Irish Channel. Last heard of twenty miles south of Coningbeg Lightship.

While the Admiralty was clearly concerned, sending out an escort to meet *Lusitania* was not an option, as the Royal Navy remained critically short of patrol vessels. Additionally, had an escort been available, the *Lusitania* would have had to have reduced its speed in order to rendezvous with it, leaving it even more vulnerable to attack. Throughout this, Captain Turner displayed a lack of concern to passengers. During the intermission of the shipboard concert on the evening of 6 May, he told them that although there had been a submarine warning, that there was 'of course ... no need for alarm'. He claimed that the following day, they would sail at a top speed, which presumably would keep them safe. Most passengers were still unaware that, due to the one boiler room being shut down, the ship's top speed was 21 knots, and not 25 knots.

At 8.00 a.m. on Friday, 7 May, the *Lusitania* was approximately 100 miles west of Ireland, and encountered a blanket of thick fog. Despite having orders to steam through these waters at full speed, Captain Turner slowed down from 21 to 18 knots due to the poor visibility. As the fog thickened, he further reduced the *Lusitania*'s speed to 15 knots, and began sounding the ship's fog horn every minute. By that afternoon, the fog lifted and the ship was within sight of the Old Head of Kinsale. Around noon, Turner brought the vessel's speed back up to 18 knots, but never returned it to its full speed of 21 knots. Turner, as on his previous transatlantic crossing, failed to heed the Admiralty's directive to 'steer a zigzag course' through the 'war zone' waters, although he was maintaining strict wireless silence. Passengers were distressed by the *Lusitania*'s apparent slow speed, commenting 'why are we not making full speed or twenty-five knots as Captain Turner told us?'

Around 1.50 p.m., some of the lookouts on duty caused some alarm when they mistook a buoy for a U-boat. However, unbeknownst to anyone, *Lusitania* was being stalked. The *U-20* had spotted the Cunard liner at 1.00 p.m. Kapitänleutnant Schwieger had been watching through a periscope, and felt he had little chance of catching the ship, as it was steaming away. Suddenly, the *Lusitania* turned thirty degrees to starboard, the beginning of a four-point bearing on the Old Head of Kinsale, a navigational manoeuvre calling for the ship to steam in a straight line for up to forty minutes so that the officers could take navigational bearings on the landmark. This unwittingly brought *Lusitania* right into *U-20*'s range.[43]

Schwieger recorded the events in his war diary. The times reported in his log were approximately one hour ahead of the time being carried on *Lusitania*'s clocks. (The format from the original document has been preserved):

7. 15.   Straight ahead the 4 funnels
2 p.m.   of a steamer were visible
                    at right angles to ours (it was steering
                    for Galley Head, coming from the SSW).
                    Ship is made out to be a large passenger
                    steamer.
2:05p.m. Went to 11 m. and ran at high speed on a
                    course converging with that of the steamer,
                    in hope that it would change course to
                    starboard along the Irish coast.
2:05p.m. The steamer turned to starboard, headed
                    for Queenstown and this made it possible
                    to approach for a shot. Ran at high speed
                    till 3p.m. in order to secure an advan-
                    tageous position.
3:10p.m. Clear bow shot at 700 m. (G. torpedo set
                    3 m. for depth), angle of intersection 90°,
                    estimated speed 22 nautical miles …[44]

At 2.10 p.m., Able-Bodied Seaman Leslie Morton was standing lookout on *Lusitania*'s forecastle when he spotted the wake of a torpedo. He made a half-hearted attempt to warn the bridge by shouting through a megaphone. Instead of waiting for the bridge to acknowledge his warning, he dropped the megaphone and ran below deck to warn his brother, who was also serving aboard. It was about thirty seconds before another lookout noticed the torpedo, and relayed the information to the bridge, where Captain Turner heard the words 'There is a torpedo coming, sir!'

It was too late. The torpedo impacted the starboard side in the vicinity of the bridge and the forward funnel, exploding loudly, and sending a column of water and debris shooting into the air, which came crashing down on the deck further aft as the ship steamed ahead.

Boiler Room No. 1 was inundated nearly immediately, and the damage was significant enough that the starboard coal bunker of Boiler Room No. 2 was also flooded. Settling by the bow as water rushed towards the forward compartments, the ship quickly took on a 15° list to starboard.

Shortly after the torpedo's impact, a large secondary explosion emanated from within the ship. After the fact, conspiracy theories emerged, without evidence, suggesting that the cargo holds were packed with secret shipments of explosive ordinance. However, the munitions that the vessel was actually carrying could not have caused a blast of that magnitude.

This secondary explosion was likely the result of a catastrophic failure of the ship's steam lines caused by the damage and flooding. After the secondary explosion, Captain Turner had wanted to beach his ship on the Irish coast which was visible and tantalisingly close, but steam pressure to the engines continued to drop steadily, and soon the *Lusitania* stopped responding to its helm.

Chaos and mass confusion quickly broke out. The task of launching the lifeboats was rendered difficult by the list of the ship. Most of the lifeboats ended up damaged or destroyed without being lowered safely to the water, upending or spilling their occupants into the frigid sea.

Within eighteen minutes of being attacked, *Lusitania* rolled over onto its starboard side. The sides of the four funnels, still attached to the ship, settled into the water. The ship then righted itself as the stern rose up into the air, emitted a 'terrible moan', and disappeared from sight. Aboard *U-20*, Kapitänleutnant Schwieger had watched as his torpedo impacted *Lusitania*, and was surprised at the deadly results and scene that unfolded, recording his observations in his log. (The format from the original document has been preserved):

Shot struck starboard side close behind the bridge.
An extraordinarily heavy detonation followed, with a very
large cloud of smoke (far above the front funnel). A second explosion must have followed that of the torpedo (boiler
or coal or powder!). The superstructure above the point
of impact and the bridge were torn apart; fire broke out;
light smoke veiled the high bridge. The ship stopped
immediately and quickly listed to starboard, sinking deeper by the head at the same time. It appeared as
it would capsize in a short time. Great confusion arose
on the ship; some of the boats were swung clear and lowered
into the water. Many people must have lost their heads;
several boats loaded with people rushed downward, struck
the water bow or stern first and filled at once. On
the port side, because of the sloping position, fewer boats
were swung clear than on the starboard side. The ship blew
off steam; at the bow the name *Lusitania* in golden letters
was visible. The funnels were painted black; stern flag not
in place. It was running 20 nautical miles. Since it seemed

3:25p.m. as if the steamer could only remain above water for a short
time, went to 24 m, and ran toward the Sea. Nor could I
have fired a second torpedo into this swarm of people who
were trying to save themselves.
4:15p.m. Went to 11m, and took a look around. In
the distance straight ahead a number of
life-boats were moving; nothing more was to
be seen of the Lusitania. The wreck must
lie 14 nautical miles from the Old Head of
Kinsale light-house ... [45]

Fortunately, Lusitania's crew were able to send out distress calls using the Marconi set before the power failed, and help was on the way. Despite Lusitania having been in sight of land, it would be several hours before many of the rescue vessels reached the scene. Although the water was approximately 52°F, much warmer than when the RMS Titanic had sunk in the North Atlantic three years earlier, many people succumbed to exhaustion or hypothermia.

Of the 1,959 people aboard Lusitania, only 761 survived. Captain Turner was amongst them, having been washed from the bridge as it submerged. One of the victims was Alfred Vanderbilt. In a twist of irony, Vanderbilt had erroneously been listed as having been aboard Titanic in some newspapers in 1912, only to actually die in a sinking a few years later.[46] His uncle, George W. Vanderbilt II and George's wife Edith were the ones who had actually booked passage on Titanic, but cancelled their voyage at the last moment.[47]

One of the passengers aboard during the final voyage was Angela Countess Bakeev, then known as Angela Pappadopoulo. She had been travelling in first class along with her husband Michael, and their friend James Baker. Angela was the only one of the group to survive. She later wrote a detailed account of the voyage and her experiences:

At the time myself and my poor husband lost in the disaster, Michael Papadopoulos [Pappadopoulo], after a voyage between Italy to visit my family and France, were in London where my husband had some business. From London in February we boarded the Lusitania at New York time together with Mr. James Baker, director of the English branch of my husband's company, the 'Oriental Carpets Manufacturers'. After two months where we were also in Canada, 1st May we decided to return to Europe with the same ship, being accommodated in cabin number B78.

Once aboard, we discovered with delight that in the cabin next to us were Mrs. Burnside and her daughter Iris, whom we met in Toronto.

The day of the 5th May passed by very pleasantly, after having dined at the Captain's table, playing cards with Mr. Vanderbilt the well known American

Michael (left) and Angela (right) Pappadopoulo. (Demetrio Baffa Trasci Amalfitani di Crucoli Collection)

millionaire who was passionate about horses, Lady Allan Montague [Lady Montague Allan] and Sir Allan Lane [Sir Hugh Lane]. That evening I insisted that Sir Lane showed us some paintings he was carrying to Europe and so we went into the cabin where I had the chance to see those works of art for the last time before they were lost forever in the shipwreck.

The day of 6th May, which would become the last happy day of sailing was memorable. Since Mike was suffering from terrible migraines that evening we had organized a small meeting with a few friends in our cabin, intervened by the Consul, Mr. Padiglia [Frederico Padilla], the Bilickes and Sir Allan Lane [Sir Hugh Lane]. Lady Montague [Lady Allan] and Mr. Vanderbilt also attended but not for long. I remember that we were joking about Mike's fear of the ship being torpedoed, when the Captain joined us and did little to calm him down. After the small private party, I accompanied by Sir Lane, reached Mr. Vanderbilt at a charity concert which I no longer remember for what cause that evening. I was there when an officer came and called me informing me that Mike crazily had slipped into one of the lifeboats to pass the night, convinced that the *Lusitania* a little while later would be torpedoed. Oh if only I had listened to my poor husband's warnings. Difficult to calm him down and thanks to Sir Lane and Mr. Vanderbilt we returned him to our cabin.

The day of the shipwreck, 7th May, seemed like an ordinary sailing day like any other, not expecting anything serious. Mike and I had dined with Mr. Padiglia [Frederico Padilla], we afterwards like always took our coffee on the veranda. With us were Mr. Baker [Leonidas Bistis] and they were just serving us coffee when we heard the first explosion. There immediately followed a second explosion and debris began to rain down all around us. Mike panicked and leaving him with Mr. Baker [Bistis], I ran to our cabin to retrieve our life jackets. I cannot say how I dared to retrieve them but I tucked money and jewels into my pockets but in moments like that one doesn't have time to think. I remember that on leaving the cabin in the darkest gloom I was forced to move along on all fours until I could find my balance, apart from the dark the inclination of the ship forced me to proceed with one foot on the floor and the against the wall to not fall to the ground. The ship was sinking at such a rate that we had just enough time to put on our life jackets before being pushed towards the lifeboats. Whilst Mike was already aboard, an officer advised me to remove my skirt in case I had to swim it would make it easier for me. At times like this one must overcome modesty and so I got into the lifeboat wearing only my petticoat.

Our lifeboat was number 17, and as soon as we were put into the sea we heard a noise like a branch snapping coming from above the bridge, and we found ourselves first of all thrown onto the steel of the ship and then into the sea. Once in the ocean I barely had to time to see Mr. Baker [Bistis] attempt to grab my husband's hand that I was dragged down even deeper by the force of the ship which was sinking. It was then that an air bubble pushed me violently towards the surface where I tried desperately to find my husband. When I realized where I was I understood that if I stayed where I was the ship would have sucked me down and I'd have drowned, and so it was that I had to swim desperately towards the lifeboats in the distance and the only thing I could think of was going home with my children. I swam in the ocean for an hour, maybe two exhausted and with a leg injury when I was rescued by a life raft. Hoisted aboard, although devoid of strength, I was aware of a Russian man with a serious injury to his arm and since travelling with Mike on his travels to Imperial Russia I had learnt the rudiments of his language, and tried to hearten him as best I could and tearing my petticoat attempted to stop the bleeding which if not would have killed him a little later.

After some hours spent on the raft at the mercy of the ocean, we were rescued by a liner and once aboard many of us were beginning to succumb to despair. My first memory aboard the liner was an officer who offered me a sherry to warm me up whilst inviting me to change my shabby soaked clothes. So it was in an officer's cabin that I changed into the jumper and trousers of the uniform of a sailor of the liner who saved us and which I jealously guard.

Since that terrible event in 1915 I have still not returned to America, and although it happened it has not exhausted my passion for travelling. Today I am still in touch with some survivors of that journey and often receive news of Lady Montague [Lady Montague Allan] who lost two daughters in the disaster who were travelling with her, and lately have become close to the Contessa de Gennes [Maude Thompson] with whom I shared experience with the Red Cross during the war.

This is an account of my experience aboard the *Lusitania* which I leave to you my beloved brothers and [unintelligible].

Asking a single commitment, at my death when and wherever it should be I want to be buried wearing the uniform of a sailor who, that afternoon in 1915 I still jealously guard.[48]

Angela wrote a poignant letter to her father shortly after the sinking, describing how she was coping with the loss of her husband, and blaming herself for his death:

Dearest Father,

How are you? I hope this finds you well and all who are at Santa Sofia. Please thank Aunt Mariantonia for me for her kindness and Uncle Rosario for his long letter of comfort which he sent me. I'm writing these few lines from Paris only now that I have retrieved my little strength and try to understand what happened. The crossing on the *Lusitania* I believe has destroyed forever my poor nerves and if I'm alive I owe and will always owe the thought to my poor children orphaned of their Father. When for hours I was at the mercy of the waves, all I could think of was them, poor little ones whom I knew already would never see their Father again. Michele disappeared into the waves in front of me and I can still feel his hand slipping from mine. The good soul of my poor husband was right in not wanting to board the ship and if he's no longer here it's also my fault. The night before the sinking in fact poor Michele had a premonition of what would happen to us all and I remember finding myself at a concert dancing accompanied by Mr. Vanderbilt, the American millionaire expert who also perished in the disaster, the Consul, Mr. Padiglia [Frederico Padilla] whom I mentioned in the last letter arrived with much anxiety to try to dissuade him from passing the night in the lifeboat … Oh my dearest Father you cannot understand the mockery which awaits our destiny, I'm sure that same lifeboat was the number on which all of us would embark the next day and which would have sunk into the ocean dragging everyone down.

I swam for hours amongst wreckage and motionless bodies and dear Father I don't believe you could ever understand what I went through until I was rescued by that small launch. The only thing which gave me strength was the thought of those afflicted orphans and the prayers to Mother and Saint Alfonzo! I believe I will never be able to erase those moments from my memory and only now I realize how my little Maria Immacolata had tried to save me. The other night I dreamt I was holding little Enrichino in my arms, and given as he will have a birthday in just over a month please give him this as a small token from me. Many thanks again for the beautiful letter which I received last Wednesday and please give a kiss to the little ones for me. I promise I will write again very soon.

Your most affectionate and devoted daughter

Angela.[49]

Scott Turner, a mining engineer from Lansing, Michigan, was another passenger travelling in first class aboard the *Lusitania*. He was on his way to Spitsbergen, Norway, in order to develop and operate mines there. Following the sinking, Turner's name was not amongst the initial list of survivors, causing his friends in the United States a good deal of consternation. Fortunately, Turner's wife had already been notified of his survival, and after receiving inquiries regarding her husband's safety, sent a telegram saying 'Mrs. Turner wires Scott is safe; had cable from him at Queenstown'. On 13 May, Turner wrote the following letter to John Munro Longyear, one of the founders of the Arctic Coal Company, who had sent a message to his wife, asking about his safety:

Approaching the Irish coast, we ran … at reduced speed – probably not over 15 knots per hour, with all port-holes open, one quarter of our boilers cold, and no precautions or escort whatever. I understand the captain disobeyed two telegraphic messages ordering him to keep 100 miles off the coast. In other words, the chump invited disaster, and the whole thing could not have been planned better if the German Admiralty had arranged it …

… The sudden list to starboard threw the 200 eighteen-inch port-holes on 'D' Deck, all of which were wide open, under water, which increased the list until 'C' deck port-holes came under. This carelessness with the port-holes alone probably sank the boat twenty minutes sooner than she would have taken otherwise.

The lifeboats were handled very badly … all my information leads me to believe that only four were successfully launched. Others were crowded full of men, women, and children, and then dropped from the davits, and this alone accounts for a large portion of the high loss among first-class passengers. Most of the people who were saved were people who did not get into the boats at all …

… I was in my cabin when the torpedo struck … the projectile struck just under me, and the ship immediately listed badly to starboard. The captain, in my presence, announced that all passengers must keep off the boat-deck, as the ship would not sink and no boats would be lowered. Later, various boats were lowered, and I was put into one about three minutes before the ship sank.

This boat, loaded with about sixty people, hung a moment on the davits, and then the fall-rope supporting the stern was let go or cut, thereby hanging the boat vertically and spilling every one into the sea, 65 feet below. The boat was then dropped on top of us, smashing it to pieces and carrying me down with it. On account of the headway of the ship, which held until she sank, this boat turned over under water like a trolling-spoon carrying me with it, and then as the bow-rope was still fast it swung with violence against the side of the ship, catching me between the boat and the ship, dislocating my left shoulder, smashing my nose, and cutting my legs badly. I was the sole survivor of this boatload.

Later I swam to a second boat, which had been dropped half way from the deck, but still contained over fifty passengers. On getting in the boat I discovered it was stove in, and it sank in about three minutes, throwing us all into the water. While the boat did not sink below the surface of the water, still the frantic passengers climbing on it caused it to roll over and over again, carrying us under with it each time, and killing some each time until there were only seventeen of us left.

I clung to this sunken boat for about four hours until picked up by the steam trawler *Indian Empire*, probably about seven o'clock, and we were landed in Queenstown at ten o'clock, and I had the dislocation in my shoulder reduced that night.

I left Queenstown at 3 o'clock on Saturday afternoon, and arrived in London at half past six Sunday morning, still in my wet clothes. Here, the doctors thought that in addition to the dislocation the bones of my shoulder had been broken, so I had an X-ray photograph taken on Monday which showed the bones to be all right. I am therefore hoping to have a very fair shoulder in time, and next week an operation on my nose will probably clear up that difficulty.

Following the sinking, Turner had been expecting to quickly return to work, but 'had no relish for crossing the North Sea until his shoulder and his nose should be in better shape'. Turner's doctor put an end to the talk of an immediate return to his business, ordering him back to the hospital for another week to 'have the bones re-broken so that the cartilages which closed the nasal passages might be set right'. Turner's shoulder was injured badly enough that he was unable to actively take part in field operations, and eventually returned to the United States.[50]

The Allies and public, stunned by the magnitude of the disaster, reacted strongly and negatively to the sinking of the *Lusitania*. The attack was instantly condemned by the British Government, who labelled it as nothing short of cold-blooded murder. The public's massive outrage was channelled towards the 'baby-killer' U-boat captains. Terms like 'Hun' were once again being tossed out by the press, and one newspaper referred to 'the atrocious conduct of the Germans', adding that the U-boat campaign was being carried out 'regardless of all considerations of humanity', and was 'a lasting disgrace to the Germans who planned it and carried it into effect'.[51] Little mention was made of the fact that Germany had repeatedly warned travellers of their intent to sink vessels in the 'war zone' waters, nor the fact that *Lusitania* was carrying munitions and war stuffs, or that Britain's blockade of Germany had forced them to utilise U-boats as a counter-blockade.

Making matters worse was the fact that of the 139 US citizens aboard the *Lusitania*, 128 lost their lives in the tragedy. Seizing on the public outcry emanating from America and perhaps hoping to gain another ally that might break the stalemate in Europe, Britain pushed for America to declare war on Germany. Once again, like with the *Falaba* sinking, the actions of a German U-boat had the unintended consequences of nearly dragging the neutral United States into the war. It is indisputable that Germany wished to avoid that possibility. President Wilson knew that the United States had to respond, but refused to overreact, instead weighing the options that were available and considering the consequences. At this stage, the American public remained fervently against entering the war, which they still considered a 'European conflict'.

While the United States debated how to react, Germany quickly published its own statement regarding the sinking. On 8 May, Dr. Bernhard Dernburg, a former German Colonial Secretary, who was regarded as Kaiser Wilhelm II's spokesman and 'official mouthpiece in the United States', was staying at the Hollenden Hotel in Cleveland, Ohio. Dernburg was scheduled to address the City Club regarding Germany's attitude in the war. While there, he issued a formal statement:

Because the *Lusitania* carried contraband of war and also because she was classed as an auxiliary cruiser and was at the disposal of the British Admiralty, Germany had a right to destroy her regardless of the passengers, which included nearly 200 Americans … Warnings given by the German Embassy in public advertisement before the sailing … together with the note of Feb. 18, declaring the existence of war zones, relieved Germany from responsibility for the loss of the many Americans …

Great Britain declared the North Sea a war zone in the Winter. No protest was made by the United States or any neutral. Great Britain held up all neutral ships carrying non-contraband goods, detaining them, buying or confiscating their cargoes.

Great Britain constantly changed the contraband lists so no foodstuffs of any kind have actually reached Germany since the war began. International law says foodstuffs destined for civil populatrion [sic] must pass. It does not recognize any right to starve out a whole people.

As a consequence, and in retaliation, Germany declared the waters around England a war zone, and started a submarine warfare. It became known in February that British ships were flying the American flag as protection.

Great Britain replied by officially declaring its purpose to starve 120,000,000 Germans and Austrians. The United States very thoughtfully tried to mediate, proposing that foodstuffs should be passed, and submarine warfare be stopped.

Germany agreed; England turned the proposal down. Then in order to protect American passengers, they were warned by public advertisement of the danger of sailing under the flag of a belligerent.

Vessels carrying contraband of war are liable to destruction unless they can be taken to a port of the country that captures them. The right of search need not be exercised if it is certain such ships carry contraband ...

The *Lusitania*'s manifest showed she carried for Liverpool 260,000 pounds of brass; 60,000 pounds of copper; 189 cases of military goods; 1,271 cases of ammunition, and for London, 4,200 cases of cartridges.

Vessels of that kind can be seized and be destroyed under the Hague rules without any respect to a war zone. The *Lusitania* was a British auxiliary cruiser, a man of war. On the same day she sailed the *Cameronia*, another Cunarder, was commandeered in New York Harbor for military service.

The fact is that the *Lusitania* was a British war vessel under orders of the Admiralty to carry a cargo of contraband of war. The passengers had full warning, first by the German note to England in February, second, by advertisement.

Germany wants to do anything reasonable so as not to make the United States or its citizens suffer in any way. But she cannot do so unless Americans will take necessary precautions to protect themselves from dangers of which they are cognizant.

What Germany has done, she has done by way of fetaliation [sic] after her offer through President Wilson, regarding submarine warfare, was turned down and after Britain declared the war was directed toward the 120,000,000 innocent non-combatants, women and children.

Americans can do their own thinking when the facts are laid before them. I have really no authority to speak. But my mission in the United States is to inform your people of the German attitude. The German Ambassador, Count von Bernstorff, can speak only in official phrases. I talk straight out, bluntly.

Dr Dernburg went on to lambast Cunard Line officials for not warning American travellers that they were carrying munitions and war contraband aboard their vessels. He accused Britain of using American civilians as 'a cloak for England's war shipments', saying that it was not reasonable that such a ship could not be sunk because there were Americans aboard.[52] Before the sinking, much of the general public had been unaware that *Lusitania* and other ships had been carrying munitions and contraband on transatlantic crossings.

Meanwhile, President Wilson and most of his advisors knew that a formal note of protest was called for. Wilson was so bothered by the incident that he isolated himself for several days, speaking only to White House staff. Some of his advisors pushed for war, believing that US intervention would 'save, rather than increase, the loss of life' in the conflict.

Secretary of State Bryan disagreed. He urged that the American response be tempered. As with the the *Falaba* incident, he did not believe the sinking justified American intervention in the war. The first note of protest to Germany was sent by the United States on 13 May. Bryan wrote to President Wilson, saying 'I join in this document with a heavy heart'. In the following weeks, Bryan 'advanced one proposal after another in the hopes of forestalling a crisis'.

Bryan, rather than supporting a call for Germany to end its submarine warfare, advocated for a warning to American citizens, telling them not to travel on 'belligerent vessels' while negotiations with Germany were ongoing. He also pushed for a protest against Britain for its ongoing interference with American trade. This, he believed, would show that the United States was remaining neutral and being impartial in the conflict. President Wilson rejected both of these ideas.

Robert Lansing, as during the 'Thrasher Incident', deeply disagreed with Bryan's approach. Lansing had personally concluded that Germany had no fear of war with the United States, stating 'Everything seems to point to a deliberate effort to affront this Government and force it to open rupture of diplomatic relations'. He argued against any measures of appeasement.[53]

President Wilson had carefully considered all of his options. Once the first note of protest had been sent, Germany dispatched an official response on 28 May, written by Foreign Minister Gottlieb von Jagow. Von Jagow argued that the sinking was regrettable, but was necessary, as the *Lusitania* was carrying munitions and war supplies to Britain, which made it a legitimate target.

The United States filed three additional notes of diplomatic protest, followed by more negotiations with Germany. In June, Secretary of State Bryan resigned, stating that Wilson's demands of accountability and ignoring of British violations of international law were leading their nation into the war. In fact, Wilson had no intention of entering the war, but wanted to impress upon Germany that further incidents endangering American lives would not be tolerated. Despite his resignation, Bryan remained a supporter of Wilson, even campaigning for his re-election in 1916. Bryan was replaced by Robert Lansing, whose fervent calls for stronger responses and even war were brushed off by Wilson. When Lansing suggested adding 'a veiled threat' to one of the *Lusitania* notes, Wilson responded that 'I do not think we need add a sting'.

As negotiations with Germany continued, Wilson backed down from some of the demands of the *Lusitania* notes. He continued to insist that German submarine commanders do everything in their power to spare neutral lives, and warned of the consequences if they failed to do so. Germany, after several additional attacks on passenger liners that inflamed public opinion further, eventually acquiesced to the demands of the United States. In late August 1915, Kaiser Wilhelm II specifically ordered Germany's U-boats to avoid attacking passenger liners without first warning them and safeguarding any passengers.[54]

Perhaps the most significant impact of the loss of the *Lusitania* wasn't the number killed, the propaganda coup it created for the Allied forces, or the way it permanently damaged Germany's reputation, but instead were the military repercussions that followed in the weeks and months ahead based on the pledge to avoid attacking passenger vessels. This signalled that the first attempt by U-boats to blockade Britain was essentially being called off, as there was no way to effectively enforce the blockade with munitions, manpower and supplies routinely being transported aboard passenger liners, which were no longer to be considered viable targets.

Based on the terrifying number of merchant ships sunk once Germany implemented unrestricted submarine warfare in 1917, it is possible that if Germany had continued to intensify rather than temper its U-boat attacks following the *Lusitania* sinking, Britain may have been unable to absorb the loss of food and supplies, and would have been defeated. Instead, German leaders, cautiously yielding to international pressure, would effectively hamstring the counter-blockade that U-boats were attempting to implement for nearly two years, failing to recognise its importance to their overall efforts against the Allies.

Following the sinking, an inquest was opened in Kinsale, Ireland by Coroner John Hogan, after several bodies had been brought ashore by a local boat, the *Heron*. The inquest's verdict was extremely harsh towards Germany:

> We find that this appalling crime was contrary to international law and the conventions of all civilized nations, and we therefore charge the officers of the said submarine, and the Emperor and Government of Germany, under whose orders they acted, with the crime of wilful and wholesale murder before the tribunal of the civilized world.[55]

The findings of the later British Board of Trade investigation into the sinking, as well as the American court proceedings, placed the blame for the disaster squarely on Germany, condemning their actions. Captain Turner was absolved of any responsibility for the sinking, despite the fact that he had ignored British

Admiralty directives such as steering a zigzag course. The court proceedings seem to have squarely reflected public opinion at the time, and the growing outrage and prejudice being directed at Germany. An example of this can be seen in the following letter excerpt, written on 23 July 1915 by an American citizen to a friend named Val, who was then serving in the British military:

> Yes, Val, the *Lusitania* affair was cold blooded murder. People over here got very concerned at first and there was even talk of war. However, a note was sent to Berlin, and a reply came back, which as to be expected, was unsatisfactory. Another stronger one was sent, and still the reply was evasive. The U.S. have now forwarded another and the contents will be published tomorrow. The papers say it is pretty strong. However, I do not think that war will result, for the U.S. could not do anything. The best way in which she can assist the Allies is to supply them with as many munitions as possible. We are having a deal of trouble over here just now with strikes at plants making munitions. The opinion is that there is German money behind the movement. I feel convinced there is, for the Huns are likely to stoop to anything to gain their end. Again, there has been trouble over in England with strikes, but I am pleased to say settlements have been brought about and the situation looks much clearer.
>
> Russia is having a pretty hard time of it – in fact she has right through the war. I hope she manages to keep the enemy away from Warsaw.[56]

In the immediate aftermath of the *Lusitania* sinking, passengers making the transatlantic crossing tended to be even more fearful than they had been prior to the tragedy, even though anxieties were already heightened due to the war. An illustration of this comes from the account of a woman named Beatie who

RMS *Missanabie*. (Authors' Collection)

was travelling from England to Canada aboard the Canadian Pacific Ocean Line's RMS *Missanabie*. Security at the pier during embarkation was tight in order to prevent sabotage, and not only would the vessel evade a submarine during the crossing, but on 8 May, it also passed through the debris field in the Irish Sea that marked where *Lusitania* went down:

May 14, 1915

Dear Nellie & Mr. & Mrs. Hill,

Thought I would write to you before leaving ship. Sincerely hope all are well Jean sea sick twice but I have never felt so well in my life. Had a nice journey from Euston to River Side Station arriving at 3.15, went on *Missanabie* through gangway after being well looked at by police, the third class were already on board Jean & I went to our births [sic] … when I said Jean I believe the floor is moving & to our surprise when we got on deck to find we were quite a distance out. I suspect it was owing to the war that we started so quietly, had a battleship, cruiser & pilot with us until night when the pilot took the mails, had tea in lounge at 4.30 everyone very brave. Made friends with Mrs. Blank & Mrs. Loughrey & their two boys who are joining their husbands in Toronto after a year's holiday, after dinner at 6.30p.m. all went on deck to see the sailors dancing. By the bye we have 300 sailors on board going to join the *Suffolk* ship (en route from for West Indies) at 10p.m. went to bed Jean up top & I underneath could not find the ladder so Jean stood on my stool & sprang in holding her head low so as not to give it a crack. Woke up at 5a.m. after a good nights sleep, had a peep at Jean & received a tap on the head & told to go to sleep as I should not get my practice here I do long to have a play. Dressing bell rang at 6.30a.m. & breakfast at 8a.m. While I was waiting for Jean to dress, Mrs. Blank's two boys & I went on deck & met up with a Mr. Wilson who is on a visit to his sister in Vancouver, introduced Jean to him after breakfast, when Mrs. Blank & Mrs. Loughrey came up & took Jean off, so Mr. Wilson & I went on upper deck & talked until eleven o'clock, then explored ship. Am sending you a book which has a good description of the boat in, so will not stop to tell you now. While at lunch 1p.m. a little boy came down to tell us the *Lusitania* had been wrecked so we all went on deck. Mr. Wilson & I just in time to see an overturned boat & a dead body also a woman with a baby tied to her, had they been alive we dare not risk so many lives for so few. The captain never left the bridge until 11.30a.m. Sunday morning with the news that so far we were out of danger, we also saw a decoy boat & submarine behind our ship darted for it but missed so were in great danger for four days & nights.

The captain said the women were splendid, only one lady fainted, but heard after she had come over for Canada to see her dying soldier son, just got there in time, so had brought the body back with her to be buried in Winnipeg poor thing ...

... Had a splendid concert Thursday, lecture for soldiers & sailors on Friday & a grand dance on Saturday, the two center tables were taken away & the floor polished, had red, white & blue lights. Leading to the dining room was a wide oak stair case which was draped with flags, it was a pretty sight to see the people walking under them, Jean had four dances & I joined in ...

Beatie described the following regarding the vessel's arrival in Quebec:

It was very pretty going through the Gulf of St. Lawrence, first we came to the Thousand Islands, it was a sight to see, then passed Mount Mavency falls [Montmorency Falls] noted throughout the world. All third class passengers & the sailors got off at Quebec, all who liked could get off so Mr. Blackshaw, Jean & I went ashore from 4p.m. till 5, did not have time to see new town so went round dock, & the old town, saw Royal Bank, Bank of Commerce & Examining warehouse also the Heights of Abram [Plains of Abraham] where we captured Quebec from the French General Wolf [Montcalm], also saw the cliff, where Montgomery threw himself over with his horse instead of being captured it is marked with a large cross ... got back to ship at 4.45p.m., so walked along to where the *Carpathia* was anchored with 2,000 soldiers on board, bound for England. My! How they shouted when they saw our ship come in, some waved their shirts from the port holes, & singing Are we down hearted No while the band played beautifully, the *Missanabie* is not taking passengers back but 2,000 troops. Reached Montreal at 12.30 Monday morning, got through customs fine ... [57]

Beatie arrived safely at home, and the *Missanabie* continued to make transatlantic crossings for the next several years.

In late May, there was another scare, this time centering around Guglielmo Marconi, inventor of the wireless telegraph, who was then serving as a senator in Italy. Marconi had travelled from Southampton, England to New York aboard the *Lusitania* that April, in order to give testimony in a lawsuit against the German telegraph company Telefunken. Prior to his trip to the United States, rumours had persisted that Germany wanted to kidnap Marconi, and had been planning to do so during his transatlantic crossing. On 23 May, Italy declared war on Austria–Hungary, as per the London Pact, and Marconi wanted to return to serve his homeland. Taking all precautions, Marconi booked passage aboard the American Line's SS *St Paul*, travelling incognito. During the voyage, the *St Paul* was chased by a U-boat. It was suspected that the submarine was on a mission to capture Marconi.

One of the passengers aboard the ship during this journey was Inez Milholland, known as the 'most beautiful suffragette'. Following the *St Paul*'s safe arrival in Liverpool on Sunday, 30 May, she wrote a vivid account of the crossing in a cablegram that was published in the newspapers. She referenced the recent U-boat attack on the SS *Nebraskan*, which took place approximately 40 miles west-south-west of Ireland on 25 May, damaging, but not sinking the vessel:

A German submarine chased the American liner *St Paul* last Saturday night right up to the Bar of the Mersey, where the submarine was driven off by British torpedo-boat destroyers …

I have this from the captain of the *St Paul*, who told it to Guglielmo Marconi and me just before we got off the boat in Liverpool Sunday morning. I do not think it was known to any of the passengers. It was known that there was likely to be an attempt made by a submarine to stop the ships and take Marconi off.

Inez Milholland.
(Library of
Congress, Prints
& Photographs
Division)

SS *St Paul*. (Library of Congress, Prints & Photographs Division)

Marconi received a warning from the Italian Consul before leaving New York and for this reason his name was kept off the passenger list and every endeavor made to prevent his presence on board becoming known. As we approached the war zone rather elaborate precautions were taken to safeguard Marconi. His name was not on either the regular list or the purser's books and there was a general tacit agreement among the passengers that if stopped by a submarine as we were all 'to lie like gentlemen'.

Meanwhile Marconi had removed all labels from his baggage and had given his private papers into my care and got into clothes suitable for slipping into a hiding place somewhere down in the bowels of the ship next to the keel, where the chief engineer said the captain himself would be unable to find him.

We had a concert that night, at which Marconi was to preside, and the program was inadvertently printed with Marconi's name as chairman, but the captain ordered all programs destroyed and when the concert began the historian, Trevelyan, took the chair and said: 'We were to have had the pleasure of Mr. Marconi presiding, but unfortunately he is not on board'.

Marconi was right there, and everybody knew it, but it was a part of our agreement to deny his presence and this announcement by Mr. Trevelyan gave a hint to everybody who had not understood before.

We had quite a lot of children on board, sons and daughters of Canadian officers going over with their mothers to join their husbands quartered in England, and there also were two very youthful brides. We saw a couple trawlers and the children tried very hard to persuade Marconi to hide.

Late on the day before we reached the war zone we heard of the *Nebraskan's* experience and then the captain wirelessed Queenstown as follows: 'In view of recent events don't you think you had better keep an eye on us?'

The answer came: 'Full speed ahead. Alter your course as much as possible. Submarines are watching the bar'.

The next morning when we landed the captain told us the submarine followed us right up to the Mersey bar. Except for the anxiety over Marconi the voyage from New York was much the same as usual.

As we approached the war zone passengers asked the captain to issue instructions to be observed in case of danger. He consented, although afraid nervousness might be increased, but the simple instructions helped greatly to imbue the passengers with the spirit of confidence.[58]

Following the voyage, American officials from the American Line refused to comment on the events, stating that they had received no word from their London agents regarding the submarine chase, and thus, would not comment on the story until they received definitive information regarding it. Guglielmo Marconi arrived overseas safely with no further ado.

Meanwhile, as the Cunard Line continued to reel from the loss of the *Lusitania*, a gaping void had been left in the transatlantic passenger service. The *Lusitania* had been the only liner of that size still operating in that capacity. Its ability to carry such a large number of passengers in one crossing was missed, even with the reduced amount of transatlantic travel due to the conflict. As a result, Cunard began making plans to return the RMS *Mauretania* to service, but it had been laid up in Liverpool during the autumn and winter months of 1914. Its interior fittings had been stripped out prior to that time, so the ship was not in a condition to return to service just yet.

Four days after the *Lusitania* was sunk, and before the *Mauretania* could be returned to service, the British Admiralty requisitioned it. The Gallipoli Campaign was going very poorly for the Allies, and casualties were racking up. Despite concerns that *Mauretania* would be torpedoed like the *Lusitania*, the pressing need to move a large number of troops to the Mediterranean convinced the Admiralty that the ship was needed.

It did not take long for *Mauretania* to be converted into a troop transport. Once the changeover was completed, Captain Daniel Dow, the former master of the *Lusitania* prior to being replaced by Captain Turner, was given command of the vessel, now known as HMT (Hired Military Transport) *Mauretania*. The ship

An Anzac troop carries a wounded comrade away from the front in Gallipoli. (United States National Archives and Records Administration/Authors' Collection)

began transporting Allied troops from England to the island of Lemnos, located in the Aegean Sea, which was being used as a base of operations for the Gallipoli Campaign. During this time, *Mauretania* completed three voyages, delivering over 10,000 troops for transportation to the front.[59]

During one of these troop-carrying voyages, the *Mauretania* barely escaped the fate that befell its sister. As the vessel was steaming along, a U-boat fired a single torpedo at it. With extra lookouts posted, the wake of the torpedo was quickly sighted, and Captain Dow immediately crash-turned his vessel to port. For a few tense moments, it appeared as if the torpedo would strike them, but the liner completed its turn just in time. The torpedo shot past the stern, missing by approximately 5ft.

The RMS *Aquitania*, which had also been laid up since early in the war, was requisitioned several weeks after the *Mauretania*. Receiving the necessary alterations, it was quickly pressed into service as the HMT *Aquitania*, joining its fellow Cunarder in that duty. On its first voyage from Liverpool, *Aquitania* carried over 5,000 troops bound for Gallipoli.[60]

Sixty-four ships were sunk or captured by U-boats by the end of May, for a total of 157,758 tons of shipping lost. Two additional vessels sustained damage, but did not sink. It was the deadliest month of the submarine war thus far. Besides the *Lusitania*, two other noteworthy attacks were on the British battleships HMS *Triumph* and HMS *Majestic*, sunk on 25 and 27 May respectively. Both warships were attacked off the west coast of Cape Helles, Gallipolli, by *U-21*, which was still under the command of Kapitänleutnant Otto Hersing.[61]

At the beginning of June 1915, even as the Western Front remained deadlocked, the Allies suffered yet another setback in the Gallipolli Campaign, being defeated in the Third Battle of Krithia. Things were going equally poorly for the Russian Empire on the Eastern Front. On 22 June, Russian forces there were in the midst of their collapse during the Gorlice-Tarnów Offensive, as German General August von Mackensen's forces once again broke through the enemy lines near Lviv, the capital of Galicia, and soon, the city was recaptured for Austria–Hungary.

At sea, despite the controversy over the sinking of *Lusitania*, passenger vessels were continuing to have run-ins with U-boats. On Friday, 18 June, the Union-Castle liner RMS *Llandovery Castle* was accosted by a submarine while steaming past a pod of whales. The details of the event were described as follows by a Mr. Gerlach, who was a passenger aboard the vessel:

> While the steamer was off Cape Finisterre on the Spanish coast last Friday morning the passengers saw a school of whales 'blowing' and cavorting to the stern of us. Suddenly I noticed we were zigzagging quite sharply, and I called the attention of a naval officer to it. As there were many women standing near, he said, 'We are only trying the compass', which struck me as being funny. The idea of a submarine being way down off Cape Finisterre, however, did not seem likely. Later the naval officer told me it was a submarine, and that he and the Captain had sighted it. The submarine showed its periscope some distance from our stern on the starboard side. Then she dived and came up to port, but could not get the right sight on us. She chased us for an hour, but lost ground, as we were going fast. Finally she gave up the race.[62]

On Sunday, 20 June, the Anchor liner *Cameronia* also had a brush with a U-boat, albeit a somewhat more harrowing one. The vessel was completing its latest transatlantic crossing from New York, when it encountered a submarine near the mouth of the River Mersey, and tried to ram it. With everyone's nerves still frayed from the sinking of the *Lusitania*, what transpired must have been very frightening.

One of the American passengers aboard was Peter Fletcher, who was travelling with his wife. He was 'an intimate friend' of Franklin K. Lane, the United States Secretary of the Interior. Fletcher was not concerned about the crossing, saying 'that it was as safe on a steamer flying the British flag as the American in view of the promiscuous attacks by the Germans on all ships'.

The *Cameronia*. (Authors' Collection)

Peter Fletcher. (United States National Archives and Records Administration/Authors' Collection)

He soon came to regret his nonchalant attitude about their safety. He gave the following account of the events:

> … on Sunday morning … a submarine periscope appeared out of the water … Naturally we were all startled. We thought of the *Lusitania* and of our chances of escaping, but no one started for the staterooms to get life preservers. We all seemed to be fascinated by the sight of the submarine. As we looked we saw the submarine come to the top of the water, and all thought our end had come. I cannot say that there was a panic aboard the *Cameronia*, but without a doubt all the passengers felt mightily shaky. We felt the steamer lurch ahead as she put on full speed, and we were all amazed to see that, instead of our ship taking a zigzag

course to get out of the submarine's way, the Captain steered right toward it.

For a moment it looked as if we were flying straight into the face of death, and I dare say the passengers must have looked quite pale. But to our amazement the submarine, instead of setting itself for attack, dived down into the water. I expected the next moment to hear the terrific crash of a torpedo underneath us, but nothing happened.

While we stood wondering what was going on the submarine popped to the surface on the other side of the ship quite near. It got a new sight on the ship, but the Captain had not been asleep, and we easily escaped through his taking a new track at full speed. It was a magnificent show of courage and cool-headedness on the part of the Captain and to this the passengers undoubtedly owe their lives. Not one of us was prepared for the sinking of the ship if the torpedo had struck her.

As the *Cameronia* proceeded into the mouth of the River Mersey, Captain James Kinnaird received word that six submarines were lurking off the south-eastern coast of Ireland and near the Mersey.[63] After the safe arrival in Liverpool, Carrol Winslow, another American passenger who had been aboard, proceeded to file a complaint with the American Consulate, and 'protested against what he considered the failure to give needed protection to the vessel so near the British Coast'.[64]

June 1915 soon came to an end, and concern began to grow amongst the Allies as U-boats began exacting an increasingly large toll. As submarine commanders improved their tactics, more and more ships were being sent to the bottom. A total of 119 ships were captured or destroyed during the month, amounting to 122,233 tons of shipping. Another five ships were damaged by U-boats, included the armoured cruiser HMS *Roxburgh*, which was knocked out of service for a year by a torpedo.[65]

By the end of 1915, Germany had lost twenty-five U-boats to accidents or enemy action thus far in the war, as British defences against submarines attacks grew somewhat more effective.[66] However, the U-boat offensive was being reinforced by the new UB-class submarines that were now in service and operating out of Zeebrugge and other harbours along the Belgian coast. These tiny U-boats, just 92ft in length, were ideal for use near the shoals and narrows of the Thames Estuary and the Dover Straits. This new class of U-boat would achieve some remarkable successes in the North Sea and Mediterranean throughout the rest of the war. Also, an increasing number of ships damaged were the result of German mines laid by the new UC class minelaying U-boats.[67]

July–August 1915

As July 1915 arrived, German forces were defeated in the final battle of the South West Africa Campaign. Things had been going poorly for the Central Powers there for some time, and this loss effectively brought the campaign in the region to an end.

Near the end of July, another international incident between Germany and the United States erupted when the SS *Orduna* was targeted by a U-boat, and barely escaped. The *Orduna* was a liner built by Harland & Wolff in Belfast, originally for the Pacific Steam Navigation Company. After two voyages, the vessel was charted to the Cunard Line. On Friday, 9 July, the *Orduna*, with 492 people aboard, was 37 miles south of Queenstown, steaming for New York, when it was attacked without warning.

The submarine fired a single torpedo at the liner, a grazing shot that missed by 10ft. It was afterwards speculated that the U-boat commander missed because he calculated the *Orduna*'s speed to be its ordinary rate of 14 knots, when in fact, it was travelling at 16 knots. The U-boat then surfaced, and attempted to sink the liner with its deck guns. Taking evasive action, Captain Thomas Taylor managed to alter the ship's course, confusing the aim of the gunners on the enemy vessel, and avoiding damage.

One of the 227 passengers aboard during this crossing was William O. Thompson, American counsel for the Federal Industrial Relations Commission, who was travelling in first class. He had been in London to consult with David Lloyd George on methods of resolving disputes between corporations and their employees by arbitration rather than force.[68] Thompson, an early riser, was on the aft end of the promenade deck when the incident occurred, and had watched the attack through a pair of opera glasses. Thompson was understandably indignant regarding the attack, as can be seen in his account, and he intended to protest the incident by bringing it before the State Department in Washington DC:

> The excitement lasted about fifteen minutes altogether, from the time of the firing of the torpedo until the last shot from the submarine fell into the water astern of the *Orduna* and sent a column of water forty-five feet up in the air … I have business to attend to in New York on Monday and will then go to Washington. I do not know exactly what forte my protest will take, but I shall lay the facts before Secretary Lansing on Tuesday and request that the United States Government take some action in the matter to protect its citizens and others, whose lives were endangered by the firing of the torpedo and shelling of the *Orduna* on July 9.
>
> I felt I had a right to return home on the *Orduna*, although she flies the British flag, because she is a passenger ship. The fact that we had no war munitions

on board fortified this opinion. Going east I travelled on the American liner
St. Louis.

The *Orduna*, an unarmed passenger ship, was deliberately attacked without
warning, pursued and subjected to shell fire. It is a little short of marvelous that
she was not sent to the bottom with all on board. About half an hour before
the submarine was sighted, a small bark crossed the bows of the *Orduna* from
starboard, which Baron Rosencrantz told me had an American flag painted on
her side, but he could not make out the name.

Baron Marcus Rosenkrantz, a fellow passenger mentioned by Thompson,
provided additional details regarding the attack:

It had just gone 6 o'clock on the morning of July 9, and the *Orduna* was
steaming through the water at top speed, as I judged by the vibration on deck.
Suddenly my wife called my attention to a peculiar trail in the water passing
close to the stern of the ship from port to starboard. The next thing we saw
was submarine rising to the surface astern, toward the starboard side, about a
mile and a half away. No warning had been given of any kind, and when the
crew got the gun in the bow trained on our ship it began firing shells one
after another.

The first two or three shots fell astern, but when the gunner got the range a
shell went whistling over the stern of the *Orduna* and missed hitting the bridge
by thirty feet to starboard. As it struck the sea with a loud splash the spray rose
higher than the crow's nest on the foremast. The next shot fell in the water
amidships, and another close by the engine room, but none hit us. This was due
to the skill of Captain Taylor, who calculated where each shot would fall to such
a nicety that he always kept the stern of the ship toward the submarine.

There were nine shots fired in all before the *Orduna* finally got out of range
and the submarine steamed away on the horizon. The passengers were quite
calm after the bedroom stewards had awakened everybody and warned them
quietly that they might have to take to the boats, and advised them to have their
life belts ready to put on.

Lookouts Joseph Henderson and Thomas Ennis were on duty on the aft
docking bridge when the U-boat attacked. Henderson gave the following
account of the events:

... we saw the periscope on the surface of the water about a mile away on
the port quarter, and before we had time to warn the bridge a torpedo shot
through the water and passed within ten feet of the stern, under the patent log
line. I rang the telegraph to warn the officer on the bridge and then pointed

down to the water from the overhang to indicate the torpedo, while Ennis ran along the upper deck and shouted to the bridge to look out for the submarine.

About eight to ten minutes later I saw the submarine rise to the surface a mile and a half astern toward the starboard, just outside the wake of the ship. Presently a shot was fired from his gun on the port side, which fell quite short. The second came closer than the third and exploded in the air. The fourth shot was in range, and passed right over my head, so near that I could hear it whistling through the air; but the Captain had swung the ship in time. It fell into the water about thirty feet to the starboard of the foc'sle head. The next shot fell into the water amidships, close to the engine room, about twenty feet away, and another shot exploded near the starboard quarter, but did no harm. The other three shells, making nine in all, fell into the sea astern, as the submarine had fallen off then, and was soon out of sight astern.

The attacking U-boat was described as one of the older models by Captain Taylor, and was unable to keep up the pursuit of its faster prey. During the shelling, passengers were ordered to go below deck for safety, but not all complied. The *Orduna* safely resumed its voyage, arriving in New York with no further ado. This incident had been the second time in as many crossings that *Orduna* had been molested by U-boats.

One of the passengers aboard during this voyage was Travers Browne, who was just returning from the Western Front after having served a year with the British Mechanical Transport Corps. He was due to stay at Narragansett with his family, until September 1915, when he was scheduled to return to France to serve in the British Flying Corps. Of interest, Browne's wife was the daughter of Charles and Frances May Fowles, who were amongst the first-class passengers who died aboard the *Lusitania*. His wife, forced to deal with the worry of her husband serving on the front on top of grieving over her lost parents, must have been greatly relieved when he reached home safely.

Those aboard *Orduna* were so thankful for their narrow escape, that on 10 July, while still at sea, a group of first-class passengers wrote a letter to Captain Taylor saying, 'We feel that it was entirely due to your skill, your resourcefulness, and unfailing pluck that we escaped', and 'We thank you, and we hope that your brilliant conduct under shellfire and in the face of grave danger will receive elsewhere the reward and praise it so well deserves'.[69]

Following the incident, which was protested by the United States due to the number of Americans aboard, Germany claimed that the U-boat had in fact signalled *Orduna* to stop, but it had been ignored. The attack could not have come at a worse time, as tensions remained high following the sinking of the *Lusitania*, and the United States and Germany were still in the midst of the negotiations regarding it.

In response to the claim that *Orduna* had been warned, United States officials stated that 'irrespective of whether or not a signal was given to halt', what the actions impressed upon them was that 'German submarines had not abandoned their attempts to destroy enemy passenger vessels, whether carrying contraband or not, and that American citizens seemed still to be subject to hazards, from which, under previously accepted rules of international law, they should be immune'.[70]

The *Orduna* incident was one of the events that led President Wilson to further increase pressure on Germany regarding their submarine campaign in the wake of the *Lusitania* tragedy, eventually leading to Germany's detrimental change in U-boat tactics.

As July 1915 rolled to a close, heavy fighting continued between Austria–Hungary and Italy, the latter who had declared war on them in May. Italy suffered two consecutive losses to them in the Isonzo region, with heavy casualties on both sides.

At sea, despite the changing tactics following the *Lusitania* disaster, U-boats continued to sink merchant shipping. A total of ninety-six ships would be captured or sunk during the month, equalling 121,294 tons. Over half of the U-boat related deaths in July came in the sinking of the Italian armoured cruisers *Amalfi* and the *Giuseppe Garibaldi*.[71] Most of the attacks continued to occur in the waters south-west of Ireland and England, and in and around the North Sea. U-boats were still under orders to avoid the nets and mines of the Dover Barrage, so little submarine activity was taking place in the English Channel.

One of the most successful U-boat commanders during July was Kapitänleutnant Ernst Graeff, commander of *U-36*. During the month, he and his crew managed to sink or capture fourteen vessels. However, their success and luck were about to run out. On 24 July, *U-36* stopped the Danish steamer SS *Luise*, when another merchant vessel approached the scene. The crew of *U-36* fired a warning shot, and signalled for it to stop. Unbeknownst to Graeff and his crew, this vessel was the HMS *Prince Charles*, and was actually a Q-ship, a heavily armed merchant ship with concealed weaponry, which was made to look like an easy target to draw submarines in, and then open fire at close range.

U-36 pulled within 600 yards of the *Prince Charles*. Once it was reasonably close, the decoy vessel's commander, Lieutenant William Mark-Wardlaw, unmasked the vessels deck guns and opened fire. The U-boat was struck aft of the conning tower, and tried to dive, but the *Prince Charles* scored several more hits before it could do so. *U-36* then began to sink by the stern. Kapitänleutnant Graeff was injured, and approximately eighteen of *U-36*'s crew perished. Initially, the SS *Luise* tried to go to the aid of the survivors, and the *Prince Charles*, mistakenly believing them to be a German resupply vessel, opened fire. Eventually, Lieutenant Mark-Wardlaw's vessel picked up fifteen survivors from the submarine. Kapitänleutnant Graeff gave the following description of the incident:

Royal Navy sailors demonstrate how hidden deck guns can be sprung on unsuspecting U-boats. (*Southampton Pictorial*, 1919/Authors' Collection)

... *U-36* stopped the Danish steamer SS *Luise* and was in the process of destroying part of her cargo when we sighted a steamer approaching ... proceeded toward the steamer and hoisted ... signal to stop and send across your papers ... we fired a round forward of her bow. The steamer stopped and swung out a boat.

As the *U-36* closed ... the steamer suddenly opened a heavy, accurate fire from hidden guns. We attempted to dive ... During that time the steamer scored several hits on the pressure hull.

As the *U-36* went under, water entered through several shell holes ... As the *U-36* regained the surface the crew abandoned her ... and went over the side. One round hit the conning tower killing the helmsman and wounding Kapitänleutnant Graeff and the navigator. Throughout the abandon ship, the steamer continued to fire ...

The British did not cease firing when the *U-36* sunk, but continued firing into the swimmers with artillery and rifle fire ... the SS *Luise* approached ... and lowered a boat to pick up the swimmers. The British shifted their fire to her ...

A half hour later the British ship returned, lowered a boat and picked up the survivors. The time lapse ... was about forty-five minutes. During that time half the men who had safely abandoned the *U-36* were killed by gunfire or drowned. The British also fired into the SS *Luise* because they thought she was a German resupply vessel.[72]

The *U-36* was the first victim of a Q-ship operating unassisted by any other vessels. While not an overwhelming success, the British strategy of using heavily armed merchant vessels as decoys gave U-boat commanders one more danger to be concerned about. However, the strategy was maligned by some, since it was thought that the use of such tactics would further discourage U-boat commanders from adhering to prize rules, since by warning ships before sinking them, they could be opening themselves up to an ambush. Despite the early success, U-boat commanders soon adapted to this tactic. Throughout the rest of the war, Q-ships proved to be a largely ineffective weapon, sinking approximately fifteen U-boats and damaging around sixty, while around thirty-eight Q-ships were lost on duty.[73]

At the beginning of August 1915, things looked grim for Russia on the Eastern Front. After Austria–Hungary recaptured Galicia, the Russian Army initiated a strategic retreat from that city and Poland in order to buy time, which became known as the 'Great Retreat of 1915'. Around 750,000 Russians were taken prisoner. By the end of the month, all of Poland was in Austro-Hungarian and German hands. Their forces continued to press east.

On the Gallipoli Peninsula, things continued to go very poorly for the Allied invasion forces, and little progress was being made. Attempting to reinvigorate the failing campaign, the Allies launched a new, last-ditch offensive between 6 and 21 August. This became known as the Battle of Sari Bair, or the 'August Offensive'. This plan also ended in failure. For the remainder of the Gallipoli Campaign, the front lines remained static, and no more major advances were attempted by the Allies. The losses had proven too grievous.

At sea, on 13 August, a horrible tragedy took place. The troopship HMT *Royal Edward* was on a voyage from Alexandria, Egypt, to the island of Lemnos. The former Canadian Northern Steamship Company liner was loaded with troops bound for combat in Gallipoli when it was torpedoed by *UB-14*. The ship sank by the stern in six minutes, taking around 866 men with it.[74] One of the lucky survivors was Harry Ross, 'of the engineers' staff':

The *Royal Edward*. (*The Illustrated War News*, 1915/ Authors' Collection)

I was off duty … and at nine o'clock was below in my room, when I observed through the porthole the wake of a torpedo, about 70 or 80 yards away, and in less than a minute it had struck the vessel on the port side, aft the engine-room. The noise of the explosion was terrible, while the rushing in of the water was overwhelming. There was soon a list to starboard, and all the lights under the decks were out.

Ross managed to 'scramble up through the hatchway' in the dark, a feat made even more difficult by the list. He did not have time to grab his lifebelt, so he clung to a piece of timber and leapt into the sea as the vessel plunged under. Large amounts of debris cluttered the water around the ship, and Ross felt that many of the casualties were caused by men being beat-up against the wreckage by waves. After a considerable amount of time in the water, Ross managed to clamber atop a capsized lifeboat with a group of other men until they were rescued by the HMHS *Soudan*.[75]

On 19 August, the White Star liner SS *Arabic* was sailing from Liverpool, England, to New York. The *Arabic* had successfully operated as a passenger liner for over a decade, and was under the command of Captain William Finch, a very rotund, yet competent commander. As the ship steamed along on a zigzag course, it came across a stricken merchant steamer, the SS *Dunsley*. The vessel had been stopped and shelled by *U-24*, under the command of Kapitänleutnant Rudolf Schneider, and was slowly sinking. Unbeknownst to anyone aboard the liner, the submarine was still on the scene. Captain Finch had received a wireless message informing him that all aboard the *Dunsley* had been evacuated, so he proceeded on the course toward America. They were approximately 50 miles south of the Old Head of Kinsale.

On board *U-24*, Kapitänleutnant Rudolf Schneider, who had been preparing to fire on the *Dunsley*, spotted a 'grey hulk' on the eastern horizon and began observing it, but was unable to make out any markings or flags. Suddenly, the ship turned, and headed bow-on towards the surfaced U-boat. Schneider, who had been attacked

Captain William Finch. (Library of Congress, Prints & Photographs Division)

by another vessel in a similar fashion days earlier, was convinced that the ship intended to ram them. He fired a single torpedo, which struck the ship.

While it was interpreted as an attempt at ramming, the *Arabic* had simply made a change in course while sailing along a zigzag course. In fact, nobody on board *Arabic* had even sighted *U-24*. Passengers and crewmembers' first sign of trouble was the approaching wake of the torpedo before it struck aft, causing massive damage.

The *Arabic* began sinking by the stern, and within ten minutes, was gone. Forty-four people died in the sinking, including two Americans. Aboard *U-24*, Schneider watched the evacuation and sinking, but was unaware of his victim's identity, recording in his logbook simply as 'an unknown freighter, of approximately 5,000 tons, probably carrying passengers'.[76] He did not know that his actions would spark yet another international incident between Germany and the United States.

The *Arabic* was the first White Star Line vessel lost in the First World War to enemy action. One of the survivors of the sinking was 19-year-old passenger Charles Frederick Kresser of England, who was travelling to America to stay with his family in Oakland, California. He gave the following account of the sinking:

> I will take my oath that the *Arabic* was torpedoed. Furthermore, I will swear that the torpedo was fired without reason, as the *Arabic* was proceeding on its way toward this country [United States] at the time it occurred. Why, no one on *Arabic* knew that there was a submarine boat in that vicinity. As a matter of fact, no person on the steamer saw the submarine boat before or after the sinking of the *Arabic*.

When told that Germany was claiming that the vessel had been sunk in self-defence, Kresser continued:

> That is only one more German lie to escape responsibility for a barbarous and criminal action. That statement is most certainly untrue. Neither Captain Finch of the *Arabic*, nor any one else on the liner, knew that there was a submarine near us.
>
> It was 9.25 o'clock in the morning, and I had just finished my breakfast. I was walking on the *Arabic*'s decks, looking over the starboard side. A greenish-white streak in the water toward the vessel's stern warned me of an approaching torpedo. We were just passing the freight steamer *Dunsley*, which the Germans had just shelled and which was slowly sinking. Having received a wireless message telling of the vessel's shelling, and that all aboard were safe, Captain Finch was proceeding directly on his way toward America …
>
> I shouted upon seeing the streak of the torpedo through the water. An explosion followed, and the *Arabic* immediately began to sink at the stern. It

was then that Captain Finch displayed supreme courage and cool-headedness. Jumping to the gunwale of the boat, megaphone in hand, he began to issue orders, which were obeyed to the letter by the crew.

Although the torpedo had been exploded about 100 feet from the stern, wrecking the engine rooms, the engineers did not leave their posts. The crew did great work in placing the passengers in the small boats. Everything was orderly … All credit for this wonderful order and coolness is due to Captain Finch and his crew.

The *Arabic* sank fast. I was in the last boat to leave, and I looked back to see Captain Finch, megaphone still in hand, standing on the gunwhale [sic]. It was a wonderful, though fearful sight to see him go down with his vessel.

The boat in which I was got away from the *Arabic* too late and we were capsized. The fact that all had taken the precaution to strap on lifebelts is all that saved us from death. In some manner, Captain Finch rose to the surface, and we took him into the boat which had picked me up after the vessel which I left the *Arabic* in had capsized. After drifting about for four hours, we were picked up by two British mine layers and taken to Queenstown.

This crowded lifeboat was photographed from the deck of the *Arabic* during the sinking. (*Illustrated World Magazine*, 1917/Authors' Collection)

Kresser then told of how he completed the journey to the United States aboard the SS *St Paul*:

I took no chances this time. The American flag was painted all over the *St Paul*, and they played searchlights on those paintings all through every hour of darkness, so that there would be no possible chance of the Germans making a mistake as to the flag under which the boat sailed.[77]

Kresser's story made the front page of the California papers once he finally arrived safely in Oakland, but since it wasn't printed until 9 September, it was overshadowed by headlines about German Zeppelins once again bombing London, and the recent developments on the Eastern Front.

Another survivor of the sinking was Second Officer Frederick Steele, who wrote the following affidavit:

I came on the bridge at 8 a.m … I sighted a vessel on the starboard bow, about seven miles away … which we later ascertained was the *Dunsley*. On approaching nearer to the vessel we found out that the vessel was sinking, going down by the head … The captain of the *Arabic* ordered me to work out a position for the *Dunsley*, so I worked one up … The captain told me to ring up the Marconi room and to tell the operator to send out a message at once that a steamer had been attacked and was sinking … When I came out of the chart room, I went to the starboard side of the bridge and passed the remark to the captain that he must be about somewhere waiting for us – meaning the submarine. We had five men on the lookout at the time. After speaking to the captain, I walked to the starboard end of the bridge and immediately clearly saw a bubbling disturbance in the water, and I also saw a torpedo traveling towards the ship, which apparently had been fired to hit her about the engine room. … I state positively that the *Arabic* never attempted to go to the *Dunsley* to affect a rescue. The *Arabic* was on a varying course, according to the commander's orders, as a precaution against submarine attack. Immediately after the torpedo was sighted the order was given 'hard a starboard' which turned the *Arabic* away from the presumed direction of the submarine. I further make oath and say that at the time the *Arabic* was struck by the torpedo she was moving away from the *Dunsley*.[78]

Several American citizens who survived the sinking also gave depositions regarding the incident at the American Consulate in Liverpool. One of them was a man named William Cummins:

I, William Cummins, first being duly sworn, do depose and say as follows … I was on board the SS *Arabic* when she was torpedoed in the Atlantic, and that I was on the top deck, close to the captain's bridge, looking at the steamer which had already been disabled by shell fire. I saw the track of the torpedo, and also saw the torpedo strike the side of the vessel. I heard the captain distinctly state to all in hearing to get life belts and go to the boats, which I lost no time in doing. I further assert under oath that the vessel was not warned, and am positive that no one on board saw the submarine. That I got into boat No. 8, commanded by the boatswain, and was taken to Queenstown by the British cruiser *Magnolia*.[79]

Another one of the American citizens filing an affidavit was Claude M. Roode:

… about 9.30 a.m., August 19th, I was on 'B' deck about amidships, and about 200 yards away I saw the track of a torpedo coming, and in my estimation the track was moving at a slight angle to the *Arabic*. I ran forward, as I was apprehensive that the torpedo would strike that part of the vessel where I was standing. The track of the torpedo was the first intimation of danger.

That I state positively, under oath, that I know the ship was not hailed by any vessel at about this time, and that no warning whatsoever of any kind was given prior to the sending of the torpedo against the *Arabic*. That after the explosion I assisted by placing life belts on two ladies, and then entered number 3 boat, and was finally landed at Queenstown, whence I proceeded to Liverpool.[80]

Several other American passengers gave affidavits attesting to the same facts: that *Arabic* had not been warned prior to being torpedoed, and that it was in no way attempting to aid the *Dunsley* when it was attacked.

Captain Finch also filed an affidavit following the rescue, and stringently protested the German claim that his vessel had tried to ram the submarine:

William Finch … doth depose and say as follows … That the *Arabic* was struck by a torpedo without warning previously given. That no submarine was seen by the *Arabic*. That the *Arabic* did not try to ram the submarine. That the *Arabic* could not have rammed the submarine had it desired to do so. That there was no time or opportunity to have done so. That the *Arabic* did not try to escape. And further, that there was neither time nor opportunity to escape if it had been desired to do so.

I further make oath and say that at 9.25 a.m., Greenwich Mean time … I sent a wireless message … that there was a vessel nearby that had evidently been torpedoed … and that there were two boats with sails set steering towards the land, evidently from the distressed vessel. At the time the *Arabic* was torpedoed I was two miles away from this vessel, on a zigzag course, and was going away from her – not towards her. Five minutes after sending this message referred to I observed a torpedo from the starboard side of the Bridge at a distance of about three hundred feet, a little before the Beam. We noticed the torpedo bubbles and a streak from the torpedo coming towards the *Arabic*. The *Arabic* sunk in about ten minutes after the torpedo struck her.[81]

The consequences of the sinking of the *Arabic* were immediate and tragic. On 19 August, the same day that the *Arabic* was sunk, *U-27*, commanded by Kapitänleutnant Berhard Wegener, stopped the SS *Nicosian*, a merchant vessel which was carrying munitions and mules for the British Army. Wegener waited until the *Nicosian*'s crew abandoned ship before beginning to shell the captured vessel. *U-27* had stopped and sunk four vessels the previous day, strictly adhering to prize rules in doing so.

While this was taking place, another vessel arrived on the scene. The ship was beat up and worn looking, with American neutrality markers present, and was

The *Arabic* sinking by the stern, as photographed by Professor Alfred Still from one of the lifeboats. (Authors' Collection)

flying the American flag. While it looked harmless, the ship was in fact the HMS *Baralong*, a Q-ship in disguise. Lieutenant-Commander Godfrey Herbert was the commanding officer. The *Baralong*'s crew was infuriated, as they had been just twenty miles from the *Arabic* when it sank and received the distress call, but had been unable to locate the survivors. The sinking of the passenger liner and the death of innocents aboard it had their blood up. Unfortunately, the crew of the *U-27*, who had nothing to do with the sinking, was going to be the target of their wrath.

Steaming closer, the *Baralong* raised a signal indicating that they were going to rescue the *Nicosian*'s crew. Kapitänleutnant Wegener acknowledged the signal, and moved to intercept the vessel. As *U-27* came around the *Nicosian*'s bow, the *Baralong* and the submarine were steaming on parallel courses. Just then, the *Baralong* lowered the American flag and neutrality markings, hoisted its Royal Navy ensign, and sprung its guns on the unsuspecting submarine.

Lieutenant-Commander Herbert gave the order to fire, and the *Baralong*'s gun crews quickly fired thirty-nine shells into *U-27*, causing the submarine to roll over and sink in under a minute. Only fourteen crewmembers managed to escape the submarine as it plunged under, and all of them had been in the conning tower, or manning the two deck guns at the time. The British sailors continued firing into the submarine even after Herbert gave the order to cease fire. According to American witnesses who were crewmembers of the *Nicosian*, the British crewmen then opened fire on the German sailors in the water with rifles and pistols.

The German crewmembers had been attempting to reach the *Nicosian*, and most were killed in the water as they struggled to reach safety. Five or six, including Kapitänleutnant Wegener, managed to climb up the lifeboat falls and board the ship, and hid in the engine room. Lieutenant-Commander Herbert sent a group of twelve Royal Marines over to the ship, under the command of Corporal Fred Collins, instructing them to 'take no prisoners'. As soon as the marines found the Germans' hiding spot, they shot them on sight.

According to one eyewitness, Kapitänleutnant Wegener ran to a cabin on the upper deck and hid in the *Nicosian* captain's bathroom. The Royal Marines broke down the door with the butt of their rifles, but Wegener 'squeezed through a scuttle and dropped into the sea. He still had his life-jacket on and put up his hands in surrender. Corporal Collins, however, took aim and shot him through the head'. Collins himself later claimed that after Wegener was dead, Lieutenant-Commander Herbert threw a revolver in his face, screaming 'What about the *Lusitania*, you bastard!'

Following the incident, Herbert filed a report with the British Admiralty, claiming that the German sailors were killed because they were going to scuttle the *Nicosian*, and that if he hadn't stopped them, it would have been negligence on his part. The Admiralty attempted to censor the details since the actions taken could be considered war crimes, but several American crewmembers from the *Nicosian* had witnessed the events from their lifeboats, and later spoke to reporters about it when they arrived back in the United States.[82]

In the US, President Wilson was disturbed and disgusted upon hearing of the incident, saying 'Isn't this one of the most unspeakable performances? It's horrible'. Secretary of State Lansing called Britain's conduct 'shocking', but stopped short of filing an official protest.[83]

Germany was incensed when they found out what had happened, labelling it nothing short of 'cowardly murder'. The German Government filed an official memorandum protesting the incident on 6 December 1915. They demanded that the *Baralong*'s captain and crew be tried for the murder of the unarmed sailors in a British naval court martial.

The response from Britain's Foreign Secretary Sir Edward Grey was considered 'full of insolence and arrogance' and was dubbed 'a monument of England's shame'. Grey suggested that the incident could be grouped with three 'German outrages' that occurred in the same forty-eight hours as the '*Baralong* Incident', including the sinking of the *Arabic*, an attack on a stranded British submarine in neutral Dutch waters, and allegedly firing 'shrapnel at the crew of the steamer in their boats' after the SS *Ruel* was sunk, and proposed that an investigation by an American Naval Tribunal be conducted to look into all four events.[84]

Even the British press was not completely satisfied with this response by their government. The *Manchester Guardian* praised Foreign Secretary Grey's suggestion of an American Naval Tribunal, but rightly noted that 'the British note does not pretend to be a reasoned reply and only refuses to admit the accuracy of the German version'.[85] After receiving the response, the Imperial German Navy allegedly put the *Baralong*'s crew on the 'black list', meaning they were to be shot on sight in retaliation if captured.[86]

Elsewhere, the sinking of the *Arabic* rekindled the smouldering sentiment of those in the United States and international community against Germany, at a time when some of the uproar over the *Falaba* and *Lusitania* sinkings was just beginning to subside. Foreign Policy Advisor Edward House advised President Wilson to act, and Secretary of State Lansing stated that relations with Germany ought to be severed.

President Wilson tactfully rejected the counsel of both, in order to avoid inflaming the situation. Following this, House wrote in his diary 'I am surprised at the attitude he takes. He evidently will go to great lengths to avoid war'. While further action was debated, the United States issued a strong protest over the sinking.

Soon, German Ambassador von Bernstorff began to display anxiety, mirroring the state of those in the German Foreign Ministry, whom the press described as behaving 'as if they have lost their heads'. German officials were evidently very concerned by the American reaction to the sinking. President Wilson ordered Lansing to continue negotiations with the German ambassador.

To the surprise of many, von Bernstorff disclosed that the German Government had previously issued private orders to its submarine commanders to obey prize rules, and to avoid sinking large passenger liners, whether from neutral nations or not. When these orders were issued by Kaiser Wilhelm II on 6 June 1915, following the uproar caused by the sinking of the *Lusitania*, he had commanded that his orders were not to be disclosed publicly. To ease tensions, von Bernstorff said that he would issue a declaration recommending that Germany make an open pledge that ships would no longer be sunk without first receiving a warning. President Wilson insisted on a further promise that 'efforts would be made to provide for the safety of passengers and crew'.

Ambassador von Bernstorff publishing his declaration did not end the crisis. When Germany offered an official explanation for the sinking, it did not confirm the ambassador's declaration that ships be warned before being sunk, and the crews' safety provided for. Publicly, Wilson hoped that a compromise could still be reached. Privately, the president was described as being deeply troubled by 'the labyrinth made for us by this German frightfulness'.

Wilson made it clear that he was willing to accept nothing less than a disavowal of the *Arabic* sinking from the German Government, coupled with a pledge to not sink any unarmed vessels without warning. This pledge was unacceptable to German military leaders who knew that blockading the British Isles was crucial to the war effort, and that this would effectively neuter their efforts. To be effective, U-boats *had* to sink vessels without warning, or they would be putting the submarines and their crews at undue risk.

Waiting patiently, President Wilson ultimately received not only a satisfactory disavowal of the *Arabic* sinking from Germany, with the U-boat commander eventually receiving a reprimand, but also a declaration that regulations on U-boat commanders would be 'so stringent that the reoccurrence of incidents similar to the *Arabic* case is considered out of the question'.[87]

German Chancellor Theobald von Bethmann-Hollweg. (*Collier's*, 1917/Authors' Collection)

Behind the scenes, the German leadership had been split on whether to settle matters with the United States. Chancellor Theobald von Bethmann-Hollweg feared American intervention in the conflict if Germany's current submarine warfare tactics were continued. Ambassador von Bernstorff had recently warned 'I fear I cannot prevent rupture this time if our answer in the *Arabic* matter is not conciliatory'. Even the Netherlands' entry into the war on the side of the Allies seemed liked a real possibility, as they had disagreed with Germany's submarine warfare policies previously, and were now declaring that 'Germany's war aims threatened the independence of Holland'.

One of the individuals on the other side of the internal debate was Secretary of State of the Imperial Naval Office Alfred von Tirpitz who was an advocate of implementing wholly unrestricted submarine warfare, arguing that such a policy could break Britain's blockade of German shipping lines. Von Tirpitz stated that the torpedoing of large passenger liners could not be prevented with any certainty unless U-boats were ordered not to operate in the 'war zone' waters any longer, which he viewed as unacceptable, as it would render the U-boat campaign completely ineffective. Writing to Kaiser Wilhelm II, he stated 'so long as preventing a conflict with America matters to us', that the entire campaign would have to be abandoned.

Von Tirpitz's pleas were supported by others in the German Government such as his ally Admiral Gustav Bachmann, Chief of the Admiralty Staff, who was also a strong advocate of unrestricted submarine warfare, regardless of the political consequences.

Despite this, Chancellor von Bethmann-Hollweg was able to get the Kaiser to issue a new order to the U-boat fleet on 27 August, stating 'henceforward any passenger vessel whatever, not only the large ones, shall only be sunk after warning and safeguarding of passengers'. U-boat commanders complained immediately. With the new orders in place, Kapitänleutnant Otto Steinbrinck of the *UB-18* told an American journalist that he 'had let forty ships in the [English] Channel go by', which he otherwise could have sunk.

Also on 27 August, Secretary of State of the Imperial Naval Office von Tirpitz offered his resignation, writing that evidently, Chancellor von Bethmann-Hollweg attached no value to his services and advice. Chief of the Admiralty Staff Bachmann had tendered his own resignation. The Kaiser refused to accept Tirpitz's offer, since he was so popular with the German people. However, he did accept Bachmann's in September 1915, reassigning him to his former post as commander at Kiel. Bachmann's behaviour and tactics during the debate had 'displeased the Kaiser'. His position of Chief of the Admiralty Staff was soon filled by Admiral Henning von Holtzendorff, who was 'known not to be a U-boat fanatic', and was believed to hold a similar position on the issue to that of his predecessor.

Admiral Henning von Holtzendorff.
(*Collier's*, 1917/Authors' Collection)

Shortly, another order was issued stating that no U-boats were to be stationed off the west coast of England, where passenger vessels were likely to be. Operating in those waters was too risky, as more mistakes would prove in the coming months. The possibility of confusing passenger vessels for viable targets was very high, as were inadvertent American casualties, which led U-boat commanders to refrain from attacking ships in many instances. Tirpitz wrote privately to the Kaiser protesting this decision, and detailing his objections. Wilhelm II responded with a sharply worded rebuke:

> America must be prevented from taking part against us as an active enemy. She could provide unlimited money for our foes … As Chief Warlord I had absolutely to prevent this event from occurring. That was wise policy. For that reason I had with a heavy heart to impose *restrictions* in order to achieve that goal … First the *war must be won*, and that end necessitates absolute protection against a new enemy; how that is to be achieved – whether with more or less sacrifice – is immaterial, and *my business*. What I do with my navy is my business *only*.[88]

On 1 September, Ambassador von Bernstorff received permission from Chancellor von Bethmann-Hollweg and Foreign Minister Gottlieb von Jagow to officially release the '*Arabic* pledge' to US Secretary of State Lansing. The pledge read: 'Liners will not be sunk by our submarines without warning, and without safety of the lives of noncombatants, provided that the liners do not try to escape or provide resistance.' President Wilson was extremely relieved and pleased with the resolution to the crisis. His popularity in the United States soared.[89]

By late September 1915, the focus of Germany's submarine warfare would shift largely to the Mediterranean Sea, which was rich with targets, with far less of a chance of American passengers or vessels being hit. It also allowed Germany to take some pressure off their Austro-Hungarian and Turkish allies who were fighting in Eastern Europe and the Mediterranean theatre. For the next two years, U-boat operations in the Mediterranean would prove a stunning success. Meanwhile, U-boat operations would be largely suspended not only in the English Channel, but also off the west coast of England. Submarines operating in the North Sea were ordered to adhere stringently to prize rules. Germany had diffused the latest crisis with the United States, effectively ending their blockade of Britain in the process. As Tirpitz put it, 'We continued the campaign in a form that could not live and yet, at the same time, could not die'.[90]

In the days following the *Arabic* sinking, the SS *Cameronia* was crossing from Liverpool to New York. Three of the passengers aboard were William J. Johnson, and his sisters Lizzie and Minnie, all from Belfast, Ireland. The family was heading to Gaston, Oregon, and had two older brothers fighting in the war. Both had already been wounded, one in Gallipoli, the other in the Marne. One of the sisters described the voyage, illustrating the tense scene on board other passenger liners following the *Arabic* sinking:

> We left Liverpool on the Cunard liner *Cameronian* [sic] and while going through the danger zone we were accompanied by two warships … We heard rumors that there was a submarine in our vicinity and, being just a day or two

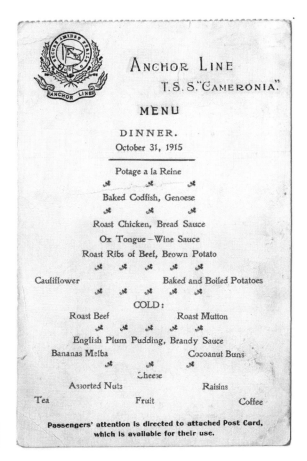

A rare dinner menu from the SS *Cameronia*. (Authors' Collection)

after the sinking of the *Arabic*, there was some consternation on board … the passengers were drilled in the use of the lifebelts, every person, even the babies, having one on, and then … was assigned to a certain lifeboat.

My brother and we two sisters were assigned to the same boat … and we knew just what to do in case of a torpedo attack. The lifeboats were in position on deck, so there would be the least possible delay in filling and lowering them … Sunday night the warships left us and we were told that all danger from the submarines was past.

The next day during the sports on deck a big crowd of passengers gave three cheers for the captain of the *Cameronian* [sic] for bringing them safely through, and there were also three cheers for President Wilson and the United States.[91]

The *Cameronia* would go on to be requisitioned as a troop transport in January 1917, and would meet a tragic end, being sunk by a U-boat in April of that same year, with loss of life.

Near the end of August, with the failure of the Gallipoli Campaign, the need for the Allies to ship as many troops to the Mediterranean slackened. However, with the high number of casualties in Gallipoli, there was a much greater need

A lifeboat struggles to get away from the *Cameronia* as it sinks, as a man climbs down a set of falls in the foreground. (*The Graphic*, 1917/Authors' Collection)

The *Cameronia* plunging under. *(The Graphic,* 1917/Authors' Collection)

Cameronia survivors struggle to keep afloat atop flooded and capsized lifeboats. *(The Graphic,* 1917/Authors' Collection)

for shipping wounded troops back home to England. As a result, the HMT *Mauretania* and *Aquitania*, both of which had been serving as troop transports, were to be converted into hospital ships.

Work quickly commenced on the vessels, with their interior spaces receiving particular attention, converting them into large operating theatres and patient wards. The hulls of the Cunarders were painted white, the funnels yellow, and the hulls had green bands applied, with red crosses marking the purpose of the ships so that they wouldn't be attacked by U-boats or enemy vessels. After its conversion, *Aquitania* had the capacity to carry 4,182 wounded, plus medical staff and crewmembers. Both vessels were now titled the HMHS *Mauretania* and *Aquitania*.

HMHS *Mauretania*. (Authors' Collection)

HMHS *Aquitania*. (Authors' Collection)

Captain Arthur Rostron. (Library of Congress, Prints & Photographs Division)

The Admiralty appointed Captain Arthur H. Rostron as master of the *Mauretania*. Rostron was famous for having been the captain of the RMS *Carpathia* when it rescued the *Titanic*'s survivors in 1912. He was initially disappointed to be put in charge of a hospital ship, as he had not yet tired of what he dubbed 'the chase', relating to 'the excitement of wondering whether we should get through or this time have a tin fish in our sides'.

While no longer viable targets of enemy combatants, the *Mauretania* and *Aquitania* would see a lot of action transporting wounded troops in the closing months of 1915 and early into 1916. The *Mauretania* made three voyages between Southampton and the Mediterranean during this span, carrying over 8,500 medical staff and wounded troops. Ironically, some of the wounded were likely men shipped to the front on the very same ship.[92]

As August 1915 came to a close, the number of ships lost or captured by U-boats during the month was 121, for a total of 200,667 tons. This was the largest number of ships lost to U-boats in a month thus far in the war, as new restrictions on submarine activity by the German Government had not yet made a significant impact. An additional five ships were damaged. The most successful U-boat commander in August was Kapitänleutnant Max Valentiner of the *U-38*, with thirty vessels sunk, and one damaged.[93]

September–October 1915

In September 1915, there were some new developments on the deadlocked Western Front. On 25 September, the British and French Armies launched the largest offensive to date, marking the beginning of the Battle of Loos. This action saw the first use of poison gas by Britain in the war. It also saw the first large-scale use of Kitchener's Army units, the 'New Army' that had been created at the recommendation of British Secretary of State for War Horatio Kitchener.

Lasting until October 1915, the offensive failed to meet its objectives. Britain suffered approximately 50,000 casualties, and German losses were placed at roughly half that number, despite the fact that their forces had been significantly outnumbered. On 26 September, German machine-gun positions cut down so many men from Kitchener's Army that they eventually stopped firing, to allow the British troops to withdraw with their wounded. The following day, author Rudyard Kipling's only son, who was serving in the Irish Guard, was killed, and his body was never recovered.[94]

At sea, things had been relatively calm following the 'Arabic pledge'. However, another significant sinking was about to take place, which threatened to undo all of the diplomatic work that was accomplished after the Arabic was sunk. On 4 September, the Allan Line's RMS Hesperian was beginning a voyage from Liverpool to Montréal, Canada. Besides passengers and cargo, the ship was carrying wounded Canadian troops home.

Around dusk, the Hesperian was approximately 85 miles off Fastnet Rock, Ireland, and was being watched by Kapitänleutnant Walther Schwieger aboard U-20. Schwieger, who had sunk the Lusitania in May, watched as the vessel steered along on a zig-zag course toward him. Even though he could not identify the ship or its purpose, and even though U-boat commanders were under direct orders not to attack passenger liners, Schwieger fired a single torpedo at it.

Lifeboats stacked on the deck of RMS Hesperian. (Authors' Collection)

The *Hesperian* sinking after being torpedoed. (Columbia Basin Institute of Regional History Collection)

At 8.30 p.m., the *Hesperian*'s starboard bow was struck. The resulting explosion tore through the ship's engine room, blasting water and debris up onto the bridge and boat deck, causing significant damage. The ship immediately settled by the head and took on a list, and steam from the ruptured lines obscured the decks. Captain William Main calmly ordered the ship stopped, an SOS signal sent, and gave orders to man the lifeboats. Despite it being dark, the crewmembers and passengers reacted calmly, and most of the lifeboats were lowered without incident. However, one boat capsized while it was being lowered, spilling its passengers into the sea, where thirty-two of them died. The evacuation was completed in under an hour.

British ships rescued the survivors during the night. Captain Main and a skeleton crew stayed behind on *Hesperian* in an attempt to save it. They hoped that despite being low in the water, the ship could be beached or taken under tow. Unfortunately, attempts at towing it to safety failed, and it sank on 6 September, not far from the final resting place of the *Lusitania*. Ironically, the body of Frances Ramsey Stephens, a widow who was a victim of the *Lusitania* sinking, was aboard, and was being transported to Canada so that she could be buried with her husband. Stephens' body went under with the ship, marking the second time, once in life and once in death, that a vessel she had been travelling aboard was torpedoed by Kapitänleutnant Schwieger and *U-20*.

One of the survivors of the sinking was Major H. Barres, a Canadian officer from the 14th Battalion who was returning home, along with twelve officers and thirty-eight other men, to recuperate from wounds received in combat. He gave the following account:

I was sitting, in company with brother officers, on one of the upper decks after dinner about 8.20 p.m., and was smoking a cigarette.

Suddenly I heard a loud detonation, the liner at the same time trembling terribly. All at once an enormous column of water about 50ft in height was shot up into air, and before we could realise what had occurred it came down on deck with a terrific thud, flooding the deck and drenching myself and my brother officers. With the downpour of sea water were several pieces of iron.

Captain Main was on the bridge when the torpedo struck the ship, and his first order was to lower away the lifeboats, and see that all the women and children on board were first safely placed in them.

He also gave instructions to have the SOS wireless sent across the waters, appealing for assistance, and, in addition, he had rockets fired to attract the attention of any vessels in the vicinity. The Morse signals were also used. [95]

An affidavit signed by four of the *Hesperian's* officers, Captain William Main, Chief Officer Alexander Maxwell, First Officer Charles Richardson and Second Officer William F. Reid, gives more details regarding the sinking:

… Dusk was closing in rapidly at the time specified when an explosion took place against the starboard bow No. 2 bulkhead, admitting water into compartments 1 and 2. The vessel sank about ten feet within four hours.

The explosion occurred within about eight feet of the surface, throwing a mass of water and steel fragments on the deck. From the steel fragments preserved it is indubitable that the explosion was caused by a torpedo and not by a mine. The characteristic odor of high explosive was noticeable.

No warning of any kind was received by the *Hesperian*. The track of a torpedo approaching the vessel was not observed by any of the ship's officers. They thought that on account of a failing light it may not have been possible to have seen it. No submarine was sighted before or after the explosion.

A 6-inch gun mounted on the stern of the *Hesperian* was painted a service gray, and would not have been conspicuous even at a short distance, and the officers think it could not have been observed at all through a periscope.

On board the *Hesperian* were forty Canadian soldiers, including officers, all either invalided or in attendance upon those invalided … No American citizens were among the passengers so far as known. One cabin steward, N. J. Dallas, was an American citizen.

Very slight panic or confusion existed, and the boats and lifesaving apparatus were in readiness and worked well. Wireless signals, siren, and rockets brought a British warship on the scene by 9.30, and two other Admiralty vessels before 10.30, but the *Hesperian* was not under convoy, and had not spoken to an Admiralty ship prior to the torpedoing. [96]

A surprising account of the *Hesperian* sinking comes from a 10-year-old Austrian child named Rudolph Gorog. Gorog, who was asleep during the evacuation, was somehow overlooked, and when he woke up, all of the passengers had abandoned ship, leaving only Main and his skeleton crew aboard:

> On Saturday night I left my mammie in her state room and went to mine, when I quickly tumbled into bed and was soon fast asleep. I slept so soundly that I did not hear the torpedo striking the ship, nor did I hear the explosion.
>
> The noise of the rushing passengers did not wake me. In the morning when I awoke I went to my mammie's berth to say good morning to her and to get my boots. When I got there the room was empty. I grabbed my boots and rushed on deck, where I did not see them, nor did I see any of the other passengers, and only one or two of the crew.
>
> I spoke to one fellow, and inquired where my mammie was. He asked me where I had come from. He also told me that the ship was sinking. He brought me to the captain, who was surprised to hear my tale, and explained that my mammie and my sisters had left the ship and gone to Queenstown in a steamer. He appeared very sorry for me, but cheered me up, saying: 'Little man, we must take care of you'. He put a lifebelt round me. I was in the steamer for two days, wondering whether I should see my mammie again, and I did, and am glad.[97]

The outcries following the sinking of the *Hesperian* were immediate, since it was a passenger liner and was sunk without any prior warning. They labelled the attackers 'pirates'. The outrage was understandable when one considers that the '*Arabic* pledge' was released just days earlier. The German Government explained the sinking by stating that the liner was armed, which was true. President Wilson regretted that in the first diplomatic note regarding the *Lusitania* sinking, he had condemned attacks on 'unarmed' ships, while Lansing had recommended the wording be 'unresisting', leaving a loophole which Germany now exploited.[98]

Publicly, the situation was resolved after Germany reiterated the '*Arabic* pledge'. However, Kapitänleutnant Schwieger's actions had once again threatened to draw the United States into the conflict. Once Schwieger and the *U-20* had returned to port in Wilhelmshaven, he was treated with disdain by his superiors for having disobeyed the Kaiser's direct orders not to attack passenger liners, and was sent to Berlin to explain himself. Schwieger would later complain about his treatment after the sinkings.

Torpedoes were not the only danger to ships. Even vessels from neutral nations, such as the Netherlands, faced risks. On 22 September, the Nederland Line's SS *Koningin Emma* was returning from Java in the Dutch East Indies, laden with passengers, mail and cargo. When it was approximately 2 miles away from the Sunk Light Vessel near Harwich, England, the vessel's bow struck a mine that had been laid by *UC-7*, and began listing heavily. The ship was evacuated, although a small number of crewmembers returned to try saving it. Rescue ships were soon

A cribbage board made from a piece of floating debris recovered after the *Koningin Emma* sinking. (Authors' Collection)

on the scene. Plans were made to tow the vessel up the River Thames to beach it in the shallows, but it capsized and sank near Shipwash Sands, approximately twenty miles off Harwich.

A newspaper account of the sinking recounted the dramatic details of the incident:

From the accounts of survivors it appears the *Koningin Emma* left Deal for Amsterdam in the finest weather, at 5 a.m. on the 22nd … At ten minutes to ten the ship was steaming at full speed – the English pilot had left a quarter of an hour earlier – when a terrible crash was heard, immediately followed by a heavy explosion which hurled everything in the fore part of the ship into the air. One of the crew states two derricks, weighing 2 tons each, were hurled into the air and fell with a terrific crash on the deck. The vessel had run upon a mine. Everyone, men, women, and children, hurried up on deck. Any panic was, however, stilled by the calm and able action of captain and officers who during the voyage had frequently practiced what they had now to do. It was only seven minutes after the accident that the boats were launched. There were various vessels in the neighborhood, including British torpedo boat destroyers and the *Batavier IV*, which hastened to take the shipwrecked people on board. This also was done in complete order, so that no single accident happened. The people picked up by the British destroyers were afterwards transferred to the *Kambangan*. Only a few passengers saved any luggage, and then only a very small quantity. The ship's papers were saved, and the cashier succeeded in saving the cash and valuables.

When Captain Braat saw that the vessel did not immediately sink, he decided to do what he could to save her. Returning on board with the crew, as much of the mail as possible was taken off, though twenty bags were lost. All the steam pumps were set to work to keep the vessel afloat. The idea was to get her on a sandbank and thus keep her from sinking. The entire cargo, consisting of maize, coffee, tobacco, tea, rubber … was lost.

A group of the passengers rescued from the vessel later expressed their gratitude to their rescuers in the following letter:

Before leaving England the undersigned felt it a duty to say how grateful they were for the kind treatment they met with on board of HMS *Lurcher* and *Ganges II* after the wrecking of the *Koningin Emma*. It is above our praise to relate the gallant rescue work H.B.M.'s [His British Majesty's] ships, and specially the *Lurcher*, rendered to the doomed mail packet, but we wish to say that we were not surprised at all to find out afterwards the glorious roll of fame of the little *Lurcher*, which shall remain in future in our eyes a great ship. It is certainly not her dimensions, but it is the virtues and the qualities of her commander and crew which classify her as A1 in the great British naval history book.[99]

In September, the British Admiralty determined that a vessel with a larger capacity to ship troops was needed, particularly since the *Mauretania* and *Aquitania* were now being employed as hospital ships. On 1 September, they formally requisitioned the RMS *Olympic*, which had been laid up in Belfast for the past ten months. The vessel, which needed a fair amount of maintenance work since it had been sitting unused in dirty water, was quickly converted into a troopship, capable of accommodating more than 6,000 troops.

While officers would be berthed in the first-class cabins on C deck, the luxurious public rooms and spaces elsewhere on the ship were to take on a much more utilitarian appearance. Amongst other changes, the second-class library was converted into a hospital with 100 beds, the third-class smoking room and general rooms underneath the poop deck were transformed into sleeping accommodations for 200 troops in hammocks, and the famous first-class dining room and D deck reception room were to be utilised as hammock and mess arrangements for 1,804 and 1,499 soldiers respectively.

White Star Line's Captain Bertram Fox Hayes was placed in command of the troopship, now dubbed the HMT *Olympic*. Once in Liverpool, defensive guns were installed on the deck of the ship, both fore and aft. Initially, the vessel retained its normal White Star Line livery, but soon, the funnels of the ship were painted grey, with the tops remaining black. The *Olympic* began its first trooping voyage to the Mediterranean on 24 September.[100]

As September 1915 came to an end, it was clear that the tighter restrictions on targets led to the number of ships sunk or captured plunging from 121 in August, to just sixty-five in September, for a total of 145,520 tons of shipping lost during the month. An additional five ships were damaged. More sinkings began to take place in the Mediterranean as the U-boat campaign shifted its focus to that region.[101]

October 1915 saw another battle in the Isonzo region, resulting in an Austro-Hungarian victory over Italy. The month would also see Bulgaria enter the war on the side of Germany and the Central Powers. Germany and Austria–Hungary's new ally promptly joined them in invading Serbia.

At sea, even with submarine activity on the decline in the North Sea and waters surrounding the British Isles, there was still peril. On 3 October, the Nelson liner SS *Highland Warrior* was on a voyage from London to Buenos Aires, Argentina. It was carrying passengers, gold bullion and meat, the latter of which comprised the majority of the cargo. The seas were rough, and the ship grounded itself and stuck fast to a rock outcropping as it steamed along. With the heavy wave action, the crew feared their ship might be dashed on the rocks, so an SOS was sent. The passengers and lifeboats were lowered into the churning sea.

The *Highland Warrior*'s distress call was picked up by the nearby HMAHS (His Majesty's Australian Hospital Ship) *Karoola*. Built by Harland & Wolff in 1909, the former McIlwraith, McEacharn & Co. liner, and veteran of the Sydney to Fremantle Australian passenger run, had been requisitioned as a troop transport in May 1915. Currently, it was serving as Australia's No. 1 Hospital Ship, transporting

A uniform patch from a crewmember of the *Karoola*, indicating the ship's status as Australia's No. 1 Hospital Ship. (Authors' Collection)

HMAHS *Karoola*. (Authors' Collection)

wounded Australian troops between Alexandria, Egypt, England, and back home to Australia. It had the capacity to carry 460 patients. When Captain W.C.E. Morgan was informed of the *Highland Warrior*'s situation, he had the *Karoola* head for their location. The crew would soon prove that a hospital ship was good for more than just transporting the wounded.

Arriving on the scene, everyone went into rescue mode, and despite the rough seas, were able to save the passengers of the *Highland Warrior*. Captain Morgan knew the *Karoola* intimately, and would end up commanding the vessel for a total of nineteen years in his career.[102] This familiarity with his vessel and crew surely aided the rescue efforts. After the passengers were transferred, the *Karoola* stood by while the *Highland Warrior*'s cargo of bullion was removed. Some of the latter's crew remained aboard in an attempt to save their ship.

One of the people aboard the *Karoola* during the rescue was Private Fosard, of the Australian Army Medical Corps. He gave an account detailing the rescue:

We went on our way from Gibraltar to London, and had been out about two days when the wireless operator received the SOS signal. Lt. Col. R.G. Craig of the Army Medical Corps held a consultation with the command and it was decided to go to the assistance of the ship in distress. When we reached the scene we found it was the *Highland Warrior*, engaged chiefly in the meat trade. The ship was piled up on the rocks, and just as we got there they put off six boats in a very heavy sea. The boats contained all the women and children who were on board.

We found it impossible to lower the gangway owing to the big waves, so we hit upon an ingenious plan. We lowered a derrick from the ship's side with a coal basket attached to a rope. The basket was swung out about 20 feet, and then two women or a woman and a child were fixed in the basket and hauled on deck. The work took two hours but we had the satisfaction of saving 35 women and children. The crew decided to stand by the ship, and we left amid a great deal of cheering.

We landed the women and children at Devonport two days later. On the same trip we picked up two enemy boats. We took them on board and landed them at Southampton.[103]

Another person aboard the *Karoola* during the rescue was Lance Corporal Harold Beechey, from Friesthorpe, Lincolnshire, England, who was in Wales, recovering from an illness. He wrote the following:

5 October 1915

3rd Western Hospital, Ninian Park, Cardiff

My dear mother,

Arrived here this afternoon from Southampton. Left Alexandria 24th September. I came over on number 1 Australian Hospital Ship *Karoola*. Had a fairly good journey but one or two little incidents. Had a very fine view of Gibraltar by moonlight – it looked very impressive and the searchlights lit up the ship like day. Then we picked up a wireless message from the *Highland Warrior* – but after searching round for some hours we found her fast on the rocks near Corunna, Spain, and took off the passengers, nine of them, bound for South America. Then most of us, more or less seriously, got ptomaine poisoning from something in the food. I got off fairly light though I had some nasty spasms of pain in my little tummy the last few days. Everybody got over it luckily. I have been sent home for a couple of months to recuperate. I'm fairly all right but pretty weak and get fagged with very little exertion. I don't know how long I shall be in this hospital but you might write straight back and I will let you know of any change of address. I expect I shall be sent to a convalescent home in a few days. Love to all and tell them to write here. I shall have at least a fortnight at home when I get fairly fit.

Love Harold

PS I suppose you got my field service postcard telling you I was being sent back to the base sick which I sent off about the beginning of September – same trouble as before.[104]

Tragically, Beechey would be killed by a bomb in Bullecourt, France on 10 April 1917 at the age of 26. Beechey and seven of his brothers fought in the war, and five of the eight siblings were killed. One of the surviving brothers was seriously wounded and permanently disabled in combat.

The total number of ships sunk or captured in October 1915 fell to forty-two, for a total of 84,614 tons. Another five ships were damaged. The location of U-boat related attacks shifted heavily to the Mediterranean, as Germany's submarine fleet continued to abandon operations near the British Isles.[105]

November–December 1915

In November 1915, another battle raged in the Isonzo region. The outcome was yet another Austro-Hungarian victory over Italian forces. Elsewhere, by the end of the month, the Serbian Army, trying to defend against the invading Central Power forces, completely collapsed. The Serbian troops began retreating to the Adriatic Sea, where they would be evacuated by Italian and French naval vessels.

At sea, the French Line's SS *Chicago* had just completed a voyage from New York to Bordeaux, France. As was often the case regarding transatlantic crossings during the war, the voyage was far from what most passengers were accustomed to from their pre-war travels. Richard Harding Davis, who was a special correspondent to *The Indianapolis Star*, was travelling aboard the ship. Davis gave a detailed account of the voyage, although his story was overshadowed by headlines in the paper regarding the land war, and the 'Serbs near disaster'. His account, tinged with bigoted language of the period, reveals the surreal circumstances of wartime travel, racial prejudices of the day, and heartbreaking scenes of soldiers heading for the front being parted from their loved ones:

> While still 600 miles from the French coast the passengers of the *Chicago* of the French line entered what was supposed to be the war zone. In those same waters, just as though the reputation of the Bay of Biscay was not already sufficiently scandalous, two ships of the same line had been torpedoed. So, in preparation for what the captain tactfully called an 'accident', we rehearsed abandoning the ship.
>
> It was like the fire drills in our public schools. It seemed a most sensible precaution, and one that in times of peace, as well as of war, might with advantage be enforced on all passenger ships. The captain of the *Lusitania* was asked to hold such a drill and refused. In his case, as it happened, it would not have helped the passengers, because the ship listed so badly that on one side the boats were held under water, and on the other were stranded high and dry in the air as though they were on the roof of a skyscraper. But had the *Lusitania*

A deck gun on the stern of the SS *Chicago*. (Authors' Collection)

not listed, a rehearsal of taking to the boats would have hurt no one and might have saved many lives.

In his proclamation, Commandant Mace of the *Chicago*, borrowed an idea from the New York fire department. It was the warning Commissioner Adamson prints on theater programs and by which he casts a gloom on patrons of the drama by instructing them to look about them for the nearest fire escape. Each passenger on the *Chicago* was assigned to a lifeboat … Women and children were to assemble on the boat deck by the boat to which they were assigned. After they had been lowered to the water the men, who meanwhile were to be segregated on the deck below them, would descend by rope ladders. Entrance to a boat was by ticket only … If you lost your ticket you lost your life. Each of the more imaginative passengers insured his life by fastening the ticket to his clothes with a safety pin.

Two days from land there was a full-dress rehearsal, and, for the first time, we met those with whom we were expected to put to sea in an open boat. Apparently those in each boat selected by lot. As one young doctor in the ambulance service put it, 'the society in my boat is not at all congenial'. The only other persons originally in my boat were Red Cross nurses of the Post unit and infants. In trampling upon them to safety I foresaw no difficulty. But at the dress rehearsal the purser added six dark and dangerous looking Spaniards. It developed later that by profession they were bull fighters. Any man who is not afraid of a bull is entitled to respect. But being cast adrift with six did not appeal. One could not help wondering what would happen if we ran out of provisions and the bull fighters grew hungry. I tore up my ticket and planned to swim.

Some of the passengers took the rehearsal to heart, and, fully dressed, remained all night on deck. As the promenade deck is directly over the cabins, not only they did not sleep, but neither did anyone else. The next day they began to see periscopes. For this they were not greatly to be blamed. The sea approach to Bordeaux is flagged with black buoys supporting iron masts that support the lights and in the rain and fog they look very much like periscopes. But after the passengers had been thrilled by the sight of twenty of them, they became so bored with false alarms that had a real submarine appeared they would have invited the captain on board and given him a drink.

While we still were anxiously keeping watch, a sail appeared upon the horizon. Even the strongest glasses could make nothing of it. A young, very young Frenchman ran to the bridge and called to the officers, 'Gentlemen, will you please tell me what boat it is that I see?'

Had he asked the same question of an American captain while that officer was on the bridge, the captain would have turned his back. An English captain would have put him in irons. But the French captain called down to him, 'She is pilot boat No. 28. The pilot's name is Jean Baptiste. He has a wife and four children in Bordeaux, and others in Brest and Havre. He is 50 years old, and has a red nose and a wart on his chin. Is there anything else you would like to know?'

At daybreak, as the ship swept up the Gironde to Bordeaux, we had our first view of the enemy. We had passed the vineyards, and these chateaux the name of which every wine card in every part of the world helps to keep famous … on a barge I saw a man in a black overcoat with brass buttons wider apart across the chest than at the belt line, like those of our traffic police in summer time, I thought it was a trick of the mist. Because at present the uniform … is not being worn much in France. Not if a French sharpshooter sees it first. But the man in the overcoat was not carrying a rifle on his shoulder. He was carrying a bag of cement, and from the hull of the barge others appeared each with a bag upon his shoulder. There was no mistaking them. Nor their little round caps, high boots and field uniforms of gray green. It was strange that the first persons we should see … in France, should not be French people, but German soldiers.

… to walk the streets of Bordeaux, saddens as well as delights. There are so many wounded, there are so many women and children all in black. It is a relief when you learn that the wounded are from different parts of France, that they have been sent to Bordeaux to recuperate and are greatly in excess of the proportions of wounded you would find in other cities. But the women and children in black are not convalescents. Their wounds heal slowly or not at all.

At the wharves a white ship with gigantic American flags painted on her sides and with an American flag at the stern was unloading horses. They were for the French artillery and cavalry, but they were so glad to be free of the ship that … they kicked joyously, scattering the sentries, who were jet black Turcos. As one of them would run from a plunging horse, the others laughed at him with that contagious laugh of the darky that is the same all the world over, whether he hails from Mobile or Tangiers, and he would return sheepishly, with eyes rolling, protesting the horse was a 'boche' (German).

Officers, who looked as though in times of peace they might be gentlemen jockeys, were … identifying the brands on the hoof and shoulder that had been made by their agents in America. If the veterinary passed the horse, he was again marked, this time with regimental numbers, on the hoof with a branding iron, and on the flanks with white paint. In ten days he will be given a set of shoes, and in a month he will be under fire.

Col. Rene DeMontjou, who has been a year in America buying remounts, and who returned on the *Chicago*, discovered that one of the horses was … a very bad 'substitute' … His teeth had been filed, but the French officers saw that he was all of 18 years old.

The young American, who … was checking out the horses, refused to be shocked. Out of the corner of his thin lips he whispered confidentially: 'Suppose he is a ringer … Suppose he is 18 years old, what's the use of making a holler? What's it going to matter how old he is, if all they're going to do with him is get him shot?'

That night at the station … many recruits were starting for the front. There seemed to be thousands of them … There was one group that was all comedy, a handsome young man under 30, his mother and a younger girl who might have been his wife or sister. They had brought him food for the journey; chocolate, a long loaf, tins of sardines, a bottle of wine, and the fun was in trying to find any pocket, bag or haversack not already filled. They were all laughing, the little fat mother rather mechanically, when the whistle blew … it was as ominous as though some one had fired a siege gun. The soldiers raced for the cars, and the one in front of me, suddenly grown grave, stooped and kissed the fat little mother. She was still laughing, but at his embrace and the meaning of it, at the thought that the son, who to her was always a baby, might never again embrace her, she tore herself from him sobbing and fled, fled blindly as though to escape from her grief. Other women, their eyes filled with sudden tears, made way, and with their fingers pressed to their lips, turned to watch her.

The young soldier kissed his wife, or sister, or sweetheart, or whatever she was, sketchily on one ear, and shoved her after the fleeing figure.

'Guard mama' he said. It is the tragedy that will never grow less, and never grow old.[106]

The SS *Ancona*. (*Collier's*, 1917/Authors' Collection)

The German soldiers that Davis saw were prisoners of war who were being utilized for labour.

On 4 November, the Society di Navigazione a Vaporetti Italia liner SS *Ancona* was on a voyage from Messina, Italy, to New York with a full compliment of passengers. The ship was about to become the latest victim of the growing Mediterranean U-boat operations. When passing Cape Carbonara, Sardinia, the *Ancona* was shelled and then struck by a torpedo from *U-38*, commanded by Kapitänleutnant Max Valentiner. He was known for shelling ships without warning, causing great controversy.

U-38 was a German U-boat commanded by a German officer, but was flying an Austro-Hungarian flag, since Germany had not yet declared war on Italy. The *Ancona* sank, taking 200 lives with it, including nine of the twelve Americans aboard. Cecile Greil, an American passenger aboard the *Ancona*, later gave a deposition revealing her experiences and the details of the sinking. There initially seems to have been some

Cecile Greil. (United States National Archives and Records Administration/Authors' Collection)

concern about her objectivity due to her partial German ethnicity, although the examiners were satisfied that she was not sympathetic to any of the warring nations when she was asked about this:

Deposition of Cecile Greil, November 18, 1915

Cecile Greil, after having been duly sworn to tell the whole truth and nothing but the truth, doth depose and say:

1st Interrogatory. What is your name and the place and date of your birth?
Greil. To the first interrogatory she saith: My name is Cecile Greil; I was born at New York on the 13th of July, 1873.
2d Interrogatory. What is your present place of residence?
Greil. New York City.
3d Interrogatory. What is your profession?
Greil. I am a doctor of medicine.
4th Interrogatory. Where did you take your degree?
Greil. I took my degree at the Medical College of New York City.
5th Interrogatory. State whether you are married, and if so, state name, nationality, and place of birth of husband.
Greil. My husband's name is Clemens Greil; he is a naturalized American citizen, and was born in Germany, in the Province of Westphalia.
6th Interrogatory. What was your father's name, nationality, and place of birth?
Greil. My father 's name was Ignatius Frank; he was an American citizen, and was born in the State of New York.
7th Interrogatory. What was your mother's name and place of birth?
Greil. My mother's name is Ernestine Frank, and she was born at Strasburg, in the Empire of Germany.
8th Interrogatory. What was the nationality of the parents of your father and mother?
Greil. My father's parents were Austrian and my mother's family German. I have met members of my mother's family from Berlin.
9th Interrogatory. Have you any special sympathy or dislike of any belligerent power?
Greil. No, I have no special liking or aversion to any belligerent power.
10th Interrogatory. What was the date and purpose of your last departure from the United States?
Greil. I left the United States on the 23d of August, 1915, for the purpose of seeing and nursing a sick friend in Italy.
llth Interrogatory. What was the date, where and place from which you sailed on the *Ancona*?

<u>Greil.</u> I sailed on the 5th of November from Naples on the *Ancona* for New York via Messina.

<u>12th Interrogatory.</u> Was there any noteworthy events during your trip on the *Ancona* prior to the attack by submarine which may have had any possible bearing on said attack?

<u>Greil.</u> Shortly after leaving Messina at about 7 o'clock on the 6th of November while at supper a man in uniform came to door of saloon and called to captain to come out without saluting. The captain poured out a tumbler of wine which he drank and then left table hurriedly without apology. My definite impression was that something was wrong, and I did not see the captain again.

<u>13th Interrogatory.</u> State fully all the facts relating to the attack on the *Ancona* that you witnessed.

<u>Greil.</u> I had just finished lunch at about 12 o'clock when I saw a number of sailors rushing on the deck, the six gentlemen, two ship doctors, and four first-class passengers who were at the table jumped up and ran on deck; as they ran out the engine stopped or slowed down and I supposed there was something wrong with the engine. I then went to the dining room window on the left-hand side of the vessel and saw the submarine to the left of *Ancona*, near enough to distinguish about a dozen figures on its deck and six cannons but not sufficiently near to distinguish faces.

A U-boat circling a merchant ship that it has ordered to stop. (Authors' Collection)

The first shot I heard crashed in the fore part of the vessel, while I was looking out of the window, I heard timbers breaking and shrieking. The dining saloon was in the rear of ship and I went forward on deck to see what had happened. Before I could go to the forward part of the ship shots were fired in rapid succession. When I got forward on upper deck I found a number of dead and wounded, there might have been 20 or 25. Steerage and second-class passengers had rushed to upper deck to get in boats and had been injured there. I saw no shots strike vessel but heard them strike and I saw debris. I also saw wounded persons fall from bridge, among which was Signore Spinnachi, a first-class passenger, who is still missing. I believe a number of guns were fired on submarine as I saw people fall on different parts of upper deck.

Then I went down to purser's cabin to get money which I had deposited the day before. I found purser's cabin wrecked and purser lying unconscious on floor before his desk. When I returned to upper deck I found the staircase by which I had descended had been shot away. I then went through second cabin and went up another staircase. I saw dead and wounded in second cabin. I entered my stateroom intending to get my passport. My passport was in a trunk under my bed and while I was stooping to draw out my trunk a shot passed through port hole window shattering glass and I heard missile pass over my head. My chamber maid, panic stricken, was standing before my door and the missile struck the upper part of her head, she fell dead before my door. I then decided to leave ship at once, I put on my life belt, cap, and sweater and went on deck.

Boats were being lowered. The first two were full and would not take me. I then crossed to other side of deck to look for boat and saw one in the water close to ship in which I recognized chief machinist and two ship doctors. I called to them to take me and they called jump. I jumped about 50 feet and landed uninjured in boat. I saw missiles strike people in boats besides the *Ancona* and people fall in water from boats. After boats pulled away from vessel they were not fired on and I believe the killing of persons in boats was unintentional. I had on my wrist watch and noted time when boat in which I was pulled away from vessel, it was 12.30 and bombardment of vessel lasted 20 minutes longer. As bombardment commenced at a few minutes after 12 it must have lasted about 45 minutes.

About 15 minutes after the cessation of bombardment the submarine which was circling around vessel fired a torpedo which struck the *Ancona*. I saw a cometlike form going through the water, saw it strike vessel causing a violent explosion and throwing huge jet of water in air. The *Ancona* listed to one side and sank at 1.32 by my watch. My watch was correct as I compared it with watch of chief engineer and found it correct.

Six other boats of the *Ancona* were in sight all the afternoon. The boat which I was in was picked up by the French naval vessel *Pluton* at about 7 o'clock p.m. and the survivors of *Ancona* were disembarked at Bizerta at about 11 p.m., but being a physician I remained on board all night attending to wounded.

Everything possible for the comfort and care of the survivors was done by the officers of the *Pluton* and the French authorities. Special courtesy was shown to myself as a woman and an American citizen.

14th Interrogatory. Can you testify as to whether any notification was given to *Ancona* before attack was commenced?

Greil. No.

15th Interrogatory. Can you testify as to whether any attempt to escape was made by *Ancona*?

Greil. The vessel commenced to slow down almost simultaneously with the rush of sailors on deck and before I had heard the first shot. The vessel vibrated and the engine must have stopped or greatly reduced its speed, my impression is that the engine was stopped. The first shot I heard struck the fore part of vessel. I can give no other testimony as to whether there was any attempt to escape.

16th Interrogatory. Was firing rapid and continuous while bombardment lasted, have you an approximate idea of number of shots fired?

Greil. Firing was rapid for approximately twenty minutes; then firing was at longer intervals. I can give no information as to number of shots fired.

17th Interrogatory. Were over fifty shots fired?

Greil. Yes, I feel confident that over fifty shots were fired at *Ancona*.

18th Interrogatory. Was loss of life chiefly due to method of attack, to panic of passengers or to any lack of control or efficiency on part of officers or crew of *Ancona*?

Greil. A number of persons were killed or wounded by bombardment, there was considerable loss of life due to panic of passengers, and there was lack of control on the part of officers of ship. Of course, effective control was difficult under the circumstances. I saw one lifeboat capsized because a pulley stuck.

19th Interrogatory. Did you meet or have any knowledge of other Americans on board?

Greil. No, I know there were no Americans in first or second cabins, and there were none among survivors as far as I know. I inquired if there were any.

20th Interrogatory. Were there any citizens or subjects of neutral states whose testimony would in your opinion be of value on the *Ancona*?

Greil. There are none that I know of.

21st Interrogatory. Did you see a flag on submarine and, if so, describe the flag.

Greil. I could see a red and white flag on submarine but can not describe the flag.

22d Interrogatory. Is there anything else relating to the destruction of the *Ancona* you wish to state?

Greil. No, I believe my statement as to what I saw is complete.

> Sworn to and signed before me at Tunis on November 18, 1915.
> (Signed) DEAN MASON,
> American Consul, Algiers.[107]

It appears that Greil, being tactful, held back some information about her experiences, because in a later written account, she graphically described additional details:

> … I went toward the bow of the ship. I descended the staircase … A large part … had been shot away – and the horror of what I saw at the bottom of it made me instantly forget what I was going for. There lay three or four women, four or five children, and several men. Some of them were already dead, all, at least, badly wounded. I made sure two of the children were dead. The purser sprawled limply across his desk, inert, like a sack of meal that has been flung down and stays where it lies. He had been shot in the head. The blood was running bright like red paint, freshly spilt, down his back, and his hair was matted with it. The first series of shots had wrecked this part of the ship, breaking through and carrying away whole sections of the framework. I tried to get back up the stairs … in the slight interval of time … enough additional shells had been discharged to finish the wreck of the staircase. I saw that this was not … 'legitimate warfare', but wholesale and indiscriminate massacre …
>
> … I found a poor old woman at the foot of the stairs, huddled in prayer. Her thin, gray hair straggled loose over her shoulder. I recognized her as a woman I had got acquainted with in my search for a fellow-citizen to join me in the first cabin. She was 65 years old … She had seen two sons off to the war, and was now going to a third who had emigrated to America and lived in Pennsylvania. It was the first time she had ever crossed the ocean. She was sick of the thought of war. In the New World she would find peace and comfort for her old age, with her 'Bambino', as she still called the grownup man who was her son. So when I saw her lying there I was possessed of but one idea – to get her off alive. I told her to come with me, that I would protect her. She acquiesced, but her fright was so great that she hung limp as if she had no spine while I halfdragged her to the first cabin deck …
>
> … A boat was being lowered. It had been swung out on the davits. It already seethed full of people. And more men and women and children were fighting … to get into it …

… At the sight before her the old woman grew frantic with unexpected strength. She suddenly jerked loose … and … ran with all the agility of fear and jumped overboard. Others flung their bodies pellmell on the heads of those already in it … Some, in their frenzy, missed … and fell into the sea. To make the horror complete, the boat now stuck at one end, tilted downward, and spilled all its occupants into the sea, ninety or a hundred at once … Perhaps if only I had some of my jewelry I might be able to bribe my way to safety in some such crisis.

I made my way back to my cabin again. There were people dead and dying on the deck. I saw one man who had started to run up the gangway to the officers' deck come plunging down again. He had been struck in the back of the head. Somehow or other, I just felt that my time had not yet come. This conviction enabled me to keep my wits about me. In my cabin … As I was searching for my valuables my chambermaid appeared in the doorway; half a dozen times I had met her rushing frantically and aimlessly up and down.

'Oh, madame, madame – we shall all be killed, we're all going to get killed!'

'Maria', I advised as quietly and soothingly as I could, still stooping over my trunk; 'don't be so mad, get a lifebelt on, and get up out of here'. Before she could speak again she was a dead woman. A shot carried away the port-hole and sheared off the top of her head. It finished its course by exploding at the other side of the ship. If I had not been stooping over at the time I would not have lived to write this story.[108]

Backlash from the sinking of the *Ancona* targeted Austria–Hungary, since the submarine had been flying that empire's flag. With nine Americans killed, the US State Department wired the Austro-Hungarian Government in Vienna demanding to know why the ship was attacked without warning. Foreign Minister Stephan Burián von Rajecz's response was that the *Ancona* had tried to flee, and that the large number of deaths were due to 'condition of panic incident to Latin blood'. Not satisfied with this, the United States pressed the issue, and Germany, desperately trying to maintain American neutrality, urged von Rajecz to accede to their wishes.

The Austro-Hungarian Government eventually agreed to pay an indemnity, and promised that Kapitänleutnant Valentiner would be disciplined. This was a meaningless statement, since Valentiner was a German officer and not Austrian. The Austro-Hungarian Government also requested that German U-boats refrain from attacking passenger vessels while flying the Austro-Hungarian flag.

While another incident was avoided, President Wilson was troubled, saying 'I think the public are growing uneasy because of our apparent inaction in what seems a very aggravated case'. Secretary of State Lansing wrote that 'American public opinion is become more bitter and … this state of affairs cannot continue much longer without the gravest consequences'. The administration continued to struggle with the fine line between appearing weak and hard-line diplomacy. While the citizenry was growing more uneasy, only a small segment of the population favoured war.[109]

Meanwhile, on 9 November, the Leyland Line's SS *Californian*, requisitioned in the preceding months by the British Admiralty to serve as a troopship, was completing a voyage between Salonica, Greece and Marseilles, France. The ship was torpedoed by *U-35* while off Cape Matapan, but managed to stay afloat long enough for Captain William Masters and nearly everyone aboard to safely abandon ship. One crewmember was killed. The loss of the Leyland liner was given additional coverage in the press, because the ship was infamous for its connection to the *Titanic* disaster in 1912. The article conveying the details of the loss also mentions the increasing intensity of submarine activity in the Mediterranean:

> Three more British vessels and the French steamer *France* have been sunk by German submarines, which some time last week passed through the Straits of Gibraltar and into the Mediterranean Sea. As has been the custom recently, the announcements today did not contain the scene of the sinkings, but it is almost certain that most, if not all of them, occurred in the Mediterranean.
>
> That Great Britain has taken steps to resist this new submarine warfare is indicated in a dispatch from Morocco which reports the destruction of two German submarines by a British cruiser.
>
> A third U-boat is said to have been captured in a disabled condition, according to a dispatch from Athens, which says: 'The newspaper Kairol says it has received assurance from a reliable source that British torpedo boat destroyers captured a German submarine in Greek waters last week, taking the crew prisoners. The submarine, with its engine damaged, was caught between Crete and Cythera and towed into Mudros'.
>
> … The War Office made the following announcement tonight … : 'The outward bound transport *Mercian* was attacked by gunfire from an enemy submarine in the Mediterranean. She reached harbor safely with casualties of twenty-three killed, thirty missing, and fifty wounded, who were landed and are in a hospital'.
>
> The British steamers destroyed were the *Californian* of 6,223 tons, the *Clan McAlister* of 4,835 tons, which was last reported in London on Sept. 13, and the *Moorina* of 3,159 tons.
>
> The *Californian* was a Leyland Line steamer, 447 feet long, 53 feet beam and 30 feet depth, built at Dundee in 1902. Many months ago she was taken over by the British Government.

The *Californian* figured prominently in the story of the *Titanic* disaster, having been near the scene of the wreck, but not having gone to the rescue. Lord Mersey, in presenting the judgment of the British Board of Trade Court of Inquiry into the *Titanic* disaster, mentioned the *Californian* as having seen the *Titanic*'s signals at a distance of eight or ten miles, and declared she could have reached the sinking liner without serious risk and have saved many lives. The *Californian*'s master, in a subsequent statement declared that the signals from the *Titanic* had not been recognized by the officer in charge as distress signals.[110]

All three of the British vessels mentioned in the article as being sunk were attacked by *U-35*.

Mines laid by U-boats continued to be as much of a threat as torpedoes. On 17 November, the HMHS *Anglia* was on a voyage from Calais to Dover. The former London & South Western Railway Co. liner had been converted into a hospital ship after the outbreak of war, and was carrying 390 injured officers and soldiers back home to England. At 12.30 p.m., the *Anglia* was 1 mile east of Folkestone Gate when it struck a mine laid by *UC-5*. The large explosion tore the hospital ship open, and it took on a heavy list that made evacuation difficult. As the ship began settling in the water, the nearby torpedo gunboat HMS *Hazard*, along with the collier *Lusitania*, helped in the rescue efforts. Despite this, 134 people were killed in the sinking.

One of the passengers aboard the *Anglia* was Private James MacKinnon, a soldier in the 9th Gordon Highlanders. MacKinnon had been shot at the Battle of Loos and was being transported home to recover. He was further wounded in the mine explosion, and spent time in the frigid water before being rescued, which wreaked further havoc on his health. While he was convalescing at Kitto Relief

HMHS *Anglia* sinks after striking a mine. *(Illustrated London News*, 1916/Authors' Collection)

Hospital in Surrey, he corresponded with Marion Howard, an American woman who wrote to random Allied soldiers before the United States entered the war, attempting to boost their spirits and morale. MacKinnon wrote the following letter to Howard, describing his experiences on the *Anglia*:

Dear Madam,

Your parcel was safely received on Friday having been forwarded on to me from Mrs. MacKinnon. I must thank you very much for your kindness the vest is fine (some vest) and all the things in the pockets. I may tell you I am in the Gordon Highlanders + got pretty badly at the Battle of Loos. I was shot through the left lung then when I was coming home on the Hospital Ship *Anglia* she struck a mine in the English Channel so I got a bit of a smash three of my ribs were broken beside a dip in the water which I have never got right over. I was up yesterday for the first time for six months. I felt a bit queer but I expect to get alright soon. It will be a while yet before I am able to leave hospital. I am not in a hurry to get back to the front again I have done my bit.

　　Thanking you again for your kind present it always cheers us up to be remembered.

Yours Gratefully,
No 4544
Pvt. J. MacKinnon
9th Gordon Hnds.[111]

For the month of November 1915, sixty-four ships were sunk by U-boats, totalling 156,992 tons. An additional four ships were damaged. The vast majority of sinkings during the month took place in the Mediterranean. One of the most successful U-boat commanders in November was the reviled Kapitänleutnant Max Valentiner of the *U-38* with fourteen kills.[112]

In December 1915, Britain made several significant decisions regarding the war. The first was John French being replaced by General Douglas Haig as commander-in-chief of the British Expeditionary Force, following French's forced resignation. This change in command was partly due to scrutiny that French received over his handling of the reserves at the Battle of Loos, followed by British Secretary of State for War Kitchener's call for an investigation into the bungled offensive. It was also clear that the British Government was growing tired of the deadlock on the Western Front, and lack of progress in the war in general.

The second major turn of events for Britain was the decision to evacuate Gallipoli. In November, Secretary of State for War Kitchener had personally inspected the front lines at Cape Helles and Anzac Cove, and found that the Ottoman forces there were still firmly entrenched. In order to prevent more unnecessary losses, Kitchener recommended the evacuation of Allied forces. The order to begin this process was given on 7 December, and the removal of troops was completed on 9 January 1916. The evacuation was carried out swiftly and without a hitch, and was widely considered the most successful aspect of the entire Gallipoli Campaign.[113] Many ships were called upon to transport the evacuating soldiers back home.

At sea on 30 December, the Peninsular & Oriental Steam Navigation Company liner SS *Persia* was in the Mediterranean, on a voyage from London to Marseilles, and then on to Bombay, India, carrying passengers and general cargo. When the ship was approximately 71 miles south of Cape Martello, Corsica, it was torpedoed by Kapitänleutnant Valentiner and the *U-38*. No warning was given. The vessel immediately took a sharp list to port, sinking in less than five minutes. Three hundred and thirty-four people were killed in the attack including the captain, and the survivors struggling in the sea would not be rescued until late the following evening.

The survivors were eventually taken to Alexandria, Egypt. While there, several of the American passengers contacted the American Consulate. Consul Wilbur Keblinger received a direct phone call from Charles H. Grant, an American citizen who had been aboard the *Persia*. Keblinger later documented the phone call, in order to pass along the relevant details of the incident to Secretary of State Lansing. After speaking with Grant, the consul was transported out to the *Hannibal* to meet with the American survivors and to take affidavits from several others. In a letter to Lansing, Consul Keblinger wrote the following:

> ... I have the honor to report as follows in regard to the sinking of the P&O liner *Persia*. At 5.30 o'clock on January 1st, 1916, Mr. Charles H. Grant telephoned to the Consulate. He stated that he was an American citizen, a survivor of the *Persia*, and was then on board of the HMS *Hannibal*, having arrived at Alexandria about an hour before. The *Hannibal* is permanently anchored at Alexandria in the outer harbor for defense purposes. This was the first advice or information of any kind I had of the

Charles Grant with his wife. (United States National Archives and Records Administration/ Authors' Collection)

disaster. I immediately set off for the *Hannibal* in a launch from the USS *Des Moines* … On arriving … I found the British Vice Consul of Alexandria in conference with the survivors who had been brought to Alexandria by the British armed trawler *Mallow*. I was informed that one hundred and fifty-one persons had been brought in, which made up the contents of four of the *Persia's* boats that had been picked up.

All told the same story: An explosion while at luncheon; a hurried endeavor to put on life belts and report to the lifeboat stations that had been previously assigned to the passengers; a rapid list of the ship to port and subsequent sinking in about five minutes; no vessel or craft of any description seen by anyone before or after the explosion. None of the officers of the *Persia* were interviewed. Those who had not gone ashore had retired.

Mr. Grant then told me that Consul McNeely, of Aden, had been on board. Mr. Grant stated that he and Consul McNeely were at luncheon when the explosion occurred. Both hurried to their cabins for life belts. Consul McNeely's cabin was on the port side of the deck above the dining salon, at the entrance to which they parted. Mr. Grant did not see Mr. McNeely again. One of the survivors told Mr. Grant that he had seen the Consul swimming, but Mr. Grant could not recall who his informant was.

Commander Blakely having kindly extended the hospitality of the *Des Moines* to Mr. Grant, I conducted him aboard, where he remained until his departure for Cairo, on January 6, 1916. My telegram to the Department … contained all of the details it was possible to gather at that time …

On the morning of January 2, 1916, telegrams from the Department and Consul General Skinner at London requesting information in regard to the disaster were received. Prompt replies were transmitted.[114]

With this letter, Keblinger also enclosed the survivor affidavits that he had taken. The first one was given by British passenger John W.E. Douglas-Scott-Montagu, Second Baron Montagu of Beaulieu, who had been travelling with his mistress Eleanor Thornton, who did not survive. Thornton was the model for the famous 'Spirit of Ecstasy' figure that adorns the hood of all Rolls-Royce automobiles.[115] In his affidavit, the baron was particularly vivid in his description of the sinking:

The voyage of the *Persia* had been a very successful one up to the time of the accident, and everyone was very comfortable and happy …

About 1.10 p.m. on Thursday, December 30, just as we were sitting down to tiffin there was a terrific explosion just abaft the main saloon; the smell of explosives at once told us what had happened, and I realized the ship had been torpedoed; the passengers at once went to fetch their life belts, and go to their stations without any sign of panic or fuss. When I got to the station allotted for

No. 6 boat, on the port side, I saw boats being lowered on that side, but owing to the list of the ship, for she had begun to heel over very considerably, I at once realized that it was impossible to get into any boats on the port side as the ship was lying over on them, and still retained too much way ... With great difficulty I then climbed up the starboard side, trying to pull with me a lady passenger who happened to be near me; the ship was then practically on her beam ends, and this was about three minutes after she had been struck.

The ship now began to sink rapidly by the stern and I was swept off my feet by the rush of water along the promenade deck, going overboard on the starboard side. The ship then sank and I was sucked down a long way, striking my head and body against several pieces of wreckage. It seemed a very long time before I came to the surface again, though I was conscious of rising very quickly, owing to the extreme buoyancy of my Grieve Waistcoat, which certainly at this moment saved my life. Just before the ship foundered there was the usual and inevitable uprush of steam and smoke from the engine room and stokehold.

To show the rapidity with which the vessel went down I do not think more than four minutes could have elapsed from the time of her being struck to the time she disappeared. I am convinced that the commander, the officers and the crew did all that was possible to be done under the terrible circumstances.

When I had recovered my senses sufficiently to look around I saw the sea covered with struggling human beings but very little wreckage, and as far as I could see there seemed to be only three boats afloat in the water. There was nothing to indicate the presence of a submarine nor did I see any sign of one

Water pours onto the promenade deck of a torpedoed merchant vessel as a lifeboat rows away in the background. *(Collier's, 1917/Authors' Collection)*

while on the *Persia* subsequent to the torpedoing and previous to the sinking of the vessel. I then swam towards a signal locker I saw floating in the distance and to which was clinging the ship's doctor, who appeared in a stunned condition, as his head appeared to be injured in some way; on reaching it I found it would not support more than one person so I left the doctor on it and swam towards a boat floating upside down about fifty yards away, her bottom being covered with native seamen, far too many for the boat to support. I managed, however, to climb up and get astride of the keel band on the extreme end aft and from this position I saw a boat a short distance off, picking up people, and shouted to them to come and help us, but they rowed away, but as there were cries of help from all sides I make no complaint about them not coming to our assistance.

About one hour after the disaster there were on our upturned boat four Europeans left, besides about twenty native crew, the remainder having dropped off as they became too weak to hold on. The boat at this time was righted by a big wave, and we managed after great difficulty to get into her. I then realized that not only had she a large hole in her bottom, but that her bows were split open as well, probably smashed in the lowering. She was also in a state of extreme instability for the air tanks which showed she was one of the life boats were some of them smashed and others perforated and the smallest weight on the starboard side of her tended to capsize her again, which before we were picked up happened several times. About sunset we were most of us sitting up to our knees in water, and there remained when the sun went down of the original number in the boat, thirteen native seamen and firemen, two Goanese stewards, one Italian 2d class passenger, one Scotchman, also a 2d class passenger, one English Steward, named, Martin, and myself, i.e., nineteen only.

Had it not been for Mr. Alexander Clark, the Scotch passenger, and Martin, the steward, who more than once helped me to climb back into the boat, after she capsized so often, I should have had no chance. At sunset I managed to stand up in the boat and have a good look around and saw only one boat to the eastward about one mile away and one or two survivors still clinging to wreckage to the southward of us. Though there was not much wind there was a considerable swell on and nearly all the time the sea was breaking over us. Before the night was half gone several more natives died in the boat from exhaustion, and as the bodies were washed about in the boat we had to throw them overboard. About 8 p.m. a steamer passed with her saloon lights all showing, about one mile to the southward; we tried to attract her attention by shouting, and the other ship's boat, to the eastward, burnt two red flares, but she took no notice, possibly thinking it was a ruse of a hostile submarine. When the moon rose about 2 a.m. I saw one or two more natives had died, including the doctor's Goanese servant, who was sitting on the gunwale of the boat next to me.

At dawn next morning, Friday, the 31st, there were only eleven, all told, left in the boat. The Italian passenger then helped to pick out more bodies at his end of boat. About three hours after sunrise we saw a two-funneled and two-masted steamer to the southward, and our hopes again raised. We managed to hoist a piece of torn flag on the one oar left in the boat, as a signal, and saw the ship's boat to the eastward, which seemed to be floating well, do the same. The ship passed westward bound about three miles away but either did not see us or suspected a ruse. We saw nothing for the rest of this day. One of the native crew about noon managed to get a tin of biscuits from the locker in the boat under the thwarts, and we managed to eat a little of this. We then had been nearly thirty hours without food or water – that is, since breakfast the day before. We saw nothing of any ship for the rest of the day. Personally I felt the heat of the sun, for except a small khaki scarf which I had in my pocket I should have had no protection, as none of us had any coverings for our heads.

At sunset on Friday we had practically given up all hope of being saved, and I found it a great struggle to keep awake and hold on, as the tendency to drowsiness was almost irresistible. We capsized again about 7 p.m. owing to the instability of the boat, and in this capsize we lost the tin of biscuits and the red flares we hoped to use that night. About 8 p.m. we saw the masthead lights of a steamer, the ship that eventually picked us up, far away to the eastward, and presently I could discern her side lights, which showed me she was coming pretty nearly straight for us. When she got close to us we started shouting in unison, and when she was about half a mile away she ported her helm, stopped her engines and appeared to be listening. We knew now like other ships she expected a ruse and dare not approach until she made further investigations.

After some time she came up closer to us and we heard the first human voice shout out to us; she also blew her whistle; this was about 8.30 p.m. When she came closer we tried to explain that we were helpless and had no means of getting alongside. Eventually the captain (Captain Allen) of this ship, which proved to be the Alfred Hold steamer *Ning Chow*, bound from China to London, very cleverly maneuvered his ship alongside our wreckage and threw two lines to us, thus hauling us alongside. Bowlings were passed round us, and we were hauled on board.

The captain and his officers did all they could for us and I consider it a very plucky act on their part, for they knew they were in the danger zone and ran the risk of being torpedoed themselves. I should mention it was Mr. Allen Maclean, the 3rd officer of this ship, who was the officer of the watch at the time and who first appears to have heard our cries, and our being saved is mainly due to him. Once on board we began slowly to recover from the exposure and injuries which we had been subjected to, and we eventually arrived at Malta at dawn on Monday, January 3. We were sent on to St. Paul's

Day for examination and brought on to Valetta in a steam trawler, where we were met by Captain Andrews, the P&O Co's agent, who showed us every consideration and kindness.

I consider that our being saved at all is an absolute miracle, as we were fast approaching a stage of complete exhaustion, and the chances of the *Ning Chow* passing over the spot so close were infinitesimal, and the same may be said of any other vessel. In conclusion I would again state that everything possible was done by the commander, officers, and crew of the ship during this terrible crisis ... [116]

The second affidavit enclosed in Consul Keblinger's correspondence was from Charles L. Martin, who had been a steward on the *Persia*:

... I was serving at table during luncheon in the dining saloon when at about 1.10 p.m. there was a violent explosion which shook the boat from stem to stern and I realized at once that the ship had been torpedoed. Immediately after the explosion I rushed to get in my life belt and then to my station, which was No. 5 boat on the starboard side. The chief engineer was also at boat station No. 5 but it was impossible to lower the boat owing to the listing of the ship to the port side. As the ship listed more to port I held on to a boat davit on the starboard side and after a very few moments I was sucked into the water.

When I came to the surface I was dazed and floated around for a while, but finally managed to get to an upturned boat which was occupied by about 20 or 25 persons, mostly lascars (Indian sailors). We were taken up by the *Ning Chow* about 8.30 p.m. of Friday, December 31, 1915, and brought to Malta. My experience after getting to the lifeboat was similar to that of Lord Montagu, which is described fully in his affidavit.

During the time I was on deck immediately after the explosion and while in the water and later in the lifeboat I saw no sign of a submarine. The *Persia* has a 4.7-gun mounted aft, but so far as I know it was not used as there was no sound of a report previous to the torpedoing and afterwards there was not sufficient time to use the gun, the ship going down within five minutes after being hit, nor could it have been used owing to the great list of the vessel. [117]

The *Persia*'s surviving officers gave affidavits in front of Commissioner for Oaths John A. Donnison on 20 January 1916, including Geoffrey S. Wood, the ship's second officer. The affidavit was then sent from Foreign Secretary Sir Edward Grey's office to American Ambassador Walter H. Page, to help the American Government obtain all of the facts pertaining to the tragedy:

... On the 30th December last I went on watch at noon and found the captain in personal charge of the navigation. There was a seaman on the lookout in the crow's nest, another on the forecastle, and an A.B. and a lascar on duty at their stations, also looking out on the lower bridge, one on either side in addition to the A.B. with me at the wheel. There were also three of the gun's crew on the poop aft … two A.B.'s aft and one marine gunner.

At 1.10 p.m. Captain Hall was on the lower bridge, and I then saw the wake of a torpedo approaching (four points on the port bow) the ship, a second before she was struck. I had not sighted a submarine myself nor had anything been reported to me nor was any warning given. As soon as the ship was struck I attempted to give the five-blast signal on the whistle which had been agreed upon to order all to their boat stations, but could not work the whistle, as the steam had gone. I then ran down to the lower bridge and asked Captain Hall if I could help with the secret dispatches, and he answered, 'No; I am attending to them myself; get out the port boats as quickly as possible and look after your passengers'.

I left the bridge and went aft, as directed, taking my life belt on the way. The Captain had been personally in charge of the navigation all the day directing and verifying the courses and had not, I gather, been down to the saloon to lunch. The weather was fine, but the sea was choppy and it would have been difficult to see the periscope of a submarine, although all were on the alert for such a contingency. The torpedo struck the ship on the port side just abaft the forward funnel and probably fractured the bulkhead separating No. 3 hold (one of the largest holds) from the stoke hold.

After the first explosion caused by the torpedo there almost immediately followed another explosion, and as I saw no second torpedo I concluded one of the boilers had blown up, partly because of the quantity of steam which was rising … and also from the fracture there was in the deck through which coal and ashes had been blown.

There were 20 boats on the *Persia*, 10 on either side of the ship, which would accommodate nearly 1,000 people and sufficient, even with the starboard boats out of service, to accommodate all the persons on board.

One of the boats on the port side No. 6 was blown away by the first explosion, but the crew were going to their appointed stations, as prearranged, and when I reached the poop Nos. 14 and 16 boats were already being properly lowered. I then looked to the two inside boats and found their gripes had been already released so as to enable them to float when the ship went down, so I went over to the starboard side to see if anything could be done to release any of the boats there, and found the third engineer trying to clear away No. 15 starboard boat, which had a number of people in it, but the boat, owing to the ship's list, was caught on the eyebrows of the ports, so I called out to the people in the boat to jump into the water, which was the only thing for them to do. I saw No. 14 port boat clear, but No. 16 was sunk by the ship's davits cutting it as the vessel went over. The *Persia* went down under my feet, and when I got into the water, I saw two empty boats floating with no one in them ... evidently ... the gripes of which had been released to admit of their floating when the ship sank. I swam to one of them and just as I got hold of it it turned turtle, and I then went to the other, got into it, and picked up altogether 43 people from the water, subsequently taking five more out of the Chief Officer's boat, which was overloaded.

Everybody behaved exceedingly well, both passengers and crew, and if there had been only a few minutes' more time we should have, I believe, saved pretty well everybody on board.[118]

The United States had a special interest in the *Persia* sinking, since two American citizens had been killed, including Consul Robert McNeely. After being pressed by the United States, both the German and Austro-Hungarian governments restated their willingness to be bound by international law and to adhere to prize rules, but failed to accept responsibility, even though the '*Arabic* pledge' had been violated. The French ambassador observed that Germany and Austria–Hungary seemed 'to believe [the *Persia*] sank of its own accord, committing a kind of suicide'. Kapitänleutnant Valentiner, despite having a track record of violating international law, was unapologetic. His logbook entry regarding the attack revealed that he believed the vessel to be a troopship when he attacked.

Even though the sinking of the *Persia* distressed the US Government, it failed to produce as virulent a reaction as some of the previous sinkings had. This may have been because President Wilson was distracted by allegations and suggestions of German espionage within the United States. This included claims that entrenched spies were spreading propaganda within the country, inciting work stoppages at munitions plants, and meddling with America's chemical and metal industries. President Wilson had also learned of 'conspiratorial dealings between German agents and Mexican revolutionaries'.[119]

Even though the United States did not continue to press the issue regarding the *Persia*, the Allies were not as willing to drop it. They were furious at Kapitänleutnant Valentiner. The fact that just three of the nineteen children aboard *Persia* were saved was used to characterise the U-boat commander as a 'butcher'. As a result of what they saw as repeated and blatant violations of international law and decency, after the war, Valentiner was added to the Allied list of war criminals. He was eventually tried by a German court, but was acquitted of all charges.[120]

In the month of December, forty-seven ships were captured or sunk by U-boats, totalling 118,617 tons. Another four ships were damaged. As had been the trend, the majority of sinkings took place in the Mediterranean. As 1915 drew to a close, it was clear that the war was far from over. For the year, 755 ships were sunk or damaged by U-boats.[121] This was at the cost of twenty U-boats lost in action, as the Royal Navy began to search for more effective ways of defending against submarines.[122] Germany manufactured a total of fifty-one new U-boats in 1915 now that the importance of submarines had been established.[123] Although there was a relative respite from Germany's submarine warfare in the last three months of 1915 compared to the earlier months, it was clear from how things were proceeding on land and at sea, that it was going to be a long conflict, much longer than anyone could have fathomed at the onset of the war.

3

The Waning and Resurgent U-boat Offensive, 1916

January–February 1916

On 9 January, the Gallipoli evacuation was officially completed. On the Eastern Front, Serbian forces had retreated to the island of Corfu in the Adriatic Sea, which was occupied by the Allies on 11 January. Austro-Hungarian forces launched an offensive on the Kingdom of Montenegro, which capitulated, and was soon occupied.

Near the end of the month, on 24 January, Vice Admiral Reinhard Scheer was appointed commander-in-chief of Germany's High Seas Fleet. He took over from Admiral Hugo von Pohl, who was suffering from liver cancer and was too ill to continue his command. Scheer wanted to employ Germany's navy much more aggressively than the tentative von Pohl had, believing that a combination of increased U-boat operations, Zeppelins for reconnaissance, and High Seas Fleet activity harassing the Royal Navy would force the British to take action, thus abandoning their blockade of Germany. Scheer also began to lobby the Kaiser for a switch to unrestricted submarine warfare, which was rejected.[1]

Thus far in the war, Great Britain had been fighting with an entirely volunteer-based army. However, owing to a high number of casualties, plus the need to reinforce the French Army on the Western Front, Britain was desperate for a fresh injection of fighting men. As such, the Military Service Act was introduced on 27 January, calling for the conscription of men aged 18–41, unless they met one of the disqualifiers, such as being married, widowed with children, serving in the Royal Navy, working as a minister, or involvement with a number of other listed occupations. In May, conscription was extended to married men as well. The bill was immediately controversial. British citizens protested that it was a blatant violation of their rights, while some military commanders argued that men forced to serve against their will would be far less effective soldiers than volunteers. However, the British armed forces had little alternative but to enact a draft given the rate of attrition their forces were receiving.

In early January, Red Cross nurse Sister May Chalmers of New Zealand had just completed a voyage to the island of Lemnos aboard the former Union-Castle liner *Braemar Castle*, which was serving as a hospital ship. Once they had arrived at their destination, Chalmers was transferred aboard the brand new hospital ship HMHS *Britannic*. The *Britannic*, sister ship to the giant White Star liners *Olympic* and *Titanic*, had originally been intended for the passenger service. However, the British Admiralty formally requisitioned it on 13 November 1915, because another large-capacity vessel was needed to carry the mounting number of casualties back from the front, even with the *Mauretania* and *Aquitania* also serving in that capacity.

The largest British liner ever built to that point was not yet complete, as it had been under construction in the Harland & Wolff shipyards when war broke out, causing progress on the vessel to grind to a halt. The shipyard had more pressing orders to tend to involving contracts with the Admiralty. Since the ship had its engines and machinery in place, the completion and conversion into a hospital ship was going to take approximately four weeks, or so Harland & Wolff estimated. The *Britannic*'s hull, which had never been completely painted in its intended White Star Line livery, was rusty and dirty from sitting out in the open.

The completion of the vessel quickly became the focus of the shipyard. The corrosion was cleaned off and the hull was painted white, with a green stripe around it, broken only by three large red crosses on each side. Green lights were installed to illuminate the band at night. Two additional red crosses, smaller than the ones on the hull, were attached to the promenade deck on each side, and would be illuminated red at night so that U-boats or enemy vessels could readily identify it as a hospital ship. The funnels and masts were painted yellow. The interiors of the ship were hurriedly finished, so not all of its intended luxurious fittings were installed. For instance, the public rooms and promenade decks were converted into operating theatres and patient rooms.

Only five of the eight planned sets of giant gantry davits, unique to *Britannic* amongst the trio of *Olympic*-class liners, were installed, with smaller Welin-type davits utilised instead to finish the job more quickly. The ship's completed lifeboat arrangements consisted of forty-one wooden lifeboats, fourteen Englehardt collapsible boats, and a series of floats placed around the boat deck, each capable of holding twenty-five persons. The need for all of the lifeboats is evident when one considers that once completed, the *Britannic* would have the capacity to carry 4,473 persons, including 3,309 casualties, 489 medical staff and 675 crewmembers. When all was said and done, Harland & Wolff had completed work on the *Britannic* three days earlier than their original four-week estimate.

Captain Charles A. Bartlett was given command of the vessel on 13 December 1915, and the HMHS *Britannic* embarked on its maiden voyage on 23 December. Between arriving in the port of Mudros at Lemnos on New Year's Eve 1915 and departing on 3 January 1916, *Britannic* had taken on around 3,300 wounded soldiers from smaller hospital ships and shore-based hospitals.[2] It was before departing for Southampton that Sister Chalmers came aboard. Writing from the newly opened Oakland Hospital near Walton-on-Thames, England, she gave her impression of the new hospital ship:

> It is truly a lovely place; if the boys are not happy they should be. They love this place [Walton] and always leave it with regret, and certainly life is made very nice for them, and they have beautiful food …
>
> We had a most interesting trip over. We went to Madras [Mudros] by the *Braemar Castle* and joined the *Britannic* there. The latter is a most wonderful ship. It must be like a floating palace in peace times, when properly fitted up. The cabins are like small rooms with two nice bedsteads in, and every luxury, but if she was wrecked I should think she would be nothing but a death trap. We met an enemy submarine and saw the periscope, but they evidently decided to leave us alone, though they have threatened to sink the *Britannic* because of her size.[3]

The *Braemar Castle*, the vessel Sister Chalmers was transported to Lemnos on, would strike a mine on 23 November 1916, killing four people. Damaged, the hospital ship was beached to prevent it from sinking. It was later re-floated, and

HMHS *Britannic*. (Authors' Collection)

reports in the British press sparked outrage when it was claimed that the ship was intentionally torpedoed, which was not true.

By the end of January 1916, just twenty-nine ships had been sunk or captured by U-boats, an eleven-month low due to the new restrictions the German Government had imposed on its submarine commanders. An additional eight ships were damaged.[4]

On land, February 1916 brought with it the beginning of a major German offensive. Even with significant progress on the Eastern Front, the Western Front remained a bloody stalemate. German Chief of the General Staff Erich von Falkenhayn believed that a massive attack on Verdun, a narrow stretch of land with historic sentiment to the French, would allow Germany to inflict massive casualties on the French Army.

The Battle of Verdun was launched on 21 February. Much to Germany's surprise, French resistance was significantly greater than anticipated. The battle was not a quick one, and in fact, would become the longest-running engagement of the war and one of the bloodiest, dragging on until December 1916. The battle saw the first widespread use of flamethrowers by the German Army, who utilised them to clear out French trenches.[5]

One estimate places the number of French soldiers killed and wounded around 377,321 and the number of German casualties around 337,000.[6] Nothing was accomplished by either side, except for turning the Verdun into a complete wasteland, and instilling a greater sense of resolve in both armies. The battle also inspired the British Army to launch the Battle of the Somme in July 1916, with the intention of relieving the German pressure on the French.

At sea, things remained relatively calm in February, with the U-boat campaign struggling to retain traction with the new restrictions placed on it by the German leadership. After completing two voyages carrying wounded troops in January, and after arriving safely in port at Southampton on 9 February, the *Britannic* was laid up at the pier until the middle of March. With the number of wounded troops moving through the Mediterranean slackening, there was no immediate need for the massive hospital ship's service.

Britannic would complete one more voyage beginning on 20 March, and by 11 April, the medical personnel had been transferred to other ships. The vessel would sit idle in an anchorage off Cowes for weeks, before eventually being moved to Southampton and back to Cowes, and then on to Belfast in May. Likewise, the lessening demand for hospital ships led to the *Mauretania* and *Aquitania* being laid up, waiting to be released back to the Cunard Line, or for the British Admiralty to find another use for them.[7]

While the actual war at sea had been quiet compared to 1915, the war of words over submarine warfare was still raging. On 11 February, the *North German Gazette* printed the text of an official German memorandum, which alleged that 'armed

P. & O. S.S. "Maloja" leaving Sydney.
(12,500 TONS, 16,000 HORSE-POWER.)

SS *Maloja*. (Authors' Collection)

British merchantmen have an official order to treacherously attack Germany submarines wherever they meet them; that means, to mercilessly wage war against them … enemy merchantmen carrying guns are not entitled to be regarded as peaceful merchantmen. The German naval forces … will receive an order to treat such vessels as belligerents'. The British paper *The Times*, in its response to the German memorandum, stated that while Germany protested merchant ships having any means of protecting themselves, 'these German instruments of war, contrary to every usage of law of nations … had for months shelled innocent merchant ships without notice or pity'.[8] This sabre rattling did little more than reinforce the positions of both nations as they currently existed.

Despite things being relatively calm at sea, there were still losses being inflicted. On 27 February, the Peninsular & Oriental Steam Navigation Company liner SS *Maloja* was on a voyage from London to Bombay, India, carrying general cargo, and was in the Dover Straits. The vessel was armed with deck guns, but only for defensive purposes. When the ship was 2½ miles south-west of Dover Pier, it struck a mine that had been laid by *UC-6*.

The ship took on an immediate starboard list, and the engines were run full astern to arrest the forward momentum. The captain gave the order to abandon ship, passengers began being loaded into the boats, and an SOS was sent out. However, due to extensive and quick flooding below deck, the engines could not be stopped. The ship, stuck in reverse, began to move astern at 8–9 knots, and the list eventually reached 75 degrees, rendering the lifeboats useless. The ship sank in about twenty minutes, taking 122 people with it. The Dover tugs *Lady Brassey* and *Lady Crundall* were the first rescue ships on the scene.

One of the passengers aboard the ship was Ralph Foster, from Kansas. He gave the following account of the sinking:

> I was promenading the deck well forward about 10.20 o'clock Sunday morning, when I heard a slight report. I thought it was a gun firing a blank shot until I saw debris falling. Even then the concussion had been so slight that I concluded an accident must have happened to some other ship nearby.
>
> I rushed back immediately toward the stern of the *Maloja*, but before I had taken a dozen steps the ship began to list, and I started toward the lifeboat that had been allotted to my cabin. It was so full of people, most of them Lascars, that I saw it was likely to be swamped. So I went below for a lifebelt. I put on my overcoat and the lifebelt and also took my passport.
>
> By this time – hardly three minutes after the explosion – the passageways below were awash. I returned to the lifeboat and tried to shove it clear. Two of the white crew of the steamer were standing by to lower the boat, but only a steward and myself were making an effort to push it off the ship's side. We could not get the boat clear of the railing on account of the heavy list of the *Maloja*.
>
> Everybody then piled out of the lifeboat. Most of them slid across the deck and into the water on the other side. The deck was inclined to such a degree that we could not stand. I grabbed an oar and slid down the deck into the water. The waves were so strong that I found I could not swim in them and was washed back against the side of the ship.
>
> Finally I managed to reach a capsized boat a few feet away and crawled onto it. From there I could see in the water near me several bodies of persons who were bleeding about the head. One Lascar was being ground between a lifeboat and the ship's side. A big swell had washed me off my insecure perch. I knew what would happen to me if I stayed on the side of the ship I was on, so I managed to get to the other side and clung to the railing until only the davits were projecting out of the water.

Ralph Foster. (United States National Archives and Records Administration/Authors' Collection)

I then pushed away from the steamer and swam a few yards to a boat which had five or six Lascars in it. When I looked around the last of the davits of the *Maloja* had disappeared. We had no oars and the waves kept breaking over the boat. When it began to sink we swam to another capsized boat and clung there until a boat from a destroyer took us off.

When we came alongside the destroyer I noticed that the swells seemed to bob us up and down ten or twelve feet. I looked at the clock on board the destroyer and saw it was 11.30 o'clock.

The only terror or excitement shown aboard the *Maloja* while they were trying to lower the boats was on the part of Lascars and some children who had become separated from their mothers. One child who was on deck was blown to pieces, an officer told me.

One thing which made an impression on my mind while I was clinging to a capsized boat was a 'Teddy Bear' which was floating about. The coxswain of the boat which picked us up rescued the toy, saying 'I must have that for my kid'. [9]

Meanwhile, the Empress Transportation Company of Midland, Limited liner SS *Empress of Fort William* was relatively near the *Maloja* when it struck the mine, and saw that it was in distress. The ship was on a voyage from Tyne and Wear, England to Dunkirk with a cargo of coal. Attempting to go to the *Maloja*'s rescue, the *Empress of Fort William* struck another mine laid by *UC-6*. The ship began to settle in the water and sank in forty minutes, but everyone was able to be safely evacuated. Captain W.D. Shepherd, the master of the ship, gave the following account of the sinking:

It was at South Shields that we loaded what was the last cargo for *Empress of Fort William*, and sailed on the afternoon of Feb. 25, 1916. We left the Tyne during a southeast gale, with bad weather all the way. We made the Downs about 9 a.m. on Feb. 27, 1916, where some 200 ships were anchored (what a target for a British submarine were the position reversed). Dodging, without anchoring, until we got our clearance, we were off in the van of the ships going south. But there were faster ships than us, and among them was the large P&O liner, *Maloja*, pronounced 'Maloya', which passed us, just after we had passed the South Goodwin lightship. We admired the ship as she passed, but felt no envy of the officers in charge.

I asked my first officer, Mr. Bray, how he would like to be on her, and bound to India. His reply was, he would rather be where he was. I think, at that time we both felt we would rather be in the thick of things. She passed us close to, going double our speed, and soon drew well ahead until she was perhaps about three miles from us. As I did not continue to watch her, I did not see what happened, but soon I noticed that she seemed to be in trouble,

owing to the way she was heading, as she was well off the course she should
be steering.

I called Mr. Bray's attention to her, but bless him, he is not the man to see
trouble if he can help it, and he gave as his opinion that she was all right. It
was soon only too evident, however, that *Maloja* was sinking; and acting on my
order, Mr. Bray sprang aft, in a way that would give many a younger man a lead,
to tell Mr. Udall, the chief engineer, to give *Fort William* all he knew.

As he did so, I turned to the man at the wheel – 'a bad young boy', the
parsons might call him, but a good British sailor – and said, 'You don't mind
taking a chance, Orr?' Promptly his reply came back: 'She's steady on the P&O
boat, Sir. If we pick up one we'll do something'.

To the second engineer, Mr. Jenkins, who happened to be on deck, I shouted,
'Get all your men up, boat station', and although he sometimes calls them
'ginks', when he is annoyed, they certainly jumped for him that day. Then the
mate, when he came forward was told the same, and Mr. Halifax, although
off watch and asleep, after keeping eight hours the previous night, must have
dreamed the order, as it was only seconds until he was at his boat half dressed.
Not one man aboard asked 'why?' All jumped – and jumped quickly.

Then we got it! I was looking aft at the time, to see that all were at the boats,
when suddenly there was a most violent explosion; as I write I can hear it, with
a rending, tearing sound, followed by the hatch coverings off No. 7 hatch being
thrown, in a dense cloud of coal well over the masthead.

Then, stillness; and when the dust had cleared, I was astonished to see my men
working away clearing the boats as if nothing had happened, or so it looked
from where I was standing.

The rate at which the stern sank made it only too evident that *Empress of Fort
William* had got her deathblow, and I think our first feeling was one of sadness
that such a harmless but useful ship should be sunk in such a way, without
warning of any sort.

Next came the feeling of self-preservation, and we were not sorry to see one
of our torpedo boat destroyers making for us at something under 40 knots an
hour. After the first excitement, during which there were some rather amusing
incidents, no member of the crew showed any undue haste to leave the ship,
and all obeyed orders implicitly, with the exception of the first engineer, who
had to be told more than once to come out of the engine room.

However, most of us got away in our starboard lifeboat, while the remainder
were taken off by a boat from the destroyer. On board the destroyer we were
well cared for, warmed up in defiance of the King's regulations, and given
opportunity to dry our rags. We were soon landed at Dover, and a cheerier
or better behaved shipwrecked crew never landed anywhere, and not one of
them ever gave any trouble, not even old John Murray, the donkeyman. Now

they have gone their different ways, all have sailed again, and some have been shipwrecked again but none is downhearted.[10]

Losses to U-boats remained relatively low as February came to an end. Fifty-one ships were sunk or captured by U-boats during the month, totalling 109,483 tons. Additionally, five ships were damaged. The majority of U-boat related incidents took place in the North Sea and the Mediterranean. Following the outrage over the sinking of the *Persia* back in December, Kapitänleutnant Max Valentiner and the crew of the *U-38* were back in action, sending eight ships to the bottom during the month.[11]

March–April 1916

On 1 March, the British Admiralty released the *Mauretania* back to the Cunard Line. They were so confident that the liner would no longer be needed that they paid Cunard around £60,000 to refit the ship for passenger service. The *Aquitania* was similarly released from service on 10 March, and Cunard received £90,000 to refit the liner. Harland & Wolff was contracted to do the job at their Southampton facilities.[12]

On land, Germany declared war on Portugal on 9 March, which then entered the war on the side of the Allies, sending troops to the Western Front. In the Isonzo region, the Italian Army launched another offensive due to pressure from France, ending in yet another Austro-Hungarian victory.

At sea on 5 March, the French Line's SS *Rochambeau* was completing a voyage from New York to Bordeaux. With the French Line's SS *France* having been requisitioned as a hospital ship, the *Rochambeau* had assumed a key role in the line's transatlantic service. One of the passengers aboard during this particular crossing was William Y. Stevenson, an American travelling to Europe to serve as an ambulance driver on the Western Front. He wrote a detailed account describing the voyage in his diary, and the conditions and perceived irritating traits of some of those on board:

> *March* 5, 1916. On board French Line SS *Rochambeau*. Carrying three bundles, a bag, a bunch of rugs, and A.B.'s luncheon taken at the Holland House, I boarded the *Rochambeau* with some effort yesterday just as the whistle sounded, while I kissed various people good-bye. For a week I have been doing nothing else. This teary sob-stuff gets on one's nerves, particularly when one is scared to death anyhow … I met a number of nice people – a Frenchman, a priest, and a silk buyer; the latter wept most of the way out of New York Harbor, recalling 'the wife' at home, and giving out a lot of maudlin stuff. I inquired how long

SS *France* in dry dock.
(Authors' Collection)

he expected to remain abroad and he said, 'Ten days'! Since then I have disliked him intensely. He kicks about the food too! I have not, as yet, met the other Ambulance men. There are about six, but they keep to themselves.

Thank Heaven, the bartender knows how to mix a dry martini. I've got a fine stateroom. The food is poor and scanty, but I expected that. The ship is shorthanded and very deep in the water – even carrying freight piled high on the after deck. Only one good-looker aboard and the Captain has already nailed her – curses! I've met a nice Englishman who is going back to his mother to die. He has lung trouble and prefers mother to his wife and family and Reading, Pennsylvania, as a place to finish off. His mother lives at Grenoble, in the Alps. One Frenchman ordered onion soup this morning for breakfast. Everybody left the table. I got a bully lot of farewell letters, gifts, and telegrams … It's nice to find one has so many friends, but why do they all give one shaving kits?

March 8. Nothing doing yesterday. Met most of the Ambulance men – nice fellows – R.T. Roche, the aforesaid Captain of Princeton Crew in 1911, Austin B. Mason, of Boston and of hurdles fame at Harvard, 1908, and William Dwight Crane, of New York and Harvard … Cargo mostly ether and oil; also munitions. There is a heavy roll – racks on table; many dishes broken; tramp steamer caused excitement, likewise hot air about possible German raider. The boys are trying to get up a concert with a 'busted' piano and no one to sing. Just met an American Ambulance man. Was in the Pont-a-Mousson Section and got Croix de Guerre. He used to do newspaper work. He is now with a 'bunch' from Pittsburgh backed by a rich woman who wishes to drive her own car at the front. She's got a swell chance …

March 9. Still no news as to how the fight went at Verdun. Expected surely some information … but if the Captain has received any, he is keeping it dark. More German-raider scares, when passing several freighters. I have met a nice old Italian returning from America where he was buying horses for his government. One of his sons already has been killed in the Battle of Trentino. Another son also is at the front ... The sea has calmed down again ...

Funny how people act on these raider rumors – women get excited, men pretend to be very calm and joke nervously about being marooned on a desert island a la Robinson Crusoe. The only one I'd like to be marooned with seems to have made a date with some one else. The old Italian has great respect for the Germans, says they are the best business men – not bright, but very efficient. He thinks that neither side has as yet been even moderately weakened and looks for the war to last at least two years more. Almost every one else thinks a year should end it.

March 10. At last news from Verdun. French still holding. Also news of British and Russian gains. Several ships (Allies) sunk; and one German boat reported escaped from internment at Bordeaux. This aroused some uneasiness, as that is our destination. I have given all my books to the sick Englishman, as he says he can't get anything but French literature at Grenoble. Met a returning French officer – Comte de Portanier de la Rochette. He has been ten months in the trenches without so much as a scratch. Has been on an eight days' leave in the United States! Met a former Philadelphian, by name Josiah Williams, a doctor, who has been in the war since the start ... Was in the Battle of the Champagne tending first poste de secours. Very interesting. He thinks the French have them licked now ...

March 11. Quite rough. De la Rochette says that in the Champagne battle, when they captured German trenches, he, himself, found seven dead Germans chained to their machine guns. Head winds and seas will make us a day late at least. The silk merchant is seasick, so we've had a respite on 'the wife back in the States' stuff. I've met a young woman of uncertain vintage who is on her way to Monte Carlo. Spends her time knocking American efforts to help France; says the Ambulance men only go over for notoriety's sake. I let her rave on, and when she was all through, bid her good-night, remarking that I was doing that myself. I hope it taught her a lesson.

March 12. The Catholic priest and some of his friends announce that they will not attend the concert because little 'blondy' collected the money. The ladies are rabid. One went to the priest and told him she understood that his job included being charitable to sinners as well as others. Priest very sheepish and presented a French novel for the auction! The little blonde, of course, is a professional; but she has done more than any one else in the way of getting up things for the wounded. The sea is so calm that several people I had not seen before turned up on deck. Imagine being in an 8x10 hole for eight days. Passed several tramps. Boats have been swung out and most people expect to sleep for the next two nights more or less fully dressed. We are now in the War Zone. We hold the auction and concert to-night.

March 14. Anchored at the harbor mouth and came up late. After much red tape got off boat ... There is quite a movement of troops, and trains are crowded. The reserves are all in the old red pants and caps, the new war pale blue being only used at the front. The new metal helmet is almost a replica of the old pikemen's casques, only enameled a pale dull blue-gray, and the comb is applied instead of being all of one piece. It is very light and of tough steel ...

At Poitiers we saw the first train-load of German prisoners; most of them were thoroughly satisfied to be out of the war. I must admit, though, that the tales of their being starved were not borne out by these men. They looked quite healthy. We also saw a train of Red Cross cars carrying wounded to the south for recuperation. Only the slightly injured, however ... [13]

Around this time, following pressure and heavy lobbying from commander-in-chief of the High Seas Fleet Reinhard Scheer, Kaiser Wilhelm II agreed to a new submarine policy. Scheer had convinced him that only by lifting some of the restrictions on U-boat commanders could victory at sea be achieved over Britain. The Kaiser agreed to a 1 April start date for a new campaign, but changed his mind just days after making the decision. Chancellor Theobald von Bethmann-Hollweg had persuaded him that such a move would only instigate the United States.

As a concession to the militarists who were pushing for the implementation of unrestricted submarine warfare, the Kaiser did agree to a more vigorous U-boat campaign to begin on 15 March, provided that prize rules would be strictly adhered to. Disgusted with this latest turn of events, Secretary of State of the Imperial Naval Office von Tirpitz finally resigned, citing 'procrastination in the conduct of war'. His resignation temporarily weakened the lobby for unrestricted submarine warfare. Making matters worse, some U-boat commanders, having already received the Kaiser's initial orders, had left their bases and were beyond wireless range by the time he reneged and issued his new orders. This would cause further problems. [14]

As the war proceeded, the Royal Navy was developing new ways to counteract the threat posed by U-boats. One which held promise was the development of depth charges, underwater explosive devices designed to be dropped from a ship or airplanes to cripple or sink submarines. Experimental designs had been around for several years, but the first effective depth charge was not ready until January 1916. Manufacturing of the devices proved slow, so anti-submarine vessels initially carried just two depth charges each. [15]

The Q-ship HMS *Farnborough* was the first vessel to successfully use the weapon when it sank *U-68* off the Irish coast on 22 March. Germany became aware of the existence of depth charges following several unsuccessful attacks on U-boats using them the following month. Only two more U-boats would be

Dropping a depth charge while racing at full speed over the
spot where an enemy submarine has just submerged
© I.F.S. from N. Moser, N.Y.

A destroyer escort drops depth charges over the location where a U-boat just submerged.
(Authors' Collection)

sunk by depth charges in 1916, both in December.[16] The weapon held promise,
but was not yet widely available enough to make a significant impact.

Near the end of March, the HMT *Olympic* was transferred by the British
Admiralty from the Mediterranean service onto the Liverpool–Halifax route.
The reason for this move was that the Canadian Government was looking to
charter vessels to transport large numbers of Canadian troops to England. Rather
than being laid up, this kept the troopship in service. The *Olympic* departed
Liverpool on its first voyage in this capacity on 22 March. The ship continued
to make crossings for the rest of spring and summer, without encountering any
enemy action.[17]

On 24 March, the Chemins de Fer de l'État Français passenger ferry SS *Sussex*
was crossing the English Channel from Folkestone, England to Dieppe, France.
The ship was sighted by *UB-29*, under the command of Oberleutnant Herbert
Pustkuchen. On his current patrol, Pustkuchen had sunk a French ship at anchor
on 19 March, a neutral Norwegian and Danish steamer on 20 March, and a
British vessel on 24 March.[18] Sighting the *Sussex*, Pustkuchen believed that it
was a minesweeper, based on the ship's 'long black' silhouette. He fired a single
torpedo from 1,400 yards, which struck the *Sussex*'s bow. The resulting explosion
completely blew off the bow of the ship from just in front of the bridge forward,
killing fifty people, including women and children.

Hot debris rained down on the deck of the ship, and the *Sussex* listed
precariously. Miraculously, it managed to stay afloat, although some of the

SS *Sussex*. (Authors' Collection)

passengers and crewmembers abandoned ship and were lowered away in lifeboats while awaiting rescue. The evacuation was far from smooth, with the crew being described as 'unorganised' and 'unprepared'. One of the lifeboats was overloaded and capsized once afloat, drowning a number of those aboard. Part of the issue may have been the fact that Captain Henri Mouffet remained on the bridge for some time following the explosion. However, considering that the ship disintegrated from just in front of the bridge forward, it is likely that he and any survivors there had been incapacitated. Once it was seen that the remnant of the ship was going to float, Captain Mouffet called the lifeboats back to the ship, although some had returned on their own before this order was given.

After rescue ships arrived, the survivors were taken to Dover, while the *Sussex* was towed stern-first to Boulogne. Initially, Germany denied responsibility for the torpedoing, insisting that only a warship had been attacked in the region, and that the *Sussex* must have struck a mine. However, while the vessel was being salvaged, fragments of a German torpedo were found in the wreckage, removing all doubt.

One of the surviving American passengers was Edward H. Huxley, president of the United States Rubber Export Company. He made the following comments regarding the sinking:

If Germany admits torpedoing a steamer near that position on March 24 in the Channel it will be their undoing, because the *Sussex* was the only vessel there at

… I went to the United States Embassy in London and made my deposition, and I was told that … photographs of the *Sussex* and of the pieces of the torpedo with the statements of survivors were being sent to the State Department on the *St Paul*.[19]

Another American passenger aboard the *Sussex* was the journalist Edward Marshall. He graphically described the attack in his affidavit:

There is no doubt in my mind that the vessel was torpedoed. I myself did not see the approach of the weapon, but I heard one of the higher officers … say to a British naval passenger that he had seen it and the quartermaster, who was on the bridge with the captain, stated to a friend of mine … that he, the captain, and others on the bridge saw the wake of the approaching torpedo and steered the ship so that it might if possible escape.

There seems to be absolutely no support for the floating mine theory … Not long before the shock … we had passed floating wreckage, indicating the destruction of a vessel. From the deck … this flotsam seemed to be bailed tobacco, but that is a mere guess. Concerning the identity of the shattered ship which bore it I have been unable to learn anything.

I was sitting in the smoking room when the shock came. I was very definitely jarred and was aware instantly that we had been blown up, but was not seriously shaken. At a table just aft of where I sat … a heavy man was thrown high into the air, coming down head first upon the chair on which he had been sitting with force sufficient to break the chair.

Of course, I hurried to the outer deck. The sun was shining brightly, the sea was very far from rough … but a strange, uncanny sound was in the air vibrant, chilling. It was a moan from the ship's company. I heard no screams.

There was no mad panic. Women became hysterical and some men lost their heads, but … There was amazingly little excitement, but there was something quite dreadful, which was the lack of training on the part of the crew. Captain Mouffet was on the bridge.

The vessel was probably struck just aft of the bow … between a third and a quarter of the ship was cut off as with a

Edward Marshall. (United States National Archives and Records Administration/ Authors' Collection)

mighty knife. I reached the outer deck in time to see this severed portion of the vessel before it slowly, unsensationally sank.

Still there were no screams but the curious moans as of many people in slow pain grew louder. Women kept their heads amazingly. Mrs. Dorothy W. Phillips Hilton, daughter-in-law of the late Judge Hilton, of New York, came up to me. 'I can't find my daughter', she exclaimed. 'I had seen her walking with a beautiful young girl about 22'. I went with her about the deck to look for her, but we could not find her anywhere.

The crowd about the boats had become dense immediately after the stunned pause which followed the explosion. From the very first I had not the slightest thought of trying to get into a small boat and so … I was only an interested and presently a horrified spectator. The captain was on the bridge. Probably the concussion somewhat stunned him for a few moments, for the ship literally had been sheared away just forward of the bridge, so near to it in fact that the foremast had gone down. He was not panic stricken but like a man whose brain is dulled.

Subordinate officers were very competent but immediately were confronted by an utterly unseamanlike crew … Some of them began to work at the lines about the davits from which the boats swung, but they worked incompetently. Passengers helped them incompetently. Still there was no panic.

The bow of the *Sussex* was blown off by the torpedo. (*Illustrated London News*, 1916/Authors' Collection)

… one of the boats touched water. Then there was a rush for it … Presently it was overloaded and without much difficulty was cast off and floated free of the vessel … It then seemed certain that the vessel … would sink and I called to some one in the boat to get to a distance thinking that otherwise the suction of the drowning vessel might take her down with her. But no one heard me.

The crowd within the boat was not behaving well … Presently she capsized. I have no idea how many of her company were drowned. For a time they floated, struggling very briefly, for I am told the water was intensely cold. Then they began to perish one by one, a few being picked up by other boats which had been lowered and drawn near. In the meantime gratings had been thrown overboard in large numbers. I saw only one person borne up sufficiently by one. On one of these gratings a strange thing occurred. A young woman deliberately disrobed and then plunged into the sea.

… At the other boats there was a succession of heart-breaking scenes. Some women dropped their children into waiting arms and then jumped after them. Some men endeavored to slide down the ropes – a ticklish business for the boat was rolling and as often as not they presently hung between the small boats and the ship. This meant they must be crushed.

Two of the boats got clear away but came back to the *Sussex* when their inmates saw that she still floated and that the small boats probably would not float long …

Meanwhile the wireless had been re-rigged, some of its stays having been carried away by the explosion. It crackled out its SOS. The sky grew overcast. A sail appeared and rockets were sent up. The sail made the slightest sign that those who governed it had seen us. Later I learned that it was that of a wind jammer which had been helpless as the breeze blew to come to our assistance but had picked up one of the boats …

… Disagreeable affairs developed. Some of the crew appeared with champagne bottles in their pockets and staggering. This did not become as serious as might have been the case, for the ship's officers took the liquor from them and cast it into the sea.

I went among the wounded. Their injuries were freakish. Both of one man's legs were twisted until his feet pointed backward. Another's face had been blown in by the explosion and presented an extraordinary spectacle. He was unconscious.

In the meantime now and then we went to the ship's rail, but could not see that she was settling. The sea was rising.

I went below, having done all that I could and having fallen once or twice upon the slippery deck. There, in which I think must have been the steerage of the ship, we huddled, shivering, some [sic] women sobbing, one or two definitely crazed, shrieking constantly, a few children crying, but now weakly, and moans coming from the slightly injured.

Presently we saw a light. Then, after hours of what amounted to dull misery, a trawler drew alongside. The transfer of the wounded was attempted, but was quite impossible, for the vessel bobbed about amazingly. Presently passengers were pulled aboard the little rescue ship … It was obviously impossible for me to get aboard the trawler as it had been for me to attempt to get into a small boat, although some new-made friends came to me, asking me to make the effort. Presently, having taken all that she could and nearly all the women and children, she drew off and the dull waiting recommenced.

It was ended by the appearance of a British destroyer. It pulled up alongside and made fast, although the rising sea now and then crashed it against the wrecked side viciously. I was among the last to be passed from one ship to the other.

The voyage into Dover was a quick one. At Dover the wireless already had assembled an ambulance train of motor cars. Our landing was made by crossing a British hospital ship at whose side within the harbor the destroyer moored, and on this hospital ship the living wounded were disposed in part, a few being taken to a hospital ashore. The ambulance train conveyed the balance of us to hotels.

It would be difficult to describe the indignation which was felt by the American survivors. Down among the mail bags on the lower deck we held a little indignation meeting while we waited for the rescue ship …

During the course of this extraordinary gathering I endeavored to take evidence as to whether we had been torpedoed or had struck a mine … One of the seamen who was in the boat with Alfred Legresly, of the island of Jersey, which, after drifting for some hour, returned to the *Sussex*, told him that he could positively swear that he actually saw the torpedo as it came … A woman passenger, whose name I did not get because she fainted had made a similar statement to me before we left the *Sussex*.

Further evidence that it was a torpedo and not a mine came to me after we had boarded the destroyer, where an officer informed me that a bit of the torpedo had been picked up on the *Sussex* not far from the grim place in which eight or nine sailors asleep in the forecastle had been blown to bits with the compartment in which they rested.

It is impossible to speak with too much enthusiasm of the kindness of the officers and men of the destroyer. Their tenderness in handling the wounded, their gentle care for the few women who were taken aboard the vessel, the reverence with which they treated the two who died as we sped in toward Dover, their skill and willingness to risk their own lives and limbs during the transfer of the passengers from the disabled vessel to the little iron ship alongside, all were notable.[20]

Surprisingly, the *Sussex* was later repaired, and used by the French Navy. Amongst the dead was the noted Spanish composer and pianist Enrique Granados Campiña. He reportedly drowned after leaping out of a lifeboat in a failed attempt to save his wife Amparo, who he saw struggling in the water. Several Americans were injured in the attack. While no Americans died, outrage in the United States was surprisingly greater than when the *Lusitania* was sunk. When Germany initially denied having sunk the *Sussex*, claiming that it hit a mine, it made matters worse.

Many newspapers were calling for the United States to break off relations with Germany. Even the *New York Evening Post*, which tended to push near-pacifist viewpoints, said 'We have had something too much of all of this, ever since the day of the monstrous crime of May 7, 1915; the time has come for making an end of it'. President Wilson was not yet ready to cut off relations with Germany. However, he was prepared to deliver a cautious ultimatum.[21]

On 17 April, Wilson authorised Secretary of State Lansing to deliver his official note to Germany on the matter. It stated that 'The commanders of the Imperial Government's undersea vessels have carried on practices of such ruthless destruction which have made it more and more evident as the months have gone by that the Imperial Government has found it impractical to put any such restraints upon them as it had hoped and promised to put'.

The massive damage done to the *Sussex*'s first-class dining saloon. (*Illustrated London News*, 1916/Authors' Collection)

The note issued a solemn warning, saying 'Unless the Imperial Government should not immediately declare and effect an abandonment of its previous methods of submarine warfare against passenger and freight carrying vessels, the Government of the United States can have no choice but to sever diplomatic relations with the Central Empires altogether'. There followed a series of contentious and ill-tempered diplomatic exchanges between Washington DC and Berlin.

However, Germany ultimately yielded, as Kaiser Wilhelm II and many in his government still feared US intervention in the war, including Chancellor von Bethmann-Hollweg. Ultimately, their viewpoint won out, although some still wanted the implementation of unrestricted submarine warfare. On 4 May, Germany issued the '*Sussex* pledge'. In it, the German Government renewed its vow that passenger ships would not be targeted by U-boats. Unlike the '*Arabic* pledge', Germany expanded this policy to state that merchant ships would also not be sunk unless the presence of weapons could be established, and not before the provision of safety for passengers and crew could be provided. President Wilson and the US Government were largely satisfied by this response, and yet another major crisis was defused.[22]

Overall, March 1916 saw an increase in the number of ships sunk by U-boats. Seventy-four ships were sunk or captured during the month, equalling 169,271 tons of shipping. An additional seven ships were damaged.[23] Of note, a potentially tragic incident was averted on the morning of 23 March, when Kapitänleutnant Paul Wagenführ and the crew of *U-44* had the *Mauretania* in their sights with four torpedoes loaded, and let it pass unscathed.[24]

In April 1916, the long-running First Battle of Kut ended after the British–Indian garrison in Kut, Mesopotamia, was starved out, facing a humiliating surrender to Ottoman forces.

In April, U-boat commanders were operating under the Kaiser's 15 March orders to implement a more intensive U-boat campaign. The '*Sussex* pledge' was still a month away and had not yet impacted the submarine war. Because of this, April would see a tremendous upswing in the number of attacks on merchant shipping.

At sea, the American Line's SS *Philadelphia* was beginning a crossing from Liverpool to New York. One of the passengers aboard the ship was Sherwood Eddy, a missionary returning from Europe after attending five YMCA conventions and several evangelistic meetings. The voyage would not be a smooth one:

> At Aden we found a battle in progress outside the city. As we came through the Suez Canal it was lined with British troops, where they are concentrating nearly half a million men to meet the proposed attack from the German and Turkish forces. At Port Said we took on a big gun for defense, astern. The

gunner was one of forty-three survivors from the torpedoed *Hawk* [*Hawke*]. The man opposite me at the table had, during the year, been in two ships that were torpedoed and in one wreck. As the submarines had just sunk our sister ship, the *Persia*, in seven minutes without warning, by the captain's order we had to have life preservers ready night and day. We left the usual course, skirting the coast of Africa and zigzagged every day to escape the submarines. By night we steamed full speed ahead in the absolute darkness with no light showing, running the risk of collision, in order to escape the submarines …

I sailed from England on the *Philadelphia*, as a neutral American vessel, in order to save my family from anxiety. The first night we ran into a sailing vessel, and sank her, losing half our boats, our mast and one propeller. Strangely enough this collision occurred at the point where I was shipwrecked at Holyhead twenty years ago when the Cunard *Cephalonia* went down. We then put back to Liverpool and I started again on the White Star *Adriatic*, skirting the coast of Ireland. We had a convoy, but received a wireless communication that a submarine was in our neighborhood. The surface of the water was covered with oil which they had thrown out to dim the periscope of the submarine. Next morning we learned that they had caught the submarine instead of her catching us. After ten days of storm and head winds, we finally landed safe and well in New York.[25]

Elsewhere, Sergeant Wilfred C.C. Satchell, an Anzac troop who had fought in Gallipoli, was stationed on the Western Front. Satchell would eventually receive an officer's commission. He would later be awarded the Military Cross by King George V himself for his actions at the Battle of Amiens in 1918. Having experienced the horrors of combat, Satchell's primary concern was not his own safety, but that of his brother Raymond, who was also serving his country. He did not believe that his brother was cut out for front-line duty, and was concerned about what the strain of having two sons serving on the front would do to his mother. As a result, he pressed Raymond to seek out a transfer to the HMAHS *Karoola*, and was thrilled when he heard that he was attempting to do so. He wrote to his mother regarding this on 6 April:

I was so glad to hear that Ray is making an attempt to get on the *Karoola*, a signaller here used to work on her and a lovely boat it is too. It will be much less worry for you too dear if he can get home occasionally, and just the thing for Ray – He is not as strong as I and would find the work (i.e. on the front) at times a great tasc [sic] on him, I'm not boasting mum, I'm just telling my earnest opinion … If Ray gets on the *Karoola* ask him that Fred McDonald 'Lizzie' they call him he says would like a letter from some of the sailor men. His address is the same as mine, of course the number is different but that doesn't matter leave it out, but address it signallers.[26]

Satchell's brother never ended up serving on the *Karoola*, and instead was transferred to the Australian Field Ambulance Corp on the Western Front. Satchell believed that his brother would be safer serving aboard a hospital ship. However, considering that many hospital ships were involved in accidents, hit mines, or were even torpedoed during the war, they were far from a safe post. As an example, the *Karoola* itself had been fired on earlier in the war when entering Port Phillip Bay, Victoria, Australia, before sunrise. The *Karoola* was not showing the regulation signal, and troops at Fort Nepean fired a shot across the bow. The crew quickly corrected their omission and a tragedy was averted.[27]

While diplomatic wrangling over the *Sussex* attack was still taking place in April, U-boat commanders continued to wage an intensified campaign against merchant shipping. In the month, ninety-eight ships were sunk by U-boats, totalling 209,612 tons. An additional twelve ships were damaged.[28] This was the largest number of ships sunk since August 1915, a fact which concerned the Allies.

May–August 1916

With the '*Sussex* pledge' in effect in early May 1916, submarine commanders were forced once again to adapt to new restrictions and rules of engagement. However, this did not necessarily make the transatlantic crossing safer for ships. Sixty-six vessels were sent to the bottom during the month, equalling 123,736 tons. Two additional ships were damaged. This was a drop in the numbers compared to May, but proved that the pledge had not completely neutered the U-boat campaign. It had just made it much more difficult to execute. A large number of attacks took place in the Mediterranean, reflective of the shifting of many submarines to that region over the previous months.[29]

The end of May was marked by the Battle of Jutland, a large-scale confrontation between the Royal Navy and Germany's High Seas Fleet. Lasting from 31 May to 1 June, it was the largest naval battle in the conflict so far, and would prove to be the only full-scale surface engagement between the opposing fleets during the entire war.

The clash, which took place off the coast of Denmark, was initiated by Germany, following commander-in-chief of Germany's High Seas Fleet Reinhard Scheer's plan. Scheer knew that the Royal Navy could not be confronted directly, but that its blockade of Germany, which was having a significant impact on soldier and citizen alike, needed to be broken, or the war would be lost.

Scheer's plan was to deploy Admiral Franz von Hipper's battlecruiser group to lure out the Royal Navy battlecruiser squadron based in Rosyth that was commanded by Admiral David Beatty, and lead them right into the path of the High Seas Fleet where they would be destroyed. U-boats had been positioned to ambush the British ships along the way, but somehow their enemy managed to sail past them undetected.

On 31 May, Admiral Beatty's squadron encountered von Hipper's battlecruiser group, and in the ensuing surface battle, lost two of his battlecruisers with great loss of life. As the Royal Navy ships fled north, the pursuing German vessels were dumbfounded to discover that they were being lured towards the Royal Navy's Grand Fleet, under the command of Admiral of the Fleet John Jellicoe. The Grand Fleet was thought to have been too far north to intervene. Scheer ordered the German vessels to retreat, and only a brilliant series of manoeuvres prevented them from being decimated by the British ambush.

As night fell, Admiral of the Fleet Jellicoe ordered the British fleet turned away from the fleeing Germans. This seemingly inexplicable order was due to Jellicoe's fear that Scheer was leading him into a U-boat trap, and the mistaken belief that Germany had developed torpedoes which did not leave a telltale trail in the water. This allowed the German ships to escape.

Kaiser Wilhelm II and Germany were quick to declare Jutland a victory, since they had sunk more capital ships than the British did. Addressing the High Seas Fleet after it returned to Wilhelmshaven, the Kaiser said 'What happened? The English were beaten. You have started a new chapter in world history'. Overall, Germany lost eleven ships and over 2,500 men, while Britain lost fourteen ships and over 6,000 lives. Meanwhile, Admiral of the Fleet Jellicoe claimed that Britain had won, since more of the Royal Navy ships remained seaworthy after the battle.

The lasting impact of the battle was that although Germany had sunk more British ships, the Royal Navy retained its dominance of the North Sea. Britain soon regained, and in fact, surpassed, the naval strength that it had prior to the battle, while Germany's fleet needed more time to recover. With another head-on confrontation out of the question, the High Seas Fleet would not directly confront the Royal Navy again during the war. If Germany was to break the blockade, it would need to find another way of doing so. The internal pressure to implement wholly unrestricted submarine warfare began to be waged anew … [30]

One of the unexpected results of the German operations surrounding the Battle of Jutland would cost Britain dearly. On 29 May, U-75 was lying in wait around the exit routes from Scapa Flow. Knowing that they could not cover all of the possible areas where the Grand Fleet could slip out of its anchorage, Kapitänleutnant Curt Beitzen laid mines in an area where he thought they might pass by. This would allow the submarine to move on and patrol elsewhere.

Meanwhile, with things going badly on the Eastern Front, the Allies feared that the Russian Empire was on the brink of collapse. This would allow Germany to fight a one-front war and focus solely on the Western Front. As a last-ditch

The view from a U-boat on patrol. (Authors' Collection)

effort, Britain decided to send Secretary of State for War Kitchener to Russia on a diplomatic mission to try salvaging the situation. On 5 June, he set sail aboard the armoured cruiser HMS *Hampshire*, which had fought at the Battle of Jutland. The cruiser and its destroyer escort encountered a serious gale, and conditions were adverse enough that the smaller destroyers were ordered back to port to avoid being damaged. With the seas so rough, it was believed that U-boats would be no threat to the *Hampshire*.

As the ship sailed along, it steamed directly into the minefield laid by *U-75*, and was torn open by a tremendous explosion, sinking in minutes. Due to the gale conditions and the quickness with which the ship sank, 643 of those aboard perished, including Kitchener and his staff.[31] There were around twelve survivors.[32] Perhaps the last person to see Kitchener alive was Seaman Charles Rogerson:

> I saw Captain (Herbert) Savill help the crew clear away the galley. The captain was calling to Lord Kitchener to go into the boat, but owing to the noise and wind and sea Lord Kitchener apparently failed to hear him.

When the explosion occurred, Lord Kitchener walked calmly from the captain's cabin and climbed the ladder to the quarterdeck. I saw him walking quite coolly and collectedly, and talking to two officers … He quietly awaited the preparations to abandon ship …

Owing to the rough weather, no boats could be lowered … Some men got into the boats, thinking that if the ship went down the boats would float, but the ship sunk by the head, turning a somersault forward, and engulfing the boats and those in them.

When I sprang on to a raft, Lord Kitchener was still on the starboard side of the quarterdeck … So little time elapsed between my leaving the ship and her sinking that I feel certain that Lord Kitchener went down with her while standing on the deck.[33]

Author Edwyn Gray described the sinking and consequences in the following manner:

Despite an intensive search no trace was ever found of Kitchener or any member of his staff. Britain's greatest army leader, a legend in his own lifetime, had fallen victim to the U-boats, his mission unaccomplished. Nothing could now save Russia from revolution and surrender.

U-75, without being present or firing a single shot, had made her momentous contribution to the pages of world history.[34]

In June 1916, Russia launched a massive offensive along the Eastern Front. This operation became known as the Brusilov Offensive. The major aim was to draw German troops away from the Western Front and to take pressure off the Italian forces struggling against the Austro-Hungarian Army in the Isonzo. Russian troops initially experienced tremendous successes, but the offensive was doomed once German forces reinforced their allies.

The battle would end up being one of the bloodiest in history, and although the Russian Army failed to meet its objectives, Germany was forced to halt its offensive in the Verdun and send troops to the Eastern Front. Additionally, the Austro-Hungarian Army was so weakened that it was unable to play a significant offensive role in the war again. Despite achieving a tactical victory, the massive losses further weakened Tsar Nicholas II's ability to maintain support and control amongst the Russian citizenry, as public opinion continued to turn sharply against the war.[35]

At sea, seventy ships were sunk by U-boats during June 1916, totalling 113,247 tons. Three additional ships were damaged. The vast majority of the attacks on shipping took place in the Mediterranean, with most of the rest taking place in the North Sea.[36] Meanwhile, the HMHS *Britannic* continued to sit idle in Belfast,

Tsar Nicholas II. (*Collier's*, 1917/Authors'
Collection)

and on 6 June, the ship was released back
to the White Star Line by the British
Admiralty, who paid the latter £76,000
for its refit into a passenger liner. The
vessel was moved to Harland & Wolff's
Belfast shipyard, where work on this task
began slowly.[37]

Meanwhile, with the Royal Navy
blockade of Germany cutting off critical
supplies, a team of German designers
and scientists came up with a novel idea:
They designed a 213ft long merchant
submarine that would be capable of
carrying relatively large amounts of
freight and cargo, serving as a blockade-
runner of sorts. The first of these was the *Deutschland*, which had been launched
near the end of March. The unarmed *Deutschland* left on its first voyage from
Kiel, Germany on 23 June 1916, carrying a cargo of dyes, medical drugs, precious
stones and mail. The vessel snuck through the English Channel undetected, and
was somewhat of a sensation in the press when it arrived safely in Baltimore,
Maryland in early July. The submarine returned to Germany laden with zinc,
silver, copper and nickel which were desperately needed for the war effort.

Britain and France soon protested the use of submarines as merchant vessels,
citing that there was no way to inspect their cargo. The neutral United States
rejected this argument, saying that submarines, provided that they were not
armed, would be regarded as any other merchant vessels would be. Rear Admiral
Degouy of the French Navy took to the American press to protest the use of
submarines as cargo vessels, saying that there could be torpedo tubes, mines and
weapons hidden in the hull and skin of the vessel, and that the submarines could
even be capable of ramming other ships and sinking them. His complaints were
brushed off, and the *Deutschland* continued its mission. Unfortunately, submarines
serving as cargo vessels proved to have too small a cargo capacity to counteract
the Royal Navy's blockade of Germany, but they certainly proved to be a strong
propaganda coup.[38]

July 1916 brought with it the Battle of the Somme, which for many was
the battle that best symbolises the horrors of trench warfare during the First

The crew of the merchant submarine *Deutschland* received a hero's welcome upon reaching Bremen. (*Collier's*, 1917/Authors' Collection)

World War. The battle, which began on 1 July, was a massive British and French offensive near the River Somme in France. The French Army had been taking severe losses in the Battle of Verdun, which was still ongoing. The Allies decided that an offensive to the north would draw German forces away from the Verdun battlefield, relieving the pressure on French troops there.

The battle would drag on until November 1916, and would become an increasingly brutal battle of attrition, marked by mud, nightmarish artillery bombardments, barbed wire, and bloody, murderous hand-to-hand struggles over tiny patches of territory and trenches. The forces taking the trenches were frequently so thinned during their assaults that the enemy troops they displaced were often able to regroup and retake the same territory not long afterward. Coming over the top of the trenches, opposing forces were mowed down by machine gun fire like blades of grass before a scythe.

Over the course of the battle, the Allied forces, who were considered victorious, had managed to advance a mere 7 miles deep into enemy territory along the 30-mile-long battlefront. All sides involved suffered horrifying losses. Germany may have had up to 600,000 soldiers killed and wounded defending the ground they held, French casualties numbered 194,451 or higher, and British Commonwealth forces suffered around 419,654 casualties. French losses at the Somme were overshadowed by their losses during the Battle of Verdun. However, the cost of the Allied victory greatly damaged British morale. People began to refer to those killed as the 'lost generation', and to many, the Battle of the Somme would be considered the greatest tragedy Britain had ever suffered in its military history. It ranks amongst the bloodiest battles in human history.[39]

At sea, the war was in some ways mirroring the brutalities on land. On 28 March 1915, the Great Eastern Railway passenger ferry, SS *Brussels*, had been ordered to stop by *U-33*. However, rather than comply and lose his unarmed vessel, Captain Charles Fryatt had turned his ship toward the submarine in an attempt to ram it. This was as per the instructions issued to merchant captains by the British Admiralty. *U-33* was forced to crash dive to avoid being sunk, and the *Brussels* narrowly escaped. For his actions, Fryatt, who had previous run-ins with submarines, was awarded a gold watch that was engraved in recognition of his actions. Germany was outraged that a non-combatant had acted aggressively toward a U-boat.

The incident came back to haunt Fryatt, as the *Brussels* and its crew would be stopped and captured on 23 June 1916. Fryatt was arrested and interned at Zeebrugge, Belgium, after the engraving on his watch and other items revealed his previous actions. Fryatt was put on trial, found guilty and sentenced to death, with the execution being certified by Kaiser Wilhelm II himself. The execution notice read as follows:

No 12.   Le S. S. Brussels coulé à l'extrémité du môle et son héroïque capitaine Fryatt, capturé
par les Boches le 23 juin 1916 et fusillé le 27 juillet 1916.
The S. S. "Brussels" sunk near the extremity of Zeebrugge-mole, and her heroic
Captain Fryatt, who was captured by the germans on the 23d of June 1916 and shot
on the 27th of July 1916.

A postcard commemorating Captain Charles Fryatt. After being captured by Germany, the SS *Brussels* was renamed *Brugge*, and scuttled in 1918. It was raised and repaired after the war, and later renamed *Lady Brussels*. (Authors' Collection)

Notice: The English captain of the Mercantile Marine, Charles Fryatt, of Southampton, though he did not belong to the armed forces of the enemy, attempted on March 28th, 1915, to destroy a German submarine by running it down. This is the reason why he has been condemned to death by judgment this day of the War Council of the Marine Corps and has been executed. A perverse action has thus received its punishment, tardy but just …

Fryatt was executed on 27 July by a firing squad. He left behind a wife and seven children. International outrage was immediate.[40] The anger and disgust is completely understandable when one considers that during the actions that he was put on trial for, Fryatt had acted defensively after being threatened by a submarine. With his killing, the First Battle of the Atlantic had reached a new low, seemingly reflecting the horrors being committed on land. By the end of July 1916, ninety-five ships were sunk or taken as prizes by U-boats, totalling 114,715 tons.[41] This increase in sinkings was reflective of the intensified U-boat campaign that the Kaiser had agreed to. The U-boat war was beginning to look resurgent.

Meanwhile, the *Aquitania* remained in Southampton, where it had been since being released back to the Cunard Line in March. The ship had been undergoing an extensive refit to return it to passenger service. However, late in July, with the Mediterranean theatre becoming more active, the Admiralty requisitioned the ship to serve as a hospital ship again. This decision was made despite the fact that the lengthy conversion back into a passenger liner was nearly complete and would have to be undone.

The *Aquitania* would serve as a hospital ship for the remainder of the year, being paired up with the HMHS *Britannic* once more. By the end of 1916, the Mediterranean theatre slowed down again. As a result, the *Aquitania* would be laid up in the Solent for all of 1917. During its career as a hospital ship, the *Aquitania* had managed to transport around 25,000 wounded troops home to England.[42]

Also near the end of the month, the British began implementing a rudimentary convoy system. The system involved having a group of merchant or troopships travel together with destroyers or other naval escorts, in order to provide protection and a screen against submarines and enemy vessels. The need for such a system became apparent as losses to submarines continued to increase. Australia had formed the first large convoy of the war in October 1914, when ten Anzac troopships joined up with other Australian ships, and received an escort from Australian and Japanese naval vessels in their crossing. Japan was a member of the Allies and lent support, particularly in the form of convoy escorts. However, the convoy system had not yet been fully developed or utilised by the British.

On 24 July, Britain organised a convoy of ships travelling on the Holland–Harwich route, to protect neutral shipping from the Netherlands. The convoy

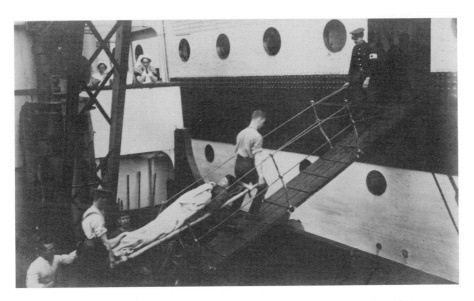

Nurses watch as a wounded soldier is loaded aboard the HMHS *Aquitania*. (Authors'
Collection)

was successful, as only one ship, which fell behind the group, was lost to U-boats.
Convoys travelling on this route would thereafter receive destroyer escorts,
and later in the war this was supplemented by flying-boat patrols. Despite the
success of this initial convoy, the British Admiralty would not approve the use of
a full convoy system to protect merchant shipping until the following year, once
skyrocketing losses to U-boats forced their hand.[43]

Meanwhile, the danger from mine-laying U-boats was an ever present threat,
and as the number of ships claimed by this method increased, so did the public
anger over the tactics being used. On 30 July, an unnamed individual wrote a
message to friends on the back of a postcard with a picture of the minelaying
U-boat *UC-5*, which had sunk the *Anglia*. It had been captured some months
earlier. Brimming with anger, the short message lambasted the Germans:

> Dear friends, hoping you are all well and am glad to tell you that I am all right
> at present myself am sending you the photo of this captured assassin German
> of course and I don't know what these creatures think of themselves with their
> foul tricks this submarine is not of a fighting one but a sneak laying out death
> for everything that comes along friend or foe.[44]

In August 1916, Italian forces won a minor victory over Austrian troops in
the Isonzo, although the latter had shifted their forces elsewhere to prevent
unnecessary losses. Regardless, the victory boosted Italian morale. A suddenly

UC-5. Note the mine chutes fore and aft the conning tower. (Authors' Collection)

confident Italy declared war on Germany on 27 August, finally living up to their obligations as laid out in the London Pact. Romania entered the war on the side of the Allies that same day.

On 28 August, the British Admiralty requisitioned the *Britannic* once again, as the front in Salonica began to increase action in the Mediterranean. As with the *Aquitania*, work was underway to convert the ship for its intended purpose as a passenger liner. The job of doing so had been moving at a slow pace, and how far it had proceeded is unknown. Work was halted, and the vessel was converted back into a hospital ship. Captain Bartlett was placed in command of the ship again. The HMHS *Britannic* would not depart on its next voyage until 24 September, and would have an entirely new medical staff, since all the previous crew who served in that capacity had been transferred elsewhere when the ship was released by the Admiralty.

At sea, August would continue the trend of intensification of the U-boat war. By the end of the month, the total number of ships sunk or captured shot up to an alarming 148, totalling 182,815 tons. Four more ships were damaged. This was the highest number sunk by U-boats in any month of the war thus far.[45]

As the submarine campaign continued to regain its momentum, Germany convened a conference at Pless on 30 August. With the continued stranglehold of the Royal Navy blockade of Germany causing significant supply and economic problems, and with no progress on the Western Front, Chief of the Admiralty Staff von Holtzendorff proposed an unrestricted submarine warfare campaign.

Chancellor von Bethmann-Hollweg once again stated that this would drag America and other neutral nations into the war on the side of the Allies. Foreign Minister Jagow and others agreed, stating that if U-boats were fully unleashed 'Germany will be treated like a mad dog'. Von Holtzendorff's argument was clearly moot for the time being and no decision for a change in policy was made, although approval was given for building twenty-one additional U-boats.[46]

September–October 1916

In September 1916, the Battle of the Somme continued to rage, and saw the first use of tanks en masse in combat. The Italian Army, emboldened by its recent successes, launched a new offensive against Austro-Hungarian forces in the Isonzo. However, the attack was halted following heavy casualties. Despite this, the Italian forces continued to wear down Austro-Hungarian troops.

At sea, U-boat commanders continued to wage intensified submarine warfare, and were finding more and more clever ways to sink merchant vessels, while still adhering to prize rules. Perhaps the best example of this was Kapitänleutnant Carl-Siegfried Ritter von Georg and the crew of U-57. On the night of 24/25 September, U-57 surfaced approximately 20 miles off the English coast, and the crew found themselves amongst a British fishing fleet. On the previous afternoon, von Georg had sunk the Norwegian steamer SS Laila, and had taken its captain and crew aboard his submarine.

Since von Georg was under orders not to attack merchant vessels without first warning them, he thought of a novel approach to the situation: he asked the Norwegian captain to row the Laila's lifeboat over to the nearest fishing vessel and order the crew to abandon ship without raising the alarm or warning the rest of the fleet, or they would be fired upon. The Norwegian captain readily agreed. Von Georg described these events, and what followed in the log book for U-57:

> I approached the last steamer … and ask the Norwegian Captain of the Laila to do me the favor of rowing to this last steamer … and informing him that a German vessel is in attendance, and whose captain is ordering him to leave his vessel immediately, along with all his crew and all his papers, and come back alongside. Any refusal to follow this order would result in the U-Boat using its weapons against it.
>
> I made the Captain of the Laila aware that I had no right to order him to approach the fishing steamer, but that he would be doing me a great service if he acceded to my request. The Captain gladly carried out my request. The Laila boat and a boat from the steamer came back with the crew of the

Fisher Prince. The fishing vessel continues to make way, with lights on display, nothing unusual is on board. I decide to use the *Fisher Prince* to assemble the crews of the remaining fishing vessels and then to destroy the steamers. An immediate attack would have merely caused the remaining vessels to flee … Oberleutnant zur See von Ruckteschell, two junior officers and two men were sent back to the *Fisher Prince* with its crew … In the event of the slightest reluctance to follow a command, the U-Boat – which would be following closely behind – would make use of its armaments. It was never my intention to remain close … I merely wanted to ensure the captains obedience by making this statement.[47]

Von Georg's bluff worked, and one by one the fishing vessels were approached in the darkness and boarded. Each time, the U-boat commander's warning was delivered to the crew by his sailors, and the captains of the fishing vessels and steamers agreed to abandon ship without raising the alarm. The ships were scuttled by opening their scuppers, or destroyed by artillery fire. After daybreak, von Georg began sinking the remaining trawlers by firing a warning shot, signalling them to stop, and then allowing the crews to abandon ship before shelling them until they sank.

As each ship was sunk, the survivors rowed their lifeboats over to the *Fisher Prince*, which was being used as an oversized lifeboat for the crews of the sunken vessels. Eventually, the Belgian steamer SS *Tromp* came along, and after being boarded and searched, was allowed to take the crewmembers of the sunken vessels on board. When all was said and done, von Georg and the crew of *U-57* had managed to sink twenty-one vessels and disable one more. Von Georg stated that 'Without endangering a single life we had polished off a neat batch of potential minelayers and sweepers and antisubmarine craft'. His exploits surely rank as amongst the most inventive and daring of the U-boat war up to that point.[48]

Von Georg was not the only U-boat commander who had found ways to work around the restrictions placed on them. Overall, in September, U-boats sank or captured 195 ships, totalling 250,200 tons. This was another monthly record. Six additional ships were damaged. There were increasing levels of U-boat activity in the English Channel and close to the British Isles once again, and the number of sinkings in the Mediterranean had not slackened.[49] The losses in merchant shipping were beginning to concern the British Government greatly, as supplies were already tight, and it was feared that the increasing number of losses might soon reach unsustainable numbers if the trend continued.

Near the end of the month, on 29 September, the RMS *Mauretania* was once again requisitioned by the British Admiralty. This time, the vessel was to be utilised as a troop transport. In October and November 1916, the ship made two voyages in that capacity, carrying 6,214 Canadian troops from Halifax to England,

Captain David Miller. (Authors' Collection)

bound for the Western Front. During one of these trips, coaling ports that were improperly battened down led to the boiler rooms flooding, and the ship was nearly lost. Following these voyages, the *Mauretania* was laid up once again, this time in Scotland, and would not be recalled to service until 1918.[50]

October 1916 saw yet another Italian offensive in the Isonzo, which was quickly repulsed by Austro-Hungarian forces. The futile onslaught in the region would be renewed again in November, which resulted in a limited Italian advance, at great cost. The struggles in the Isonzo would last through 1917, a total of twelve battles.

In England, Zeppelins continued to bomb London at night. Between 2 September and 2 October 1916, there had been four such raids. Up until 2 October, there had been forty-four Zeppelin attacks on London during the war in total, killing 431 people and wounding 1,146.[51]

HMT *Franconia* sinking, as photographed from one of the lifeboats. (Rich Turnwald Collection)

At sea, more and more ships were continuing to be sunk by U-boats. On 4 October, the Cunard liner HMT *Franconia* was on a voyage from Alexandria to Marseilles. Operating as a troop transport since February 1915, the *Franconia* was not carrying any troops on this particular leg of its voyage. The ship was spotted by *UB-47*, which fired a torpedo into it. The ship began sinking quickly, and Captain David S. Miller gave the order to abandon ship. One of the crewmembers aboard the vessel at the time was Assistant Purser William Gerson, whose experience at sea had already included witnessing the aftermath of the *Lusitania* sinking from the Liverpool Shipping Office, and also the troop-landing at Gallipoli. He gave the following account of the sinking, which claimed the lives of twelve crewmen:

Our ship had thus far escaped going down to the wharves of Davy Jones, and during our voyaging from the Persian Gulf to the English Channel and to Bombay and return, we gave little thought to the idea of being 'pipped' by a German submarine. Some of my mates were fatalistic enough to think that in the tube of some underwater craft was a torpedo labeled *Franconia*, but they were little worried. There was our boiler-maker who had served forty-one years at sea and who was to complete his final voyage upon reaching the home port, who predicted – without fear – that he would never live to draw his pension and die in a sailors home. We laughed at his prediction. As for myself, whose every worldly possession was with me on the *Franconia*, I felt that I had been born under a lucky star. It did not seem possible that anything could ever take our ship away from us, the *Franconia* – not England – was my home, and many another shared this sentiment. As though in preparation for her final sacrifice, the *Franconia's* engines were overhauled, her bottom scraped and painted, and a new coat of war-gray paint was applied by her sailors. Everything had been done to put her in beautiful condition, and as she left Alexandria, Egypt … she was the pride of every man aboard, from the cabin-boy to the commander, David S. Miller …

As our ship steamed from Alexandria to Malta, the first leg of the triangle run, every precaution was taken to outwit the U-boats with which those waters were known to be infested. Watches were doubled – two men in the crow's nest scanned the Mediterranean for the white foam which would mean 'periscope ahoy'. Captain Miller religiously followed Admiralty instructions to keep the ship on a zig-zag course. Not a ray of light found outlet from the ship at night. No one carried a lighted cigarette or pipe on deck under the penalty of court martial. The quartermaster steered with the aid of a shaded compass.

Despite these precautions none of us felt down-hearted, not even Sammy Bostock – the boilermaker – who was to find his way to Davy Jones's locker before another 24 hours has passed, nor Engineer Gus Lawlor who was to escape with his life and a bottle Scotch whiskey when the torpedo came.

And so October 4, 1916 dawned over the Mediterranean as clear and warm and as beautiful a day as we could have wished … All about me were busy, and I spent my own time making out pay-rolls and government papers, quite unaware of the uselessness of it all. Ship's inspection was about to start when, without the slightest warning, a terrific explosion occurred, about twenty feet for'ard throwing me out of my seat. Instantly darkness closed in about me. The dynamo had been crippled, and like every other man on the ship, I thought, 'She's got it!' Perhaps it was the tension of the moment, but although I was to learn the meaning of fear at a later date, I felt none whatsoever as I realized disaster had overtaken us.

The odor of gun powder or TNT almost overpowered me, and I knew straightaway it had been released by the exploding torpedo. A succession of crashes followed the return of the ship to a horizontal position, the forward part of the boat having been lifted almost out of the water.

Within thirty seconds I was at my post behind Captain Miller on the bridge. The skipper's courage and training stood him in good stead in the moment, only a deathly pallor betraying his anxiety. His first order to me was, 'See if you can see the submarine'. As the vessel had now taken a list to starboard I looked on that side for evidence of a periscope. Fritz was keeping himself well under cover, but upon looking beneath the bridge I could see a patch of discolored water which indicated that our stokehold had been pierced. Soft coal was pouring into the blue waters of the Mediterranean.

By this time the quartermaster had given four tugs of the ship's whistle cord, four piercing blasts sounding the order, 'Abandon ship!' My thoughts turned to the radio operator. 'How about giving Cobham our position?' I asked the captain who was supervising the lowering of boats. In answer he made for the chartroom, seized a pair of compasses, roughly figured out the longitude and latitude of our position and scrawled it upon a piece of paper.

Seizing the paper from his hand I hastened down to the Marconi cabin where Cobham was already sending out the SOS, in which message he now incorporated our position …

Returning to the bridge, the Captain bade me to call the engineer on the telegraph, not knowing how things were below. But although I blew lustily on the speaking tube, I could hear nothing but the swish of water, and the sound of distant voices, and so reported to the Captain who replied, 'Never mind'. He knew no one could stay below after the for'ard stokehold had been pierced. Engineer Lieutenant Samuel Birks then made his appearance reporting that nothing could be done in the engine-room, and that unless 'up for'ard' had caught it, everyone was out. As a matter of fact, thirteen men had been killed outright by the explosion.

My next task was to return to the Marconi cabin to find out whether replies has been received to our SOS. Cobham informed me that the destroyer *Shelldrake* was coming up and would be on the scene in an hour.

After reporting the message to the Captain, I reminded him that he neglected to put on a life-belt. 'That's alright', he replied. 'Can you swim Gerson?' I told him that I could and silently mumbled my prayers. Feeling a great deal of affection for the old man, I could not take his answer as a finality and dashed down to his cabin for a life-belt. There I noted his pet canary had been killed by the shock, its cage lying on the floor and the bird motionless. The little incident impressed itself upon me, for the old man was a lonely sort of chap who had found a real presence in the companionship of the songster.

Again I rushed down to the Marconi cabin, where I found that not only the *Shelldrake* but also the *Dover Castle* was rushing to our assistance. With a look of anxiety on his face, Cobham said 'I hope the old man won't forget me!' His duty chained him to his post until orders released him. Before returning to the Bridge, I enjoyed with Cobham the last cup of cheers quaffed on the *Franconia*. Then it was that I remembered the ships records which alone could enable a checking up of survivors and against orders made my way through the darkened ship to the desk which I knew them to be unfailingly kept.

The trip below included my worst moments on board the *Franconia*. Feeling my way through the listing ship's passageways, I feared that the ship would now turn over, the flooding in through the portholes. The darkness oppressed me. Time and time again I knocked myself against objects loosened by the explosion. Only after what seemed hours did I reach the paymaster's office, thrust my hand into an open drawer and withdrew the papers. My desire to regain daylight swiftly became an obsession and only as I reached the bridge and the sunlight again did the horror fade. The Captain's smile as he saw me place the records underneath my life-belt, more than compensated for the trip below.

The ship was now listing heavily. Lifeboats circled about us in the blue waters below, with boat number 13, to which the Captain was assigned, standing off ready to take us off at the last moment. The foc'sle head for'ard was almost submerged and the heavy 6 inch gun astern assumed the elevation of an anti-aircraft gun. Its breach had been thrown overboard (by Admiralty orders) and the gunners had left the ship.

'Dusty' Miller, thirty-two years at sea, skipper of a sinking ship, now became fidgety for the first time. There was no fear in his face – only regret. 'I think it's time to go,' was all he said. The *Franconia* meant more to him than anything in the world. As though performing some last rite, we left the bridge and made our way along the boat deck to the point where a rope ladder had been suspended. 'Come on, Sparks,' was his call to the wireless operator who must have heaved a sigh of relief as he tossed off his ear-phones and joined the silent assembly outside his cabin. There he assured us that the streaks of black smoke on the horizon were from the destroyer *Shelldrake* and the hospital ship *Dover Castle*. Silently we started to clamber down the rope ladder and I felt it an honor to precede only the captain. Just as he put his foot over the rail he paused, patted the rail affectionately and said, 'Good bye old girl. I'm going to leave you!' Reaching our boat, the oarsmen rowed us out some 200 yards from the ship, upon which the waterline steadily mounted.

Rapidly the *Franconia* approached the final moment. Her nose disappeared under water, her stern rose and then followed the weirdest sight I have ever seen. Further and further under water slipped her nose until the waves almost washed over her bridge. Then she gradually straightened herself and her stern rose clean out of water to an angle of 75 degrees, an awe-inspiring picture against the blue sky of the Mediterranean. Then this mammoth ocean liner started to dive. A muffled roar reached our ears as the boilers exploded blowing the for'ard funnel … into the sky.

Then one bulk-head went, and the *Franconia* shot down. Again a bulkhead snapped and hurried the ship on her passage. The after-mast crumpled back against the deck and the 6-inch gun crashed through the deck-house. To see our old ship twisted and torn as though she were made of cardboard was a terrible sight. The last bulkhead now gave way and she slipped quietly under water. Our home was gone. *Lusitania* reports had led us to expect a suction, but except for a few waves and loose wreckage there followed nothing to indicate that the *Franconia* had gone down.

Within two hours after sinking (while the destroyer *Shelldrake* was stalking the U-boat) we were picked up, and safely housed aboard the hospital ship *Dover Castle*. There it was my duty to call the roll and place an ominous black cross next to the names of those failing to answer, and for the first time we learned for certain that Boilermaker Samuel Bostock and twelve of the 'black squad', or coal passers, had met death. At sun-down we held a combined memorial and thanksgiving service on the boat deck … [52]

Meanwhile, across the Atlantic, some submarine crews had begun to sink merchant shipping provocatively close to the eastern coast of America, but outside of the United States' territorial waters. On 8 October, the New York, Newfoundland & Halifax Steamship Company liner SS *Stephano* was travelling from St John's Newfoundland to New York with general cargo and passengers. When it was approximately 3 miles east of the Nantucket Lightship, it was spotted by the crew of *U-53*, which began pursuing the vessel. Shortly before 6 p.m., the submarine's crew began firing warning shots across the *Stephano*'s bow with its deck gun from approximately a half mile away. The ship quickly stopped.

This image of a U-boat was captured from the deck of a merchant vessel torpedoed by it off the shore of the United States. (Authors' Collection)

The U-boat's commander, Kapitänleutnant Hans Rose, gave Captain Clifton Smith time to abandon his vessel, and the latter began the evacuation immediately. While this was happening, US Navy destroyers arrived on the scene, in response to *Stephano*'s distress calls. Being from a neutral nation and seeing that the U-boat was adhering to prize rules, they stood by and did not interfere.

While their intended victim was being evacuated, the *U-53* spotted and turned its attention to the Dutch steamer SS *Blommersdijk*, which it ordered to abandon ship and then proceeded to sink. Coming back alongside the *Stephano*, German crewmembers boarded and searched it. After they were clear, the *U-53* shelled the vessel, then fired a torpedo to finish the job. The ship sank in seven minutes, with no loss of life. All of the *Stephano*'s survivors were rescued by the destroyers standing by.

Following the sinking, Captain Smith described the events:

We were about three miles east of the Nantucket Lightship and 42 miles from the mainland when I first saw the submarine. This was at 5.55 p.m. I was on the bridge. The weather was somewhat hazy and it was a little dark, but I could make her out plainly. She was about half a mile away, and was lying next to a fairly large ship …

She fired a shot across our bows and I slowed down. There were four such shots fired altogether … None of them hit us. There were two American destroyers near us by about this time. I ordered the boats lowered, and prepared to abandon ship. There were 97 passengers and 67 crew, and we used six out of eight boats. While we were doing this the submarine went under the lee of the *Stephano*. I could not see much of her, but could tell her by her lights that she was going along by the side of the ship.

When we were in the boats it was dark, but we saw the submarine leave the *Stephano* and go off about a mile and a half and sink a freighter. We could not make out what vessel it was … but we saw her sink.

Then the submarine returned … She fired thirty shots into the hull … but they apparently did little harm. They did not even put the dynamo out of commission, and the vessel remained fully lighted. Then the submarine drew off and fired one torpedo. The *Stephano* went down in seven minutes after being hit. We were later picked up by the destroyer.[53]

Sylvia Carew, a passenger from Halifax, gave a detailed account of the sinking. She had been on her way to New York to visit a friend:

It was about 6 o'clock, and I was … giving my order … in the dining room, when I heard a shot … Every one went on deck and every one was frightened. But there was no panic.

After the first shot came another across the bow of the *Stephano* from the submarine, which could be seen lying low in the water, with its red and green lights burning. Persons … on deck … had seen the United States destroyers approaching, but had thought that these were simply on maneuvers … But those who had been below now saw them for the first time and such thought … ran along lines as to … whether they were enemy ships. One of the officers of the destroyer said later that the vessel had come so swiftly from Newport that all the paint on its funnels had been burned off by the intense heat from its fires.

The lifeboats were manned at once. I rushed to my stateroom and got together what things I could. But they made me leave my bag behind, so all that I had was what I wore … There was no disorder about the lifeboats. The children were crying and their parents were comforting them as best they could and the talk of the Spanish crew rose shrilly above everything, but there were no signs of panic.

We got into the boats by rope ladders, held taut from below, and there was a heavy swell to the sea. Those boats on the side toward the destroyer were towed to it by a launch, but those on the other side – the side toward submarine – had to be rowed. I was on the side toward the destroyer.

It loomed up grayly through the dusk and we could not tell its nationality … We who were British subjects wondered if we were to be made prisoners … But as we got nearer in the lifeboat we saw that the flag was the Stars and Stripes and there was a sigh of relief. It took just eleven minutes for all the passengers to be taken from the *Stephano* to this destroyer and to the other ones which had come up.

… climbing down the rope ladders into the boats and getting aboard the destroyers the principal trouble was the ladders and the sea. If it had been an hour later, when the sea became even rougher than it was, we might not have gotten aboard at all.

Then we stood on the deck of the destroyer and watched the *Stephano*. Nobody had thought to shut off her lights, as she was only a short distance away, she could be seen plainly. And the other ship – it was either Norwegian or Dutch – which had been ordered by the *Stephano* to stand by, we could also see.

We waited a long while. The Germans had not boarded the *Stephano* before we left and we had not seen any of them. Perhaps we had to wait so long because they found a good dinner waiting them on board. While we were standing by, the submarine came nearer to us … For a moment I wondered if it was going to sink us. I knew that it wouldn't, but I couldn't help wondering as it came nearer and nearer. Then it went away again.

It must have been 9 o'clock when the submarine began firing. It fired thirty shots – we counted them – into the *Stephano*, but she did not sink. Whether the water cocks had been opened I don't know.

Then there was a crash amidships and the *Stephano* began to slide into the water, her bow rising into the air. I have seen pictures of sinking ships like that, but I never knew what it was until I saw the *Stephano*, outline against the moon, going to the bottom. Just before she disappeared steam escaped into the siren and it gave two shrill cries, just like the cries of a human being. The destroyer also stood by while the submarine sank the other vessel, which turned its bow into the air as the *Stephano* had done as it slid into the depths.

Miss Carew then related how she had previously visited the cemetery in Halifax where the victims of the *Titanic* disaster were buried, and was struck by the fact that so many of the 'graves are marked by numbers, for the men and woman who sleep there are nameless'. With this in mind, when she had boarded the *Stephano*, Carew had tied her money in a chamois bag, and also put a card in it bearing her name and her father's name and tied it around her neck.[54]

Following the sinking, some parties raised an uproar since there had been American passengers aboard. However, the *U-53* and its crew had adhered strictly to international law throughout the incident, and no lives were lost. Accusations in the press such as 'First Warning is Solid Shot', alleged that Germany had violated the '*Sussex* pledge'.[55] In fact, as Captain Smith's account clarified, the first shots were fired over the bow of the ship, and none struck it.

Afterwards, the British Government was upset with the United States for having stood and watched the *U-53* sink the two ships without intervening or attempting to detain it. The American Government responded that as a neutral nation, they had no cause to do so since the submarine had been operating well within international law, and had seen to the safety of those aboard before sinking the vessel.[56]

On 26 October, the Furness, Withy & Company ship SS *Rappahannock* was travelling from Halifax to London carrying a cargo of grains, deals and general goods. The ship was stopped about 70 miles from the Scilly Isles by *U-69*. The submarine was commanded by Kapitänleutnant Ernst Wilhelms. The crew was allowed to abandon ship, and the *Rappahannock* was torpedoed and sunk. The U-boat then left the scene, abandoning the survivors in the lifeboats to their fate. None of the thirty-seven crewmembers were ever seen again. The fate of the vessel was unknown until a body was washed ashore on 8 November, and floating debris and cargo of the type that the vessel was carrying was sighted by another vessel on 9 November, 60 miles off the Scilly Isles.

The British Admiralty condemned what they were certain was a U-boat attack saying 'If the crew were forced to take to the boats in the ordinary way it is clear that this must have occurred so far from land, or in such weather conditions, that there was no probability of their reaching the shore. The German pledge not to sink vessels "without saving human lives" has thus once more been disregarded, and another of their submarines has been guilty of destructive murder on the high seas'.[57]

Germany denied having left the *Rappahannock*'s crewmembers to die, and much later, on 27 January 1917, the German Government in Berlin issued the following official statement:

> The English steamer *Rappahannock* was forced to stop by a German submarine … following a pursuit of some length, and sunk after the crew had been given ample time to leave the vessel … The safety of the crew, who had entered the boats, appeared to the commander of the submarine to be guaranteed, in as much as the life-boats were in good condition and well equipped with sails and provisions, and were able to reach land quickly and safely in view of the favourable sailing wind, which pointed towards land, and the slight sea.[58]

Why the survivors never reached land is a mystery, although it seems likely that they experienced bad weather and were all drowned. Whether Kapitänleutnant

Wilhelms abandoned them in adverse conditions, or if the weather changed after he left the scene is impossible to tell. While the British claims that prize rules had been violated in this case are uncertain at best, it is evident that some U-boat commanders were disregarding their superiors' orders, as unannounced attacks on neutral shipping and British merchant vessels were on the rise.

By the end of October 1916, a staggering 199 ships had been sunk or captured by U-boats, totalling 357,923 tons of shipping. Five more ships suffered damage in attacks. The English Channel was once again a battleground, and the 'war zone' waters of earlier in the war saw increasing numbers of losses, while the pace was kept up in the Mediterranean.[59] The number of ships sunk was yet another monthly record in the war, and the voices of concern amongst the Allies over the resurgent German submarine campaign continued to grow.

November–December 1916

On 7 November 1916, President Woodrow Wilson narrowly won re-election. One of the more important slogans of his campaign was 'He kept us out of war', to appeal to American voters who wanted to avoid entering the conflict in Europe, and to avoid a conflict with Mexico, with which there were tensions. On 18 November, the horrific Battle of the Somme finally came to a conclusion, with both the Allies and Central Powers bloodied.

At sea on 12 November, the HMHS *Britannic* had departed Southampton on its sixth voyage to the Mediterranean, bound for the island of Lemnos, where it would take on wounded Allied soldiers and personnel. After arriving in Naples, Italy on 17 November, the ship took on coal and water. Unlike on previous outbound voyages, there were no passengers aboard the ship, which allowed the medical staff to have free reign. Typically, it was the policy to keep passengers and medical staff separated, which prevented the latter from being allowed into certain spaces while aboard. A storm hit Naples, and Captain Bartlett wisely decided to postpone the departure until conditions improved. The storm continued to rage until the afternoon of 18 November. *Britannic* finally resumed its voyage, although the weather and seas made things extremely uncomfortable.

By the next morning, conditions were fairly clear, and the ship's speed was increased. The medical staff were rushing around to make preparations for the wounded that they were due to receive. On the morning of 21 November, the *Britannic* was sailing through the Kea Channel, off the Greek island of Kea. The weather was sunny and clear, the deep blue waters were calm, and the mood aboard was relaxed.[60]

Many were just settling down for breakfast and enjoying the beautiful day. One of these crewmembers was Violet Jessop, who had joined the war effort by

The *Britannic* while anchored in Southampton. (*Southampton Pictorial*, 1919/Authors' Collection)

volunteering as a junior nurse in the British Red Cross. Jessop had previously served as a stewardess aboard both the *Olympic* and *Titanic*. Her career had been very eventful thus far. She was aboard the *Olympic* when it collided with the HMS *Hawke* in 1911, survived the *Titanic* disaster the following year, and was aboard when the *Olympic* rescued the HMS *Audacious*' crew earlier in the war. She described the jovial atmosphere aboard in the following way:

> Everybody scrambled down to breakfast, talking and joking, for breakfast time was quite the nicest, friendliest time aboard … the animation of good spirits … was noticeable everywhere. Banter was rife, even at the austere commanding officer's table … [61]

Suddenly, at 8.12 a.m., an explosion shook the ship. Jessop described it as a 'dull, deafening roar'. Crewmembers and nurses leapt up from the tables immediately, to see what had happened. Many near the bow believed that the ship had been torpedoed. Others further aft felt a slight jolt, and believed the ship had struck a smaller vessel.

she cracked her head hard against a solid object. Once she reached the surface
and drew a deep breath she said 'I opened my eyes on an indescribable scene
of slaughter', and quickly shut them again out of revulsion. She saw a man in
uniform with his head cracked open 'like a sheep's head served by the butcher,
the poor brains trickling over on to khaki shoulders'. Severed limbs and bodies
drifted past.

At 8.35 a.m., Captain Bartlett realised the stricken liner would never reach Kea
in time to be beached, so he ordered the engines stopped. His command came
just in time, as a third lifeboat was drifting toward the propeller, which halted
right before the boat reached it. The occupants had to push off the now still
propeller blades to get clear. Unaware that boats had already left the ship without
permission, Bartlett gave the order to abandon ship.

Even with the list and previous disorder, the majority of the remaining
lifeboats were lowered away quickly and safely, although the list interfered with
the lowering of the boats on the port side, which lay against the *Britannic's* hull.
By 9.00 a.m., the starboard list was so great that the davits could no longer be
used. However, most of those aboard had already got away safely. The crew
lowered away twenty-eight of the lifeboats and two motor launches total. The
motor launches began picking up survivors out of the 70°F water, including
Violet Jessop.

The *Britannic* continued to settle by the bow, but at a slower rate than earlier
in the sinking. As such, Captain Bartlett made a last-ditch attempt at saving the
ship, ordering the engines restarted, and once again tried to make it to Kea.
Unfortunately, the ship's rudder was no longer responding and as the propellers
rose further out of the water, they could no longer provide adequate forward thrust.
Bartlett saw that their efforts were futile, and ordered the ship stopped for good.
The ship's steam whistles were blasted, signalling any remaining crew to abandon
ship. Bartlett was then washed into the water as the bridge submerged, swimming
to a nearby lifeboat, where he began organising the survivors and rescue efforts.

As it settled, the *Britannic* rolled over on its starboard side, and its four funnels
began collapsing and heading to the seafloor below. At 9.07 a.m., the last portions
of the ship dipped below the surface. The *Britannic* would be the largest ship sunk
during the First World War. The survivors would be rescued by Greek fishermen,
Royal Navy vessels, or by making it to shore on their own. Miraculously, although
the *Britannic* had sunk in a mere fifty-five minutes, much faster than its sister ship
Titanic had in 1912, just thirty people were killed. The timing of the sinking
was lucky, as no patients or passengers were aboard. If the ship had sunk when
returning to England with a full load of wounded soldiers, the death toll would
likely have been much higher.[63]

John B. Atkinson, one of the two chaplains who had been aboard the *Britannic*,
gave the following account describing the events:

It was my privilege and joy to serve on the hospital ship *Britannic* as Church of England chaplain. Never shall I forget the lovely sunrise and the 'oily' seas of November 21, 1916. My duty took me at 7 a.m. to the lounge to officiate at the daily celebration of the Holy Communion. The joy of that service would have been impossible had not an all-wise Providence blocked the future from our knowledge. After the service there was half an hour to wait for breakfast. Little groups of cheerful women feasted their eyes on the bleak but wondrously coloured Islands of the Aegean Sea. At the sound of the gong all made their way to the dining saloon to partake of the last of the excellent meals which were such a feature on the *Britannic*. Not more than five minutes had elapsed before an ominous crash was heard. Owing to the great length of the ship and the distance between the place where the blow was received and the dining saloon the noise of the blow from the torpedo was not in the least like what one would have imagined it. Instinctively all stood up, but in a few minutes we sat down again. Then the clear voice of a captain in the Royal Army Medical Corps rang out, giving the order for all to go to their cabins. Led by that most courageous of matrons, Miss Dowse, QAIMNS [Queen Alexandra's Imperial Military Nursing Service], the whole … filed out in the steadiest possible manner. In a very-short time we were all on the boat deck. Life jackets were adjusted, and then all stood in perfect calmness awaiting the next order. Yon it came. 'Ladies, this way, please'. As they passed aft on the starboard side I saw the last of the heroic nurses at close quarters. Three boats took them safely from the sinking ship. As we saw them lying in the distance on the calm sea, we, who still remained on the rapidly sinking ship, felt pleased to think that these brave women now stood every chance of being saved. This brief account I feel it my duty to write. It is given to few to witness such courage, and to those to whom it is given there falls the obligation to acknowledge it. In the disaster no one saved more than that in which they stood up. No one complained. If loss had been incurred something had been trained, an imperishable record of the bravery and heroism of British womanhood.[64]

Another account of the sinking was given by Matron E.A. Dowse, a veteran of the Boer War, who saw to the evacuation of the female nurses during the sinking:

The ship had all the hospital marks, and was fitted up like the best shore hospitals. It is impossible to understand why the ship was attacked. We were bound for Mudros, and when the disaster occurred we had everything ready to take the sick aboard there. I had with me seventy-six nursing sisters, mostly belonging to Queen Alexandra's nursing staff, together with four stewardesses. They are all English, and happily all were saved. We had no patients aboard, excepting a few of the staff, who were slightly ill. We were able to carry these on deck and get them away.

The explosion occurred when we were at breakfast. We heard something, but had no idea the ship had been hit or was going down. Without alarm we went on deck and awaited the launching of the boats. The whole staff behaved most splendidly, waiting calmly lined up on deck. We were two hours in the boats. The Germans, however, could not have chosen a better time for giving us an opportunity to save those aboard, for we had all risen. We were near land, and the sea was perfectly smooth.[65]

In another account, Dowse recalled how all of the nurses had left behind their medals and belongings, and how many of those sitting in the lifeboats awaiting rescue 'were suffering from strain' and 'became distracted'.[66]

Another crewmember who had been aboard the ship was Archie Jewell who, like Violet Jessop and another crewmember, John Priest, was a survivor of the *Titanic* disaster. Jewell had served as a lookout aboard *Britannic*'s ill-fated sister ship. He wrote the following in a letter:

It [the explosion] made her shake all over. I very soon knew what was up when I saw the water coming in and the smell of powder. Before I knew where I was a man came rushing out of a cabin door right where she was struck and ran right into me and stuck me with his head just over my eye and cut it right open so I was blood all over.

The poor fellow was so frightened he did not know what he was doing. I don't know what he was or if he was saved or not. I ran up to the boat deck and then some one tied my eye up so I was like old [Lord] Nelson, only one eye.

We started to lower away the boats and then the order was passed around to stop lowering and then they started to move the propellers. I think they were going to try and run her ashore but she started to go down by the head very quick so we started lowering the boats again and then she took a big hit to starboard and we had a hard job to get the port boats out.[67]

Sadly, Jewell would die on 17 April 1917 while serving on the defensively armed ambulance transport HMHS *Donegal*, when it was torpedoed and sunk by *UC-21*. Fellow *Titanic* and *Britannic* survivor John Priest was also aboard the ship at the time, but survived.

Following the *Britannic*'s loss, many were quick to accuse Germany of having torpedoed the ship. In fact, the best evidence supports that the *Britannic* struck one of the mines documented as having been laid in the area by *U-73*. Evidence of this minefield, including mine anchors and chains, was found in the region near the wreck using sonar scans during an expedition led by the late Carl Spencer in 2003.[68]

No evidence has ever emerged from a log book, etc. that a U-boat fired a torpedo at a ship fitting *Britannic*'s description on the date and in the region it was sunk. Tellingly, Captain Bartlett himself assumed that the ship had struck a mine since his vessel was clearly marked as a hospital ship and since there was no geyser of water, which is typically caused when a torpedo strikes the side of a vessel. Regardless, the *Britannic*'s loss was yet another blow to the White Star Line, which had now lost two of the three massive *Olympic*-Class liners. *Britannic* would have been the largest passenger liner in the world at the time, but never had a chance to serve its intended purpose.

Following the sinking, the *Britannic*'s nurses were recognised for their calmness and valour during the sinking. An example of this is a letter written in recognition of the service of a Miss Smith, one of the ship's nurses:

2nd January, 1917.

Dear Miss Smith,

It has been decided that a note shall be made on your Record of Service of your conduct on the occasion of the sinking of the *Britannic*.

I feel, however, that occasion should not pass without conveying to you my personal appreciation for your services and my conviction that you have, by your conduct, added lustre to the records of the Nursing Service.

Yours very truly,
    Alfred Keogh

Director-General
Army Medical Service[69]

By the end of November, U-boats had managed to sink or capture 195 ships, totalling 348,627 tons, building on their successes in recent months. Twenty additional ships were damaged.[70]

In December 1916, the terrible Battle of Verdun finally ended in a tactical victory for France, but both France and Germany suffered great losses. Meanwhile, with losses in merchant shipping beginning to add up, many in the British Government and Admiralty were becoming alarmed. Former Admiral of the Fleet John Jellicoe had been appointed First Sea Lord in November 1916, and was just beginning to serve in that capacity. David Beatty replaced him as Admiral of the Fleet. Prior to being appointed to his new position, Jellicoe had written to the Admiralty expressing grave concerns over the losses of shipping to U-boats, citing 'the ever increasing menace of the enemy's submarine attack on our trade'. The Admiralty responded that 'No conclusive answer had yet been found to this form of warfare … perhaps no conclusive answer ever will be found. We must for the present be content will palliation'.

When Jellicoe was appointed as First Sea Lord, he was specifically charged with defeating the U-boat menace. The increased rate of sinkings had spurred British researchers to explore new countermeasures. Hydrophones, underwater listening devices that could detect U-boats, were in development, and depth charges continued to be improved, although the rate of manufacturing and quantity available to ships remained completely insufficient when compared to the number needed. Unfortunately, Jellicoe was very opposed to the implementation of a full convoy system, despite the promise that just such an approach showed as a U-boat deterrent. Jellicoe and the Royal Navy did, however, set up the Anti-Submarine Division in December 1916 to find new ways of combating the growing threat.

Another big change for Great Britain occurred on 5 December when Prime Minister Herbert H. Asquith resigned. Asquith, who was considered an ineffective wartime leader, had formed a coalition government in 1915. However, he was not strongly supported by members within his own Liberal party, by the Conservative party, or even by the press. Because of Asquith's apparent ineffectiveness, Secretary of State for War David Lloyd George, who had succeeded Lord Kitchener in

British Prime Minister David Lloyd George. (*Collier's*, 1917/Authors' Collection)

that capacity, plotted with other Conservative party members to force Asquith's resignation. George and others within the government had wanted to implement additional conscription of troops, and George demanded an inner war cabinet which Asquith would not be included in. Asquith protested, so George took the other Conservative party members and left the coalition in response. With little remaining support, Asquith resigned, being unwilling to serve under anyone else. George succeeded Asquith as Prime Minister two days later on 7 December.[71]

Also on 5 December, Germany and the Central Powers made a public 'peace offer' to the Allies, stating in a note that they were willing to have discussions on the matter, and should their enemies refuse, that 'the odium of continuing the war will fall on them. War-weariness … will then grow and generate new support for the elements that are pushing for peace. In Germany and among its Allies, too, the desire for peace has become keen'. However, the note, viewed as arrogant and insolent in tone, was received with scepticism by the Allies. The rejection of the offer pushed the German Government towards the implementation of unrestricted submarine warfare, in order to end the war quickly.[72]

At sea near the end of December, Karl Walter, a former musical and dramatic critic for the *Kansas City Star*, was heading to the war in Europe. He had resigned his position at the newspaper in November to join up with the British Army. Walter was travelling aboard the America Line's SS *St Louis*. Walter's account tells of the mood that Americans had toward the war at this stage of the conflict, when it had not yet directly affected the majority in the United States. He also references the SS *Vaterland*, which was still being interned in New Jersey:

SS *St Louis*. (Authors' Collection)

The young American ambulance driver looked across the table. 'Gee!
Zeppelins!' he murmured, as if they were something good to eat.

Of course there weren't any for dinner that night. They never are nowadays,
although they frequently get as far as the east coast, it is said.

The loss of the afterglow that beautiful winter evening was our first wartime
sacrifice, the first unavoidable sign of the times ... [73]

In December, a new monthly record was set, with 209 ships sunk or captured by
U-boats, for a total of 346,798 tons of shipping lost. Fourteen additional ships
were damaged. However, the ever-increasing number of ships falling victim to
submarines was not the biggest story as December drew to a close. With the
Royal Navy blockade of Germany putting severe strain on the German populace
and threatening it with starvation, and the catastrophic number of troops lost in
battles that year, the situation was getting desperate.

The German leadership knew that a significant change in strategy was needed.
To that aim, Chief of the Admiralty Staff Henning von Holtzendorff drafted a
memorandum on 22 December 1916 stating that it was a necessity for wholly
unrestricted submarine warfare to be implemented at the earliest opportunity.
His memo contained a statistical analysis indicating that if Germany could sink
an average of 600,000 tons of merchant shipping per month, numbers which
he considered imminently attainable, and could maintain this level of losses for
five months, that Britain would be forced to begin rationing food, and soon,
would have no choice but to sue for peace. It was expected that such terrible
losses would also deter two-fifths of shipping from neutral nations trading with
England from continuing to do so due to the high risk.

Von Holtzendorff's analysis indicated that an intensified U-boat campaign that
continued to operate under prize rules would only be capable of reducing the
shipping reaching England by half of what unrestricted submarine warfare could
– not nearly enough. Speaking to this point, he said 'I consider it unthinkable
that the current English leadership under Lloyd George, who is absolutely
determined, could be forced to make peace on these grounds'. Von Holtzendorff
made a strong case that the ongoing arming of merchant ships would soon
offset the number of losses U-boats were capable of inflicting if they continued
adhering to prize rules, a very reasonable point.

Von Holtzendorff pointed out another unexpected factor which could
favourably impact Germany if unrestricted submarine warfare was implemented:
in 1916, there was a poor crop yield, which left grain supplies low. He reasoned,
based on a study by Dr Richard Fuss, the renowned director of the Magdeburg-
based banking institute, that unrestricted submarine warfare could starve Britain
into submission quickly. The projected losses of merchant shipping would not

allow Britain to receive the necessary amount of grain imports and to sustain the war economy simultaneously.

Von Holtzendorff acknowledged that this strategy would risk America entering the war on the side of the Allies. But if the unrestricted U-boat campaign was begun soon enough, England could be forced to seek a peace agreement before America could fully mobilise its military enough to impact the outcome of the war. He stated that 'Therefore my conclusion is that a campaign of unrestricted submarine warfare, launched in time to produce a peace before the harvest of the summer 1917 – i.e. 1 August – has to accept the risk of American belligerence, because we have no other option. In spite of the diplomatic rupture with America, the unrestricted submarine warfare is nevertheless the right means to conclude this war victoriously. It is also the only means to this end'. Von Holtzendorff took care to point out that the arrangements necessary for an unrestricted submarine warfare campaign could be carried out within three weeks' time.[74]

Overall, 1,517 ships were sunk or damaged by U-boats in 1916.[75] The number of U-boats lost in action totalled twenty-two.[76] The number of new U-boats built during the year was 108, which would prove to be the highest number built by Germany in any year of the war.[77] As the year came to a close, the stage was set for the most horrific portion of the First Battle of the Atlantic. Germany had been forced into a corner, and would not be content to roll over and quit. The coming year appeared ominous indeed.

4

Unrestricted, 1917

January–February 1917

People awoke on New Year's Day 1917 to headlines such as, 'Allies Decline to Enter Peace Talk; Disclaim Blame'. The *Bay City Times* of Michigan went on to say that the 5 December 'peace offer' from Germany was just a 'war maneuver'. As this was being debated, the Cunard liner-turned-auxiliary transport HMT *Ivernia* was sunk by *UB-47* with over 120 lives lost. The commander was William Turner, who had been captain during the *Lusitania*'s final voyage. The sea was becoming more and more strewn with wreckage and bodies with each passing week.

Dr Charles Riley, the Anglican Archbishop of Perth, was travelling as Chaplain-General of the Australian forces and later gave an account of the sinking:

> I was in the smoke room reading when the shock came. Every bit of glass in the room was shattered to atoms. I went upstairs and saw that two boats on the starboard side had been smashed to atoms. There was a great volume of smoke and water, and we were given to understand that the men below had been killed. They began to lower the boats, and into mine twice as many got in as should have done. In this boat there was no officer or sailor, so I had to take charge, and I was delighted when I got the whole crew safely aboard a trawler. There was only standing room on the trawler, and we had to stand for 10 hours while being towed into harbour. I am often asked, what does it feel like to be torpedoed. I can only say I cannot explain, but I hope it will never occur to me again.[1]

A similar story was told by survivor W.H. Field in a letter home to his mother:

> The *Ivernia* was attacked at 10.50 a.m. on New Year's Day. The sea was rough. The torpedo struck the engine-room, killing all the stokers except one, who had come up on deck three minutes before for a smoke. We threw rafts and boxes overboard. I jumped into the water, and with others was rescued by a

Survivors from HMT *Ivernia* struggle to stay afloat in the ocean and in a swamped lifeboat. (Authors' Collection)

destroyer. There were many terrible scenes. I would much rather be in the trenches than go through, the experience again.[2]

Meanwhile, on 9 January, the Pless Conference was held. This was a secret meeting between the Kaiser, Chancellor von Bethmann-Hollweg and the German military leadership to determine the direction of the war. With gridlock on the Western Front, and the Royal Navy blockade literally starving out the German populace, a drastic change was needed. Chief of the General Staff Paul von Hindenburg argued that the 'war must be brought to an end by whatever means as soon as possible'. Soon the conversation turned to unrestricted submarine warfare, and to Chief of the Admiralty Staff von Holtzendorff's December 1916 memorandum on the subject. The scene proceeded in the following way:

> Everyone stood around a large table, on which the Kaiser, pale and excited, leaned his hand. Holtzendorff spoke first, and, from the standpoint of the navy, both well and above all in confidence of victory. England will lie on the ground in at most six months, before a single American has set foot on the continent; the American danger does not disturb him at all. Hindenburg spoke very briefly, observing

German Chief of the General Staff Paul von Hindenburg. (*Collier's*, 1917/ Authors' Collection)

only that from the measure a reduction in American munitions exports had to be expected. Bethmann finally, with a visible inner excitement, set forth once again the reasons that had led him in the past to cast an opposing vote against a U-boat war beyond the limits of cruiser warfare, namely concern about the prompt entry of America into the ranks of our enemies, with all the ensuing consequences, but he closed by saying that in view of the recently altered stand of the Supreme Command and the categorical declarations of the admirals as to the success of the measure, he wished to withdraw his opposition. The Kaiser followed his statements with every sign of impatience and opposition and declared in closing that the unrestricted U-boat war was therefore decided.[3]

On 25 January, the armed merchant cruiser HMS *Laurentic* was on a voyage from Liverpool to Halifax. Initially built for the Dominion Line as the *Alberta*, it was transferred over to the White Star Line before its launch. The one-funnel vessel served primarily on the Liverpool–Montreal route until she became a troopship in 1914, transporting Canadian soldiers. The ship struck two mines laid by *U-80* and sank, killing 354 of those aboard. The vessel's commander, Captain Reginald Norton, gave the following account:

… I was on the bridge when a violent explosion occurred abreast the foremast on the port side, followed twenty seconds later by a similar explosion abreast the engine room on the port side. Nothing was seen in the water prior to the explosion. The ship was steaming at full speed ahead. No lights were showing.

I ordered full speed astern, fired a rocket, gave the order to turn out the boats and tried to send a wireless call for help but found that the second explosion had stopped the dynamo.

… One hundred and twenty [survivors were in the water] … To the best of my knowledge, all the men got safely into the boats. The best of order prevailed after the explosion. The officers and men lived up to the best traditions of the Navy.

At about 45 minutes after the explosion, prior to leaving the ship, I went around the vessel below with an electric torch and satisfied myself that there were no men in the ship. The vessel was then very low in the water. At last when I entered a waiting lifeboat bumping dangerously alongside the ship was sinking, but owing to the darkness and rough weather we did not actually see her sink.

… Possibly some were killed in the engine room, but I have been unable to ascertain that owing to the fact that no survivors are left of the men on watch. I know that all the men got up from the stokehold. The deaths were all due to exposure, owing to the coldness of the night. My own boat was almost full of water when we were picked up by a trawler the next morning.[4]

Following her sinking, *Laurentic* was referred to by divers as, 'The Gold Ship' due to the large numbers of gold bars carried aboard its final voyage. Most of these were later recovered.[5]

Meanwhile, President Wilson made another attempt at peace terms while addressing the Senate on 22 January. To the horror of many, on 31 January, Germany announced 'ruthless' submarine warfare starting at midnight on 1 February.[6] This was in compliance with the Kaiser's signed orders. Upon hearing the news, Chancellor von Bethmann-Hollweg privately declared that 'Germany is finished', a view echoed by many in the German civilian government.

In January, a total of 211 ships equalling 376,874 tons were sunk or captured by U-boats, a new record. Eleven additional ships were damaged. With the start of unrestricted submarine warfare imminent, the number of ships sunk was about to increase dramatically.[7] Germany had no fewer than 111 U-boats on patrol at the beginning of the month, and manufacturing continued to be increased to meet the new demands of the war.[8]

At the beginning of February 1917, the news that Germany was implementing unrestricted submarine warfare dominated headlines. In New York, the RMS *Laconia* was about to begin a crossing to Liverpool. The twin-funnelled liner was the pet ship of Cunard officials, according to its purser, Charles Spedding. Due to set sail on 17 February, it was held up due to paperwork and the crew lost half a day.

A surviving daily newspaper printed aboard the ship on 24 February gives the news of the day. British Prime Minister George announced further import restrictions when submarine parts were found at Cartagena, resulting in the

RMS *Laconia*. (Authors' Collection)

arrest of three Germans. Most notably, it was reported that, 'only a miracle can indefinitely postpone a creation of something approaching a state of war between the United States and Germany'. Meanwhile, the passengers and crew indulged in a rousing concert which was detailed in the newspaper:

> Isolate half a hundred human beings on a steamer in mid-ocean, open a room large enough for their convention … throw in one piano, pour in one wholesome measure of willing charitable-ness … stir to a dual patriotic boiling point, and then set aside to cool in pleasant memory—the concert of February 22nd, in the Lounge aboard the S.S. *Laconia*.
>
> The programme opened with two excellent selections by Mr. W. Ballyn whose rich baritone carried the pleasing story of 'Tired Hands' and 'Nuthin'. Mr. F. Paulding was roundly applauded for his rendering of 'When the Ebb Tide Flows'. 'Leet'el Grey Hom' in de wes' afforded ample opportunities for the delicious pronunciation of Miss Mitsie Marsa. Mr. Arthur A. Holland expounded the alphabet through the whole gamut of oratorical writhing, and inflections.
>
> Mr. Charles S. Wood, with eyes directed steadfastly towards the lounge hearth, sang 'For Ever and For Ever', until relieved by the presentation of flowers. Mr. J. Harris made the sea more lovable, even to the mal-de-mer club, with his 'I Love to be a Sailor' and 'I Want to Marry-arry' presented with mirth provoking comments that would make one Lauder turn green. Master Morwood Howie, with the keyboard at the level of his chin, accomplished a pianoforte solo with great promise. 'Le Credo du Paysan' afforded a vehicle for the pleasing baritone of Mr. H. C. Braun. Mr. Sewell H. Gregory sang 'John Peel' with an earnestness that started the audience unconsciously humming the old English hunting song.
>
> The Rev. F. Dunstan Sargent, the able organiser of the Concert, was chairman, and spoke eloquently on behalf of the Seaman's Institution of Liverpool, and afterwards announced the collection, which netted £14 7s. 7d. Mr. W.A. Trethowan sang 'The Skipper' to unstinted applause. Miss Phyllis Barker proved the efficacy of the kind, if insincere remark over the violent and gruff one, in her recitation of 'The Matinee Hat'. 'Before the Dawn', sang by Mr. John B. Newman, was well received. Miss Mitsie Marsa rendered in French, 'Berceuse de Jocelyn' and evoked well earned applause. 'The Charge of the Light Brigade' as charged by Mr. H.B. Pope afforded ample grounds for the preference of charges against some of the elocutionists he imitated. Miss Marsa and Mr. Wood indulged in affectionate tableaux while the latter sang 'Bid Me to Love' con expressione. A piano duet entitled, 'Sweet Smiles' by Master Morwood Howie and Miss Catherine Howie was greatly appreciated. Miss B.M. Finlay and Mr. J.P. Savin played the accompaniments. The concert concluded with the singing of 'God Save the King' and 'America' by all present.[9]

On 25 February, the *Laconia* was west of Ireland when it was struck by a torpedo from *U-50*, commanded by Kapitänleutnant Gerhard Berger. The vessel managed to stay afloat, and time was given for the *Laconia's* passengers and crew to abandon ship. Twenty minutes later, another torpedo was fired into it to finish the job. Since there were US citizens aboard the vessel, the attack was a sign that the new U-boat campaign was indeed underway.

While at the American Consulate in Queenstown on 27 February, several of the *Laconia's* surviving officers and crewmembers filed an affidavit in front of Consul Wesley Frost:

We, W.R.D. Irvine, captain; A.W. Robertson, chief officer; H. Morrison, first officer; G. Jones, second officer; and C.T. Spedding, purser; of the late British S.S. *Laconia*, being duly sworn, do affirm:

That the *Laconia* cleared from New York on February 17, 1917, bound for Liverpool, with a general cargo (including cotton, foodstuffs, and nonexplosive munitions), with 77 passengers and 217 officers and crew.

That on February 25, 1917 at 10.53 p.m. G.M.T., or 9.50 p.m. A.T., the vessel was torpedoed without any warning whatever, on the starboard side in No. 5 hold aft of the engines and listed to starboard. The passengers and crew took to the boats without disorder, although owing to the list, the starboard boats got away with least difficulty and consequently carried most of the women and children.

That the ship's way was stopped immediately when the vessel was struck by the torpedo to facilitate in taking to the boats. Approximately twenty minutes after the first torpedo, when most of the boats were clear of the ship, a second torpedo was fired, striking the *Laconia* on the starboard side fair amidships. At the time she was torpedoed, the vessel was making a speed of approximately 16 knots per hour. Her navigational lights were not showing and no other lights out board. The lights were extinguished at once. The ship sank about 60 minutes after the first torpedo had struck.

That some 12 boats got away, and that as far as is known 12 lives were lost in taking to the boats. The sky was overcast, so that it would have been utterly impossible for the submarine to have seen the protecting 4.7 gun on the stern of the *Laconia*. As there was not the slightest prior intimation of the presence of the submarine there could be and was not the slightest attempt to escape or resist the submarine. The wireless apparatus was put into service immediately upon the impact of the first torpedo, and was in touch with Admiralty vessels immediately. Nine rockets were also sent up to indicate the vessel's position. The sea consisted of heavy swells, with a height of 10 to 12 feet from trough to crest, and there was a rather light breeze with considerable chill in the air as the night wore on.

That the submarine came alongside the lifeboat which was in charge of
Officer Coppin and asked for the Captain, and made inquiries concerning the
ship's cargo. No offer of assistance was made and no inquiry as to casualties. As
the ladies in the boat were apprehensive, the submarine Officer, who spoke
excellent English, reassured them and said that the Admiralty patrols were on
their way to the scene and would reach it in a very few hours.

That the Admiralty vessel reached the boats between 3.30 and 5 a.m.,
February 26; and gradually took on board their occupants, the operation being
very difficult by the heavy swells. In one boat, No. 8, there were deaths from
exposure.

The *Laconia*'s third officer, Joseph Coppin, filed the following affidavit at
the American Consulate in Liverpool on 2 March in front of Consul Horace
L. Washinton:

> ... I was extra third officer of the Cunard S.S. *Laconia* ... All went well until
> the evening of Sunday, the 25th, when at about 9.30 the *Laconia* was torpedoed
> by a German submarine ... The *Laconia* was torpedoed without warning. She
> carried one gun in the stern for defense purposes. Her cargo was mainly cotton
> ... Fifteen minutes after the torpedo hit the *Laconia* about seven boats were clear
> of the ship, and I was in No. 13. Shortly after this the submarine fired another
> torpedo into the *Laconia*, and then a little while afterwards the submarine came
> within speaking distance of the life boat in which I was and inquired as to
> the tonnage of the vessel. The reply from the boat stated the tonnage of the
> ship at eighteen thousand. The submarine then said a patrol would pick us up.
> The submarine left us and we were picked up by a patrol boat about 4.30 on
> Monday morning after suffering seven hours' exposure in an open boat.

In his affidavit, Gerald Kennedy, the *Laconia*'s surgeon, described the conversation
with the U-boat's commander. His affidavit was filed the same day and at the
same location as Washington's:

> ... about twenty minutes after we had left the ship the submarine ... came
> alongside, and ... hailed our boat and called 'pull alongside'. A general
> conversation in our boat then resulted, a number of people making replies
> to the general effect of the best method of bringing the boat alongside the
> submarine.
>
> There was a big swell so we were unable to get alongside of the submarine on
> account of the danger, but we did get within about five yards. The conversation
> from the submarine was conducted by one man, and this person, as well
> as I could see, was leaning out of the conning tower. His tone was entirely

impersonal. I assume he was the Commander of the submarine. He spoke English fairly well.

The first question he asked was 'What is the tonnage of your ship?' Somebody forward in the boat replied that the tonnage was 18,000 tons. He then asked the name of the vessel, and it was shouted out generally *Laconia*. The third question he asked was the tonnage again. There were general replies, repeating the tonnage. He then shouted back, confirming our reply, '18,000 tons'. The fourth time he repeated '18,000 tons' with evident pleasure at the size of the ship.

It appeared to me that he did not know what was the vessel he had torpedoed, as he seemed particularly pleased on ascertaining that it was so large a ship. His fifth question was, 'How many passengers were on board?' We answered 78. I think the next thing he said was that there would be a patrol out in between two or three hours, which would pick us up. The submarine then went on its way.

That when we were drawing near the submarine prior to the above recorded conversation taking place, some of the occupants of my life boat were fearful that the submarine intended shelling the boat and said excitedly, 'They are going to fire on us'. I then heard a man on the submarine laughing derisively at the natural apprehension and agitation of the occupants of the boat ... [10]

Another one of the survivors was Jacob Fotheringham, a businessman from Sydney, Australia. He gave a very detailed private account of the sinking after the rescue. His account is tinged with racially insensitive language which was common during the time period:

We left New York Harbour ... Sunday morning, February 18th ... and there was much discussion as to when we should get to Liverpool. The first information we got was on the following Sunday night at dinner, when the wireless man came down and handed the Captain a message ... The Captain was quite unconcerned and laid the message on the table and went on with the course he was having. After dinner he ... said, 'I can relieve some of your gentlemen's curiosity, for I may inform you that we shall be docked at Liverpool before 8 o'clock Monday night'. Everybody was delighted. He went away to the bridge, as he was very rarely off it the whole of the time ... there was a suggestion that we should get up a Testimonial for him, on account of the strenuous time he had had. It was agreed to quite unanimously ... It was suggested that we should buy some pieces of plate engraved 'From the Passengers of the *Laconia*' and the date. It was left in my hands to get the subscriptions by Monday morning ... we had a four at Bridge, which we played every night. We had just got into the first rubber when the bang came. It wasn't a terrible explosion, but you could hear the glass everywhere. Everybody jumped up and made a rush. We had been drilled, of course, every day, in what we were to do … I was on boat No. 8. I went to the cabin and got my overcoat. Fortunately we hadn't dressed for dinner that night. I got my life-belt and cap and writing case and wasn't very long in getting on deck. There was no disorder at all … There were a few kiddies, who all had their life-belts on. One little fellow had on a little jersey suit and a life-belt, an exact copy of mine in a smaller edition, and he looked the funniest character on deck. He was always very proud of himself when he did his boat drill.

I went to our boat and found Mrs. [Mary] Hoy and Miss [Elizabeth] Hoy, rich people in Chicago, there. They were very reserved people who kept to themselves pretty much. Some of the sailors were in the boat and some of the firemen were getting the tackles ready and these ladies didn't know what to do. We had to step over another raft to get into our boat – a lot of oars tied together. We handed the ladies into the boat and I asked about a Mrs. Harris, who was missing, because I knew the number of passengers there should have been. Some of them said they thought she was in another boat so I went round to see if I could find her. No one had seen her. Then I ran across an old fellow [Moritz Marcuse] who had had an operation for cataract and could hardly see. He was floundering about on deck so I … asked him the number of his boat. He told me it was No. 10 and I was only just in time to get him in. I hadn't time to look for Mrs. Harris … as they were getting ready to lower our boat. The other boats were lowered and away, with bright red lights. They were launched properly and were full of people and were rowing away from the ship.

Something went wrong with No. 10 boat; it was stuck up a bit … but they eventually got it into the water and got away … I called to No. 10 boat to tell them not to row away yet. It was a huge mistake. They should have stood by till they saw we were alright; They were all talking at the same time in our boat, There was an engineer giving orders and a couple of sailors and a fireman all ordering and nobody seemed to know what to do. There was absolute confusion. One of the sailors said 'Are the plugs in the boat?' That shows what a farce our boat drill was, for it was the first time I knew that the plugs were not always in a boat. One sailor said 'Yes, they are alright', but I do not believe they were in the boat …

They started to lower for'ard first. They let her go and she went down and we were at such an angle that we had to hold on to the seats to hold ourselves in … No one was in charge so I thought I had better take charge myself. I said 'Don't lower any more; try to lift it', to the man who had lowered the boat. He said he couldn't because it was choked. Somebody said 'Cut it away; has anybody got a knife?' I said "For God's sake don't cut it; climb up the rope and see what is wrong with it'. They said it was quite free … There was a ridge round the ship and we had got jammed on to that and were really resting on a ledge. The only thing we could do was to try and push the boat off. I said 'Get a couple of oars out. Has anyone got a knife?' They were all tied down in about ten places. Nobody had a knife. I had a little bit of a pen-knife and I cut away and got an oar out eventually and we pushed on to it. I said 'Let her go off there now' and they let her go suddenly and she came against the side and of course that did the damage. It must have knocked off about 6 feet and sprung a plank and did tremendous damage. They started to lower away and we struck the water and she buried, I suppose, about a quarter of the boat's nose in water and then she righted herself. We were just over our ankles in water. That would not have mattered but … we could not get away from the ship; we kept hanging on to the side of her … we couldn't shift her and I found the water coming up to my knees. If I could have got a rope I would have climbed back to the ship but I missed it. Some of the women screamed out, 'The boat is sinking. Pull back to the ship'. I said 'We can't get back to the ship … Get clear of it so that it doesn't come down on our boat'. We righted again and I looked up and found the ship was over the top of us and she seemed to drop about 5 or 6 feet all at once. I made a desperate effort with the oar … and we gave her another push and we got past the ship altogether. By this time the water was floating over both gunwales. Of course she kept afloat the whole time, but we were in water all the time. When we got away from the ship I said, 'See if you can find the lanterns or the lamps', but they couldn't find them at all … One of the passengers had a little electric torch and we flashed that, but nobody saw us. We organised a call for help but there was not a sign of anybody and we gradually drifted away and saw the boats going away from us in an opposite direction till we must have been more than a mile from any of them. By this time one of the passengers, a Manchester man [William Robinson], very delicate, became very sea-sick. He was at the other end of the boat and they tried to hold his head up for some time, but the waves were coming over us because we were in a fairly big swell. Every time the waves came over us the women screamed and this man was in a terrible state until he just collapsed into the boat, face downwards, and was dead in about ten minutes. He floated out of the boat … All the time Mrs. Hoy and her daughter would stand up in the boat. They would have been just as safe if they had sat down, but they wanted to keep out of the water as far as possible, as they were up to their knees when standing. But if they had sat down it would have been much safer … for every time the boat gave a lurch they grabbed at each other. The engineer and I jumped over the side of the boat … and we got the boat straightened up; but Mrs. Hoy moaned and got in a terrible state and she gradually collapsed and fell back in the boat and that was the end of her. The daughter was screaming about her Mother and threw herself on top of her Mother, and they were really drowned in the boat and did not die from exhaustion, though it was cold enough to have killed them in that time. Then there was a big n****r. He [Tom Coffey] was from the very start almost dead with fright and all he did was to pray 'Jesus, save me, save me for the Lord God's sake. Oh, ma poor old Mother, ma poor old Mother'. I shut him up because the other woman was getting into hysterics too. This n****r kept boring into me. He had his head right under my chin and he was trying to get me out of my position. I had to stop him by just giving him a blow on the head. He was lying right across me and I couldn't get him off for he was 15 stone. Afterwards he rolled over and became unconscious and the water was coming over rapidly, so whether he was drowned or absolutely died from fright, I do not know, but in about an hour's time he was as cold and dead as could be. I said to the engineer that we had better do something for we could not keep that dead weight in the boat. I asked him if he could get to the two ladies, because he was, nearer than I was. He … could not move because he had got his foot caught but afterwards he got to the ladies and said they were both dead. I asked him to give me a hand with the n****r and we had a terrible job to get him overboard and were pretty tired and exhausted. Then we got across to the ladies and by that time the other woman, an actress [Mitsie Marsa], saw what we were doing and started to scream at us. She said 'What are you doing, what are you doing? You wretches, you beasts!' That was awful. I tried to calm her. I told her that if any of us were going to be saved our only chance was to get anybody who was dead out of the way. The man [Cedric Ivatts] the actress was with was in a bad way and she was trying to hold him up. She was all the time thinking of nothing but him. She was holding his head up, and she got her handkerchief out and tied it round his head and was trying all she knew to keep the water from him. She asked whether I could make something for his head to lie on. I put an oar across and his weight kept it down. She took something off herself and put it under his neck, and she hadn't very much on, either, for she was in evening dress, and she laid him down there and he was, by that time, unconscious. When she saw us getting rid of the other bodies she laid across him and put her cheek down on his face and laid there a long time. She either slept or fainted; there was no movement for an hour and a half. Before I put the n****r overboard the storeman asked me to give him the n****r's life-belt because he hadn't got one himself … it took me a terribly long time to undo the knots. I got it off … and I believe that saved the storeman's life, for he was only in his singlet and pants, no boots or shoes or stockings, and was shivering with cold but the life-belts are very warm … There were four of us left … and we huddled close up together to keep warm … Then a fireman who had been talking to himself for a while started raving. He got up and screamed and went right clean mad. He didn't know what he was saying and he used the most foul language and before I knew what was happening he had gone overboard. The worst part of it was that when he went overboard he dragged with him the man who had the torch, which we were saving till we could use it with some chance of doing good with it. The man who owned the torch let it go to save himself and so our only light was gone. I thought we were done then for we could see the three flash lights in different parts and we knew there were three boats picking up the others. All the other boats had a light and I could pick out the 7 different lights at different times and as each light disappeared we knew another boat had been picked up, till the whole of the boats had been picked up, including the Captain's boat. We were told afterwards that the Captain said there was one boat missing ... The patrol boat said they couldn't do anything in the dark ... so all they could do was to hang round till morning. Another of the firemen was the next to go. He was sitting right beside me ... I saw him gradually getting weaker and I tried to prop him up several times, trying to raise his head on my knees. But at last ... he died, never opening his mouth or struggling. I left him for a long time, but he was quite cold when we put him overboard. Then I would have put the friend of the actress overboard, for I knew he was dead, but I hadn't the heart to do so when she was laying on him trying to keep him warm.

... the whole night didn't seem more than an hour to me, but the Captain said afterwards it was because I was so busy and he believes that saved me after the flash lights had all gone out and we were left absolutely in the dark, the engineer said, 'I think I have had enough'. I said, 'What do you mean?' He said 'I am not going to suffer; I would rather finish it now'. He held out his hand and shook hands with me. I said, 'For God's sake don't do that. While there is life there is hope. You are as strong as I am and I don't feel I am going to die yet. It is a thousand to one we shall be picked up if we can hang it out'. He said, 'I would rather finish it now without suffering'. I said, 'Don't be silly'. He said, 'Take my advice and you will too'. I said, 'I won't while there is a breath left in me' and just shortly afterwards one of the sailors said, 'There is day breaking'. I said, 'That is not day breaking yet; it won't be day for another four hours yet'. He repeated 'That is day breaking'. I had my watch but I never thought it would be going, but it had not stopped. I took it out to look but we couldn't see. We waited about half an hour and then we saw it was 5.15, that was really 6.15, because we hadn't altered the time. It ... began to lighten up and about a quarter of an hour afterwards one of the sailors yelled out, 'There's a torpedo boat' ... I could not see anything. He said, 'Wait till we get up on the next wave' and then I saw three of them, we could just see them, apparently about six miles away. I just began to realise then that we were going to be saved. I thought they would get us within another hour and I felt I could last another hour even if the boat went from under us; for she had been gradually settling and even our part was under water then and I was afraid every minute some of the water-tight compartments would give out and she would have gone down. They told me that just after we were taken out of her the boat went down; there was not much left of her. When we saw the boats I said, 'Let's try to rig up something that will be seen'. To a big n****r in front of me who had said nothing the whole time and had kept perfectly quiet, I said, 'Can you get that oar out?' He said, 'I can't move my legs'. I said 'Never mind about your legs, your arms'. He said, 'No, I can't'. The only other thing he had said all the time was when I had asked him to help me lift one of the bodies and he replied, 'No, I never touch no dead men', and he wouldn't put a hand on one of them. He wouldn't help to lift the oar up, so I asked one of the storemen, and finally it took three of us to lift it up, for we were dead meat. The n****r had a hard black hat and I had often heard that a black object could be seen waved about better than a white one. So we tied the hat on to the end of the handkerchief, and knocked a hole through the brim of the hat to secure it. The n****r said, 'Don't you take my hat'. I threatened to knock his head off if he didn't shut up. The three of us waved the thing round and round … They didn't take any notice and I thought they couldn't see us … All of a sudden a flash light was thrown right across us. I said, 'That's alright, he has seen us'. Two of the boats raced up to us, trying which could get to us first. It seemed about an hour, but I suppose it was about 20 minutes. They had picked up all the other boats … When they saw the condition we were in they wouldn't risk bringing the boat to us and we saw each of them lower a boat and there was race to see who would get to us first. It was the finest thing I ever saw. One boat got a good way ahead of the other and called out to us, 'Don't anybody move, lay there, don't attempt to move'. There wasn't one of us who could move. I had no feeling from the waist downwards; I didn't know I had legs on me. They came along on a big swell and we lost sight of them now and again. Then just as they were coming down, one of the sailors jumped clean overboard with rope and landed beautifully … He landed just … across the boat, and got the rope round the woman [the actress] like lightning and pulled her through the water and she was on the vessel in two seconds. Another one took the man who was with the actress, thinking he was alive. Then they took an elderly man [Arthur Naylor] who was in our boat. I was the second last to be taken. When the sailor got up to me he saw me trying to move and told me to sit still. (Both boats had got up to us by that time and were on each side of us.) … I just remember someone getting me by the back of the neck and I came down on an anchor and then I found had legs! They got us over to the ship and had the greatest trouble to get us on board because the sea had got up very strong by then and I was afraid the companion-way they had lowered would be smashed; they had to be very careful maneuvering it. They put ropes round each of us and got hold of the rope and held on to us. We got knocked about a good bit. I went against something not very soft. When they got me on deck, two of them put their arms under me and carried me along down below, close to the stoke-hold. It was quite warm. They laid me down on the floor and lifted my head up and one man said, 'Get outside of this', which was a glass nearly full of rum, with some hot water and sugar, and he poured it down me. That brought me round a bit and I felt much better. They took off my boots and clothes and lifted me into a big tub of hot water and then I ached some-thing fearfully … it was worse than the violent pains in my stomach. The hot water relieved these, but it only lasted for about ten minutes and they laid me down on deck and a couple of them rubbed me very hard and dried me and got a flannel jacket, a big pair of woolen drawers and lifted me up into a hammock and I think I must have been asleep in about three minutes. From 7.30 to 4 o'clock I never woke. When I awoke some of them were there and they said the Captain had been down about a dozen times and he was much annoyed because I was a saloon passenger and had been put to sleep amongst the sailors. He came to me and said he was very sorry. I told him I had been ten times more comfortable than if I had been in his bed, and added I couldn't have been better looked after. He asked me to come and have some dinner with him when I felt inclined, but I told him the sailors were going to look after me. I told him they had been so kind that I did not like to leave them. They might not have liked it and would have felt it was very ungrateful. I didn't feel much inclined to eat anything so they gave me some more rum.

The actress was still alive, but she was unconscious and was nearly naked when they rescued her. They stripped her and put her in warm water and rubbed her and wrapped her in warm blankets. They buried the man at three o'clock in the afternoon off the vessel, before she became conscious. She was very bad all night and they had to get a nurse for her, when we were taken to a hotel at Bantree. Before we were landed there we picked up another boat-load from a sailing ship that had been torpedoed and they told us there was still another boat missing, so we waited till 1 o'clock before they started to bring us in when they got a wireless saying the other boat had been picked up. We got in there at 11 o'clock at night. The whole of the township were on the pier. They had a hearse waiting for the body and the actress saw it. When she first woke up on the patrol boat she had been terribly bad and wanted to do away with herself, and tried to open an artery in her arm. She talked of nothing else but the man the whole time. A couple of cars were waiting for us, to take us to the hotel.

The Captain told us afterwards that it was about a quarter to ten when we were torpedoed. He immediately shut the engines off and put the lights out, just temporarily. A little while after he put the lights up again. Then he gave us the five blasts of the whistle and he saw all the boats get away, but he didn't know their condition. He went down into the hold to see in what condition the ship was and he found she was on fire. He had the hose turned on to put the fire out. He kept some of the crew with him. There was not much water coming in and he reckoned he could have saved the ship and got her towed to port. He had the wireless operator on board all the time and he had been told that the patrol boats would pick us up, as they were on their way … Then the Captain went up on the bridge … He had every hope of getting the ship off, when the next thing he saw was a submarine within 200 yards and one of the boats was close to it. The Captain of the submarine asked in good English what was the name of the boat. He knew quite well but wanted to make sure. He sent another shot right into the engine room and everything went into darkness. The steward was waiting for the Captain and asked if there was anything else to do. The Captain said no, and told the steward to look to himself then. They had one boat waiting … and the steward said, 'Shall we wait for you'. But the Captain said, 'No, you will pick me up alright'. He took off his uniform and put on other clothes in case the Germans did get hold of him. He saw everybody was off and ten minutes after the second torpedo he jumped over himself … The boat had waited for him and he got in it. When he saw us he said what a terrible time we must have had and added he didn't know how any of us were alive. He told me I ought to have had the V.C. [Victoria Cross].

The Cunard Company did everything they could and, so did the hotel people. We were told to go to the store and get everything we wanted. They had dried all my clothes on the patrol boat beautifully, though the clothes were shrunk looked a bit dilapidated. I got a shirt and collar and handkerchief from the store.

We afterwards met the other passengers, over 200, that had landed at Queenstown. We joined their train at Cork and they did give us a reception. The other boats had been alright and had had only just an exciting adventure. One little boy of eight years [Robert Morwood Howie] was asked what he thought of it when the torpedo shock came an answered, 'It is a wonderful experience, isn't it?' They were told at Queenstown that there were only five survivors from our boat and Reginald Downing said at once, 'I'll bet Fotheringham is one'. We afterwards met Mrs. Harris and I told her she had born under a lucky star. She had gone to another boat because Major Owen had made her go with him.[11]

Fotheringham was said to have 'never properly recovered' from the effects of exposure and the stress of the events he experienced. He was just 58 years old when he passed away in 1924.[12]

Assistant Purser William Gerson, as detailed in the previous chapter, had already survived the sinking of the *Laconia*'s sister ship *Franconia* in 1916. During the war, it was not entirely unusual for crewmen to be sunk multiple times. In the following account, he detailed his second wreck:

Sunday, February 25 dawned. To me, it meant that usual run of routine duties including divine service, but … conversation veered around to the German threat. That night we were to enter the danger zone; and incidentally to pass through the major physical crisis of our lives.

When the dinner gong sounded at six bells, I took my usual place at the head of a table in the dining saloon with four ladies and two gentlemen as my companions. Three of the young ladies [Margery Chapman, Dorothy Chapman and Margaret Monro] who were from Philadelphia [sic] showed their anxiety, but said nothing at first. Next to me sat a most self-confident English matron [Annie Marguerite Howie] and two very cheerful American traveling salesmen.

… one of the Philadelphia ladies addressed me, 'Is there much danger tonight, Mr. Gerson? We heard that you were torpedoed not long ago'. Her question fell like a bomb-shell in our midst. The English matron was not to be shaken from her self-confidence, however … 'I am not afraid. My children will take their baths as usual and get into their bed clothes'.

After completing my walk, I returned to the office and met Engineer Harry Hurtle and Engineer Teddy Mitchell. Together we adjourned to my cabin for an after-dinner highball.

We talked and smoked together, now pausing to catch strains of music from the lounge deck where the orchestra was playing … Mitchell was about to leave, and just as I was saying, 'Good night, Teddy', we heard a terrific thud aft. My first reaction was the thought that the *Laconia* had … caught a mine in her propeller. Instinctively, I thought of the darkness which had settled down upon the *Franconia* when the torpedo came, for the cabin lights here on the *Laconia* remained brilliantly lit.

With an instant I was assured something was wrong, for bedlam had broken out. Ladies … rushed past me to the boat deck. Taking up the cry, 'Abandon ship', I proceeded to the cabin of the self-confident matron. Sure enough, her children (Robert Morwood, Catherine and Howard Howie) were in their night clothes, and … their mother refused the deadly seriousness of the situation.

Snatching up from the bed, her 7 year-old girl … I wrapped it in a blanket and started for the boat deck. I had determined to take the child in lifeboat 2 with me, but the ship had listed so badly that Captain Irvine had ordered the port boats abandoned which meant transferring the child to one of the boats on the starboard side – already well filled and some of them departed. The child put her arms around me, whimpered a bit, but seemed to trust me as I gave her over to eager hands reaching out from one of the life-boats.

Teddy Leake, the second steward … assured me … that the little girl's mother and the other children had been safely placed in one of the boats. I could now direct my attention to other passengers and presently a young woman (Mitsie Marsa) who had already been placed in a life-boat became violently hysterical. Why she picked on me I don't know, but she jumped out of her boat, threw her arms about my neck and let out the most piercing shrieks I have ever heard!

Captain W.R.D. Irvine. (Authors' Collection)

This was too much! I pushed her away, and adopting a rue de guerre, crashed my right to her chin, knowing that this alone would bring her to her senses. She fell to the deck, and after picking her up, I passed her back into the life-boat just as it was being lowered away ... This was the first (and only) time I ever struck a woman, but it was done as a last means of saving her life ... suffice to say she ... proved grateful afterward for my assistance. An open life-boat is better than sinking ship!

Racing down the companionway, I made certain that no passengers were below and returned to find that the last lifeboat had left the ship. Then it was that that I did some real, hard thinking. The deck lights had been switched on to facilitate the lowering of the lifeboats, and those of us who were left realized that the *Laconia* made an easy target for Fritz who was certainly hanging about to shoot another torpedo into her and insure her end.

Two of us stood on deck together – Fourth Engineer Steele and myself. Below we could hear below the bumping of the ship's lifeboats against the ship's side as they were disentangled from their davits ... Worst of all, a flood of light streamed out from the shelter deck just below us, cutting off any vertical view we might have had of the water close to the hull.

'Well, I'm going!' said Steele, grabbing one of the davit ropes preparatory to sliding down ... A moment later, I heard a dull thud and an outcry. Steele had gotten hold of the wrong rope, and had dropped ... seventy feet through the air, crashed into a lifeboat and smashed his backbone.

Sensing the grim outcome of his fall, I determine to wait for the ship to go down and take my chances of ... being saved by floating debris. Smoking ... I paced nervously up and down, knowing at least that when the *Laconia* went, her captain and chief officer would be with me in the water. A moment later, Grinrod, the captain's valet touched me on the shoulder. He attended to the 'old man' to the last.

'What are you going to do, Sir?' he asked anxiously. I told him my plan to wait for the ship's sinking ... I faced almost certain death, and I wondered why I had not given up the sea following the *Franconia* ... people said, 'Why don't you lay off it, Bill?' Naturally, my thoughts turned homeward. Grinrod was thinking of his wife and children. His remark, 'I'm a married man, Sir!' told me that, and

I realized come what might, my duty was to set some sort of example for him. I told him nothing about Steele, but said, 'Come along with me', walked over to the edge of the deck at another point …

'Well, I am going to jump Grinrod. Will you follow?' I said to the captain's man. He gave me his word that he would do so and closing my eyes tightly, I jumped. It seemed an eternity until I reached the water. One thought crowding all others from my mind, 'Will I hit anything?' I struck the water, my first sensation being that of a chill. Gasping for breath, I looked about and saw a lifeboat perhaps six feet away. A moment later Grinrod followed and together we struck out for the boat, I was not to see him again until we landed in Queenstown. Catching hold of the life-line encircling the boat, I made my wrist fast in a half-hitch, so that when the ice-cold water should wear down my last resistance, I would not go under. 'Get me out' I pleaded. A flashlight turned on my face and Harry Turtle, boilermaker recognized me. 'We'll get you out, Bill' he said, and but for [him] … I would not be alive today. The boat was now ordered to clear the ship's side, as Fritz's second torpedo was expected at any moment. Eventually a halt was called and the bow of the boat was turned to meet the waves head-on.

… Harry Turtle, together with a couple of sailors … pulled my feet toward the keel … The lifeboat already contained sixty-one passengers including a dying Negro, but there was 'room' for one more. I was to remain in the water a while longer, however.

A terrific roar was now head from the *Laconia*. All lights suddenly went out and the great Cunarder slowly settled down. The second torpedo had struck … Our hopes were then raised by the appearance of what we took to be a steam trawler, but which we quickly recognized as the U-boat still circling its victim.

'Come along side!' came the sharp command from the U-boat commander. 'We cannot. We have women and children on board,' was our reply. 'What is the name of the ship?' '*Laconia*'. 'What is the tonnage?' 'Eighteen thousand'. A long interrogation followed, after which the submarine commander volunteered the information that a British destroyer would pick us up within two hours and a half, curtly bade us 'Good night' … and his craft disappeared beneath the waves. His work had been well done.

Renewing my struggle to climb on aboard the lifeboat, the water gradually lost its chill, a purple light revolved before me and I fell unconscious. My next sensation was that of lying in the bottom of the boat where I had been laid for dead after being pulled out. Reaching out my hand I discovered later that the companion next to me, in a similar position, was a dead Negro. My feelings were hardly pleasant at this point, but my movements informed the passengers that I had 'come to life' and I was hoisted up to a saint. My memory of this remains blurred, but I recall thinking that unless I revived myself by getting hold

of an oar, things would go black before me again. Feeling gradually returned to
my limbs and I began to pull on the oar while Harry Turtle spoke words of
encouragement.

Then came a voice which I recognized as that of one of the young ladies from
Philadelphia. 'Hello' I mumbled. A cry of delight followed from one, re-echoed
by the other two, 'Pass this over to him', said one, holding out a flask, which a
sailor instantly grabbed from her hand … Before he could drain it, however, she
snatched it back and poured its contents down my throat.

One of the young ladies wrapped her woolen muffler about me and I was able
to do a man's share of the rowing throughout the next seven hours, taking my
turn at bailing out the water in the boat. The waves were high … Towards dawn
we spied a search light sweeping the horizon … We now burned red flares
continuously feeling sure that the searchlight was directed from a destroyer, and
soon distinguished the port and starboard lights of what proved to be H.M.S.
Laburnum. Within a quarter of an hour, we had maneuvered our craft alongside
of her. And with rescue at hand, I fell unconscious; awaking to find myself safely
aboard the rescue ship … Seventeen hours later we reached Queenstown.

As I was being carried on a stretcher down the gangplank following Engineer
Steele, I saw my friend the Englishwoman once more. She gave me just a
glance, saying coldly, 'Who is that?' Informed that I was the assistant purser, she
murmered coldly, 'Too bad!' That was her way of thanking me![13]

American survivor Arthur T. Kirby, a lawyer from Bainbridge, New York, told a
poignant tale of the aftermath of the sinking after arriving in Liverpool aboard
the *Lapland*. A familiar tune triggered bad memories:

Arthur Kirby's *Laconia* immigration card, which he carried off the sinking ship. (Authors' Collection)

On the Tuesday before the *Lapland* sailed we survivors of the *Laconia* had a dinner at the Hotel Barclay in London, and the chief music played was 'Poor Butterfly' the tune that was on the talking machine when we were torpedoed. I'm sure that tune will ring in our hearts as long as they beat.[14]

President Wilson had much to digest following the sinking; amongst the twelve victims were two prominent Americans. The 'overt acts' he had spoken of were coming to fruition. Additionally, Arthur Zimmermann, the Foreign Secretary of the German Empire, was exposed as trying to recruit Mexico against the United States when British Intelligence intercepted his plans. Although tensions between the United States and Mexico were high, the Mexican Government ignored the proposal. The message was initially dismissed by many as a hoax, and later, after it was admitted to be genuine, the German Government claimed that it was a 'what if' only, in case America declared war on Germany. This did little to calm the uproar.[15] Zimmermann's coded telegram said the following:

We intend to begin on the first of February unrestricted submarine warfare. We shall endeavor in spite of this to keep the United States of America neutral. In the event of this not succeeding, we make Mexico a proposal of alliance on the following basis: make war together, make peace together, generous financial support and an understanding on our part that Mexico is to reconquer the lost territory in Texas, New Mexico, and Arizona. The settlement in detail is left to you. You will inform the President of the above most secretly as soon as the outbreak of war with the United States of America is certain and add the suggestion that he should, on his own initiative, invite Japan to immediate adherence and at the same time mediate between Japan and ourselves. Please call the President's attention to the fact that the ruthless employment of our submarines now offers the prospect of compelling England in a few months to make peace.

Signed, Zimmermann[16]

Woodrow Wilson went before Congress on 26 February to bring them up to speed on the current situation and his thoughts on the matter, making the following statements:

You will understand why I can make no definite proposals or forecasts of action now and must ask for your supporting authority in the most general terms. The form in which action may become necessary cannot yet be foreseen. I believe that the people will be willing to trust me to act with restraint, with prudence, and in the true spirit of amity and good faith that they have themselves displayed throughout these trying months; and it is in that belief that I request that you will authorize me to supply our merchant ships with defensive arms, should that become necessary, and with the means of using them, and to employ any other instrumentalities or methods that may be necessary and adequate to protect our ships and our people in their legitimate and peaceful pursuits on the seas.[17]

Wilson was considering a policy of 'armed neutrality', fully arming merchant vessels for defence against U-boats rather than rallying support for an all-out declaration of war. Privately, he believed that Germany was likely to treat US shipping as the enemy regardless, but that most of the American public would approve of such a step.[18] Following his speech, that day's edition of the *Fort Worth Star-Telegram* described it as the next step towards war.

By the time February 1917 came to a close, U-boats had sunk an incredible 301 ships during the month, totalling 506,057 tons. Twenty-seven other ships were damaged. It was by far the deadliest month of the First Battle of the Atlantic thus far.[19] A few weeks into unrestricted submarine warfare, and U-boats were already coming close to matching their monthly goal of 600,000 tons of shipping sunk. Britain was feeling the loss of supplies and materials. If the rate of sinkings could be increased, things would begin to look very grim for the Allies.

March–April 1917

In March, the first of two revolutions were taking place within the Russian Empire. The uprising had broken out spontaneously, without any true leaders. The Russian people, fed up with economic problems and the high level of losses and hardship being suffered in the war, had finally had enough. The Russian Army soon sided with the revolutionaries, and on 15 March, Tsar Nicholas II abdicated the throne. A provisional government was appointed, but another revolution, this time led by Bolsheviks, would rock the country that autumn. Russia's position in the war continued to grow more tenuous, which when combined with unrestricted submarine warfare, greatly disconcerted the Allies.

On 19 March, the Union-Castle liner *Alnwick Castle* was torpedoed and sunk by *U-81* while on a voyage from London to Cape Town. The ship was carrying passengers and a cargo of silver. Forty individuals were lost. The following letter written by Captain Benjamin Chave to the ship's owners was published in the English newspapers. It describes a typical experience of the sort that merchantmen had to go through during the war:

London. Gentlemen, –

With deep regret I have to report the loss of your steamer *Alnwick Castle*, which was torpedoed without warning at 6.10 a.m. on Monday, March 19, in a position about 320 miles from the Scilly Islands.

At the time ... there were on board ... 100 members of my own crew and 14 passengers, the captain and 24 of the crew of the collier transport *Trevose* whom I had rescued from their boats ... the previous day ... their ship having been torpedoed ... two Arab firemen being killed by the explosion, which wrecked the engine room ...

I was being served with morning coffee at about 6.10 a.m., when the explosion occurred, blowing up the hatches and beams from No. 2 and sending up a high column of water and debris which fell back on the bridge. The chief officer put the engines full astern, and I directed him to get the boats away. All our six boats were safely launched and left the ship, which was rapidly sinking by the head.

The forecastle was now (6.30 a.m.) just dipping, though the ship maintained an upright position without list. The people in my boat were clamoring for me to come, as they were alarmed by the danger of the ship plunging. The purser informed me that every one was out of the ship, and I then took Mr. Carnaby from his post, and we went down to No. 1 boat and pulled away. At a safe distance we waited to see the end ... Then we observed the submarine quietly emerge from the sea, end on to the ship, with a gun trained on her. She showed no periscope – just a conning tower as she lay there silent and sinister. In about 10 minutes the *Alnwick Castle* plunged bow first below the surface; her whistle gave one blast and the main topmast broke off; there was a smothered roar and a cloud of dirt, and we were left in our boats, 139 people, 300 miles from land. The submarine lay between the boats, but whether she spoke to any of them I do not know. She proceeded northeast after a steamer which was homeward bound ... and soon after we saw a tall column of water, etc., and knew that she had found another victim.

I got in touch with all the boats, and ... I was satisfied that every one was safely in them. The one lady passenger and her baby three months old were with the stewardess in the chief officer's boat. I directed the third officer to transfer four of his men to the second officer's boat to equalize the number, and told them all to steer ... for the Channel. We all made sail before a light westerly wind, which freshened before sunset, when we reefed down. After dark I saw no more of the other boats. That was Monday, March 19.

I found only three men who could help me to steer, and one of these subsequently became delirious, leaving only three of us. At 2 a.m., Tuesday, the wind and sea had increased to a force when I deemed it unsafe to sail any longer; also it was working to the northwest and north-northwest. I furled the sail and streamed the sea anchor … we used the canvas boatcover to afford us some shelter from the constant spray and bitter wind. At daylight we found our sea-anchor and the rudder had both gone. There was too much sea to sail; we manoeuvred with oars, while I lashed two oars together and made another sea-anchor. We spent the whole of Tuesday fighting the sea, struggling … to … head the boat up to the waves, constantly soaked with cold spray and pierced with the bitter wind … I served out water twice daily, one dipper between two men, which made a portion about equal to one third of a condensed-milk tin. We divided a tin of milk between four men once a day, and a tin of beef (6 pounds) was more than sufficient to provide a portion for each person (29) once a day.

At midnight Tuesday-Wednesday, the northerly wind fell light, and we made sail again, the wind gradually working to northeast and increasing after sunrise. All the morning and afternoon of Wednesday we kept under way, until about 8 p.m. when I was compelled to heave to again. During this day the iron step of our mast gave way and our mast and sail went overboard, but we saved them, and were able to improvise a new step with the aid of an axe and piece of wood fitted to support the boat-cover strongback. We were now feeling the pangs of thirst as well as the exhaustion of labor and exposure and want of sleep. Some pitiful appeals were made for water. I issued an extra ration to a few of the weaker ones only.

During the night of Wednesday-Thursday the wind dropped for a couple of hours and several showers of hail fell. The hailstones were eagerly scraped from our clothing and swallowed. I ordered the sail to be spread out in the hope of catching water from a rain shower, but … the rain was too light. Several of the men were getting lightheaded and I found that they had been drinking salt-water in spite of my earnest and vehement order.

It was with great difficulty that any one could be prevailed on to bail out the water, which seemed to leak into the boat at an astonishing rate, perhaps due to … the pounding she had received.

At 4 a.m. the wind came … and we made sail; but unfortunately it freshened again and we were constantly soaked with spray and had to be always baling. Our water was now very low and we decided to mix condensed milk with it. Most of the men were helpless and several were raving in delirium. The foreman cattleman, W. Kitcher, died and was buried. Soon after dark the sea became confused and angry … At 8 p.m. we were swamped by a breaking sea and I thought all was over. A moan of despair rose … but I shouted to them, 'Bail, bail, bail!' and assured them that the boat could not sink. How they found the bailers and buckets in the dark, I don't know, but they managed to free the boat, while I shifted the sea-anchor to the stern and made a tiny bit of sail and got her away before the wind … the wind died away about midnight and we spent a most distressing night. Several of the men collapsed, others temporarily lost their reason; and one of these became pugnacious and climbed about the boat uttering complaints and threats.

The horror of that night, together with the physical suffering, are beyond my power of description. Before daylight, however, on March 23, the wind permitting, I managed with the help of the few who remained able, to set sail again, hoping now to be in the Bay of Biscay and to surely see some vessel to succor us. Never a sail or wisp of smoke had we seen. When daylight came, the appeals for water were so angry and insistent that I deemed it best to make an issue at once. After that had gone round amid much cursing and snatching, we could see that only one more issue remained. One fireman, Thomas, was dead; another was nearly gone; my steward, Buckley, was almost gone; we tried to pour some milk and water down his throat, but he could not swallow. No one could eat biscuits; it was impossible to swallow anything solid; our throats were afire, our lips furred, our limbs numbed, our hands were white and bloodless. During the forenoon Friday, another fireman, named Tribe, died, and my steward Buckley died; also a cattleman, whose only name I could get as Peter, collapsed and died about noon.

To our unspeakable relief we were rescued about 1.30p.m. on Friday, 23, by the French steamer *Venezia* of the Fabre Line, for New York for horses. A considerable swell was running, and in our enfeebled state we were unable properly to manoeuvre our boat; but the French captain, M. Paul Bonifacie, handled his empty vessel with great skill and brought her alongside us … We were unable to climb the ladders, so they hoisted us one by one in ropes, until the 24 live men were aboard.

The four dead bodies were left in the boat, and the gunners of the *Venezia* fired at her in order to destroy her, but the shots did not take effect.

I earnestly hope that the other five boats have been picked up, for I fear that neither of the small accident boats had much chance of surviving the weather I experienced. At present I have not regained fully the use of my hands and feet, but hope to be fit again before my arrival in England, when I trust you will honor me with appointment to another ship.

I am, gentlemen, your obedient servant,

Benj. Chave[20]

Day after day in March was a repeat of the horrors experienced by the crew of the *Alnwick Castle*. The Atlantic had become an utter killing zone, and all and sundry were liable to be targets. The number of ships captured or sunk by

U-boats during the month ballooned to a massive 379, totalling 582,066 tons, just shy of Germany's monthly target of 600,000 tons.[21] Thirty-four other ships were damaged. Appeals were made to the British Admiralty to reconsider implementing a full convoy system to escort all ships making the transatlantic crossing. As before, this request was rebuffed, as the leadership remained unconvinced of the potential effectiveness of convoys.

On 2 April, the building number of German acts of aggression and lack of consideration for American lives finally forced the United States into action. Everyone, include Germany, had foreseen this eventuality. As he prepared to meet with Congress to ask for a declaration of war, President Wilson must have thought back to the words he spoke in 1911:'No man can sit down and withhold his hands from the warfare against wrong and get peace from his acquiescence'. A few days later, Congress was ready as well and agreed that America was at war with Germany.[22] Following this, the president addressed his nation:

Do Your Bit For America

My Fellow Countrymen,

The entrance of our own beloved country into the grim and terrible war for democracy and human rights which has shaken the world creates so many problems of national life and action which call for immediate consideration and settlement that I hope you will permit me to address to you a few words of earnest counsel and appeal with regard to them.

We are rapidly putting our navy upon an effective war footing and are about to create and equip a great army, but these are the simplest parts of the great task to which we have addressed ourselves. There is not a single selfish element, so far as I can see, in the cause we are fighting for. We are fighting for what we believe and wish to be the rights of mankind and for the future peace and security of the world.

HMT *Arcadian* sinking. Note the men climbing down the falls and struggling in the water, and the two lifeboats dangling uselessly from the falls. *(Illustrated World Magazine,* 1917/Authors' Collection)

To do this great thing worthily and successfully we must devote ourselves to the service without regard to profit or material advantage and with an energy and intelligence that will rise to the level of the enterprise (task at hand) itself. We must realize to the full how great the task is and how many things, how elements (different parts) of capacity (the maximum something can be achieved) and service and self-sacrifice it involves.[23]

A byproduct of the Royal Navy's blockade of Germany was that it forced Germany into an untenable position where they had little choice but to enact unrestricted submarine warfare. This made war with the United States inevitable, something which the Allies had been hoping for, since it would tip the advantage in their favour.

On 15 April, the troopship HMT *Arcadian* was on a voyage from Salonica to Alexandria. A veteran of the Gallipoli Campaign, the ship was originally built as the *Ortona* and served as a transport during the Boer War. It was then acquired by the Royal Mail Steam Packet Co. and renamed *Arcadian*.[24] The ship was torpedoed by *UC-74*, sinking in just six minutes with the loss of 277 lives. One of the soldiers aboard was Reginald Huggins, who gave the following account:

We were not too optimistic as to our chances, but in the early evening the *Arcadian* directed her nose seawards once more, steaming out into the open without mishap. Our Japanese friends [destroyers], of course, still playing the part of protector.

Arrived at Salonika, the troops intended for that front disembarked, and … we of the Egyptian contingent put forth to sea bound for Alexandria …

Through the night we sped on our way down the Aegean Archipelago, and the following evening, a Sunday, saw our real encounter with the U-boat that had dogged us so relentlessly. Without one moment's warning, a terrific explosion occurred, made hideous by the splintering into matchwood of great timbers, the crash of falling glass and the groaning of steel girders wrenched asunder, followed by the hissing rush of escaping steam from the ship's boilers.

Having given one convulsive shudder from end to end, the great ship began to settle down on her port side with the loose deck paraphernalia slithering about in all directions and dropping into the sea. To get away easier, I discarded my military boots, and donned a lifebelt. On reaching the side of the ship and peering over, one of the two small boats which had survived the explosion was to be seen putting away full to overflowing with men. Nothing else remained but to make the descent into the sea by a rope conveniently to hand, and this I attempted.

Unfortunately, my equilibrium on the ship's rail was disturbed by someone in great haste to be among the rescued, and, falling, my arm became jammed at the wrist between two steel uprights employed as supports.

For moments that seemed long years, I was dangling from the side of the rapidly sinking *Arcadian*, but was rescued just in time from that perilous position by two comrades, one easing my weight from underneath the shoulders while the other wrenched the caught arm from the fixture.

I do not know the identity of my rescuers to this day. Seizing the means of escape, I shinned quickly down into the sea – my hands suffering badly from rope-burns, and was surprised to find the water comfortably warm. My attire consisted of trousers, shirt and socks.

The lifebelt, I found, supported my body so that my head from the chin was above water, and I looked about me, taking in the seascape. Being a non-swimmer at that time, I was unable to get clear of the ship, and her enormous bulk seemed likely to topple over upon me at any moment, supposing I was not sucked down one of the huge funnels by the inrush of water.

For a moment or two the *Arcadian* partly righted on her keel and then with much hissing of escaping steam and explosions from the boiler rooms, she slid for ever out of sight of human eyes, carrying with her hundreds of troops and her own crew caught like rats on the lower decks.

Within … minutes … from the time that she was struck all that remained of the ship was bits of floating wreckage.

It is difficult to describe my sensations during the minute or so following. Down and still further down, I was dragged by the suction till it seemed that I must soon touch bottom. I was spun round with great rapidity and swirled about in an alarming manner.

I held my breath and closed tightly both eyes and mouth, until forced by bursting lungs to take in air, I opened my mouth, getting a large helping of Aegean Sea.

At last, however, I came with a rush to the surface, and was violently ill for some time. Glancing at my wristlet watch, I found it had stopped. The time was 5.45 p.m. Large numbers of drowned, the survivors, and a quantity of wreckage were close by me … After desperate efforts to propel myself through the water, I gave up in despair, finding that no headway was being made.

The sun now was lowered on the horizon: the sea became chilly and turbulent. The heads of the survivors by this time were dotted about with great distances between, they having drifted with the wind and the currents.

After some hours, I was brought by the same means within reach of a small raft, which was clutched with considerable gusto, and I found myself in the excellent company of five officers, three Navy and two Army.

Only an occasional word was spoken. Darkness descended quickly, and the sea was bitterly cold.

Wafted across the waters, our ears received the words of the hymn 'Nearer my God to Thee'. Apparently every poor devil – more than three-quarters drowned – was doing his level best to swell the chorus on that awful night. The incident has imprinted itself indelibly on my memory.

The combined weight of our six bodies completely submerged the slender support, but, nevertheless, by arrangement we each of us managed in turn to scramble on to the raft's surface and to get for a short spell as much of our numbed bodies above sea-level as was possible in the circumstances …

… Through the ingenuity of one of the Navy officers we were shortly located. In his possession was an electric torch – quite unaffected, apparently, by its prolonged immersion – and with the instrument he proceeded to signal in the Morse code.

… We watched intently. The beam of a searchlight shot into the sky from the rescuing ships.

It swung from side to side, missing our little group again and again. Eventually, however, it found its mark.

Then quickly the lantern shut down to allow of a message to be flashed out. Slowly this was read to us by our friend with the torch. 'Will pick you up soon as possible with other survivors'.

Utter blackness again and another long waiting; this time, however, with a hope. At last there came stealing upon us the tall black bows of a ship. The 'Q' ship *Redbreast* she was. Voices hailed us from the deck. She drew swiftly alongside, and dropped a rope ladder. Down this came a couple of men, who heaved us up.[25]

One of the survivors of the sinking was Thomas Threlfall, a *Titanic* survivor. He noted that 'It was the same day of the week and the same date of the month that the *Titanic* went down, and I have come safely out of both affairs'. He praised the rescuers, and noted that the 'patrol boat had to keep circling round, for she dared not stop. As it was, the submarine fired at her a couple of times, but missed'.[26]

Two days later on 17 April, the hospital ships HMHS *Donegal* and *Lanfranc* were targeted and sunk in the English Channel by *UC-21* and *UB-40* respectively. The *Donegal*, which was serving as an armed ambulance transport, carried slightly wounded cases, all British. Of these, twenty-nine patients, as well as twelve of the crew, were missing and presumably drowned.

The *Lanfranc* carried 387 some significantly wounded patients, including, ironically, twenty-seven wounded German officers and 140 German soldiers of other ranks. Forty people were killed in the sinking. One of the survivors gave the following account:

The *Lanfranc* was attacked … about 7.30 Tuesday evening, just as we had finished dinner. A few of us were on deck when there was a crash followed by a loud explosion. In a few minutes the engines had stopped and the *Lanfranc*

from the jaws of death while fighting under the scream of their own and enemy shells in the inferno between Arras and Vimy Ridge; and all … had faced the Hun in his vilest and murderous guise when he torpedoed the *Lanfranc* without warning.

A handful of lint was given to one man with a … nasty cut on his forehead, which was still bleeding. 'I only just found out that I had it … I did feel a bit of a bump … when I was getting down the side, but forgot it after … we could see she was done for and everybody kept quiet. It was perishing cold, but I'm feeling fine now. I got twenty-eight Huns to me own rifle out there on Vimy and I wished it had been a hundred. Of course they wanted to get us to-night, but it seems to me a dirty way to do it – with a hospital ship'.

The silent calm of the long hospital train containing the survivors … seemed almost unnatural. The wounded accepted the whole thing as part of the day's work. And as the train left to take them to hospitals … the wounded offered up their thanks in the only way they knew, with a long, quivering cheer.

Are you down-hearted?' called an orderly. With a long rumbling roar of a 'No', they disappeared into the night and – England.

'Nice chap, Fritz', said a destroyer officer, as he turned away. Yes, it's 'Nice chap, Fritz', as the destroyer officer had said. Nice chap to lessen the tonnage of his enemies by resorting to the drowning of helpless men as well as nursing sisters. Nice chap to justify himself by saying the ships he sinks must have been carrying troops and munitions, for German submarines never made mistakes.[27]

The French liner *Sontay* was just one of many ships sunk by U-boats in the Mediterranean in April 1917. (*Illustrated World Magazine*, 1917/Authors' Collection)

The sinking of both hospital ships was denounced internationally. As April came to a close, U-boats had sunk or captured a record 474 ships, amounting to 886,891 tons, while damaging forty-one others.[28] The stunning amount of tonnage lost far surpassed the monthly goal. Ships were sunk around the British Isles and Mediterranean in equal measure. If the losses could be sustained for a few more months, Britain would be forced into submission. Coupled with news of a series of mutinies in the French Army along the Western Front, things were looking grim for the Allies.

May–June 1917

With the staggering losses, the British Admiralty knew something had to be done, and near the end of April, had finally approved the use of convoys in the Atlantic. There were still an insufficient number of destroyers to serve as escorts, so they would only accompany convoys in coastal waters on both sides of the Atlantic. Obsolete cruisers and armed merchant vessels would play the role of escort during the bulk of the crossings until more destroyers were put into service. Observation balloons would also be employed in some convoys to help spot submarines. The first transatlantic convoy would set sail from the United States on 24 May. The group would lose just one vessel, which had become an easy target by falling behind and becoming a straggler. Despite this, it would be several months before the Allies gained full confidence in the convoy system, and until the methods employed matured.

On 4 May, the troop transport HMT *Transylvania*, a former Anchor Liner, was torpedoed and sunk in the Mediterranean by *U-63* while on a voyage from Marseille to Alexandria. The ship sank with the loss of as many as 412 lives.[29] Reverend James Gillies of Lesmahagow, Scotland, who for two years was assistant minister at Scots Church Melbourne, was one of six chaplains on the transport. He gave the following account:

How does it feel to be torpedoed? Is a question that has been frequently asked me – for I have had recently a double experience of shipwreck. The first time was on a homeward journey from the East. I thought that, after being shipwrecked both in the Eastern and Western Mediterranean I might be looked upon as a Jonah but most of the officers who were saved along with me seemed to regard the matter in quite an opposite light ...

My second experience was tragic enough. The story of that shipwreck constitutes perhaps the greatest tragedy that has befallen a British transport since the war began. I saw the two torpedo boats of our convoy sail away, as full as they could hold; I saw all the serviceable boats launched and filled and still there were many aboard … everything that could float was thrown overboard … and some boats that were barely seaworthy were lowered as a forlorn hope. I got off the starboard side into one of these … It was a glorious evening when we sailed from the port … We had a fine ship – the *Transylvania* – with troops. We were accompanied by Japanese torpedo boats. The crews looked very capable and alert and proved very helpful when our catastrophe occurred.

After my previous experience of shipwreck I had made up my mind only to partially undress at night; but as I was feeling very tired I broke this good resolution at once and slept very soundly till 4 a.m. when we had all to parade in lifebelts. Next morning … About 20 minutes past 10 a.m. I was talking to one of the nurses who had been a previous shipmate of mine when a tremendous explosion occurred and we realised that a torpedo had struck us. A few minutes before this our ship had sounded a warning signal to the torpedo boats, and I have heard since that a torpedo had just missed us at that time. Our boat was fitted with watertight compartments and these closed automatically after the explosion.

The captain turned the ship towards the shore … but the explosion had burst the steam pipes of the engines and we could only move … with the momentum of the ship … we kept on an even keel and this allowed some of the boats to be readily launched. The nursing sisters were put aboard first. Some of the men, in the first excitement, jumped overboard and endeavoured to get on to rafts or such of the boats as were lowered. Many of these must have perished. I saw several of them crushed against the ship when one of the torpedo boats came alongside.

About fifteen minutes after the first torpedo hit us another torpedo struck and completed the shipwreck. It blew up the forward hatches and many men at the same time. After this, the ship began to fill rapidly. I think that if we had missed the second shot the ship might have floated and perhaps been able to be towed into port … It was all darkness below as the lights went out at the very first. But I found my way downstairs changed into boots, got my waterproof belt, leggings – just such things as I could carry on me – and returned upstairs … On the instructions of the second officer I got into one of the last two boats that left the starboard side and we had just moved away … when the great vessel plunged her nose in the waves, raised her screw almost perpendicularly and sank out of sight in deep water. It was an awful and a fascinating sight I could not take my eyes away though they were full of tears at the tragic spectacle … the waters had closed over her and nothing was to be seen but some swimmers and floating wreckage. The captain went down with his ship also the officer commanding the troops; the senior medical officer was on duty to the last and died at his post. The captain came to the surface and was hauled aboard a boat in a very exhausted condition. Poor fellow, I saw him brought on to the Italian torpedo boat which picked me up. He was in great pain and though he lived to reach hospital he died that night.

It was very rough for the Mediterranean. Of course we had not the terrible rollers of the Atlantic. But the waves seemed big enough to us in our poor little boats … they frequently broke right over us and every moment it seemed as if we would be swamped. Some of the boats were leaking and quickly filled. A boat with 45 nurses in it swamped and the women had to hang on for a long time with only their heads above water … every one of them … were eventually rescued at the point of extreme exhaustion. Not one woman was lost, a fact for which we were all infinitely thankful.

There were many deeds of splendid heroism … One major was on a raft and rescued so many struggling men that the little raft became top heavy. He promptly jumped into the sea, not only taking off his own weight but helping to guide the raft shorewards. He was so exhausted by his exertions that though rescued, he died before reaching the shore. Our torpedo-boats came alongside and each took off about 1,000 of the troops. I did not attempt to board either of them. There were so many young lads looking white and anxious that one had enough to do for some time trying to reassure them and got them into safety. It still seems to me wonderful, not that a few hundreds were lost, but that so many hundreds were saved under such difficult circumstances. One of the torpedo boats was narrowly missed by the torpedo that struck us the second time …

The boat I got into was badly damaged … and had no rowlocks. Some of the men took off their putties and tried to make temporary rowlocks, but we could get no purchase; it was the most difficult thing … to keep her half way on to the wind, and all we could do was just to keep afloat with drenching billows constantly breaking over us. We were some three or four hours tossing about in the waves … when an Italian torpedo-boat that had received our wireless message picked us up. All were soaked to the skin nearly all were miserably sick and almost too weak to scramble aboard. But as I hardly ever suffer from seasickness, I felt amazingly fit and after a rest and some stimulant aboard the torpedo boat I was quite ready to make myself useful again.

We were taken along to the little wardroom [officers' mess] … Some of our officers were resting in the bunks, others were hanging around almost naked for we were all dripping wet and took the chance to throw off our clinging garments. Now and again other officers were brought in some bleeding, others as sick as could be … The poor captain … was carried past, and we could see he was dreadfully ill.

… the military and civil authorities of the Italian city where we landed gave us unstinted help, and heaped most generous kindness upon us. The news of our disaster quickly spread through Northern Italy and inquiries with offers of assistance came in thick and fast … By accident, I met the representative of

Lloyds who asked if he could do anything for me. I was glad of his help and he took me to various shops where I obtained the things immediately essential. In the first shop I went to the good lady of the place would not accept a farthing. I assured her I had money to pay. 'No! No!' she said … From a shipwrecked mariner, she would accept nothing. I thanked her as best I could with a lump in my throat … Few of us will ever forget the sympathy and kindness they lavished upon us.[30]

On Sunday, 27 May, the RMS *Baltic* departed New York for Liverpool. One of the White Star Line's 'Big Four', which also included the *Adriatic, Cedric and Celtic*, the vessel was serving as a troopship. On this crossing, the passengers would include not only the first American soldiers bound for Europe, but also the headquarters staff and commander of the American Expeditionary Force, General John 'Black Jack' Pershing. Thomas W. Smith, a Lieutenant in the 1st Engineer Battalion, described the crossing:

'Report to the adjutant at 1 p.m. today'. This was the command given me by the first sergeant of Company A, 1st Engineers, on the morning of May 22, 1917 … I felt that a movement of great importance was being considered, and that … I might be given an opportunity to participate in it.

Since April 6 … well-founded rumors were to the effect that the 1st Division would be among the first of American troops to see overseas service.

RMS *Baltic*. (Authors' Collection)

United States General John 'Black Jack' Pershing.
(*Collier's*, 1917/Authors' Collection)

When I reached the adjutant's office, I found
it full of men ... representing the different
companies in the regiment. Each one was
put through a rigid examination by Captain
Ernest Graves relative to their educational
qualification and army record, until he selected
ten men. The others he dismissed.

... he believed he had selected sober,
industrious men. 'You are going on a long journey', said he. 'I cannot tell you
where, but you must not reveal this information. You may never return'.

While the last assertion was anything but encouraging, we were ... elated
upon being selected to go to France with the General, as we were sure the
battle field of Europe was our ultimate destination.

We were ordered to be ready ... but did not get away until ... May 27 ... We
arrived at Governor's Island in the evening. At noon we boarded the river boat
and steamed down the bay and waited for the White Star Liner, *Baltic*, boarding
her at 5.30 p.m. By this time the entire party (the United States Expeditionary
Force) was on board. It included General Pershing and about 10 officers, 67
enlisted men and about 50 civilian clerks.

The good ship *Baltic* was ten days in making the trip across the Atlantic to
Liverpool. The weather was fine, with a comparatively smooth sea. We were
convoyed by three American torpedo boats the last three days of the voyage.
We also had two British destroyers, but they stayed but a few hours, for they left
us to aid three freight boats which had been attacked by three submarines and
sunk. It is believed that these submarines were laying in wait for the *Baltic* and
missed us or could not attack owing to the convoy.

When the *Baltic* reached the danger zone off the Irish Coast, she took a
zig-zag course, in order to avoid the numerous submarines. However, this was
customary at all times during the war with boats while in the danger zone.

Some amusing incidents occurred when it was decided that the members of
the Expeditionary Force should don civilian clothes, loaned by the field clerks
and passengers ... to prevent the enemy from shelling the lifeboats. Should
... the *Baltic* be struck by a torpedo and the Germans detect soldiers in the
lifeboats, we knew our chances would be poor.

Arriving at Liverpool on Friday, June 8 ... we were met by an English
General and staff and a battalion of British infantry and band ... [31]

The arrival of Pershing and the Americans was big news in the press:

> General Pershing arrived in London and was greeted by Walter Hines Page, the American Ambassador; Lord Derby, secretary of the state for war; Viscount French, commanding the British home forces and Lord Brooke who would be attached to Pershing's staff. Commenting on Pershing's imminent arrival in France, Colonel Fabray described the General's task to be an 'ardous' one.[32]

As May drew to a close, it was another devastating month at sea. U-boats had sunk or captured 386 more ships, a total of 618,184 tons of shipping, again meeting the Germans' monthly goal. Twenty-seven ships were damaged in attacks, but not sunk.[33] With the United States now in the war, Germany intended to keep the pressure up to starve Britain out before American forces could begin making a difference.

Early in June, the Second Battle of Messines raged on the Western Front. At sea, things remained equally as chaotic as on land. Convoys were helping, but they were being implemented gradually, and had yet to stem the losses to U-boats. A total of 386 ships, equalling 709,861 tons, were captured or sunk in the month, and another forty-six damaged.[34]

A U-boat victim heads to the bottom. An alarming number of merchant ships were sunk in spring 1917. (Authors' Collection)

July–August 1917

Near the end of July 1917, the Third Battle of Ypres erupted on the Western Front. Earlier in the month, diplomatic contacts between the Allies and Central Powers floating the idea of peace talks went nowhere. It was reported that German Chancellor von Bethmann-Hollweg spoke to members of the Reichstag and declared, 'I repeat that formula of peace without annexations is unacceptable to us. We declare our terms of peace. We must fight and conquer'.[35]

July came and went, with U-boats sinking or capturing 286 ships, totalling 577,645 tons, shy of Germany's monthly goal. Twenty-five more ships sustained damage.[36] The tide had slowly begun to turn, as more escort ships were made available and the Allies grew more confident in the use of the convoy system. Coinciding with this was an increase in the availability of depth charges. In July 1917, just four were available to each convoy escort. This would increase to six the following month, and then from thirty to fifty each in 1918 as production was ramped up.[37]

In August 1917, the situation remained much the same as the previous month. Shipping losses were high, but continued to flag. A total of 221 ships were sunk, equalling 523,948 tons. Twenty-one more were damaged. The monthly totals would generally decline throughout the remainder of the war.[38] U-boats were proving incapable of combating the convoy system. Korvettenkapitän Hermann Bauer had been pushing an idea that may have neutralised the effectiveness of convoys: having large submarines patrol for potential targets, and then use a powerful wireless set to coordinate the attacks of groups of U-boats working together. This tactic was actually experimented with in June 1917, but Bauer's suggestion was ultimately brushed aside.[39] More and more supplies and American troops continued to pour into European ports.

One of the more significant developments during August was the implementation of dazzle camouflage on ships. The Royal Navy had been experimenting with various forms of camouflage since the beginning of the war, mostly using different shades of grey, and other techniques such as colouring the tops of the masts and superstructures on naval vessels white to conceal their profiles in certain weather conditions. However, this was often hastily done, and less than effective.

An example is the camouflage that had been haphazardly applied to the Cunard liner *Ultonia*, prior to its sinking in June 1917. Regarding the paint job, one witness described the ship as 'smeared and dirty and utterly woebegone'. He noted that a thin coating of grey had been 'slapped over' the black hull, and how much of it had worn off, giving the ship 'a peculiar, spotted appearance'. The funnel had some experimental camouflage applied, but 'rain and salt spray had made a multi-colored mess of their work'. With merchant shipping losses to

SS *Willochra* transporting Anzac troops home after the war. The geometric patterns painted on the ship provide an excellent example of dazzle camouflage. (*Southampton Pictorial*, 1919/ Authors' Collection)

U-boats mounting, the Allies were desperate for more effective and innovative ways of protecting ships.

Notable maritime artist Norman Wilkinson, who was serving in the Royal Navy Volunteer Reserves, thought of an idea while on patrol in the English Channel the previous May. He knew that completely camouflaging ships was not practical, as smoke from their funnels gave away their position. Instead, he began thinking of ways to make it difficult for U-boat commanders to aim at ships through a periscope. Accurately firing a torpedo at a moving ship required submarine crews to correctly estimate the range and speed of their targets, followed by firing the torpedo ahead of the ship's current position, so that it would intercept the ship as it steamed ahead. The hulls of most merchant vessels were black, which made them highly visible under most conditions.

Given this, Wilkinson theorised that painting ships in confusing geometric shapes and sharp lines with strongly contrasting colours, which intersected and interrupted each other, would distort their silhouette. This would make it difficult for U-boat crews to determine the ship's heading. False bow waves, false sterns, and colours designed to hide or distort the shape of the superstructure or number of funnels were common. Even though the idea seemed highly unusual, the British Admiralty was desperate, and after initial testing on models, gave his idea a chance. The merchant ship SS *Industry* was painted in a prototype dazzle camouflage scheme, and at Wilkinson's request, so were several other vessels.

The initial successes were so encouraging, that the Admiralty, under the Defence of Realm Act, ordered all merchant ships to be painted in dazzle schemes. Wilkinson was placed in charge of a department focused on camouflage and overseeing the design and implementation of the various dazzle schemes.

The Admiralty soon began applying dazzle camouflage to naval vessels as well. In August 1917, the HMS *Alsatian* became perhaps the first Royal Navy vessel to receive dazzle camouflage. By the end of the year, approximately 400 vessels were camouflaged using this method, and the sight of a ship in dazzle camouflage would be more common than not by the end of the war. Norman Wilkinson was eventually assigned to Washington DC, so that he could consult with the newly established Camouflage Section of the US Navy, which US Naval Reserve Force Lieutenant Harold Van Buskirk was put in charge of. Van Buskirk was a fencing champion in his civilian life.

In both Britain and the United States, artists first drew up new dazzle camouflage designs on paper. Next, the schemes were applied to accurate wooden models of each individual ship. Then the models were viewed through a periscope by trained naval observers, sometimes with other models in mock convoys, to see how effective the designs were. If they passed muster, diagrams would be drawn up and sent to yard workers who would paint them on the actual ships, under supervision. The offices used in the designs of dazzle camouflage both in Britain and the US were lined with hundreds of models, each representing an individual ship and dazzle pattern.

United States Naval Reserve Force Lieutenant Harold Van Buskirk (right) and a colleague compare a mock-up of a dazzle camouflage pattern on a wooden model of a ship to the original design on paper. Scenes such as this were common in the offices of the Camouflage Section. (Authors' Collection)

The offices used in the design of dazzle camouflage in both Britain and the United States were lined with models, each representing an individual ship and camouflage pattern. (Authors' Collection)

While the ingenuity behind the designs was truly impressive, it is difficult to determine how truly effective they were. Contemporary reports suggest that the designs worked, but objective conclusions are difficult since so many variables could impact the outcomes, such as the colours and patterns used, speed and formation of the convoys, differing weather conditions, etc. It is clear that the Allies believed that dazzle camouflage was effective given its widespread use, and the fact that it remained in use, to a lesser extent, during the Second World War. Dazzle camouflage, when combined with the use of convoys and more advanced countermeasures, may have helped turned the tide of the First Battle of the Atlantic, but the full extent of its impact may never be fully known.[40]

September–October 1917

On 1 September, American sailor John E. Metzger had just completed a transatlantic crossing aboard USS *Rijndam*. The former Holland America Liner was now employed as a troop transport. Metzger's convoy had been attacked by U-boats during the crossing, and he recounted the details to his family. His account demonstrates the growing effectiveness of the convoy system, and an example of coordinated U-boat attacks:

Some place at sea

Sept. 1, 1917

Dear Folks at Home,

I am now safely returning to America. I am well in the best of health and not a scratch. Many things have taken place since I left the good old U.S.A. We made the trip over very peacefully until the 20th of August. Land was just sighted twenty or twenty-five miles from us. There were five transports and six American destroyers and two French patrol boats in the fleet. These boats met us at the war zone. One of our destroyers sighted a submarine ten or fifteen feet below the surface of the water.

The destroyers immediately dropped a deep sea bomb upon the submarine and there was a muffled explosion and I am sure she scored a hit. Our ship broke the silence then with six blasts from her fog whistle and then the other ships blew the same signal.

Before I had time to think there were guns firing from every ship. We were engaged in the greatest submarine battle ever fought. Immediately as soon as the sound of our gun fire reached the coast, French air planes came to our assistance. In the battle there were automatic revolvers, army rifles, machine guns, and guns from one in to eight inch guns. I almost forgot the Kaiser he had some torpedoes.

RMS *Adriatic* (foreground) and another member of White Star Line's 'Big Four' (third from right), both painted in dazzle camouflage, cross the Atlantic in a convoy. (Authors' Collection)

There were transports, destroyers, patrol boats, and air planes, and submarines engaged in the battle. The engagement lasted from eight thirty a.m. to eleven thirty a.m. making a total of three and one half hours.

During this time there were three or four hundred shots fired and three or four submarines sank. Every American ship and man came out without a scratch. It was a well planned attack. They put a string of mines in our path which would have sent any of our ships to the bottom if they struck one of them. Then the submarines got between the string of mines and waited for us. They will have to get up early in the morning when they get ahead of Uncle Sam.

We discovered the submarines before they had a chance to get their periscopes out of the water, after three and one half hours of steady gun firing we sailed safely to port and landed at 2.00 p.m. that day …

… Sailed from a French port Aug. 26. We came out very peacefully and not a gun was fired. On Aug. 27 a day I always will remember we caught in a storm. Our engines broke down. We lay rolling, pitching, drifting and a target for any submarine that came near for we were in the heart of the danger zone. I do not think there were many submarines for we lay there for five hours before the engines could be repaired. They were not repaired but one cylinder was taken out and then we were able to continue our voyage at a reduced speed. We got out of the danger zone and the storm and are now peacefully moving back to New York. We will be half way tomorrow.
Sept. 7

We are now nearing the Statue of Liberty. Expect to arrive some time tomorrow … I am on the morning watch and the sun is just coming out of the deep blue sea. I think we will have a nice day to finish our voyage …

With love John E. Metzger[41]

On 9 September, the RMS *Adriatic* was about to depart from New York in a convoy. The member of White Star Line's 'Big Four' was serving as a troopship, and sported a dazzle camouflage scheme. The ship carried members of the 101st Field Artillery Regiment. One of the soldiers described the crossing in detail:

… we had loaded ourselves and baggage aboard the steamer *Grand Republic* and headed out into the East River … The 'Rumor Association' which had been busily sending us to all destinations from Halifax to a southern training camp, now had it straight that we were to sail from Hoboken on the *Leviathan*, and the … steamer even seemed to point us more surely toward the piers where the huge bulk of the once-German liner was plainly showing. Any enthusiasm over the idea … was short-lived … as we slid past a stern marked *Adriatic* and climbed off onto the docks of the White Star Line.

... we were soon filing aboard in pay-roll order, each with a card showing where his quarters were and when he messed. There was some excitement when a steward steered us into the second class compartments, which we thought would do very well, until we were unceremoniously chased out and down to our proper place on the third deck forward, fairly comfortable barring an insufficiency of fresh air.

The *Adriatic* was not exactly a transport but a commercial vessel on which the Government had engaged space. Thus we traveled not as troops but as third class passengers: there is some distinction. A Royal Mail Steamer, however, is almost a part of the British Navy in time of war. We had a species of state room ... we were not on the whole crowded. Besides ourselves, there was a part of the 102nd Infantry on board, a hospital unit, swarms of unattached officers, a few civilians, and a most varied cargo said to range from gold bullion and explosives to barbed wire. We were able to verify the wire, as well as two motor trucks on the forward deck, which made excellent lounging places, and had to take the rest on faith ... There was the same clash between the sight of crowded pleasure craft bound up the Hudson and the little signs on the *Adriatic* warning how the display of a light at night might 'jeopardize the safety of the ship'. It seemed as if America had not awakened to the reality of the war and that we were bearing the whole burden alone ...

...Very few of us had ever crossed the ocean before, and in spite of submarines and all, the prospect of seeing foreign countries was most alluring.

At that time the undersea warfare was just coming under control, but it was still a strong menace and strict protective measures were necessary. We had rigid orders against showing any sort of light at night, and these extended even to cigarettes and illuminated wrist watches. We understood better when we learned that at sea a lighted match can be seen three miles away at night. Nothing could be thrown overboard which might float and so give away the path of the ship. These points were strongly impressed on us before we sailed ...

We arrived at Halifax where we were to join our convoy for the run through the submarine zone on Tuesday morning, September 11. Its harbor was crowded with ships ... Our stay was short. We wrote home letters to be forwarded to Washington and released on notice of our safe arrival on the other side, and just before sunset on Wednesday, when we were beginning to tire of the scenery, the convoy slipped slowly down the harbor. As we passed a British training ship the crew lined the rail and her band played the 'Star Spangled Banner'. Before dark we were out of sight of land.

Our convoy comprised seven ships and an auxiliary gunboat which was immediately christened the 'Plattsburg Cruiser'. One of the convoy was the *Manchuria* also carrying troops ... There were also the *Orduna* and a cattle boat known as the *Dummy* ... Our speed was limited to that of the slowest boat of the group, and probably never exceeded 10 knots an hour, while our course was a bewildering series of zig-zags.

These zig-zags were an important part of our defensive measures and proved a most interesting feature. There were apparently several zig-zag combinations to be executed on signals from the cruiser, given at irregular intervals. They ranged from simple movements for quiet waters to an intricate set of twists and turns for the danger zone, when each ship seemed to be trying to sink as many of the convoy as possible before she herself went to the bottom. Many were the hair raising moments when only a few yards separated two great ships plunging to apparent mutual destruction, and many were the false submarine rumors which had their being when the cruiser turned suddenly in a new direction as if something suspicious had been sighted on the horizon.

There was not much to do on the ship but sleep. In the morning we had calisthenics, and boat drill in the afternoon, and spent the rest of the time waiting for the dinner bell …

Two or three days out from Halifax the various outfits on board were called on to furnish extra submarine lookouts. At night this was unpleasant work for the weather was often bitterly cold, but it carried with it exemption from all other duties, always an advantage. Each lookout had a strong pair of glasses and would doubtless have seen anything that appeared. The best moment for sighting U-boats was said to be at night when they lay on the surface recharging their batteries, and theoretically visible two miles away.

Submarines, of course, were very much in everyone's mind, and life-boat drill was taken quite as seriously as it deserved. The story, however, had it that the ship's captain (who looked like King George and had an excellent reputation for fooling the subs) could not understand how we took it all so calmly. Most of the other troops he had brought across had spent all their time on deck with life belts on from the moment the ship left port, while we had not taken kindly to the belts nor shown any undue preference for the deck.

For all that, we had plenty of nervous moments. There were crowds of porpoises following the ship, and there is nothing that looks more like a torpedo than a porpoise. There was also a surprise boat drill one day. The signal – five blasts on the ship's whistle – came without a moment's warning and disturbed us, to say the least. There were, however, some who claimed to have known what it was all along. Lastly, there was an inquisitive ship which might have been almost anything unpleasant and which was finally shooed away by the cruiser.

The guard on board the ship … looked for suspicious lights, was furnished by each battery in turn. Our turn happened to fall on … our entry into the danger zone, the night before our Naval escort picked us up. An extra guard was also posted to operate water-tight doors, and every imaginable precaution was taken to cover our lights. Even the chart house was less brightly lighted, though it usually looked like a store window at Christmas time; but the number of carelessly screened port-holes seemed greater than ever…

Our entry into the danger zone brought two innovations with it. First, we were to stay on deck from 5.30 in the morning till 8 at night, barring meal times, and we were to wear life belts at all times. The halflight of the early morning makes observation very difficult and such a time is ideal for submarine attacks. Accordingly, we got up much earlier and remained at our boat stations until … the critical period was considered past. As for the lifebelts, they were not built for comfort and the general opinion was that they would be in the way if we ever struck the water.

On the afternoon of that first day we were picked up by our escort, eight British destroyers. All hands were watching for them … They took up their positions without any fuss whatever and took a load from our minds at the same time. Beside our ship they looked like toys, but very sinister toys, and whatever they did was done with an air of confidence and efficiency that was most reassuring.

So we gradually drew near the end of our trip. We suffered in silence the food which the crew seemed more disposed to sell us between meals than to serve on the table … there was a fine mist to greet us as we moved up the Mersey to disembark on a rather crude landing stage. Here we had our first glimpse of the British army in the shape of some very shiny officers and some hard-boiled soldiers with campaign ribbons for every affair back to the Norman Conquest. By 11 o'clock we were in trains of the London & Northwestern Railway and moving out through an ancient country where everything from railroad cars to houses seemed to be in miniature … we piled blanket rolls on a motor truck (they called it a 'lorry' and made two very distinct syllables out of it) and marched three miles, through streets dimmed against air-raids, to a restcamp on Southampton Common … Our part of it consisted of small conical tents … each having a circular wooden floor, large enough for six men but accommodating ten … we were at once issued blankets, but as soon as we had drawn them we were ordered to take them back to the store house again. This caused some hard feeling until we learned that the previous users had been quarantined South African Negro troops and that, in the meantime, there had been no fumigation.[42]

As September came to an end, a total of 218 ships had been sunk or captured by U-boats, totalling 351,636 tons. Twenty-seven ships were damaged. The tonnage of shipping lost to U-boats had decreased substantially from the previous month.[43] Of significance, Kapitänleutnant Walther Schwieger was killed on 5 September, presumably after his submarine *U-88* struck a British mine and sank with all hands. The U-boat commander, dubbed 'The Baby Killer' after sinking the *Lusitania*, had claimed forty-nine vessels during the war.[44]

Meanwhile, near the end of September, Johann Heinrich von Bernstorff, former German Ambassador to the US who then became Ambassador to Turkey, was embroiled in a scandal. Secretary of State Robert Lansing had revealed that von Bernstorff had previously been using money to try to influence members of Congress to prevent war with Germany.[45]

In October, Isabel Anderson, an American woman who had volunteered for service in the Red Cross, was crossing to Europe aboard the Armement Deppe liner SS *Espagne*. She gave an account describing the crossing:

> During my short stay in New York City I bought … things that I was told I might need in France, but which I afterward found I could buy just as well over there … then I went to New Hampshire to see my mother for a few days. Back again to New York, where passports were obtained, photographs taken, and letters received from the Red Cross officials … By the Red Cross regulations workers were allowed to take only a steamer trunk and a dress-suit case, and it was a masterpiece of packing that stowed away all the necessary articles in so small a space …
>
> My husband and I were very sad at the prospect of a separation but we both had war work, it was war-time, and we felt patriotic. At last, after he had made all my arrangements for traveling, he left me in my stateroom on board the *Espagne* … The gangplank was pulled up, and our ship glided out into the blackness of the night, leaving behind the twinkling lights of the great city of New York, while the enormous statue of Liberty with her flaming torch lighted the heavens. It all seemed a strange dream. Was it possible that I was quite alone and on my way to France in war-time?

> It was impossible to find my own chair on deck, so I finally took an empty one … The first night I went to bed in a real nightgown, but finding it too much work to dress in the morning, after that I slept in my clothes, as it was necessary to do for months at the front. This voyage was not different from others except in the darkness of the passageways and the complete blackness of the decks. I

Isabel Anderson. (Authors' Collection)

could not see one thing. It was positively spooky, and it made me feel more and more my absolute aloneness in the world.

The next morning we were in the midst of a wild storm and the boat plunged through the spray of high waves. I managed, however, to go down to all my meals, and found myself at a small table with a nurse who had been in France during the war, and a man on his way to Portugal to buy cork from the large cork-oak groves of that country.

On looking about, I found most of the YMCA workers exercised every day on deck, and listened to lessons in French and lectures on the sex question. The Red Cross men were rather sporty and smart-looking in their uniforms, while the Red Cross nurses reminded me of school teachers. There was a very pretty girl in khaki who caused much amusement, as it was said she planned to drive a motor, with bath-house attached, from place to place for the convenience of aviators. Hundreds of Armenians at this time were going back to fight, and every day I watched them in their tight clothes and fur caps as they were drilling in the steerage.

The voyage was smooth and warm and peaceful … until we reached the danger zone. Then it became colder and fog settled upon us. Our ship began to zigzag. We tried on our frog-like rubber life-saving suits, and all assembled on deck before the boats … Mine was No. 7. The people for that boat were far from pleasing. I did not feel like drowning with them.

Six of us women slept side by side in a corner on deck, with our passports and money upon us and our life-belts beside us – it was very warm below – and we told stories and giggled like school girls. Even if the bed was hard, it was fun to watch people prowling round in the darkness.

There was superb phosphorescence one night. Never even in the China Sea have I seen it so brilliant; the sensation was as if we were sailing over the moon or a ball of glowing crystal – it was unearthly and mysterious.

A day or so before we arrived we saw floating wreckage on the water, and the *Espagne* shot once at a supposed mine and three times at a submarine or an overturned boat in the distance. The passengers were all agog! People seized their glasses and rushed to the upper deck. We changed our course and zigzagged even more, for the supposedly overturned boat seemed to be suspiciously moving with us.

Our shots fell short of it, and it did not return the compliment. It was said, however, we were chased by a submarine that evening. As a rule, they appear at dawn in smooth weather.

The last night on board we had an auction, and people paid huge sums for trash. We sighted two French torpedo-destroyers, and then steamed up the river, past the welcome green fields and pretty houses to Bordeaux. At the docks were great French liners, and German prisoners at work, and American soldiers

be the senior and therefore in command of the troops. He outlined the guard to be mounted by the young officers.

Five posts, on night and day, was the schedule, and each relief was to be on four hours and off eight. The posts were really watches at sea. One was in the very bow of the vessel, one was on each side of the lower bridge, one was in charge of the submarine guard on the main deck, and one was on the small bridge, just above the stern's gun.

The mission of these officers was to look out for submarines, though no one knew, it seemed, exactly what he should do if by chance he should see one. The submarine guard, besides being charged with the responsibility of keeping all lights out, was to watch for the undersea craft and to open 'a murderous fire' if any became visible. Instructions were also given as to the method of lowering boats and of putting on life-belts.

That night the waters seethed and foamed and the waves ran high. It was pitch dark on the ocean and the boat rolled uncomfortably. The next morning many of those who had eaten too heartily the day before were not to be seen at the breakfast table.

Attempts were made to have the men do the 'setting-up' exercises, but the efforts proved futile, for who can do a 'full knee bend' when a ship is lurching and pitching? Too, when its motion catapults one into a donkey-engine or into one of those Victrola looking ventilators?

November 8 … that evening the good ship anchored in the outer harbor at Halifax. Submarine nets across the channel to the inner harbor had already been placed, so the *Andania* had to wait until early the next morning to go inside. Soon after breakfast the nets, which had been suspended from barges, were swung back enough to allow the vessel's passage.

She dropped anchor, and it was not long before a barge came alongside and the coaling began. Several other vessels appeared to be ready to clear. That afternoon one steamer passed slowly by. Her rails were solid lines of khaki; and when word was passed around that she was a Canadian transport taking back to the front soldiers who had recovered from their wounds, cheers were exchanged between the Americans and the men on the transport …

Then there came out of the inner harbor a grey ship, larger than either of the preceding [*Lapland*], and crowded with khaki figures. Eagerly the troops on the *Andania* searched her decks with glasses. Suddenly a soldier, disobeying orders, climbed half way up the stays … signaling by flag 'What outfit?' Instantly there came back from the other vessel 'A-L-A'. Then the band on the *Andania* burst out into the soul-stirring, blood-boiling strains of 'Dixie'. Cheer after cheer went back and forth across the ever increasing space while wigwagged messages of 'Good Luck!' were being exchanged between the Alabamians.

... The afternoon of November 9 ... the *Lapland* cleared, and that evening the *Andania* finished coaling and followed her out of the harbor. During the night of November 10 the *Andania* picked up the fleet and the next morning at daybreak took her position in line.

In the convoy there were ten ships. An auxiliary cruiser was the leader and escort. The vessels steamed in three columns, the *Lapland* at the tail end of the left column, the *Andania* abreast of her, at the tail end of the center column. The trip on the whole was uneventful. Boat drills and fire drills were held every day and life-belts had to be worn at all times.

Occasional officers' schools were held ... Combat formations were studied and the latest changes in trench warfare were discussed.

... On the night of November 17, while the ships were plowing along, Captain Dancey organized an amateur concert in aid of the Seamen's Institute. Several of the ship's crew participated as well as a number of the soldiers, and a neat sum was realized. That morning a fleet of destroyers had dashed up, circling in and out among the vessels, lending much reassurance to those aboard the ships in the convoy.

The morning of November 18 land was sighted. It proved to be the north shore of Ireland. All day the convoy sailed along the coast. In the afternoon some of the vessels headed north, but those with the Alabamians aboard turned southward down through the channel and into the Irish Sea.

The early morning of November 19 the ships passed up the Mersey River and nosed into dock space at Liverpool, England. It was about noon before the *Andania* put in at that port. Then the bands played 'Over There' and 'Good Bye, Broadway, Hello France!' The troops were glad the long ocean voyage had ended.

As the vessel lay there the men lined up along her rails and watched the unloading of a troop ship full of kilted Scotch-Canadians. The latter passed, carrying large bundles and boxes, waving and shouting to the Alabamians. 'Hey! Scottie', yelled one of the men of the 167th, 'whot yer got them skirts on fer?' The reply came back, 'For what you got your breeks on, lad?'[48]

Unfortunately, the *Andania* was living on borrowed time, and would be torpedoed and sunk by a U-boat on 27 January 1918, with the loss of seven lives.

In November, U-boats sank 152 ships, for a total of 302,374 tons of shipping lost. Twenty-two more ships were damaged. The convoy system was driving down the monthly losses to low levels not seen since 1916.[49]

Early in December 1917, the United States declared war on Austria–Hungary, escalating the former's involvement in the war. By the end of the month, Germany and a weakened Russia would sign an armistice, although the cease fire would not last.

On 7 December, the SS *Espagne* was about to depart on another voyage from New York to Bordeaux. One of the men aboard the ship was YMCA worker Harold Morton Kramer, who was too old to serve in the US Army, but was accepted to help the troops in other ways. He later described the crossing in great detail:

Then there came an early December day when I stood on the deck of a ship, the *Espagne* … as we slipped away from a North River pier and started for the great sea, beneath which lurked submarines and beyond which was the Great Adventure. An incoming vessel whistled a salute to us, their band assembled forward and played 'The Star-Spangled Banner', while the passengers of both ships lined the rails and fluttered handkerchiefs.

… That stormy night I had sorrowed because my soldiering days were past. In truth, they were—but this December evening I trod the deck of an ocean liner wearing the uniform of the Y.M.C.A., and I was bound for France to take my place beside those who were privileged to carry rifles or serve the artillery or do battle in the air – or what not. For two months I had worn the uniform, serving in Camp Zachary Taylor, Louisville, Kentucky, and then I had been accepted for overseas service.

Physical examination? Oh, yes, there had been one in New York. But – well, here I was. So let's not discuss the 'hows' and the 'whys' of that stage of my journey to the trenches. Over there was work for everybody who had the will. Possibly there were doctors in the world who believed that where the spirit was willing a man in a Y.M.C.A. uniform was an asset to the American army in France even if the flesh was weak …

A cold wind was sweeping up the river, but most of the *Espagne*'s passengers remained on deck, loath to seek the four walls of staterooms while their eyes might be banqueted with the sight of American shores …

Just as the wintry dusk was falling we passed the Statue of Liberty, presented to the people of our country by the people of France. The uplifted hand seemed waving a good-bye to us as we passed out to sea, and I wondered what was in store for me between this good-

YMCA worker Harold Morton Kramer in his uniform. (Authors' Collection)

bye and the wonderful day – if it ever came – when I should stand on the deck of another ship and interpret that uplifted hand as a greeting for my safe return.

The shores of my native land faded from view ... The ship began to yield more and more to the roll of the open sea ... I sent my goodbyes to wife, to the land of my birth, and to all that I held dear. The engines were thud-thudthudding ... four bells (six o'clock) sounded, and from some mysterious place a gong reverberated its call to dinner. I turned to answer its summons, but paused to cast another backward look ...

Slowly our ship threaded its way through the mine-fields that guarded New York. Presently our engines stopped, and I stood on deck in the darkness wondering why. Suddenly a dazzling wedge of light shot across the waves and in its glare I saw a rowboat bobbing about close to us, and a man was going down a rope ladder lowered over the side of our ship. We were 'dropping' our pilot. In a moment the tiny boat was at the foot of the ladder, I saw the pilot leap into it and wave his hand. Instantly the searchlight flashed away from us, from out of the darkness where I had last seen the rowboat came a hoarse shout, our engines began to thud again, and we were on our way across the Atlantic. I went in to dinner.

At dinner the service was excellent and cuisine all that could be asked, but it was a French ship, with French officers, crew and servants, I knew no French, and the waiters knew no English. So I ordered my dinner by pointing to articles on the menu card, which was printed in both French and English, but the success of this plan was marred by the fact that the garcon seemed unable to see straight when I pointed out my order on the card.

... My lot was the common lot of all who spoke no French. After one had ordered by the sign language one waited with considerable curiosity to see just what was brought. There was no gayety in the dining-room and no music. The passengers assumed an air of cheerfulness, but most of the smiles were as set as a design on china-ware. Everybody pretended – but nobody was deceived.

We were running without lights of any kind visible on the outside. Not even a cigarette's glow was permitted on deck ...

Not even the glow of New York's waste of light now showed on the western horizon, and I gave up my lonely after dinner vigil on deck and went inside. The passageways of the ship were dimly illuminated with carefully shaded lights, and all portholes were tightly shut and covered with heavy disks as an added precaution against the escape of a ray of light.

In the smoking-room men were talking in subdued tones, smoking much but drinking little. No hilarity of any kind here. In the salon a little company of passengers was making a brave attempt at jollity, led by two Y.M.C.A. workers, one a young woman canteen worker who was at the piano playing accompaniments for one of the men secretaries who stood at her side singing and striving to inject cheer into the group. But it was futile. The parting from loved ones was too recent, the perils of the submarine-infested sea too new and real.

'Over there! Over there!
Send the word, send the word over there,
That we'll be over, we're coming over—
And we won't come back till it's over over there!'

The splendid baritone voice rolled the words out with a snap that for a moment roused the listeners from their lethargy, and a little burst of applause greeted him. Ah, little did he know that the Angel of Fate had written his name as one who would not come back even when it was over over there. Gallant and fearless, strong and full of the joy of life he was when last I saw him near the flaming battle lines of the Luneville sector. Not long afterward he fell, killed by a shell, while serving his country in the only way circumstances had privileged him to serve.

The days passed rather wearily … Many were missing from the dining-room the first morning because of seasickness, but beyond a slight headache that remained with me much of the voyage I was fit. The *Espagne* was armed with a rapid-fire three-inch gun forward and two six-inch guns at the rear, all manned by French naval gunners. Shells were piled beside the guns, and every minute the sea was being closely scanned for submarines.

We had sailed without any convoy, the rumor being that a destroyer or some other type of fighting vessel would meet us soon after we put to sea and guard us on our voyage. About noon on the second day we sighted a ship, miles away, low down on the horizon, and the Society for the Spread of Groundless Rumors immediately announced that the stranger was 'part of our convoy'. A little study, however, proved beyond question that the ship was sailing westward, which effectually did away with the convoy story.

Let it here be recorded that the greatest abiding-place of rumors known to man is the deck of a ship a thousand miles out at sea … The convoy rumor was the first to seize the *Espagne* in its grip, and it lived all the way across the Atlantic until the day – and a truly glad day it was for all of us – when a little wasp of the sea did come dashing out to fight for us against a German submarine that was creating havoc not many leagues away …

This universal interest caused the convoy rumor to assume many – and sometimes laughable and absurd – forms. I remember well of a dear old lady who was extremely nervous because of the submarine peril, but who came to me late in the afternoon of the second day …

'I feel so much better now that I have found out about our convoy', she said, happily.

'Our convoy?' I asked, in uncertainty. 'Well, just what have you found out about it?'

'Oh', she replied, with a joy note in her voice, 'it is keeping out of sight, just below the horizon, but following us all the time, keeping in touch by wireless and ready to rush up and sink any submarines that attack us'.

'Um-m-m – isn't that great!' I exclaimed with feigned enthusiasm that found a sincere response in her soul.

Absurd? Certainly. But why destroy her peace of mind by proving the absurdity? Throughout the rest of the voyage she was calm and content in her belief that our valiant guardians were watching over us – out of sight, just below the horizon.

Again night came upon the sea, again the portholes and windows were carefully blinded, and once more we were in a world of faint light and feigned cheerfulness. Still our thoughts were behind us. We were remembering that back there were our loved ones …

Sunday morning dawned in storm and blinding clouds of rain and spray wind-driven until tiny streams found their way through the door crevices and ran down the companionways. When I opened my eyes I found the ship plunging and rolling terrifically, and also discovered that the stateroom was oppressively warm. When I sat up in my berth the perspiration started very easily, and when I dressed and started toward the dining-room I became aware that life was not all joy. Making my way to the promenade deck, I found that the sea was running mountains high, the atmosphere was muggy, and … clinging to the guard-ropes were groups of distressed-looking passengers, viewing the angry ocean. The night before it had been quite cold. Now it was like summer, the change being clue to the fact that we had entered the Gulf Stream during the night.

All day long the storm raged, and but few appeared in the dining-room. And so the day passed, with the ship plunging and rolling and creaking. Night came down early, and the wind died away, but the sea still ran high. A few tried to spend the evening as usual in the salon, but by eight o'clock the smoking-room and salon were deserted and only the staterooms knew the hum of voices – and occasionally the mournful sighs of the victims of seasickness.

Sleep was just winning me from the consciousness of all this when I heard the ship's whistle. Raising on one elbow, I listened. Yes, there it was again, low, sonorous, longdrawn … it sounded over and over again, ominously. Then another portentous fact forced itself upon me. Our engines had stopped.

… with engines stopped we lay pitching and rolling in the trough of the heavy sea – the most unpleasant sensation possible to be experienced on an ocean voyage.

Dressing hurriedly and going on deck I found our ship hove to in a world of dense fog, through which a heavy downpour of rain was coming. The whistle was sounding a warning for other ships that might come slipping through the

compelled to live for some days in a little world of their own they had as well make the best of it. So now in the evenings we were having entertainments of various kinds in the salon. We had lectures, music, moving pictures, readings, and 'stunts'. Then we would pace the dark decks for an airing before seeking our staterooms, and occasionally we would pause to lean over the rail and watch the phosphorescent display in the waters beside the speeding ship. In the foam caused by the passing of the vessel the phosphorus would flash as if myriads of tiny lanterns were being darted here and there beneath the waves. At times the water seemed to be fairly blazing.

All things must end, and so there came a time when we could say, 'Tomorrow our voyage will end'. That night was the eighth one we spent on the *Espagne*, and it was the night of our voyage, for now we were in the very heart of the danger zone, imperiled by submarines and mines …

A large number of the passengers spent this night on deck, curled up near the boats, with life-belts near their sides …

All day we had been running with all boats swung out over the sides, ready for instant launching. The rope ladders had been let down, and by each ladder there was a cluster of electric lights with a reflector to throw the light on the ladder and boat – if the power plant were not demolished by the explosion, which was not unlikely if we were torpedoed or struck a mine.

Our old friend, the Convoy Rumor … again visited us this afternoon when we sighted a three-masted ship some miles away on our right … and ahead of that ship we could discern another vessel of some sort, riding low in the water. Immediately the Society for the Spread of Groundless Rumors was on the job, and in a few minutes we were served with everything from a decoy ship and submarine to 'Our Convoy'.

The *Espagne* quickly fluttered a rope full of flag signals, but if the strangers paid any attention to them, those of us who had glasses were not able to discover the fact. Neither do I know what our signals meant. Finally the two ships disappeared below the horizon – headed westward. The convoy myth had perished once more. My glasses plainly showed me that the low-riding vessel was a torpedo boat destroyer – but beyond that fact I know nothing.

When night came I pondered on the question of whether I should remain in my stateroom or sleep on deck. For the last two nights I had slept in my berth with my clothes on, ready for any emergency. There were those who scoffed … To my mind it seemed to have become a question of some … sleeping … with their clothes on and others scoffing in their bravado and then undressing and spending the nights in sleeplessness …

Need I say that it was one of the strangest nights I ever experienced? Wrapped in my overcoat and blankets, I stretched out in a deck-chair close to the boat to which I was assigned, and with my life-belt across my knees I was as nearly ready for an emergency as it was possible to be. The decks were in total darkness, heavy clouds were hanging over us, and always there were the steady thudding of the engines and the swishing roar of the sea. And always one knew that at any instant a torpedo or a mine might blow up the ship.

Those of us who chose the deck for our sleeping-quarters that night had plenty of company. Nearly all the chairs were occupied. People groped their way about the dark deck, joked with friends as they fell over deck-chairs or friendly feet or snarled at strangers who growled when their chair was jostled or their toes trodden upon. But for the most part people were cheerful and forbearing – and under a strain … And all night long there were sleepless passengers who paced the deck, back and forth, back and forth, or around and around the ship.

Sleep came to me that night more generously than I had anticipated … Toward morning I became aware that it had turned suddenly colder, and by the peculiar lurching of the ship I knew that we were zigzagging sharply and frequently. I was awake again in time to lie cuddled up in my chair and watch the dawn come over the sea … We were then zigzagging our way up the Bay of Biscay, having swung south and come up along the coast of Portugal and Spain.

Soon after breakfast our wireless brought us the news that a British freighter had been torpedoed at dawn by a German submarine, the attack taking place about fifty miles from our present location. An hour later we were passing through waters thickly strewn with bits of wreckage, evidently from the ill-fated freighter.

A little before ten o'clock on the morning of this eventful day a smudge of smoke appeared on the horizon ahead of us, and a few minutes later our ship sent aloft a number of signal flags and broke out the French tricolor at the stern.

… we divided our attention between the unknown vessel ahead of us and the wreckage, sinister in its silent warning, all about us. That the newcomer was speedy was soon demonstrated, for it quickly rose above the horizon and bore down upon us rapidly. Larger and larger it grew until our glasses told us that it was a destroyer, coming at full speed.

In what seemed an incredibly short space of time the vessel swept past us and a mighty shout went up from our decks when we saw the newcomer run up the flag of France. Our convoy had come at last.

It was a French destroyer that had come racing to meet and guard us during the remainder of our voyage, one of the speediest wasps of the sea, mounting guns that seemed amazingly large and heavy for so small a craft …

The decks of the *Espagne* became a new world. The happy laughter of women – laughter long stifled by anxiety – rang gayly, and the voices of the men carried a new ring of joyousness. The destroyer swung back and forth across our wake, occasionally speeding up opposite us on one side or the other and then dropping back again, and as I stood and watched it and then noted the floating wreckage of the English freighter, the French flag flying from the stern of the guardian vessel took on added beauty in my eyes.

Steadily we zigzagged our way forward. The waters of the Bay of Biscay are peculiarly striking in their opalescent coloring, and numerous sudden squalls and rainstorms during the day lashed them into scenes of tumultuous beauty, sent the *Espagne* and our doughty little convoy reeling and plunging, and moistened our decks with clouds of spray that the occasional bursts of sunshine painted with the hues of the rainbow.

At 10.45 we assembled in the grand salon for church services conducted by a minister in our Y.M.C.A. party. The minister was standing with his back to the front of the boat, and from where I sat I could look directly past him through the front windows of the salon and see the crew on duty beside the three-inch gun. The minister had commenced the reading of the Scripture lesson when I saw the gunners suddenly spring to position and begin swinging the muzzle of the piece toward a new direction. At the same time the non-commissioned officer in charge turned and shouted something to the officers on the bridge, and pointed in the direction in which the gun was now being aimed.

It was a tense moment. Others sitting beside me saw the incident. But none of us wished to disturb the service that was proceeding so calmly under the leadership of the minister who knew nothing of what was transpiring out on the gun deck. So we sat with clenched hands and waited for the flash of the gun that would signal the opening of the fight which seemed to be only a moment in the future.

But the shot was not fired. The gunners crouched beside their piece ready at the wink of an eye to launch a shell, and presently we who were witnesses of the affair saw our guardian go racing past us toward the spot on which our gun was trained … I … heard the words the minister was speaking. I shall never forget the verse of the psalm he was reading: 'In God have I put my trust. I will not be afraid what man can do unto me'.

It was 3.30 in the afternoon when I saw a sailor standing well forward raise his glasses and gaze steadily ahead and slightly to the left – over the port bow … Something in his manner convinced me that it was a matter of prime interest that was engaging his attention, so I leveled my glasses in the same direction and saw – France!

… Land – after nine days of rolling sea! A squall had been sweeping about us, but now it had passed and the clouds were growing lighter. Ten happy minutes passed, and then the *Espagne* ran a bundle of bunting to the top of the forward mast, and at the pull of a string the Glory Flag – the Stars and Stripes – leaped out to the breeze … just as the dear old flag streamed out from the halyard the sun broke through the clouds and bathed it in a warm caress.

... the passengers cheered with great, ringing shouts of joy and pride and thankfulness, the French and passengers of other nationalities joining in the cheers and salutes. I am not ashamed to tell that there was a rush of tears to my eyes as I stood on the deck that afternoon and saw the wonderful flag of a wonderful land – my native land – fluttering above me. Just ahead was the land I hoped to have a humble part in freeing from a brutal invasion ...

That afternoon in the Bay of Biscay I suddenly came to realize that I loved this homeland of mine more devotedly than I had ever dreamed of before I had gone adventuring across the sea.

... Presently we found that the vessel headed toward us was the pilot-boat, bearing the man who was to guide us into the harbor and up the river to Bordeaux. Then the *Espagne* hove to and lay awaiting his coming. We were now safely within the submarine nets that guarded the approach to the Gironde River, and our gunners began packing up the shells and covering their guns with tarpaulins. The destroyer ran on past us and also came to anchor. We were no longer in need of protection.

The pilot, putting off in a rowboat from his vessel, caught the rope ladder we dropped over the side and came clambering up to the *Espagne*'s deck. Soon he was on the bridge and once more we steamed ahead. Before us the breakers were dashing against a green coast – a coast of wondrous beauty ... we were close enough to shore so that we could see the pretty villas on the hillsides.

... Close at hand was land – but over me suddenly swept the realization that it was not my land. However, it was the land of friends, and although a great loneliness came over me at the thought that the sea now separated me from my loved ones, a chastened joy was in my heart as we slowly steamed into the mouth of the river and finally came to anchor opposite the little town of Royan. Here we were to wait until an early morning hour when the tide would permit us to proceed up the river to Bordeaux.

Dusk came on, and then a wonderful thing happened. The electric deck-lights were switched on, for the first time since we left New York. As we strolled around the lighted decks happiness was everywhere, and through the open portholes – another wonder – came the sound of laughter and merriment in the staterooms. In those hours the *Espagne* was the abiding-place of light hearts.

Presently the police-boat came alongside, bearing the harbor police and customs officials, and then bedlam, pandemonium, chaos, babel – and everything else one can think of along those lines – broke loose. With the police and customs officers were a large number of porters to handle the baggage, and for some reason they had a hard time getting their boat into the desired position beside the ship. They would start to raise their gangplank to our deck and then would pull it back, amid a perfect pandemonium of shouts and orders and a wilderness of gesticulations. One instant all of the porters would be rushed to one end of the patrol-boat, and the next instant they would be wildly herded to another spot; they would shove the gangplank forward and then pull it back; they would raise it amid a babble of shouts and then lower it with a bedlam of exclamations.

… I looked down on the turbulent scene and a great wonder began to arise in my mind as to how I would ever get along in this strange land.

The gong sounded and we went to dinner and while we ate the patrol-boat got its affairs straightened out and the officers and porters swarmed aboard. And then we found that we had a strenuous evening ahead of us.

First the police and customs officials must dine, and this they did with the deliberation characteristic of the French, to whom every meal is a ceremony. After they had finished the officials proceeded with their respective duties. In the grand salon the police established themselves with our passenger list, and as our names were called we were ushered before them and presented our passports and other credentials for their vise. After they had stamped and signed them they issued to each of us … a landing permit.

In the meantime the porters … were hoisting the baggage from the hold and trundling it along the port side of the promenade deck, where it was stacked in huge piles, while others were racing up and down the corridors at the beck and call of the customs officers who were visiting the staterooms and inspecting the cabin baggage … everything … had to be … opened for examination …

On this – the starboard – side of the promenade deck a desk had been set up for the selling of railroad tickets and the checking of the baggage, which first was to be weighed on a small set of scales similar to those found in any country grocery-store in America. These scales had been dragged out on deck and put in position about twenty feet from the ticket-desk.

… Everybody American, of course, was in a desperate hurry to have his wants attended to immediately. During my service abroad – in France, in England, in Scotland, in Ireland – I discovered that by this trait one might always know an American. Despite the fact that a perfect swarm of porters had come to us on the patrol-boat they were all too few in number to meet the desires of the Americans who wanted their trunks removed to the weighing station on the promenade deck the instant the customs official had put his cabalistic mark on the pieces. As a result, porter-hunting became popular – or perhaps I should say universal, rather than popular – and a little later, after the supply had been gobbled up by the early hunters, porter-stealing became a fine art.

… Twice did my roommates and I get porters to our room, and twice did we lose them through kidnapping or other cause, so at last we decided that the three of us ought to be able to shift for ourselves and carry our own stuff to the deck. This we did.

But when it came to getting our baggage weighed we found a little the worst confusion we had yet encountered. In all sincerity I affirm that I have learned profoundly to admire the French people – but just as sincerely I affirm that their 'system' for the baggage weighing – on that voyage, at least – was chaos …

Women with hats on one ear, perspiration streaming down their faces, and hair sadly disheveled, struggled the same as men, some near to tears and others bitterly scornful. Be it said to the credit of our country that most American men did their best to ameliorate the lot of these unhappy women – but most men were encumbered with two or more pieces of baggage and had slight opportunity for being of real service to any one in distress, even though their souls may have been filled with chivalry.

And reaching the scales was no sure sign that one's troubles were ended. Just as 'porter stealing' had been indulged in down in the staterooms, so now was 'scales-stealing' practiced, and in much the same way. If one had succeeded in getting his baggage piled on the scales it was not uncommon for it to be dumped off without weighing by the scales man who had been bought by a larger tip from some one who thus succeeded in having his stuff weighed ahead of his turn …

In truth, as I witnessed one or two cases of this law of the claw and fang, of the triumph of brute force over physical weakness, I found myself wondering what might have been the result had the strong and the weak found themselves occupying an overloaded lifeboat or raft on the open sea …

Occasionally some one with a sense of humor would shout a jest that smoothed out many of the discomforts of the struggle, and now and then a Y.M.C.A. secretary would pipe up from the midst of the mass and sing a verse:

'Pack up your troubles in your old kit-bag
And smile, smile, smile'.

I was thankful for a sense of humor that carried me in good spirits through that episode. In due time I got my baggage weighed, the attendant shouted and clamored at the clerk at the ticket-desk some distance away, until an answering shout announced that the weight had been heard, I fought my way to the ticket clerk, bought my ticket for Paris, paid the amount demanded for baggage excess, a destination slip was pasted on my baggage – and I staggered down to my stateroom, exhausted, but laughing at the absurdity of it all. And for hours after I had reached my room I could hear the trampling of feet and confusion of voices on the deck above me, where the 'Battle for the Scales' was still being waged.

When I opened my eyes in the morning the *Espagne* was slowly making her way to the pier in Bordeaux. A hasty breakfast and we were out on deck in time to see the ship tie up.

At nine o'clock, in a drizzling rain, I made my way down the slippery gangplank. The voyage of the *Espagne* had ended.[50]

HMS *Attack*, which was sunk after coming to the aide of the *Aragon*. (Naval-history.net Collection)

An unnamed male survivor gave the following account of the sinking. He leapt from the sinking vessel and was hauled aboard the destroyer HMS *Attack*, which was itself torpedoed, and he found himself struggling in the water once again:

I believe that the second torpedo which sent the destroyer to the bottom had been saved for the *Aragon* … It was not until the Germans were satisfied that the troopship was doomed that they attacked the destroyer. There must have been 300 or 400 on the destroyer for it had done excellent work in pulling men out of the water and some of then must have been killed or drowned in the second attack …

The vessel disappeared within seventeen minutes of being struck, and one member of the crew said that he attributed the swiftness of the disaster to the fact that the cargo hold was practically empty. He said that the torpedo caught the vessel aft of the engine room department, shattering the shaft. Had the vessel been loaded with cargo the progress of the torpedo might have been arrested but as it was it crashed into the bowels of the ship and sent wood … and iron flying in all directions …

… Most of us on deck thought we would have plenty of time to get all the soldiers away … whilst we struggled with the lifeboats the soldiers were drawn up onto the lower deck.

The vessel had taken a very decided list and when I tell you that some of the crew were up to their waists in water whilst they were launching the boats you will realize that the work was carried on under great difficulties. One of the lifeboats was smashed in the explosion but we managed to get one set away. It was not possible to launch all the boats because of the ship's heavy list.

I shall never forget the magnificent courage of the nurses. It was a case of women first, but those nurses would have gladly given up their places to the soldiers. Two or three of them made a protest as we were hurrying them into the lifeboats. 'Let us take our chance with the Tommies' said one sister … They showed no sign of fear. Some of the soldiers gave them a hearty cheer … they should be proud of the fact that 100 nursing sisters were not only saved but that not any one of them even got their feet wet.

The other thing that will remain in my memory is the remarkable behaviour of the troops, men from all parts of the country, northerners as well as southerners, who seemed to defy death. How they sang. I have heard the chorus 'Keep the home fires burning' on many occasions but I don't think that I have ever heard it given with so much power.

And while it is a tragedy to think that so many of them went down, there are two reasons for it. In the first place the vessel sank quite unexpectedly and the second was that those who had been picked up by a destroyer went down when she was torpedoed. As mentioned in the Admiralty communiqué, what one of the seamen described as 'the last act' occupied only a minute and a half. Suddenly the vessel gave a tremendous lurch, it was the spasm of death. At that time many of the soldiers were drawn up at attention on the deck, and Captain Bateman, who remained on the bridge shouted 'Now then, every man for himself, and may God help you all'.[53]

In December, 182 ships fell victim to U-boats, equalling 400,058 tons. Thirty more ships were damaged.

Overall, 1917 proved to be the deadliest year of the war at sea. A truly staggering amount of merchant shipping was lost with the introduction of wholly unrestricted submarine warfare. A total of 3,722 ships were hit by U-boats during the year, well over double the amount attacked during the previous year.

The number of U-boats lost in action in 1917 was sixty-five.[54] Eighty-seven new U-boats were built during the year, enough to replace those that were lost.[55] However, the experience of the veteran crewmembers that were killed was the true loss.

During the height of the losses in the spring, it appeared that Britain was on the verge of starvation, and indeed it was. Food reserves, particularly grain, began to get dangerously low as the amount of food and supplies being landed safely ashore plummeted. However, later in the year the use of a full convoy system restored hope to the Allies. Shipping losses began to flag as U-boat commanders had trouble adjusting to the increasingly effective defensive formations. More and more ships were making the transatlantic crossing in safety, and large numbers of American troops were arriving in Europe every day. It was just a matter of time before they would be organised and ready to make a significant contribution to Allied efforts on the battlefield. The tide was beginning to turn.

5

Over There, 1918

January–February 1918

On 8 January 1918, President Woodrow Wilson gave his 'Fourteen Points' address to Congress, intended as an outline for how world peace should be obtained. Wilson wanted to make it clear that the United States had not entered the war due to any nationalistic disputes or ambitions, and the 'Fourteen Points' focused on topics that would likely arise during peace talks. Wilson issued his statement without consulting any of America's European allies.

Amongst other things, the 'Fourteen Points' called for an end to secret treaties between nations, a reduction in arms, adjusting colonial claims to benefit native peoples and colonists alike, and freedom of the seas. Wilson also advocated for the removal of economic barriers between nations, and the formation of a world organisation that could help provide collective security for all nations.

Part of the motivation for President Wilson's statement was to encourage Central Powers nations that an agreeable peace could be reached, and to undermine their will to continue fighting as a result. Not all of the Allied leadership was happy with Wilson's approach, but his address would directly influence the direction of peace negotiations when the time came.[1]

President Woodrow Wilson. (*Collier's*, 1917/Authors' Collection)

In January, the *Aquitania*, now emblazoned in dazzle camouflage, began serving as a troop ship. The vessel, which had been laid up for all of 1917, was requisitioned in November, and began transporting American soldiers across the Atlantic. The HMT *Aquitania* would make nine voyages between January and November 1918, carrying approximately 6,000 US and Canadian troops overseas on each crossing.[2]

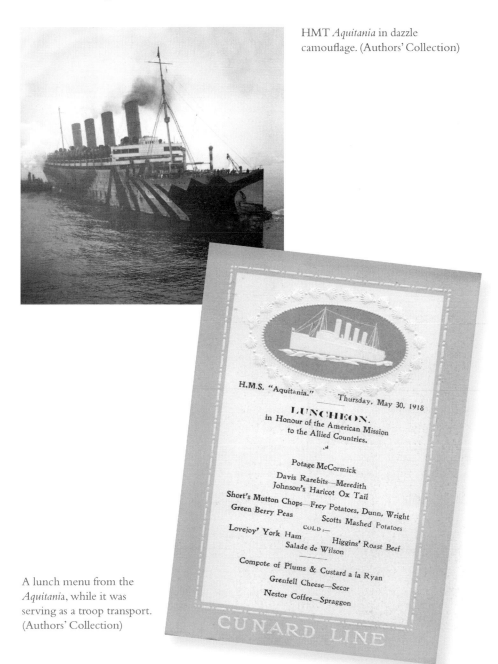

HMT *Aquitania* in dazzle camouflage. (Authors' Collection)

H.M.S. "Aquitania."   Thursday, May 30, 1918
LUNCHEON.
in Honour of the American Mission
to the Allied Countries.

Potage McCormick

Davis Rarebits—Meredith
Johnson's Haricot Ox Tail
Short's Mutton Chops—Frey Potatoes, Dunn, Wright
Green Berry Peas
Scotts Mashed Potatoes
COLD :—
Lovejoy' York Ham   Higgins' Roast Beef
Salade de Wilson

Compote of Plums & Custard a la Ryan
Grenfell Cheese—Secor
Nestor Coffee—Spraggon

CUNARD LINE

A lunch menu from the *Aquitania*, while it was serving as a troop transport. (Authors' Collection)

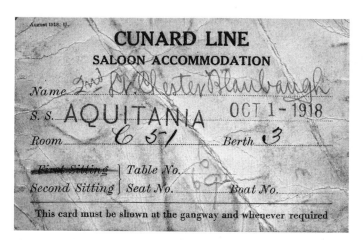

A saloon placement card from an American soldier transported across the Atlantic on the *Aquitania* in autumn 1918. (Authors' Collection)

On 31 January, American soldiers from the 114th Telegraph Battalion Signal Corps boarded the RMS *Adriatic* in New York, bound for Liverpool. The battalion, composed of men from the Philadelphia & Reading, and Erie Railroads, was organised in November 1917. The men were ultimately bound for Chinon, France, where they would establish their headquarters. One of those being shipped out was a Sergeant Fisher. He gave the following account:

> We stealthily crept on the enemy via the 23d Street pier on the East River, where we were loaded on a steam scow and taken around the island to the White Star Line's docks at West 23d Street, and there gleaned the information that we were to sail on the *Adriatic* for Liverpool, and after being lined up on the pier and given another talk on habits, drinking, etc., the Major announced that we would be searched and any man found with liquor would suffer court martial, and that if we possessed anything strong to turn it in. Results were not very good, and the talk only netted one 'petite' vial, which the C.O. handed to Colonel Erricson of the 107th Ammunition Train, who sailed with us, and the Colonel said: 'Thank you; it is just what I have been looking for'.
>
> … The food was horrible, and since finding out recently that America paid England $81.75 per man for transporting us, I have decided to ask for an $80.00 rebate.

The *Adriatic* safely arrived in Liverpool on 16 February. While in Europe, members of the 114th Telegraph Battalion Signal Corps strung telegraph wire and erected 20,000 telegraph poles, served as dispatchers, station masters, operators, linemen and maintainers at eighty stations along 300 miles of railroad.[3]

In January 1918, a total of 167 ships were sunk by U-boats, equaling 313,857 tons. Seventeen additional ships received damage. The total number of ships lost was lower than the previous month, as the Allies' refined their use of the convoy system to protect ships.[4]

In February 1918, the Central Powers launched the last offensive on the Eastern Front of the war, repudiating their December armistice with Russia. This was after some in the Bolshevik government in Russia pushed for a continuation of the war, believing that workers in central Europe were on the verge of revolution, and that they would support their nation's new workers' state.

The German offensive, titled Operation Faustschlag, or 'Fist Punch', began on 18 February and would last until 3 March. Russian forces were unable to put up any significant resistance due to the Russian Revolution and the ongoing Russian Civil War, which continued to weaken them from within. As a result, the Central Powers were able to advance 150 miles within a week, capturing large swaths of territory in the region of Ukraine, Belarus, and the Baltic States. This forced Russia's Bolshevik government to surrender.

War Commissar Leon Trotsky negotiated the armistice, which was strongly supported by Bolshevik leader Vladimir Lenin, who wanted the war to end so that they could deal with the problems within Russia itself. The Treaty of Brest-Litovsk was signed on 3 March, ending their participation in the conflict.[5] Germany was no longer fighting a full two-front war.

At sea on 4 February, the Cunard liner RMS *Aurania* was on a voyage from Liverpool to New York in ballast. The ship was launched in 1916, and had been immediately fitted out as a troopship. The British Government contracted the *Aurania* to move supplies and soldiers across the Atlantic. When the ship was approximately 15 miles north-west of Inishtrahull, Ireland, it was struck by a torpedo from *UB-67*. A trawler took the stricken *Aurania* in tow, but it became stranded near Tobermory on the Isle of Mull, Scotland. Rough seas soon broke apart the vessel and it was completely wrecked. Eight people died in the attack.

A Connecticut newspaper, *The Hartford Courant,* published details about the sinking, since quite a few people from Hartford had connections with the vessel. The article also discusses that the ship's captain, W.R.D. Irving, had been in command of the RMS *Laconia* when it was torpedoed in 1917:

News of the torpedoing of the Cunard steamship *Aurania*, target of a submarine on Wednesday, is of particular interest to many Hartford people, some of whom voyaged on her as late as in November. The ship sailed from an Atlantic port a short time before that, carrying, as her printed passenger list shows, some 1,400 men, including two units from New England and a large number of casuals, mainly officers of medical and other branches not then assigned to units, some of whom have since sent letters, extracts from which have been printed in several papers …

... When the *Aurania* sailed from an English port in November she carried among her passengers A.C. Watson [Arthur C. Watson], a traveling salesman for the Hartford-Bigelow Carpet Corporation of Thompsonville, who had been driving a Fiat ambulance for the Norton-Harjes ambulance field service, a branch which had been militarized a short time before, shifting from its semi-private status to a full branch of the Army. She also carried field service drivers who were acquainted with Captain Frederick W. Prince, Everett J. Lake and with Hartford boys who had been pupils at St. Paul's School.

The captain of the *Aurania* was W.R.D. Irvine, well known to a number of residents of Hartford. Captain Irvine had been in command of the ill-fated *Laconia* when she carried a Clark party to Smyrna, Cairo and Jaffa and the Holy Land in March 1913. On her way to these ports she anchored in the harbor of Piraeus, near Athens, preparatory to starting for Cape Helles, the entrance to the Dardenelles. Professor C.C. Stearns of California, formerly principal of the Collins street classical school here, was a passenger and took a party, including Rev. Shanley, formerly of St. Joseph's Cathedral, to the Acropolis.

When the *Laconia* neared Cape Helles, she was fired on by a Turk water battery, because Captain Irvine was flying his pennant as an officer in the Royal Navy Reserve and because the number of warships in the Dardenelles by Turkey, then at war with Greece and the Balkan states, was limited. The matter was straightened out and the ship steamed up the strait and came to anchor off the Golden Horn ...

... Captain Irvine was still in command of the *Laconia* on February 25, 1917, when his ship was torpedoed 250 miles from Fast Net Light. Two passengers lost their lives. Mrs. Hoy and Miss Hoy of Detroit, Mich., both well acquainted here, where Miss Hoy had classmates, she having attended Smith College, among such friends being Miss Katherine Ahern and Mrs. Ralph O. Wells.

The story of this tragedy Captain Irvine told [sic] to *The Courant* man in November, while on the *Aurania*, remembering the sad end of Miss Hoy, who died of exhaustion. An officer of the *Aurania* told the story of the gallant conduct of Captain Irvine at the torpedoing and said that the captain was last to leave his ship. The sinking of the ship and the loss of American lives were among the culminating causes for the entrance of this country into the war.

... Of the five ships of the Cunard Company which have been torpedoed, *The Courant* correspondent has sailed on four, the *California*, the *Laconia*, the *Transylvania*, and the *Aurania*. It was not his fortune to sail at the right time.[6]

Another one of the crewmembers aboard the *Aurania* was William Gerson, who survived for a third time after a vessel he was serving on had been torpedoed.[7]

The following day, 5 February, there was another sinking, albeit a much deadlier one. The Anchor liner HMT *Tuscania* was travelling in a convoy from New York to

HMT *Tuscania*.
(Authors'
Collection)

Liverpool, carrying over 2,000 American troops. It also was carrying general cargo such as thirty mules, supply wagons, and boxes of spare aircraft parts. The *Tuscania* had been converted into a troopship in 1916, complete with a 4in naval gun. The ship had played a significant role in the transport of American soldiers and personnel overseas. During the voyage, as was typically the case with troopships, conditions were overcrowded and uncomfortable, particularly below deck.

The convoy *Tuscania* was travelling in was deployed in five columns to protect against U-boats, and was being led by the Royal Navy cruiser HMS *Cochrane*. The ships were sailing at just 12 knots so that all of them could stay in formation. As was standard procedure the larger vessels and/or ones that were considered more important were located toward the centre of the convoy. Several of the ships were equipped with M-V sets, an early form of hydrophone designed to detect submarines up to 2 miles away. These sets were essentially composed of a series of underwater microphones placed at different points along ships' hulls.

The convoy was approximately 7 miles north of Rathlin Island, Ireland, when it was spotted by Kapitänleutnant Wilhelm Meyer aboard *UB-77*. He ordered full speed ahead to get in front of the column of ships, which were plowing through rough seas. Despite being equipped with an M-V set, nobody aboard the *Tuscania* detected the U-boat approaching. Around 6.40 p.m., Meyer fired two torpedoes at his quarry. The first struck the ship on the starboard side, exploding between the engine room and boiler room, killing thirty-nine firemen working there. The second missed the target. The ship began listing between 8 and 10° to starboard within minutes.

A distress signal was immediately sent, the ship's whistles repeatedly blasted, and distress rockets were fired. Efforts to abandon ship began with haste. Three Royal Navy destroyer escorts would respond to the calls for help, with two of the vessels coming alongside to take men off the sinking ship, one on the port side and the

A UB-III class U-boat like *UB-77* surfacing off the coast of Heligoland. (Authors' Collection)

other on the starboard side, while the third destroyer stood off at a short distance to pick up any swimmers in the water and watch for submarines.

Efforts to abandon ship proceeded calmly, but were hampered by *Tuscania's* heavy list, which rendered the boats on the port side virtually useless as they hung against the ship's hull. On the starboard side, the gap between the lifeboats and the ship was so great that many men fell into the water trying to jump across, and ended up getting crushed in between the destroyers and their own vessel. Once the lifeboats full of troops did reach the water, the wave action bashed them against the ship's side, breaking the oars and causing the boats to leak, rendering some of them helpless.

One lifeboat fell from the davits, landing on top of another heavily loaded boat and crushing its occupants. Some men struggling in the water struck out for land, and not all made it. Even the rescue ships themselves proved dangerous under the weather conditions. When the destroyer escorts arrived, some of the men who had been tossed out of lifeboats were caught in the wash of one of the rescue ship's propellers.

During the evacuation, *UB-77* eventually circled back to finish off the *Tuscania*. However, Kapitänleutnant Meyer's third shot missed the ship and passed underneath the stern of HMS *Mosquito*, one of the destroyer escorts alongside *Tuscania*. Its crew immediately sprang into action, dropping depth charges where they thought the submarine might be. In spite of the damage, the *Tuscania* remained afloat for around four hours, before plunging under bow-first with a muffled explosion. The survivors in the eleven lifeboats were later picked up by a trawler and taken ashore, while the destroyers saw to the rest. Despite the brave efforts of the rescuers, 166 men died.[8]

One of the survivors of the sinking was Lieutenant Don A. Smith, from Michigan. He wrote the following in a letter to his aunt back home:

I am at the officers' mess of the Thirtieth Irish Rifles. My work is clearing up now so that I hope to get a chance to write. Everybody is so very kind to me here, it seems as if I had been sort of handed the keys of Belfast. There are several American women here who have done wonders for our men.

You probably guessed I was on the *Tuscania*. Soon as I landed I cabled 'safe'. I'm crazy to hear from you, but have to make the best of it. I have so much to tell, but don't know how much the censor will pass. Sometime I'll send you a good account of the affair. It was rather fierce. Just twelve hours or so from Liverpool – we thought we were there. It was a great experience – one I would not care for again, but still experience. I learned many things. Torpedoed at 5.50, pitch dark, strong south wind [censored] – in Irish sea. I was looking at an atlas at the time. Had just found our position. It was a ——— of an explosion, right under where I was sitting. The 15,000-ton ship lifted and shook and the lights went out. My lifebelt, which I had carried to meals and to bed and every place, was at that moment below, so I had to go down to my cabin and get overcoat and life preserver.

Confusion, of course, but no panic. The men were heroes. They stood at their stations and all they wanted were orders. Our bulkheads held and we stayed up three hours. But every minute of the hour and a half I was aboard I looked for her to take a plunge.

We lost our men through faulty lowering of boats. The crew were supposed to do it, an officer and six men at each davit, but they showed up in but one or two cases. Our men lowered the boats and, not knowing how, they were dropped any old way, invariably filled with water, often smashed, and to get one boat away the falls often were so fouled that they had to be cut, consequently putting the three boats yet to be lowered from that davit out of business.

I saw one boat dropped onto a full boat in the water, square on. Another held at one end and dropped at the other, the men in it rolled out and the boat later took a dive among them. That was the way we lost our men – more were crushed than drowned. I watched all the boats get away and one destroyer loaded to capacity, and at 7.15, when the *Tuscania* had been afloat fifteen minutes longer than her sister ship (SS *Transylvania*) sunk last year in the Mediterranean stayed up when hit, I saw an empty boat, or rather a life raft, smashed in at both ends and full of water, but on account of her liferaft characteristics – airtight tanks – safe or sure to float at least. I was afraid the *Tuscania* would go down and in going down drag us all. Three-quarters were off and it was every man for himself.

I had no troops to look after, and I thought I'd chance the water, so went down a rope and swam to this empty boat with two privates [censored]. It was some swim and a damp spot to land. We floated, drifting with the ship, saw the second destroyer come up and get the rest, saw the *Tuscania* take fire and sink at 9.00 p.m., leaving a film of burning oil on the surface for a time – a most weird sight.

At 12 midnight by my watch, which kept going in spite of its bath, an armed trawler picked us up, just as we were expecting to be thrown on the rocks of Islay. I found matches and struck a light in the boat just in time. Five hours on a raft, wet and shaking like I don't know what! It was sure cold and disagreeable, to put it mildly. The trawler landed us at Larne, Ireland, at 8.00 a.m. next morning, in fairly run-down condition.

I helped Captain Rochey, from the Liverpool office, to get the rolls of the men saved, and thereby worked myself into being left in Ireland in charge of all men unable to be sent at once to England. About 150 sick, here and in Larue, Londonderry, Dublin and Ballymena. Had four medical officers left with me. I opened up 'Headquarters American Army in Ireland' and your nephew is boss. Funny, isn't it?[9]

Another American soldier who was aboard the vessel was Ray Stephenson, a young man from Darlington, Wisconsin. He gave the following account to papers in his hometown:

You wanted me to tell you more about the *Tuscania* … It happened February 5, 1918. We were due to land in Liverpool the following morning. About 5.30 that evening I was sitting talking to the members of my Company on the lower deck (I, myself, had a stateroom up on the upper deck). I was waiting for the supper bell to ring, when all of a sudden, the sub, or 'tin fish' as we now call them, hit us. It was a queer, deadening noise, and put the lights out immediately and water was shooting all over from bursted pipes caused by the explosion. We had been talking about the danger that we were in just before she was struck, as the men on the boat said it was the most dangerous part of the water, and was filled with mines, submarines, etc. As soon as we came to our senses, there was a mad rush for the steps leading to the upper deck. It was pitch dark outside and no lights were allowed on deck after dark at any time.

Well, in getting out of the place I was at, there were big iron posts and steel bars; it reminded me of a jail. I managed to crack my head against one of the posts, and, together with that and the excitement, I was about all in. I carried the cut and bump, as a reminder, for a couple of weeks; but I found out there was no need of anything to remind me, for I could dream constantly, night after night, and imagine I was still on the water.

I got up two flights of stairs and made for my stateroom, as I did not have my life preserver with me, due to carelessness, as we were cautioned never to appear at mess without one …

I got to my room, by luck, after feeling my way. I got down on my hands and knees and confiscated my pack and found a flashlight, then put on my life belt, and away I went to the outer deck. We were all assigned to certain places on the different decks. I had a hard time to make my way through, as the fellows were all trying to get away in the life boats as they were lowered. I was one of the unlucky ones, for when we got to our deck all to be found that looked like it might have been a lifeboat was a lot of splintered timbers. We waited and waited and saw lifeboats, one after another, being lowered and paddled away. Several smashed boats were thrown from the top deck, striking and upsetting loaded boats ready to pull away. The boys were thrown into the water and were floating around perfectly helpless, and their cries were of no use for we could do nothing.

After every lifeboat was off, things began to look pretty blue … There was not even as much as a board left for us to float on, and the only thing we could see to do was to wait and hope. Every once in a while faint lights were seen in the distance, and we did not know whether it was help coming to us or a light in some lifeboat … the night … was as black as I ever saw it. Finally it started to rain, and then the thoughts of our being in the cold, salty water made us stop and use some headwork, and do it quickly, for the *Tuscania* had already tipped considerable and was sinking fast.

All of a sudden a crash was heard on the opposite side of the boat, and, after going over, we found it to be a torpedo boat destroyer. Men were going down the ropes like rats jumping into a river. Several fell and others were crushed between the destroyer and the *Tuscania*, from the dashing of the waves. About half an hour after the first one left … a second destroyer pulled up, and it was then I made my get-away. I landed on the destroyer in good shape … I had on only a suit of underwear, shoes, shirt, and trousers when I got off, and it was a cold night, too.

Well, as we pulled out, another submarine fired at us and missed, and we were told it was sunk by depth bombs from the destroyer. These destroyers could have come to our rescue sooner had they not been loaded; but they had to go to the nearest shore and leave their crew, and thousands of gallons of oil, which they burn, were dumped out. In the first place they were not supposed to take us on; that is the rule of the sea; but they took the chance; otherwise we would have all been drowned, that is, those who had no lifeboats.

We got to Bemerency, Ireland, about 2.30 in the morning, and they had a lunch for us and then we went to bed. It was about four weeks before our Company were all together again, outside of three men – two of those were drowned and the other was McCauley, who used to drive jitney with Guy. He had pneumonia when we were torpedoed and he got away in his underwear only, and was in a hospital at Larne, Ireland, until about six weeks ago. His voice has never been the same since. We had the best of treatment in Ireland and England. We crossed from Dublin, Ireland, to Hollyhead [Holyhead], England, in a fast mail and passenger boat, escorted by two American destroyers.[10]

Wilbur S. Nutt, a soldier with the 20th Engineers, was another survivor of the disaster, although he too suffered from exposure and pneumonia following the sinking. A graduate of the Ohio State University School of Agriculture, Nutt wrote the following letter describing his experiences during the sinking:

The minute she was hit every man went as quickly and quietly as possible to his assigned life boat and I assure you it was remarkable how calm and yet how serious every man was.

Before all the life boats were lowered, cruisers came alongside and took the remaining men on board. The *Tuscania* remained on top two hours and 40 minutes, thus giving every man ample time to get off.

The boat I was in stayed close by until the *Tuscania* went down. We then made for shore only to find (but alas, too late) that we were to be cast against the rocks and be left to the mercies of God and the fate of the fearful breakers.

On seeing we were to be cast into the sea, we bid one another good-by, wished each other luck, and asked God to help us. We had given up all hope of living but a few minutes at the most. We could see the wave coming which every man knew would have us at its mercy.

In a second our boat was upset. On coming to the surface, I was quite near the upturned boat. In fact, the boat was surrounded with struggling men. I reached its side, grabbed the rope, then the boat. Just then someone grabbed me around the neck with clasped arms and a death-like grip.

With one loose arm, I grabbed the cleat on the bottom of the boat, then with one mighty leap, broke myself loose and scrambled up on top, only to be dashed off again by the second wave to pass. I was then whirled about as a stick in the water with feet and arms dangling as though they were nailed on. In the meantime, I came in contact with a board lengthwise of my body, as nice as though placed there. This I clasped tightly as possible with both arms, but it was soon thrown away from me, then a wave came in, driving me close to shore, and as it receded, I felt a rock under me, clasped it with my hands, managing to hold myself until the next wave came, lifting me onto its top. It was then I was able to scramble ashore and drag myself to safety.

It was impossible for me to walk, so crawling on hands and knees, I came to a post where I pulled up to a standing position and moved my arms and limbs until I became limbered up a little. It was probably between 1 and 2 o'clock a.m. I walked back and forth until 8 o'clock a.m. At 2.30 p.m. was able to get off my cold, wet clothes and have had the best of care ever since. I have completely recovered from an acute attack of pneumonia in the left lung.

I forgot to tell you I helped to lower the life boats, so was wringing wet with perspiration on getting into the life boat, and it was the sudden change and exposure that caused my illness. And to think my life was one of the few to be saved of 40 or 50 in this life boat! It was only a miracle … I am very glad to think that the most the Germans can do is destroy one's life.

This is a critical time, and I sincerely believe that we should make the effort to make a world peace, and even if I should be called to make the great sacrifice. I thank God for being able to do even so little.[11]

On 25 February, the HMT *Olympic* was ready to depart New York on another trooping voyage to Liverpool, the route it had been on since leaving the Canadian run. The ship underwent a refit early in 1917, and had been fitted with 6in deck guns. The ship was also painted in its first of two dazzle camouflage schemes. Large geometric shapes and designs were emblazoned on *Olympic's* hull in several shades of grey, blue and olive. The ship would be transporting American soldiers overseas, including members of the 157th Aero Service Squadron, which recently arrived in New York from Mount Clemens, Michigan. One of the soldiers aboard described the crossing:

February 12, 1918, saw us leave Mt. Clemens for our port of embarkation. It was a happy day, for the boys were anxious to get overseas and into action. We were ten days at Garden City and Mineola and even now the mention of the 'barracks' under the grandstand at the Mineola Fair Grounds will send chills up and down the spinal column. It was a 'cold, cold winter' and no mistake. These ten days were busy ones … 'til finally on February 25th the entire squadron embarked on a ship officially designated as 'Ship No. 527'. It was the White Star liner *Olympic*, bound for Liverpool.

The trip across developed very few seasick patients, as we had perfect weather. The Engineers band gave daily concerts on the deck and the life-boat drills and daily parades on the decks made the time pass quickly. The fifth day out we picked up our convoy of four American destroyers, and they were a welcome sight. There was little fear of submarines after that and the captain, a native of dear old England, after witnessing the actions of the 'Yanks' when 'subs' were sighted, expressed himself rather forcefully on the subject. The occasion came when the ship's gunners fired on a periscope and the destroyers cruised around and dropped depth bombs. Several shots were fired and those aboard lined up against the rail and gave vent to their feeling in wild cheers. 'They are either

very brave or else they are damned fools' was the captain's observation. Maybe
he was right on both counts, who knows? Tales vary as to whether there were
three submarines or only two encountered on the way over, but it makes little
difference. We were fortunate enough to elude them and finally took those
'shock absorbers', or life-belts, off when we reached Liverpool, March 5, 1918.

Immediately after debarking we were put aboard one of the funniest sights
(outside of a top sergeant being called down by the C.O.) that we'd seen since
joining the army.[12]

By the end of February 1918, 143 ships were sunk by U-boats, totalling 323,181
tons. Another twenty-two ships were damaged.[13]

March–April 1918

In March 1918, the Spring Offensive, also known as the Kaiserschlacht ('Kaiser's
Battle'), was launched along the Western Front. Initially successful, this resulted
in the largest advances in the region by either the Central Powers or Allies since
1914, and marked the first true British defeat there since trench warfare had
begun three and a half years prior.

By the end of 1917, the United States Army had just 184,000 men in France,
and by 31 January 1918, held 6 miles of the Western Front with one formed
combat division. The other Americans that had already arrived overseas were still
in training. Around 500,000 more Americans were expected to arrive in Europe
over the course of 1918. This highlights why Germany felt the need to launch a
large-scale offensive that spring, before the Allies began reaping the full rewards of
American involvement in the conflict. Furthermore, Germany had a swelling in
the number of troops they had available due to the Russian surrender, as divisions
that had been fighting on the Eastern Front were shifted westward.

Allied intelligence suspected Germany was planning an offensive, but was
caught off guard by the large scale of it. Furthermore, many British units along
the Western Front were still worn down by the battles of attrition there in
1917, and were not in any state to defend against such a large-scale offensive. As
one experienced soldier put it, 'I must confess that the German breakthrough
… should never have occurred. There was no cohesion of command, no
determination, no will to fight, and no unity of companies or battalions'.

The main goal of the Spring Offensive was for the German Army to penetrate
through the Somme region and then cut off the British Army in Flanders. This
was expected to draw British forces away from the English Channel, leaving the
ports there open to attack. Without access to the needed supplies coming through
those ports, the British Army would soon be surrounded with no means of

escape. This would force their surrender, and then France would have no choice but to seek an armistice.

This seemingly simple strategy proved anything but, as the planned targets of the attacks had to be shifted and adjusted constantly due to the changing situation and reality on the battlefront. The German Army proved incapable of moving up supportive artillery, needed supplies and manpower quickly enough to keep up with their rapid advance. Outpacing their own supply lines, and without enough food and ammunition, the offensive began to falter.

By April 1918, the real danger of a German breakthrough on the Western Front had passed. The Spring Offensive had come within a hair's breadth of success, but its failure would ultimately consign Germany to defeat. Territory that had been gained during the offensive was of little strategic value, and Germany would have trouble replacing the elite troops and number of men it had lost. Conversely, the Allied forces were being reinforced daily by the large numbers of American troops that were arriving from overseas and training for combat.[14]

Meanwhile, the *Mauretania* was reactivated in March to serve as a troop transport. The ship was once again placed under the command of Captain Arthur Rostron, who had been in command of the vessel twice previously. From that point until the end of the war, the *Mauretania*, which the British Admiralty had designated as the HMS *Tuberose* for security reasons, would carry over 30,000 American troops overseas. The vessel was painted in dazzle camouflage, with a checker-pattern emblazoned in blues, white and black on its hull, superstructure and funnels.[15]

The *Mauretania* in its dazzle camouflage scheme. (Authors' Collection)

At sea, 199 ships were sunk by U-boats in March 1918, a total of 379,406 tons of shipping. Thirty-one more ships were damaged in attacks. This was the highest number sunk by U-boats since September 1917.[16] However, the effectiveness of the convoy system and anti-submarine countermeasures continued to keep the losses of merchant shipping well below the 600,000 tons per month needed to starve Britain out of the war.

In April 1918, the USS *Leviathan* was completing a troop-carrying voyage across the Atlantic. The massive troop transport, which had begun its life as the Hamburg America liner SS *Vaterland*, was seized by the United States Government when America declared war on Germany on 6 April 1917. The vessel had been interned in Hoboken, New Jersey since the onset of the war, and more than half of the ship's German crew had decided to remain with the vessel during that time. Now that the two nations were at war, the *Vaterland*'s crewmembers were transported to Ellis Island, New York, and offered American citizenship.

The United States seized other German vessels after the declaration of war, including the interned North German Lloyd liners *Kronprinz Wilhelm* and *Kronprinzessin Cecilie*, which were eventually renamed the USS *Von Steuben* and USS *Mount Vernon* respectively, serving as troop transports. After being seized by the United States, the *Vaterland*, which had had its engines, boilers and other machinery sabotaged, began undergoing repairs and the conversion into a troop transport. The funnels and superstructure were painted grey

American doughboys on the deck of a troop transport, heading across the Atlantic. (Authors' Collection)

USS *Leviathan*. (Authors' Collection)

during this process, and the ship was renamed the USS *Leviathan* on 6 September 1917.

The *Leviathan* made its first transatlantic crossing as a troopship on 14 December, under the command of Captain Joseph W. Oman. It carried over 7,000 officers, troops and nurses to Liverpool during that particular crossing. When it was first learned that the luxurious liner was going to be converted and used as a troop transport, some scoffed, saying that it was 'roughly the equivalent of converting the Ritz into army barracks'. However, the ship's contribution to the Allied war effort during the remainder of the war cannot be understated, as during its nineteen crossings, the *Leviathan* would carry more than 100,000 American soldiers to Europe. On one crossing, the vessel's crew would have the honour of transporting General John 'Black Jack' Pershing.

Despite being returned to service, the *Leviathan* was in poor shape from sitting unused since 1914, so following the December voyage, the ship remained in Liverpool to receive repairs, and did not return to the United States until February 1918. On returning to Liverpool in March, further repairs were carried out, and the worn hull was repainted in a dazzle camouflage scheme.[17] On 22 April 1918, the ship was beginning a crossing carrying, amongst others, men from the 306th Field Artillery. One of these soldiers was Private Lawrence Henry Foster, who wrote the following letter to a friend:

DEAR OLD PAL:

Well! Well! Here's a letter from your old friend right out in the ocean.

Can you amagin [sic], Al. 'Me', who's been kicking up the dust on the old diamond, or chasing 'em over the grass in deep center. 'Me', who's never had no use for water, except what's in the pail and you know, Al I only hit that for appearances sake 'cause you know, Al, it's the regular thing to do after banging one over the garden wall. Yes, Al, I am now doing a high diving act on the high seas. Said diving being into the lunch. But I'll tell you about that later.

To begin with, we started for France from Camp Upton about 9 p.m. on April 21st. At 9 p.m. we falls out of the barracks and had roll call with full packs until 3 a.m. April 22d … Well, at 3 a.m. the foist sargent [sic] for the last time, very gently bawls 'CALL THE ROLL', and off we go for France to get the 5.30 train for Long Island City …

… Soon we pulls into Long Island City and gets on a special ferry-boat resoived [sic] for us, and when we hears that we are making for Hoboken, and that we would have a few roll calls in that good old Irish town, the boys all feel pretty good. Also pretty dry, cause it was excrushiating [sic] hot. But I guess the gink who was running the excursion was one of them bone-dry guys and we lands flat on the dock.

Well, Al, I wasn't much surprised to see that we was going to make the voyage on a boat with smokestacks. I had a tip on it from a guy who's pretty thick with the barber who shaves the Major. And what do you think the name of her was? Yes Sir! the *Leviathan*. Some giant, boy! She's the old Dashund [sic] or something like that, made over, and listen Al, the guy who give her the new name knew something, 'cause the foist [sic] part made a hit with the Irish and Algerians in the outfit. We get as far as the gang-plank and we have another long delay on the dock. But this was just military courtesy and we didn't mind. It seems the Commodore of the vessel was just dining at the time. And he takes about three hours to dine! Which is making a good job of it eh, Al? So right here is where we gets our foist [sic] knockdown to corned beef. Our Cap. commands, (1) Eats, (2) Rations! Rations is the command of execution but before he says it we have forty-two cans open, and when the Red Cross ladies hands us coffee and cake for desert, which was delightful, we calls it a meal. (The coffee and cake part of it.)

It gets to be about 2.30 and at last we move. Yes Al, she's some boat! A whale! But I hear that an Irishman drawed [sic] the plans for her. I had a laugh, Al, when one guy sees the boat and says he don't get it as how such a boat made of steel cud [sic] float. So I tells him as how the boat was made of iron, not steel. And she's made of wood inside, plenty of wood in proportion. That's where a guy's education comes in Al.

Well it don't take us long to get consigned to our staterooms, and right here, Al, is where I gets sore on the Irishman who made the plans … No doors or walls or curtains or anything on the staterooms, everything open! … I asked a naval guy on the ship, 'What's the idea?' and he says it was the 'Iron Pipe Demountable System' and I tell him I calls it, 'The Sardine System'. But then he tells me about the idea being that if the boat was captured we could be safe because the Germans couldn't get thru the ailes [sic] of our bunks. That's where I lurns [sic] something Al. But I couldn't kick, because the side of the boat I slept on has holes in it, portholes they calls 'em.

Well Al, once we gets under way there wasn't much excitement until Mess time, then all hands makes a dive for the Grand stairway what leads to the Ball-Room. That's where we dine Al, in the Ball-Room. Can you amagin [sic] it Al, privates in the Ball-Room with hand paintins [sic] on the walls and ceilings! I don't know where the Officers feed. I guess they have to take care of themselves as best they can. As I was saying Al the boys make the big rush for the lunch and every time I sees that rush it reminds me of the riots at the gates on the days that McGraw had me slated to pitch. Once we gets into the Ball-Room it's all big-league stuff Al, with Officers standing all around umpiring and any guy caught going to the plate more than three times in one inning is out. We only have two meals a day and that is enuf [sic] Al. Breakfast and dinner. For supper we have abandon-ship drill by the numbers in case the ship goes down.

And we have nifty little life-presoivers [sic] that go on like a chest protector. We was told that if the ship went down, to keep cool, and take one blanket with us, and take an Annie Kellerman off the stoin [sic] … Can you figure as how the a guy's going to swim with a blanket on him? … believe me the 'Subs' never had a chance. Our deck is decorated with guns all camoflowed [sic] and each of 'em run by the best Navals we got in West Point.

Every night we close the portholes so as no sound can get out and hold an entertainment with movies which we enjoy, Al, but most of the nights we spend trying to shave ourselves with salt water. We always have our evenings to ourselves, Al, and I spend most of 'em on deck taking in most of the scenery which is always about the same …

Well Al, old boy, I'm sorry I can't tell you just where I am, but here's a hint. One day I asks [sic] a petty Naval just about where the ship was and he says, 'We are now passing thru Military Channels'. So there's your tip, Al, look it up on the map and you can figure about where we will land. Now Al, I guess I will have to close as I just hears the whistle blow for medical exercises which we have every day.

Assuring you that I will keep in touch with you and hoping that you will give my regards to the boys in the league, and wishing you the same, I am your old Pal.

Hen.[18]

As April came to a close, a total of 138 ships had been sunk or captured, equalling 293,584 tons. Another twenty-eight ships were damaged.[19] This was the smallest number of merchant ships lost in a month since July 1916, evidence that the anti-submarine countermeasures in place were proving highly effective. The convoy system was the largest factor, as was the greater availability of depth charges, as manufacturing capability finally caught up with the demand. More airplanes were also available to patrol over convoys, which proved an effective way of detecting U-boats just below the surface. While still a worry, the amount of shipping being lost compared to how much was making it across the ocean meant that Britain no longer faced starvation, and that the Allies were still receiving necessary supplies and manpower despite U-boat commanders' best efforts. More and more American troops continued to pour across the Atlantic and into Europe. For Germany, time was running out.

May–June 1918

In May, Germany's Spring Offensive was continuing to weaken on the Western Front, and its forces were suffering from supply shortages, partly as a result of the Royal Navy blockade. Meanwhile in the east, Romania, isolated since its Russian allies surrendered, signed the Treaty of Bucharest on 7 May. This peace treaty with the Central Powers marked Romania's exit from the war.

At sea, the Cunard Line's HMT *Ausonia* was making a crossing from Liverpool to New York, in ballast. The *Ausonia* had proven a lucky vessel thus far in the war. Put into service as a troop transport in 1915, the ship was torpedoed by *U-55* in June 1917, but managed to limp to port in Queenstown with only one person aboard having lost their life. However, its luck would not hold.

On 30 May 1918, the convoy in which *Ausonia* was travelling was spotted by Kapitänleutnant Ernst Hashagen aboard *U-62*. Hashagen, a submarine ace who would have forty-eight kills by the war's end, began stalking the ships. He was hoping to pick off individual vessels once the convoy was farther out into the Atlantic, at which point the Royal Navy destroyer escorts would turn back for England, and the other ships would begin to disperse. There still were not enough escorts to travel with every convoy coming and going across the Atlantic for the entirety of the crossings. This was a new tactic being attempted by submarine commanders to combat the convoy system. Two days prior, a U-boat had been spotted near the convoy, and the destroyer screen chased and depth charged where it was last seen. This time, the *Ausonia* would have no such protection.

Hashagen soon sighted the *Ausonia* off on its own, and fired a torpedo at it, which struck aft. The vessel began settling by the stern, and Captain Robert Capper quickly gave the order to abandon ship. Once the crew had evacuated, the U-boat shelled the *Ausonia* to make sure it would sink. The submarine then came alongside the lifeboats to interrogate the survivors. *U-62* soon left the scene, abandoning the survivors hundreds of miles from shore. They would spend eight days in the open lifeboats before being rescued. Fortunately, with the amount of time until they would be rescued uncertain, the crewmen had begun rationing supplies right away at the captain's order. A total of forty-four people died in the *Ausonia* sinking, including two lifeboats full of survivors who were never seen again after being separated from the other boats.

A female stewardess, Theresa Edgar, was one of the survivors. The only woman who had been aboard *Ausonia*, Edgar had experienced a number of close calls already during the war. She had been aboard the *Mauretania* on the transatlantic crossing during the outbreak of war in 1914, when the speedy liner was pursued by a German vessel, and ran into Halifax. She also served aboard the *Lusitania* and the *Laconia* on their last round-trip crossings prior to being sunk by U-boats. Edgar gave the following account describing the loss of the *Ausonia*, and the survivors' long wait for rescue:

Captain Robert Capper.
(Authors' Collection)

Survivors from a sunken merchant vessel give some impression of what the *Ausonia*'s survivors would have looked like adrift in an open boat. (Authors' Collection)

bedraggled and half dead we were pulled aboard the warm, cozy compartments of the warship.

None of us will ever forget that wonderful breakfast, which we devoured like hungry wolves, after we had made such toilettes as the accommodations afforded.

The ship ran us into Bearhaven, County Cork. We stayed at the hotel for a few hours and then journeyed to Dublin, then to Holyhead. Crossing the Irish Sea, I thought, 'Now I can finally rest', but no sooner was I resting in my cabin when I was warned of the danger we faced, and again we drew in our breathe and steeled ourselves for any new experience that might overtake us. All the other boats made land, except the two lost sight of the first night out. One sailor boy, who had his ankles broken by a piece of wood that fell on him when the explosion occurred, we had taken into our boat. He died two days after reaching the hospital in Liverpool. The rest of us suffer at times from rheumatism or from our feet, but otherwise we are no worse for the experience.

I love the sea. I am happier on it than on land. After my husband died I had to earn my living, and I prefer this to anything else. I try not to think of that experience in a lifeboat. Perhaps if I should dwell on it I should go crazy. I do not deny it was terrifying. Crouched down in the bottom of a boat, drenched for days, not knowing what moment would be our last, was not an experience to be forgotten in a hurry. But why dwell on the past when there is so much worth living for in the future?[20]

During May 1918, a total of 163 ships were sunk or captured, totalling 310,188 tons. Thirty-one additional ships sustained damage in attacks. While most of the ships were sunk in the Mediterranean or around the British Isles, one attack did occur right off the coast of the United States.[21] By this point of the war, so many merchant ships had been sunk that it was impossible for passengers or crewmembers travelling across the Atlantic to ignore the evidence of the attacks. Masts of U-boat victims protruded from the water in and around the Thames Estuary, and despite the employment of the convoy system, the Mediterranean shipping routes were often cluttered with debris from sunken vessels. One American sailor, Ray Millholland, graphically described an example of this in the Mediterranean in 1918:

Everywhere on the surface … was mute evidence of the effectiveness of Germany's unrestricted submarine campaign. We were constantly shifting our zigzag course to avoid smashed lifeboats, drifting hatch gratings, and the odd clutter of gear that rises to the surface from a sunken ship. Occasionally a shapeless undulating mass buoyed by a cork life jacket would drift by, and a brine bleached face would stare with empty eye sockets at the glaring sun.[22]

In June 1918, American forces were gradually getting more involved in the land war. At sea, the U-boat war remained a volatile one. Despite Allied countermeasures, tragic losses were still being incurred. In fact, with things going poorly on land, many of the U-boat crews were pressed to take even bolder action.

On 2 June, a convoy was approaching England. Aboard one of the ships was Reverend Joseph Wareing of Baltimore, Maryland, a survivor of the *Laconia* sinking who was travelling with a group of Red Cross workers. As the convoy approached the 'war zone' waters around the British Isles, a group of U-boats sprung an attack, despite the destroyer escort. Reverend Wareing described the incident as follows in a press account, which was overshadowed in the papers by headlines reading 'Americans and French Continue Shoving the Enemy Back at Chézy':

Soon after we reached the danger zone our convoy was attacked by German submarines … at least two were seen.

We had a lively escort of British destroyers, however, and they were on the trail of the periscopes like a flash. Guns and depth charges began popping like giant firecrackers on the Fourth of July. Fifteen depth charges were dropped into the nest of German submarines. Whether any submarines were sunk I cannot say … but I know we did not lose a single ship. Our convoy carried a large number of American troops – I cannot tell you how many.

The conning tower of a U-boat just breaking the surface. (Authors' Collection)

When the first alarm was sounded for the passengers to go to their life boat stations late on Sunday afternoon I was in my stateroom. I had no sooner reached my station than depth charges began to explode, shaking our ship. After a few minutes of anxious waiting at the life boat stations we received the signal. 'Enemy beaten off'.

Discipline on board was superb. The troops behaved as if a submarine attack was part of the everyday routine, and there was not the slightest flurry anywhere on board. For coolness in time of emergency I do not think you could beat these young Americans. Their nerves are like steel.

Two hours later on the same day, while I was preparing for dinner, another alarm was sounded and almost simultaneously the destroyers began dropping depth charges. One landed within 500 yards of our ship and gave it a good shaking.

At no time during either attack did I see a periscope or the track of a torpedo.[23]

Daring attacks on convoys were leading to heavier losses of U-boats and their crews, and the effectiveness of the attacks continued to decrease. However, the new tactic of several U-boats coordinating their attacks on convoys and merchant shipping was predictive of the 'wolf pack' tactics that U-boat commanders would employ during the Second World War, to devastating effect. This strategy had been experimented with as early as 1917, but the German leadership had not accepted it as a feasible strategy at the time.

June 1918 also marked the beginning of construction on the Northern Barrage. This was an ambitious Allied plan to reduce the number of U-boat attacks on merchant shipping. The Dover Barrage had already made it difficult for U-boats to safely access the English Channel, by cutting off access with underwater indicator nets and mines. The Dover Barrage's effectiveness had been increased since earlier in the war. This can be attributed to the invention of more effective mines, improved minefield coverage, and night patrols equipped with searchlights. Eventually, the hazard of crossing into the English Channel proved too great, and by mid-August 1918, Germany had ordered U-boats to cease crossing into the Channel at all. This led to more and more U-boats having to sail through the North Sea and around Scotland to attack merchant shipping in the North Atlantic, or to be resupplied.

Originally proposed in 1916, and then agreed to at the Allied Naval Conference in September 1917, the Northern Barrage was envisioned as a barrier of underwater mines strung across the North Sea, between the Orkney Islands and Norway, to 'fence in' U-boats. Initially, Vice Admiral William Sims, commander of the United States naval forces in Europe, was sceptical of the project. However, his objections were overcome due to an appeal by Assistant

The shaded areas on this period map mark the locations of the Northern Barrage and Dover Barrage. (Authors' Collection)

Secretary of the Navy Franklyn Delano Roosevelt, who persuaded President Wilson to support it.

In May, the United States Mine Force began arriving at its base in Inverness, Scotland. By June, enough mines had been assembled that construction could begin. The American minelayers proceeded from their base under the escort of Royal Navy destroyers. While they were constructing the barrage, Grand Fleet vessels provided the ships with a screen consisting of a force of battleships, battlecruisers and light cruisers. Operations continued unabated until October 1918, when work was halted. Additional mines laid by Britain supplemented those laid by the Americans.

Mines assembled and ready for use in construction of the Northern Barrage sit in storage in a warehouse. (Authors' Collection)

Minelayers cruise in formation while constructing the Northern Barrage. (Authors' Collection)

When all was said and done, the Northern Barrage consisted of rows of mines 230 miles long across the North Sea, and 30 miles wide. Over 70,000 mines were used in its construction, and laid at varying depths from 0–240 feet below the surface. This proved effective against U-boats as a physical barrier, but was even more valuable given its demoralizing effect on German submarine crews. Combined with the convoy system, merchant shipping losses continued to decline.[24]

The USS *Quinnebaug* was one of the American minelayers involved in the construction of the Northern Barrage. Previously known as the Old Dominion liner SS *Jefferson*, the ship had been chartered by the United States Navy. As

USS *Quinnebaug*, formerly the SS *Jefferson*. (Authors' Collection)

with the other vessels in the Mine Force, the *Quinnebaug* was painted in dazzle camouflage to confuse U-boats. One of the crewmembers that served about the ship was a sailor named Frank. He described the accomplishments of the Mine Force in a letter to his sweetheart back home, but due to censorship, wasn't able to write about it until after the war was over. His letter brims with pride at what was accomplished:

> U.S.S. *Quinnebaug*
> Nov. 30th 1918
> 'Inverness Scotland'

Dear Little Girl:-

Just a few lines to let you know my whereabouts, and also send a couple of pictures. While of course they are only postcard pictures I think they will give you an idea of how a Okla [sic] boy looks in Uncle Sam's uniform and also kilts. I intend having some better ones made as soon as we hit the states and if they are good I will send you one.

You will notice from the heading of this letter that I am in Scotland and have been since my departure from the states. Which is now nearly seven months.

I suppose you would like to know what I have been doing during my seven months over hear [sic], and now that the censorship has ceased, and I am permitted to talk on what ever subject I wish I will state, that I have been with the mine laying fleet in the North Sea. No doubt you had read of the doings in this, this particular place which always affords a large amount of excitement to those who traverse its waters. The source of excitement being based on floating mines, submarines, or terrible storms. But so far we have been real fortunate having lost no men at sea and only having two encounters with Williams 'U' boats, in both cases managing to come out 'OK'. Our ship carries alone carries six hundred and ten mines, and there are thirteen others capable of carrying equal as many if not more. The mine laying record for this ship alone was '6,049'. We completely enclosed the North Sea there by putting an end to Williams 'U' boats. The English were greatly pleased with our work, as they had pronounced the task impossible, and in there [sic] attempt to do the job, they lost practically every mine layer they sent out. When they were told that with fourteen ships we could lay '7,000' mines in one trip, they refused to believe us. We have been awarded with a gold chevron as a distinguishing mark for foreign service. Now that we have finished our task we are going to southern England, perhaps Liverpool and from there home. And believe me I will be glad to see that Statue of Liberty again. Well sweet little girl that is all for this time. Hoping to hear from you real soon.

    I am Ever

        With Love for You

            Frank

        U.S.S. *Quinnebaug*

        c/o PM at N.Y.

Merry X-mas and a happy New Years[25]

On 27 June, the HMT *Justicia* was about to depart on an Atlantic crossing. Laid down as the *Statendam* for the Holland America Line, the vessel was requisitioned as a troopship, and then given to the Cunard Line because of the sinking of the *Lusitania*, and renamed *Justicia*. When Cunard had difficulty assembling a crew, the ship was moved to the White Star Line, which assigned the *Britannic*'s former crew to man it. An unnamed American troop from the 301st Engineers gave a description of the crossing:

We soon received the order to detrain and were formed and marched … to an East River dock, where we embarked on an old river steamer, the *Ossining*, and steamed down along the east coast … and up the Hudson. We watched the pier numbers and soon saw No. 58 in the distance. As we drew nearer, we noticed several large camouflaged steamers near the pier, the largest of which we later learned was the famous *Vaterland* … at our pier … we assembled by groups … While we were waiting, Red Cross workers … made their way through the mass of soldiers dispensing buttered rolls and coffee, while others accepted postcards and telegrams which would be released upon our safe arrival in France.

    We learned that the large, three-stacked steamer on the south side of the pier was destined to have us on its passenger list and we regarded it with interest.

An example of a Red
Cross postcard that
American soldiers
sent home to let their
families know that
they had safely arrived
overseas. (Authors'
Collection)

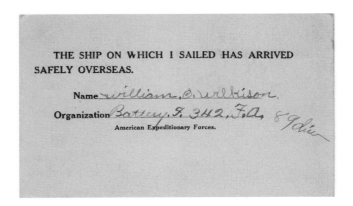

THE SHIP ON WHICH I SAILED HAS ARRIVED
SAFELY OVERSEAS.

Name *william, O. wilkison.*

Organization *Battery, F, 342, F.a,*
American Expeditionary Forces.

Next to the *Vaterland*, it was the largest of the great ships in the vicinity, and
we learned later that it was the fifth largest in the transport service. It was the
Justicia, formerly the *Statendam*, or better known as 'His Majesty's Transport
F8261' ... She had a displacement of 30,000 tons and a transport capacity of
4,000 troops. When war broke out, she had been little more than the hull and
only the first-class salons and the staterooms had been completed, making her
admirably adapted to the accommodation of troops.

Our turn for embarkation finally came and we lined up at a dock on the
pier and were given our berthing and meal tickets. The officers had first-
class accommodations, the first sergeants had second-class, and the sergeants
third-class. We found our staterooms with the aid of directions from the deck
steward. The officers were quartered by rank, three in a stateroom, and the
four first-class sergeants had a second-class stateroom on the same deck. The
other sergeants were poorly quartered somewhere in the vast hold, so room
was made for them with the other senior sergeants and this arrangement
continued throughout the voyage.

We embarked too late for the noon meal on shipboard, so it was with
ravenous appetites that we greeted supper. We found the food excellent, well
cooked, though not up to the army standard of quantity, but at that there was
no danger of starvation. We turned in early that night determined to make the
most of the clean, white sheets and pillow-cases, to which the army in war
times is so unaccustomed, before there should be any possibility of an enemy's
torpedo depriving us of these luxuries.

The next morning, the 28th of June, we were both surprised and disappointed
... to find the dark, gloomy walls of the pier still looming close to the side of
the ship. However, our disappointment was short-lived, for after dressing and
breakfasting, we went on deck and noticed the unmistakable signs of departure
... the gangplank was drawn aboard, and several puffing little tugs were drawing

alongside and making fast. Directions were shouted … and the *Justicia* moved slowly out into the Hudson and pointed her nose downstream.

At this interesting stage of the game we were all ordered below decks … The great ship was throbbing now and we were gathering speed. On each side the sky-scrapers of lower New York and the low factory buildings of Hoboken drifted past and we found ourselves in the bay. Our hearts jumped a bit as the inspiring figure of the Goddess of Liberty loomed up and then faded from view and soon we saw only a sunlit expanse of water. America lay behind; France was ahead.

We reached the three-mile limit, where the convoy was assembling, about ten o'clock and were permitted to come on deck. It was a magnificent spectacle. Twelve giant steamers (of which the *Justicia* was, however, the largest) were assuming their formation. A United States cruiser had taken its place at the head of the column and off to each flank was a torpedo boat destroyer. Encircling us, in amongst us here, there, and everywhere, were submarine chasers of the mosquito fleet and in the air above us were two hydroaeroplanes and a dirigible. While we were assembling, these planes and the balloon scouted in all directions for any signs of enemy periscopes.

At noon while at dinner the ship began to throb once more and we were off. After dinner we went on deck, with our life preservers now, for we were required to wear them at all times once we had left the three-mile limit. The planes had left us, but the dirigible was still hovering over the cruiser ahead of us and at odd intervals scouting to the flanks and far ahead. It was a peaceful scene, and … it was difficult to realize that there was a mighty fleet of submarines attempting to spot the passage of every ship in the convoy on its journey to France.

Life on shipboard was very easy compared to the rigorous training to which we had been subjected in the preceding months … The only daily routine was boat drill, held once in the morning and once in the afternoon, at which every man was required to report to his emergency station at one of the lifeboats and remain there until one of the ship's officers had checked up. It was at one of these drills that the Naval aviation officer in charge of the lifeboat next to ours, who seemed to be inflicted with an insatiable curiosity, prowled around his boat, which was hung over the side of the ship from the davits, and laid his hand on a lever in the bow of the lifeboat.

'What's this?' he inquired … and pressed the lever. The next second the cry of 'Man Overboard' went up and every one rushed to the railing. The boat was upside down in the wash of the propeller, and the officer, who was fortunately a good swimmer, had reached it and was clinging to it … there was another transport directly behind us, which slowed down enough to reach him with a rope and haul him aboard, for it is certain that the *Justicia* would never have stopped to send a boat back for him. The lives of four thousand and the safety of one of England's largest transports depended on keeping her at a great enough speed to enable her to maneuver in case of emergency.

After this event the voyage was fairly uneventful. As a rule the sea was calm … Every fifteen or twenty minutes the convoy would change its course and … assume a new formation … but these changes and the occasional passing of a returning convoy or single steamer were about all that afforded particular interest to the hundreds who thronged the deck during the day.

After the ship had been a few days at sea, one of the artillery officers of the 76th division inquired as to the possibilities of having some talks by engineer officers on artillery emplacements and dugouts. As the smoking-rooms were sufficiently large for such purposes, an impromptu class was arranged and some of the essentials in which the artillery was particularly interested were studied in detail and some practical features discussed by the engineer officers of the detachment. At the same time classes in French were conducted by French officers, who also organized a short course in trench warfare for infantry officers.

July 4 did not pass unnoticed; General Treat, in command of the troops, read the Declaration of Independence to the men and officers who had assembled in the forward part of the ship. General Donnelly spoke briefly, after which the band played such pieces as were requested by the men. General Treat was on his way to Italy for duty there; General Donnelly, as Chief of the 4th Corps Artillery, several months later, was again associated with the regiment.

Evenings were the best part of the day. As the sun sank in splendor in the western sky, the regimental band from the artillery organization which was on board gave excellent concerts …

About a week out, word made the round of the ship that we would pick up our British escort before night fell, and surely enough, in the late afternoon they appeared on the horizon and we joined them. They were destroyers of the most modern type – long, low, gray boats of a graceful slenderness and an incredible speed. They pitched and tossed in the waves which hardly made themselves felt on our great steamer, but they would rise on the crest of one and sink into its trough, out of sight, only to reappear again and go racing ahead or off to the flanks to search for the once dreaded but now hoped-for periscope. For with these watchful sea hounds on all sides of us (there must have been fifteen of them), we were very anxious for the sight of a little action.

We thought we had it when, one morning, just after we had sighted the coast of Scotland … two of the destroyers went racing off toward the Irish coast and opened fire at some invisible object. They maneuvered around for nearly half an hour, keeping up a desultory fire, and then overtook us and took their places in formation. Rumor had it that they had sighted several submarines and sunk them after a hot engagement. At any rate, we had something to write home about, for it was the first shot in the war for us … It developed, however, that no submarines had been seen. The destroyers were firing on and exploding mines which had been laid by the Germans very recently … as they were well located in the channel. Had the giant bow of the *Justicia* just ticked one of these, there would have been ample opportunity to test the efficacy of our boat drills. These waters were particularly dangerous because of the protection the barren, indented coasts afforded the submarines.

When darkness came that night, we were well down off the coast of England, and when we awoke next morning the steady throbbing of the engines below us had ceased. We rose and opened our port-holes, which of course had been kept closed at night throughout the voyage to avoid the showing of lights, and there before us was land and a real city such as we had forgotten existed. A ferry passed us close to our ship and we saw a group of people smiling and waving their hands. And the strange part of it was that there were women in the group and men in civilian clothes. We hadn't seen either for thirteen days …

We had all risen very early and breakfast was not yet ready, so we went on deck and watched the strange scene with interest. We were lying in mid-river off the Liverpool docks and ahead of us and behind us were other ships of the convoy. Some of them were already at the docks and were becoming lightened of their troops and passengers …

About eleven o'clock (it was the morning of the 10th of July), our tugs made fast and began to draw us through the narrow locks into the network of basins which forms Liverpool's docking system. As we drifted slowly along … a great crowd of gamins followed us along the pier and scrambled for the pennies which were thrown them from the ship. A stout English 'Bobbie' made slow, deliberate efforts to get rid of the gang, but when he had driven them off of the dock and around the corner of the building, up they would come again scrambling madly for pennies from around another corner of the building. Doubtless our sympathies were more with the gamins than the 'Bobbie' …

Early in the afternoon we had our packs and hand-baggage ready on deck for disembarkation, and a little later we received the expected orders. We formed on the dock and were marched through the streets of Liverpool to the Midlands Railway station, some distance from the piers. We received a royal welcome, particularly from the street urchins who coupled with their hospitality demands for American pennies, and would run beside us for blocks urging the backward among us not to fall short of their expectations of us.[26]

On the same day that *Justicia* was beginning its transatlantic crossing, one of the more blatant examples of misconduct on the part of a U-boat commander and crew took place. On 27 June, the Union-Castle liner HMHS *Llandovery Castle* was on a voyage from Halifax to Liverpool. The ship had been requisitioned as a hospital ship by the British Admiralty in July 1916, and attached to the Canadian forces. On this crossing, the *Llandovery Castle* was attacked without warning by *U-86*, under the command of Oberleutnant zur See Helmut Patzig. The vessel sank in ten minutes, approximately 116 miles west of Fastnet Rock.

The *Llandovery Castle* was sporting the standard hospital ship livery, so there is no way that the ship could be identified as anything other than a hospital ship. After the ship had sunk, Oberleutnant zur See Patzig, seeking to cover up evidence of the attack, proceeded to run down the lifeboats with *U-86*, and then had the crew open fire on the survivors. Two-hundred and thirty-four of the crewmembers aboard died, including the majority of the medical staff.

Twenty-four survivors were later rescued, and told the horrific details of the attack. Germany initially claimed that the vessel was sunk due to it carrying American officers overseas illegally – a false claim – and later denied that it had been sunk intentionally at all, saying that it was mistaken identity or that it struck a mine. Anger over the attack was immediate. Newspapers in the United States ran headlines such as 'Diary Indicates Falsity of Hun U-boat Excuses'. The diary in question was that of Sergeant Major Chenette, of Duluth, Minnesota, who was serving in the Canadian Expeditionary Force. He had crossed the Atlantic on the *Llandovery Castle* earlier in June, and wrote the following, which demonstrates how unlikely it would be for the vessel's identity to be misconstrued:

Thursday, June 6 – … Walked two blocks down to 'Pierhead', where we boarded the *Llandovery Castle*, one of the finest Red Cross boats we have. All the other men in the boat are put in 'Blues' again so in case of submarines the Germans have no cause to say they saw troops aboard. We are all assigned to lifeboats and have life belts.

  Friday, the 7th – Nice day. Pulled out at 5 a.m. Sea very smooth … All of us have to sleep in our clothes for a few days so as to be ready in case of subs. Had boat drill and lowered two boats. Men aboard with legs cut off. Bed 9 p.m.

  Saturday, the 8th – Off the Irish coast and quite a swell running but am not sick yet. Our beds are small iron ones swung between little steel tripods. The mine sweeper is an interesting appliance. At night the vessel is lit up with green and blue lights placed five feet apart clear around the deck and the Red Cross funnels on the smokestack are illuminated. There could be no rational excuse for a mistake in knowing these vessels … [27]

Some time after the sinking, the HMS *Morea* passed the floating debris and bodies of the *Llandovery Castle* victims. One of the witnesses to this tragic scene was Kenneth Cummins, who was on his first voyage to sea:

We were in the Bristol Channel, quite well out to sea, and suddenly we began going through corpses … The Germans had sunk a British hospital ship, the *Llandover Castle* [sic], and we were sailing through floating bodies. We were not allowed to stop – we just had to go straight through. It was quite horrific, and my reaction was to vomit over the edge.

It was something we could never have imagined … particularly the nurses … seeing these bodies of women and nurses, floating in the ocean, having been there some time. Huge aprons and skirts in billows, which looked almost like sails because they dried in the hot sun.

There was no chance of rescuing them – they were all dead. As the fighting ship – which we were – we were not permitted to stop unless ordered to do so by the Admiralty.

Cummins survived the war, served in the Second World War, and died in December 2006 at the age of 106.[28]

After the war, Oberleutnant zur See Patzig and two of his watch officers, Ludwig Dithmar and John Boldt, would be charged with war crimes due to the sinking. They were to be put on trial during the Leipzig War Crime Trials, conducted by Germany in 1921 as one of the requirements of the Treaty of Versailles. Only twelve individuals in total would be brought to trial during these proceedings, including Dithmar and Boldt, who were found guilty and sentenced to four years in prison each. However, Patzig had left Germany and was beyond the court's jurisdiction at that point. The judgement in the trial read as follows:

In estimating the punishment, it has, in the first place, to be borne in mind that the principal guilt rests with Commander Patzig, under whose orders the accused acted. They should certainly have refused to obey the order. This would have required a specially high degree of resolution. A refusal to obey the commander on a submarine would have been something so unusual, that it is humanly possible to understand that the accused could not bring themselves to disobey. That certainly does not make them innocent, as has been stated above. They had acquired the habit of obedience to military authority and could not rid themselves of it. This justifies the recognition of mitigating circumstances … a severe sentence must, however, be passed. The killing of defenceless shipwrecked people is an act in the highest contrary to ethical principles. It must also not be left out of consideration that the deed throws a dark shadow on the German fleet, and specially on the submarine weapon which did so much in the fight for the Fatherland. For this reason a sentence of four years' imprisonment on both the accused persons has been considered appropriate …

… the accused, Dithmar, is dismissed from the service, and the accused, Boldt, is condemned to lose the right to wear officer's uniform.[29]

The two crewmembers of *U-86* were the only U-boat crewmembers found guilty of war crimes after the war. However, they would later 'escape' on the way to the labour camp where they were to serve their sentences.[30]

In June, a total of 116 ships had been sunk by U-boats, totalling 253,236 tons. Sixteen additional vessels suffered damage in submarine attacks.[31] Despite the risks U-boat commanders were taking, they simply were not inflicting enough damage on merchant shipping to make a difference.

July–August 1918

July 1918 proved to be a momentous and very important month in the war. On 15 July, the German Army launched its last offensive of the war, marking the beginning of the Second Battle of the Marne. The German offensive failed when the French Army, supported by Italian and British troops, counterattacked their right flank using 350 tanks, inflicting severe casualties. Nine United States Army Expeditionary Force units, totalling approximately 250,000 men, also participated in the battle, under French command, and were lauded for their tenacity.

The battle would last until 6 August, and would end in a decisive Allied victory, crushing German morale. Casualties were heaviest for Germany, totalling approximately 168,000 men. The Allied casualties were lighter, with France suffering 95,000, Britain 13,000, and the United States 12,000 casualties respectively. This outcome effectively marked the beginning of the end of the war, and thereafter, most German commanders believed that defeat was inevitable.

The goal of defeating the Allies before the United States could put large numbers of troops into action had proven a failure. Between May and July 1918, the number of American troops in France had doubled from 500,000 to 1 million. It would double again by the end of the war, as convoys continued to pour troops across the Atlantic, a clear sign of the failure of the U-boat campaign as a counter-blockade of the Allies. Following the Second Battle of the Marne, Germany would be on the defensive in Europe, with the Allies advancing, and American forces now firmly in the fight.[32]

Another significant event in the war occurred in the early morning of 17 July, when Tsar Nicholas II, his wife and five children, who had been in exile and held under house arrest following the Russian Revolution, were executed by the Bolsheviks. This was done out of fear that the anti-communist White Army, the opposing side in the Russian Civil War, would liberate the Tsar and use him and his family as a powerful symbol.

At sea, U-boat attacks continued unabated, even though the outcome of the war now seemed very doubtful for Germany. On 1 July, the USS *Covington* was travelling in a convoy from Brest, France, to Hoboken, New Jersey. The

Covington began its life as the Hamburg America liner SS *Cincinnati*, and like the *Kronprinzessin Cecilie*, was interned in Boston when the war began. Once the United States entered the conflict, the vessel was seized, along with multiple other German ships that were interned in the United States, to be used as troop transports. Renamed the USS *Covington*, the vessel began shuttling thousands of soldiers across the Atlantic.

The ship was torpedoed by *U-86*, commanded by Kapitänleutnant Patzig, fresh off the *Llandovery Castle* massacre. The *Covington* took on a sharp list to port, and despite heroic efforts to save it, the ship had to be scuttled the following day. Six people died in the attack. A vivid description of the sinking was later written by United States Naval Reserve Lieutenants H.L. Jones and D.H. Garrison, survivors of the sinking:

USS *Covington* lists to port after being torpedoed. (Authors' Collection)

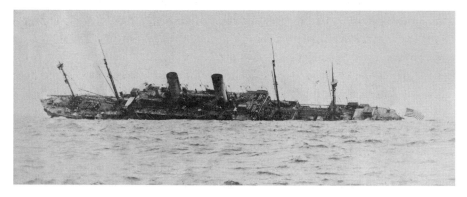

The stern of the *Covington* begins to submerge. The vessel is still flying the American flag aft. (Authors' Collection)

Sailors on a nearby ship watch as the *Covington* begins to plunge under. (Authors' Collection)

On the morning of July 1, 1918, the *Covington*, accompanied by the transports *George Washington*, *De Kalb*, *Ryndam* [*Rijndam*], *Dante Allegheri*, *Princess Matoika*, *Wilhelmina* and *Lenape*, together with a convoy of destroyers, left Brest on their homeward voyage to the United States. About 9.15 o'clock on the first night out … the men in the lookout stations on the *Covington* observed a telltale white wake rapidly approaching the ship on the port side. The officer on the bridge was immediately notified and an effort was made to avoid the oncoming torpedo by changing the course of the vessel, but without success. A few seconds after first sighted it struck the side of the *Covington* amidships just opposite the boiler rooms.

The force of the explosion that resulted was terrific. It threw up a column of water that reached the upper crow's nest on the foremast, and at the same time tore from its lashing a life-boat which hung on its davits more than fifty feet above the sea and buried it inboard against the smoke stacks. The hole in the side of the ship extended almost sixty feet in length and I can still remember the roar of the sea as it rushed through it and flooded the engine and boiler rooms. The wireless and lighting systems were instantly destroyed and everything was shrouded in darkness. By this time the vessel had lost headway and had a list of more than thirty degrees to port. It was obvious that it would be extremely hazardous to remain on board much longer and so the order was given to abandon ship.

The life-boats and rafts were quickly lowered and the men sliding down the falls or descending by means of rope ladders were taken aboard the boats or remained in the water clinging to the ropes circling the rafts, which were huge doughnut-like affairs with a hole in the middle and very buoyant. The work of abandoning the *Covington* was carried out with practically no confusion, which reflects the highest praise for the efficiency and discipline of the officers and crew. The lifeboat I commanded picked up forty men who were floating in the water nearby and then succeeded in getting five of the rafts in tow, so as to prevent them from becoming separated in the dark. Nearly all of the men in the boats were wet to the skin and were shivering in the wind. Those hanging on the rafts in the water suffered intensely from the cold and were chilled to the bone. The courage they displayed, however, was magnificent. They started to sing, 'Where Do We Go From Here, Boys', and 'Hail, Hail, the Gang's All Here', keeping this up until they were rescued two hours later by the destroyer *Smith*. One of these men clinging to a half-submerged raft had picked up the ship's puppy before leaving the vessel. As I rowed past him, he asked me to please take the poor frightened animal into my boat, which I readily did, and he thanked me through chattering teeth. Although he himself suffering greatly from the cold, his first concern was about the comforts of the small puppy. What chances had the Huns of terrifying or defeating men of this character with their stupid and inhuman campaign of frightfulness!

Captain Hasbrouck and the crews of the four six-inch guns were the last people to leave the ship. The men stationed at the after port gun, just before going over the side, fired three times at an object thought to be a submarine, but at the time it was too dark to determine whether or not any damage was done or to ascertain if it was a U-boat.

USS *Rijndam*, showing the wear and tear of wartime service. (Authors' Collection)

In compliance with standing orders, the other vessels in the convoy, with the exception of the destroyer *Smith*, immediately after the *Covington* was attacked, put on full steam and hastened to get out of the vicinity as quickly as possible to avoid the possibilities of a similar fate. The single destroyer, however, promptly came to our assistance and began dropping depth charges as she circled around our disabled ship. Finally the *Smith* began to take men off the boats and rafts, never actually stopping for this purpose, but taking them on board while still under way and then casting the boats or rafts adrift again. During the night she succeeded in picking up almost 800 of the officers and men.[33]

In July 1918, John E. Metzger was still serving aboard the troop transport USS *Rijndam*. His ship was in the same convoy as the *Covington*, and witnessed the attack on the vessel. He wrote the following account describing the events:

USS *Rijndam*

At Sea
July 6, 1918.

Dear Folks at home:

I am well and in the best of health. I am now a little better than half way back to the U.S.A. I think this ship will arrive in the States about Thursday the eleventh … There has been most beautiful weather this trip. We had very quiet trip over and never saw any submarines. My ship was in France four or five days. I was ashore twice.

I was through a couple German prison camps. The prisoners are very well satisfied. One of the German officers escaped and a couple weeks later came back with fifteen other German officers. That will give you a slight idea of how well they are treated. The German prisoners are treated better in there [sic] prison camps than they were in their own lines. I guess the war will last another year or so and then it will end. Let us all hope and pray it soon comes to an end. Us sailors are sure taking some bunch of troops across. There are many more soldiers in France than what the public think there are. The Germans have just began to think and know the Americans are coming over there and they won't come back until it is over over there. This ship sailed from France a few days ago in a convoy with seven other ships. At nine thirty the same evening a submarine came up and torpedoed the U.S.S. *Covington*. We were escorted by eight American destroyers. It did not take them long to tend to the sub. From the report they give the sub will not get another one of our ships. The *Covington* did not sink until the next day so I guess there were no lives lost. We did not stop but were many miles farther on when the *Covington* sank. The destroyers stayed with us until we got out of the most dangerous zone and then went to meet a convoy coming in the war or danger zone. The convoy has split up and all ships are for themselves now. It is a grand race for the States. We had an extra good dinner and moving pictures in the afternoon and night. There was moving pictures this afternoon and I guess there will be some more this evening. I am now on the four to eight P.M. watch and I will not get to see the movies tonight. All you can hear on board now is furlough furlough and nothing but furlough. There is a talk about half of the crew getting five days leave when we get in port. I guess that will not reach me for I would have to have five days traveling time. I will try and get another furlough this fall before it gets cold weather …

I will now close trusting in God to land us all safely in U.S.A.

Your son, Boy and Uncle John

Same address

PS: Let no news paper reporter get hold this. John E. Metzger[34]

Metzger also described the attack on the *Covington* in a typed letter that he wrote to his brother Howard on 14 July:

U.S.S. *Rijndam*
July 14, 1918

Dear brother:-

I take time and pleasure to write you a few lines. I wrote most every thing I new [sic] in the letter I sent home.

I am on duty day to day. This is a big holiday here in New York. All ships have been dressed and they sure look fine. This holiday is in honor of the French Bastille Day. I suppose you have received my telegram and the letters I sent when I arrived.

… The ships is [sic] being camouflaged now. There is fresh paint all over the ship. The weather is very warm here in New York. When you receive this I will most likely be on my way over there again …

… This last voyage I saw the U.S.S. *Covington* torpedoed and sunk the next day. There were only six lives lost. The submarine was blown to pieces by United States destroyers. This makes twice that the *Rijndam* has been in the same convoy where a ship has been torpedoed.

I may get transferred to the U.S.S. *George Washington*. If I get transferred I will let you know. The *Washington* is a much larger ship than this one.

Bethel is still on the U.S.S. *Ohio*. I got a letter from him and he is sure sick of that ship. Bethel only has three months to serve on this enlistment. I think he is planing [sic] on extending his enlistment a year but not on the *Ohio*.

Well I just had my dinner and now I feel a little better and will continue my letter. We had for dinner chicken, mashed potatoes, bread, butter, coca, cake and icecrean [sic]. I wish every day in the Navy was a holiday. This is sure some pretty day to have to stay on board this old packer.

Here is a couple pictures I took some place at sea. I have on a life preserver and gun ready to go over the side. We wear life preservers the entire trip.

Above all do not let any new papers [sic] get hold on anything that I write home. I am going to try and get a furlough again before cold weather...

Well Howard I guess I have told you most every thing I can thing [sic] of at present ... so I will close.

Love to all
John E. Metzger[35]

Contrary to what Metzger believed, *U-86* was not sunk. He probably believed this to be the case given the depth charge bombardment that the destroyer escorts unleashed following the attack on the *Covington*.

On 8 July, the USS *Leviathan* departed Hoboken, New Jersey, bound for Brest, France. The ship was carrying troops from the 314th Infantry Regiment, which was organised as part of the 79th Division of the American Expeditionary Force. One of the men aboard was First Lieutenant Arthur H. Joel. He wrote a detailed description of the crossing and conditions aboard the ship:

'By the deep line. By the deep line.' The strong bass voice of the sailor throwing the sounding line repeatedly called through the spray to the window of the wheelman's cabin. Frequently he would add the number of fathoms sounded.

From his post well forward on the gun decks, the husky 'gob' would swing the heavy weight like a pendulum, and finally, with his best effort, sling it well forward into the rough sea. Expert manipulation of the rope gave the depth of water and a guide for safety.

Until darkness and distance had obscured the Statue and maze of electric signs, the majority of the brown host held their positions on the open decks, fixing their gazes westward ... There was no information as to our destination, and the captain ... himself was certain of our course only for the time being. A warning or guiding wireless message might change our direction radically at any time. So ... the *Leviathan*, Monarch of the Seas, boldly began its lonesome journey across the Atlantic. For protection against submarines it depended almost solely upon secrecy and speed.

What an example of fate's irony! Carrying armed enemies equal in number to a fourth of the population of Lansing, Michigan, this old ocean liner, *Vaterland*, was now bent on aggression against its former owners. German signs could still be found in the staterooms.

Few people who have never seen an ocean liner have a correct idea of the makeup of such a craft. The *Leviathan* was almost a thousand feet, or a sixth of a mile, long, and a hundred feet wide, and she sank forty-odd feet in the water. Her displacement was sixty-nine thousand tons, and she had forty-six water-tube boilers. Few harbors could dock her, and she could not go under Brooklyn Bridge, or enter the Panama Canal.

Although a 'gob' – sailor – might be perfectly at home in the floating city, it was not an infrequent occurrence for a 'doughboy landlubber' to completely lose himself. Then, to his inquiry as to direction, a friendly sailor might give him the following answer.

'Sure, Jack, I'll tell you. Go up the ladder what's behind the hatch that's two compartments aft. Then go through the galley to F-26. Take the stairway to 'F' deck, swing starboard and aft again, and you're there. It's all right, Jack. Glad to help you. No! aft is that way. That's a hatch there! Sure. Don't mention it Jack'.

And finally, after several more inquiries and a great deal of wandering, just when he was more puzzled than ever, a friend might point out his bunk section within a few rods of where he stood.

The floating mass of wood and steel which made up the troop ship *Leviathan* was a complicated structure, to say the least. Horizontally, the ship was divided into floors or decks, designated by the letters from 'A' to 'H'. Beginning with the topmost deck, which contained the lobby and officers' dining room, this series ended with the lowest troop quarters below water line. Still below this deck, however, were the coal bunkers, and the engine and stoker rooms. The troop decks were divided into numerous compartments, or rooms, separated by water-tight doors. Located at various places among this maze of 'decks', compartments and lobbies were 'galleys', or kitchens, shower baths, latrines, hospital rooms, baggage rooms and sailors' quarters, the whole connected by ladders, passageways and stairways.

The troops were quartered in the 'deck compartments'. Each soldier was entitled to the privacy of a luxuriant bed made by stretching heavy mess wire across a six-by-two frame of iron pipe. Economy of space seemed to be the prime consideration, and consequently 'bunks' were arranged four deep and two wide, with just enough aisle space to allow two slim doughboys to pass each other.

Life on board a troop transport was in sharp contrast to life on a peace-time passenger boat. With the lives of over thirteen thousand men to consider, and a most dangerous course to pursue, it was necessary to take special precautions other than the ordinary rules of an ocean voyage.

Whistling was not permitted, singing after dark was forbidden, and a general order demanded absolute silence after 'taps', or bed time.

As naval men claim that it is easy to track a ship which leaves a trail of articles on the water, it was specially ordered that nothing whatsoever be thrown overboard. This offense was about as serious to a naval man as the smoking of a cigarette or lighting a match would be to a doughboy under an enemy bombing plane at the front on a dark night.

At sunset the entire ship was darkened except in certain spaces well below decks. A special blue light circuit was then used for any necessary traffic or movement.

A troop billet for the USS *Leviathan*. On the front, these indicated the deck and compartment where each soldier was to be berthed, as well as their lifeboat station, and on the back, emphasised important safety rules. (Authors' Collection)

The men were forbidden to show a light or to reflect one upon a polished surface, to use flashlights or matches on decks, or to smoke in the open night, as any of these acts might endanger not only their lives but those of their fellow passengers by attracting an awaiting submarine.

Ship information gave the following notice: 'Sea-sick cans are supplied and should be used for that purpose only. Men vomiting on deck should be made to clean it up. Men should realize it is no disgrace to be sea-sick and that anyone can feel it coming. It is a mean trick to vomit in the home of others who are all around. Use the sea-sick cans and keep the deck clean'.

It was a court-martial offense to carry ammunition, to open portholes or water-tight doors, to smoke in quarters, to be caught away from your bunk without a life preserver, or to fail to report at your designated post when the bugler sounded the signal to abandon ship.

For the soldier, the feeding or messing system was a simple matter. He merely took his designated place in a certain line of men, and followed the snake parade until he had eaten and returned to his bunk.

But to feed these thousands of men twice a day was no simple matter. The system surely was almost an ideal of efficiency, for in the one troop mess hall on 'F' deck, forward of the galley, this host of men were fed in about an hour and a half, dishes washed, finger bowls and napkins collected, and all meal tickets properly punched.

The cafeteria system was used. The troops, equipped with mess outfits, marched by outlined routes to food-serving stations, where the prunes, beans and chili sauce, canned 'Bill', and 'Java' were properly mixed in mess kits as the men passed by. No seats were provided. Garbage was dumped in cans near the exit, and mess gear washed in dish-washing cans at the washing stations. There were naturally complaints about the 'chow', for a soldier can, and usually does, at every opportunity, exercise his privilege of complaining about his meals.

For several days, while the vessel was passing through the hot gulf stream, the lower decks were most uncomfortably hot, stuffy and ill smelling. Imagine if you can, the combination of closed compartments and port holes, mid-July heat intensified by the warm ocean current, a soldier to about six square feet of floor space, and the majority more or less sea-sick. It was a three-day Turkish bath, so hot that men who lay almost naked in their bunks perspired freely. Many a doughboy lost his beans and macaroni, and took C.C. pills to help him recover his bearings.

C.C.'s were the 'pill rollers' or 'medics' universal offering to the suffering soldier for sore throat, sore feet, earache, falling hair, trench feet, mal-de-mer, and flu. Some say that C.C.'s won the war, but the M.P.'s and Y.M.C.A. dispute the claim ...

USS *Leviathan* sailing through heavy seas. (Authors' Collection)

During the four-hour watches among the bunks and sweating troops, one could easily see that the stuffy conditions were playing on the tempers of the men. Epithets of all sorts, with Italian, Austrian, and mountaineer accents, as well as in good English, were evidence of the men's feelings. And the scores of questions asked about our location on the Atlantic, our probable destination, and about dangerous submarine zones were proof enough of their thoughts.

… Anxious eyes and eyes glinting with the light of excitement searched the calm blue stretch of mid-ocean. Pulses quickened with the re-appearance of the distant, white flash in the water, and those well forward watched the training of the big guns, and waited for the first shot to rock the boat.

There followed a few moments of anxious suspense. 'Oh! hell, it's a whale spout', came the voice of a rather disappointed native of the moonshine section of West Virginia.

This, to our knowledge, was as close as we came to open dispute with submarines. However, on its previous voyage, the *Leviathan* had a close call just outside of Brest, when three U-boats suddenly appeared between the big transport and its protecting destroyers. A quick fusillade of gun fire and the dropping of depth bombs ended what was for the moment a very dangerous situation. The gun crews claim that at least one of the 'sousmarin's' never rose again …

… Until within two days of Brest harbor the *Leviathan* was more lonesome than Columbus' *Santa Maria*, which had the company of the *Nina* and *Pinta*. Secrecy, speed and expert gunners were our protection against subs.

One morning we awoke to find five camouflaged destroyers – long, narrow, super-speedy boats, painted with varicolored diagonal streaks, and as graceful as canoes. From our own monster boat we viewed these daring craft with admiration and with about the same warm feeling that one has upon meeting a friend in a wilderness or in a strange city.

How quickly and confidently the destroyers were on the trail with depth bombs ready and guns trained, whenever a whale spout, grocery box, empty boat or other suspicious thing loomed with: a telescopic view! We had good reason to be proud of our own gunners, who were the best in the Navy...

An open boat on the high seas usually means disaster. On the final lap of the journey a small life boat was passed, and later a boat load of naval officers was picked up – circumstantial evidence of the fortunes and misfortunes of a torpedoed crew. Finally, on July 15, the *Leviathan* completed the final and most dangerous lap of the journey – through the submarine-infested area along the rocky coast of Brittany, near Brest. Land was first seen in the early morning, when a rocky island was indistinctly outlined in the dense fog. The destroyers accompanied the *Leviathan* into the long, narrow channel which led to the spacious harbor of Brest, and soon the monster ship was anchored in the quiet waters of the big Brittany port.

A blue-uniformed, dapper, little port officer speeded out in his motor boat, and the lines of vision of thousands of searching eyes shifted and intersected as the soldiers intently gazed toward the foreign land where fate would decide and work out their various fortunes and destinies during the coming months of the big adventure.

So, far fine! We had escaped the U-boats and the 'chow' hadn't been bad. What was ahead mattered little. Brest from a distance didn't look half bad, so worries were packed in the ould [sic] kit bag. Future troubles didn't bother a soldier ... The worst was yet to come; so why remember sea-sickness, ill-smelling, hot quarters, saltwater baths, and restrictions of all sorts? ... Captain Jacobs of 'H' company, with a Napoleonic pose greeted Brest as he did all new places. 'Ah! ha! So this is Russia!'[36]

On 12 July, the HMT *Olympic* began another Atlantic crossing, departing New York with American troops from the 364th Infantry Division. The *Olympic* was proving to be a workhorse, and by the end of the war, would earn the nickname 'Old Reliable'. It had already survived an encounter with a U-boat on 12 May that year, which resulted in the submarine, *U-103*, being rammed and sunk. This would stand as the only known incident of the war in which a merchant vessel sunk an enemy submarine.[37] Around this time, *Olympic* had been repainted in a second dazzle camouflage pattern, consisting of more distinctive geometric shapes and lines, coloured black, blue and blue grey. Two of the soldiers on board

Workers applying dazzle
camouflage to HMT
Olympic. (*Illustrated
London News*, 1919/
Authors' Collection)

The *Olympic* in its second
dazzle camouflage scheme.
(Authors' Collection)

on 12 July crossing were Bryant Wilson and Lamar Tooze. They described the voyage in detail:

Out into the broad Hudson, the boats chugged and then turned their snouts downstream. Soon we found ourselves opposite the great city and amid a host of strange objects, daubed with color, which we immediately recognized as camouflaged ships. On the western shore lay numerous army transports among the Hoboken piers, but it was toward the east we turned and drew up at Pier 59 with many a thrill. For there lay a huge leviathan, out-measuring anything else on the horizon.

The ferryboats spewed forth their great throngs which immediately filled the enormous pier buildings and began a savage attack on bushels of refreshments which thoughtful organizations had provided.

Then began the entry into the ark, which proved to be none other than the great *Olympic*, now masquerading under a coat of badly-blended brown and black and yellow paint and sailing under a number instead of a name. To our delight, two hundred nurses of feminine gender were sent up the gangplank. They were to make a pleasant trip twofold more pleasant.

Once aboard, a trip of exploration was in order. We sometimes thought that the object in placing us aboard such a huge ship was threefold: first, to accustom us to the gentle practice of locating billets with ease, for there were several thousand hammocks aboard and all looked alike and were apparently distributed in haphazard fashion; secondly, to get us in practice for strenuous marching later on, for the ship, being 890 feet long, required more than a quarter of a mile's hike to circle it, a thing one had to do every time he set out to find either his hammock or his chow; thirdly, to break us into the delights of dugout life, for the old boat boasted twelve stories, five of them under water. But the floating palace of peace days, now remodeled as a troop transport, had many items in her favor, namely, she could carry the whole regiment of 3,600 men with a sanitary and ammunition train thrown in; she was fast and traveled alone rather than in a convoy, thus being able to develop her full speed; she was so huge that those few who harbored any submarine fears felt that it would take a whole school of torpedoes to sink her.

We remained motionless … until nine o'clock on the morning of Friday, July 12th, when the giant craft began her long journey. Simultaneously with her first shuddering movement, each one took unto himself a bosom friend in the form of a life preserver, which, on the pain of a turn in the brig, was always to be worn except when sleeping. Out on the high seas, the guards' favorite diversion was to keep a sharp lookout for some luckless officer of high rank who had forgotten his life-belt, or who carried it in his hand instead of on his back.

… Instead of a stealthy fade-away in the dark, the great ship, crowded with soldiers, sailed majestically through the busy harbor in broad daylight, the object of the gaze of thousands on boats and on land and the subject of much cheering and waving. In the outer harbor a vast throng of camouflaged freighters were assembled in convoy formation, heavily laden with supplies. Past them we gradually pushed our way out into the misty deep until the famous statue, symbolic of that liberty for which we were to fight, disappeared from sight.

But with the fading from view of the metropolis, our attention was turned to a slim, sleek craft which appeared to be running circles around us. It proved to be a convoying destroyer of particularly jaunty appearance because of the brilliance of its yellowish streaks of camouflage. Almost simultaneously, a dirigible balloon appeared over us and two or three aeroplanes hummed industriously about. The dirigible remained as sky escort until four in the afternoon when it turned back, but the trim little destroyer was still cutting the waves in wide sweeps ahead of us when the fine summer day gave way to darkness. With the coming of morning, the destroyer had also disappeared and the *Olympic* zigzagged across the seemingly deserted ocean for five days, quite alone.

Many factors contributed to make the ocean voyage a pleasant one … Excellent weather and calm seas favored us. Aboard ship there was abundant talent for entertainment. And the possibility of a peep at a submarine added another little thrill to our adventure.

In order to guard against the piratical 'tin fish', a rigid guard was maintained. A comprehensive system for manning the lookout posts and the watertight compartment doors was in operation day and night. The guard personnel … numbered into the hundreds … scores of soldier eyes constantly searched the surrounding waters for a possible periscope of a U-boat. Six big guns, alertly manned, pointed across the waves in various directions in a very menacing and businesslike way.

When a call was made for entertainers, the result would have pleased a Belasco. Several performances were given. The ship's captain allowed the men to crowd together and enjoy the music and stunts out on the exposed decks even while in the danger zone. The enlisted men were entertained from seven to nine in the evening and then the stage was shifted to the dining saloon for a nine o'clock performance for the officers and nurses.

Services were held in three different parts of the great ship Sunday morning, July 14th. We were fortunate in having on board with us some notables of the New York financial world and also Mr. Herbert Hoover. These men consented to speak to us in the evening and one of the striking statements made that night which indicated the critical outlook for the Allies was 'the one thing for which we are praying is for the fall of snow to stop the Germans!' Little did we realize that the day upon which those words were spoken was the first day of the

Herbert Hoover, the head of the United States Food Commission, and eventual President of the United States. (United States National Archives and Records Administration/Authors' Collection)

ever-memorable week which marked the breaking of the last great German offensive upon the stone wall of Allied resistance, and the beginning of Foch's counter-attack which was to bring victory before the fall of snow.

Before Mr. Hoover appeared to speak to the large throng of men gathered on the aft deck, Chaplain Lyman Rollins, a veteran of several months' service in France, told us of experiences with the Huns, amusing and otherwise. Then when the Honorable Mr. Hoover, feeder of a world, mounted to the searchlight platform, and was introduced, some irrepressibles on the lower deck shouted, 'We don't want Hoover. He feeds us tripe for breakfast!' Mr. Hoover laughingly disclaimed the honor of being sponsor for the serving of that breakfast delicacy and proceeded to tell us about the simple job of rationing a world.

Speaking of tripe reminds us of some of the exchanges constantly going on between soldiers and the ship's crew – exchanges of postcards, tobacco, and also of fists. One sailor suddenly found himself in Dreamland when he chose to remark, in the presence of a horny-handed American Sergeant, that 'the next war would be between the two "yellow" races, the Japanese and American.' No charges were preferred. Again, after champion 'midget' Sepulveda of Company 'A' had put to sleep a husky deck hand who refused to obey orders, some of the crew were heard to remark, 'If the smallest bloody man in the outfit can fight like that what could the big guys do?'

The announcement that we were at last within the danger zone only added to our thrills of interest. Thousands of pairs of curious eyes searched the surrounding waves for a possible Hun periscope. One grizzled member of the ship's crew, after watching the actions of this Wild West bunch, delivered himself of the following: 'Well, I'll be hornswoggled! It's many a load of troops I've seen cross in this old boat, but never a gang like this. Generally about this time, one can see a lot of Bibles in evidence and scared looks on the owners' faces. But if we sighted a submarine this minute, every American on the ship would be crowding the rails to see her, and, if she succeeded in launching a torpedo, all that these doughboys would do would be to watch its course and yell "Raspberry!"'

But no subs appeared. However, those in command were taking no chances. Every day throughout the trip, alarms were sounded, boats were manned, watertight doors were closed, and all rushed to their appointed posts.

Upon entering the danger zone, the ship's paravanes were lowered into the water. These were contrivances shaped like torpedoes, equipped with wings which held them out at an angle of forty-five degrees from the ship's prow, to which they were attached by steel cables. They were placed low enough in the water to intercept the cables of any mines in the ship's course and the paravane cables, extending out from the ship, would not only ward off the deadly mine head but would force the mine cable into the saw-tooth mouth of the paravane which would promptly sever it and cause the mine to float on the surface where it could be easily destroyed.

We awoke, the morning of Thursday, July 18th, to the fact that five U.S. destroyers had surrounded us and were convoying us through the last lap of the journey … The destroyer which first sighted us, signalled our presence to the others by means of a dense smoke cloud and soon we were surrounded by our speedy little zigzagging friends. On the aft end of the nearer boats could be seen an 'egg' breakfast for the Huns – neat piles of depth bombs ready to be dropped into the haunts of enemy subs. These gave us great assurance of safety but the thing that delighted our hearts the most was the sight of the American ensign which seemed to breathe a message from home.

Toward midnight of the eighteenth we sighted the light at Scilly Isle on our starboard side and the light at Land's End on our port side. The moon was out just enough to aid the U-boats but we successfully crossed the 'ships' graveyard' and morning found us in sight of the Isle of Wight.

At the entrance to the harbor leading to Southampton, the ship was stopped, paravanes hoisted on deck, and a pilot taken aboard. The scene before us was suggestive of the grim war being waged against the submarine. The sea was filled with destroyers, P-boats, friendly submarines, hydroplanes, buoys marking mine fields, and nets. Out of the shallow water protruded the masts of a recent victim of the underseas wasps …

Proceeding into the harbor, we passed through the opening between the nets near Portsmouth and lay to for several hours awaiting the tide. Finally we slowly made our way up the channel to the piers of Southampton, reaching our destination at five in the afternoon of July 19th. We had arrived at the very port from which the *Mayflower* had sailed with our forefathers three centuries before. We were now returning, many thousand strong, to aid our Mother in her fight for the liberty which that ancient band had set out to seek.[38]

HMT *Olympic* and other ships in dazzle camouflage docked at Southampton. (*Illustrated London News*, 1919/Authors' Collection)

One factor that is rarely considered when it comes to troop ships are the atrociously crowded and malodorous conditions below decks, with the public rooms and spaces packed with thousands of soldiers. A good description of this comes from the account of Will R. Bird, a Canadian soldier of the 42nd Canadian Infantry Battalion who sailed for England on the *Olympic* in October 1916:

> We were marched on board the *Olympic* at dusk and sailed for England on Friday, October 13, which date made some of the lads miserable. Being last on the boat we were consigned to the smelly depths of 'F' deck, where the hammocks were strung so closely it was necessary to crawl under them on hands and knees. The odours were terrible. I went up on deck at once and watched some Lascars emerge from a ladder way. A moment's chat with them informed me that one could use the ladder to go to any deck, even the upper boat deck which was out of bounds to us. So around ten that night two figures went up the ladder to the forbidden territory, quickly untied the covers of a life boat and got into it. There we slept in clean fresh air, and in the morning were down below again as our fellows were astir, swearing about the foul air that had more than twenty of them sick.[39]

On 17 July, the Cunard liner RMS *Carpathia* was on a voyage from Liverpool to Boston, and was in the Celtic Sea. The ship had been used as a troop transport

This image from a United States troopship gives an idea of the crowded and claustrophobic conditions below deck on troop transports as soldiers made the transatlantic crossing. (Authors' Collection)

The submarine *U-55*, which sunk RMS *Carpathia*. (Eddy Lambrecht Collection)

during the war, but on this particular voyage, was carrying only passengers. The ship had been travelling in a convoy, but by now, the escorts had departed, and the other ships began splitting up. At around 9.15 a.m. the ship was sighted by Kapitänleutnant Wilhelm Werner aboard the *U-55*. He fired two torpedoes. One slammed into the port side, penetrating the No. 4 hold and the stoke hold below the bridge. The second exploded near the engine room, disabling the ship's engines, and preventing it from escaping. Two firemen and three trimmers were killed below deck, and two engineers were badly scalded.

Carpathia began settling by the bow and listing to port. Captain William Prothero gave the order to abandon ship. The other vessels in the convoy escaped at high speed to avoid falling victim to *U-55*, but sent out a distress call on behalf of the stricken vessel, which was unable to do so on its own. After the passengers and crew had abandoned ship, the U-boat circled around and fired a third torpedo into the stricken liner. The *Carpathia*, famous for rescuing the *Titanic* survivors, was gone within minutes. The survivors in the lifeboats were picked

Captain William Prothero. (Authors' Collection)

A rare image from the personal photo album of an officer-engineer who worked on U-boats shows RMS *Carpathia*'s final moments. The photo is labelled in part '*U 55* … sinks the 12,000 ton steamer "*Carpathia*"'. (Eddy Lambrecht Collection)

up by HMS *Snowdrop* which was fairly quick to arrive on the scene. One of the crewmembers aboard the *Carpathia* gave a description of the events:

The passengers had just finished breakfast and it was a beautiful summer morning, when about 9.15 a torpedo struck us near No. 3 hatch forward. Two minutes later another torpedo struck right in the engine room and killed five of the crew who were at work there. We could see the submarine. It was a big two-masted vessel, quite the latest type of U-boat.

The *Carpathia* did not seem to be very badly damaged by these two explosions. She was taking in water, but I think she would have lasted for hours, and she might even have been towed into the harbor if the U-boat had not got busy again.

A quarter of an hour after the first torpedo had been discharged a third was fired and caught us near the gunner's rooms. A big explosion followed. We could then see that the *Carpathia* was doomed. She settled down rapidly after that, and, at about 11 a.m., disappeared.

Meanwhile perfect discipline had been maintained on board. There was no panic among the passengers. The officers had the whole situation well in hand, and the passengers and crew, with the exception of the five men who had been killed, were away from the ship and safely in their boats within a quarter of an hour after the first torpedo struck us. We were picked up by a warship about midday.

Another crewmember insinuated that the U-boat was approaching the survivors in the lifeboats when the rescue vessel arrived, saying 'The U-boat I am sure would have opened fire on our boats if a mine sweeper had not come up. She seemed to be training her guns on us'.[40]

A medal presented to Captain Prothero. The inscription reads 'Captain William Prothero, Liverpool Shipwreck + Humane Society, for bravery at the *Carpathia*'s sinking, 17 July 1918'. (Kalman Tanito Collection)

When Captain Prothero described the sinking in his affidavit, he refuted the claim that the U-boat approached the survivors:

I, William Prothero ... do herby make oath and say:-

That I was captain of the British S.S. *Carpathia* at the time she was torpedoed;

That I have read the foregoing affidavits ... and concur in the same as being substantially a correct account of the circumstances stated except as may hereinafter set forth ...

... That the ship's speed at the time was the speed of the convoy which was ten knots;

That the *Carpathia* joined the convoy at Liverpool;

That when attacked the ship was zig-zagging;

That the convoy was composed of seven vessels none of which were American ships;

That the *Carpathia* carried one six-inch gun aft;

That the submarine did not fire on the vessel as stated in the foregoing affidavit, the third torpedo sinking the ship;

That the submarine appeared after the ship had been abandoned but did not speak to any of the boats, submerging on the appearance of the patrol;

That the submarine was at least 500 [sic] feet long, mounted two six-inch guns, one forward and one aft. There were three men in the conning tower ...

... That I destroyed all codes and confidential documents.[41]

On 19 July, the troop transport HMT *Justicia* was heading from Liverpool to New York in a convoy. On this crossing, the *Justicia*, which was painted in dazzle camouflage, was in ballast and was being escorted by two destroyers. Despite this, *UB-64*, commanded by Kapitänleutnant Otto von Schrader, managed to evade the destroyer screen and fire a torpedo into the ship, which exploded in the engine room, killing ten men. The ship was stopped so that the damage could be assessed, and the destroyers began to search for the U-boat, dropping depth charges. *Justicia* took on a list, but was staying afloat with its watertight doors closed.

Destroyers began to escort the vessel to safer waters. However, von Schrader was not so easily dissuaded. A veteran U-boat commander, he would ultimately sink or capture fifty-eight ships during the war. Despite the escorts, he was able to fire two more torpedoes into *Justicia*. Again, the ship failed to sink. With its engines disabled, the vessel was largely evacuated, save for a skeleton crew. Most of the crew of the ship were former *Britannic* crewmembers, who once again found themselves abandoning ship.

Much to everyone's surprise, the *Justicia* still did not sink, but was unable to proceed under its own power. It was taken in tow by the HMS *Sonia*, with the intention of grounding it in the shallow waters. A few hours later, the *UB-64*

HMT *Justicia* finally sinks after receiving a fifth and sixth torpedo strike. Clearly it was a well-built ship. (Ioannis Georgiou Collection)

Edward Butt. (United States National Archives and Records Administration/Authors' Collection)

attacked once more, slamming a fourth torpedo into *Justicia*. Still the vessel refused to sink, and von Schrader was forced to abandon his pursuit, since his vessel was damaged in the subsequent destroyer counterattack. He did however report the *Justicia*'s position to another submarine in the area.

The following morning, 20 July, the *Justicia* was targeted by *UB-124*, which managed to catch up to the vessel, hitting it with two more torpedoes. The U-boat was sunk in the resulting destroyer bombardment, but all but two of its crewmembers were rescued and taken prisoner. The fifth and sixth torpedo finally proved too much, and the *Justicia* rolled over on its side and sank. Clearly, it was a well-built ship.

Edward H. Butt, one of the passengers on the SS *Melita*, another ship in the same convoy as *Justicia*, witnessed the initial attacks on the vessel by *UB-64*. His description of the events were as follows:

… Passengers on a British liner arriving here today said that last Friday their ship gave battle to a German U-boat 750 miles off the New Jersey coast and last night fired three shots at what is now believed to have been an American submarine. Apparently neither undersea craft was hit.

SS *Melita*, from which Edward Butt witnessed the attack on the *Justicia*. (Authors' Collection)

The stern of the *Melita*. (Authors' Collection)

This liner was one of several which were being convoyed with *Justicia*, when that vessel was torpedoed off the North Irish Coast on July 19. According to the passengers, a torpedo which hit the *Justicia* passed astern of their own ship, and narrowly missed another merchantman before finding its goal.

E.H. Butt of Augusta, GA, a brother of Maj. Archibald Butt, who lost his life on the *Titanic*, described the liner's three encounters with submarines.

The first, he said, came on July 19, two days after the merchantman, convoyed by destroyers, left a British port.

'We crowded on all steam and zig-zagged as, in company with our convoying destroyers, we left the scene in a race to save ourselves', said Mr. Butt. 'We heard during the night that the *Justicia* and destroyers were fighting the U-boats, and later learned that her struggle to survive had failed'.

Mr. Butt said that the ship met no more submarines until last Friday at noon, when 750 miles off the New Jersey coast the ship's guns began firing at an object apparently several miles away.

'This was a super-submarine', said Mr. Butt. 'It made no attempt to come nearer, and, after firing solid shot, which fell short at least 1,000 yards began to fire shrapnel'.

The exchange of shot lasted about 45 minutes according to Mr. Butt, who said the U-boat then submerged and was not seen again.

At the same time ... said, another submarine engaged a British freighter in the same waters, and it was thought the U-boat was sunk.

'If so, the Britisher got a good one', said Mr. Butt. 'For these boats are super-submarines which depend more on destruction by gun fire than by torpedoes ... We got our next shock last night', he said. 'In a smooth sea a big submarine broke water not three miles away and at once our gunners fired three shots at the boat while our commander signalled: "Who are you?"

'The shots fell close to the boat and we could see the flutter of flags. Finally our commander signalled to the gun crews to cease firing and we came on, leaving the submarine on the surface. Rumor on board had it that the latest U-boat was an American'.[42]

Overall in July 1918, U-boats sank or captured 130 ships, totalling 298,267 tons. Twenty-eight additional attacks damaged vessels.[43]

On 8 August 1918, the Hundred Days Offensive began on the Western Front. This was a series of offensives by the Allies against the Central Powers, the start of which was marked by the Battle of Amiens. The Hundred Days Offensive would last until 11 November 1918, and would result in the German Army largely being forced out of France and back beyond the Hindenburg Line. The end result would be Germany seeking an armistice, but there was still a lot of hard fighting left to go.

At sea on 15 August, the cruiser USS *Minneapolis* departed Philadelphia and was sailing to New York. The ship had been serving on transatlantic convoy duty, and was preparing to escort a new group of ships overseas. Dangers from U-boats were a constant worry, even this close to the American coastline. One of the sailors aboard was Art White, who wrote the following description of the short journey:

Brooklyn New York
Aug 17 1918

Dear Mother

Well we arrived safe dropped anchor in upper harbor New York, fine place lots to see.

We left Philly thurs morning at 10.15 and arrived in N.Y. friday morning 8.45.

Had a fine trip down the Delaware river and bay entered the Atlantic just before dusk, the gunners maned [sic] their guns waching [sic] for subs but good fortune failed to see any. Our run from the Delaware Bay to New York was mostly at night. We had a race with a battleship for about 50 miles but lost out.

In the lower harbor N.Y. we must of passed over thirty ships French, English and other nationalities loaded down with American troops, if they don't leave for a few days, why we might go with their convoy across with them.

I am now over in Brooklyn at the Y. I have a 36 hr leave, we left the ship in motor sailor's [sic] landed at Satten Island [sic] from their [sic] we took a ferry boat to N.Y. from their [sic] I took a subway to Brooklyn bridge, crossed it to Brooklyn on a street car got off at the Y.

Well I guess I'll close will write later.

> Your loving son
>> Art
>
> U.S.S. *Minneapolis*
> c/o P.M. New York

P.S. Give my regards to all the folks. Haven't received that bag yet can't Joe hurry it up for we might leave soon and I would like to have it.

> Art.[44]

Once the USS *Minneapolis* finally departed with a convoy on 21 August, the transatlantic crossing was not without incident. Art White described the journey in detail in another letter to his mother the following month. One incident that he witnessed reveals a new tactic that American forces were using to decoy German U-boats and then ambush them:

At last we have dropped anchor in New York, it is just 30 days ago when we left. It was 12 p.m. wed the 21st of August. Our convoy was made up of twenty ships, French, British and American. On our first day out we were on the top side looking for excitement.

The 2nd day or the 22nd at sea two hydroplanes came out from New York to see that every thing was ok, in the afternoon we sighted a sailing vessel who wouldn't answer our signals. Our captain took no chances so he sounded general quarters which means get ready for the enemy, at 12.30 p.m. we found it to be a American ship which was towing two American subs which were submerged they were waiting an attack from a German sub, you see if a German came up to sink the vessel why these two American subs would ponce [sic] on the kaiser sub and destroy it. Aug 23 at sea 11 p.m. we left the convoy sighted a deserted whale boat about five miles off, we circled around it watching it all the time for you know that Germans play all kinds of tricks. Our gunners fired eight 4" shots at it expecting to explode a mine or rooting out a sub this happened 300 miles out …

... Aug 25 at sea Sunday about 900 miles from N.Y. we washed our bags and hammocks, also transferred a armed guard man to a merchant ship whose gunner was sick, we took the sick man aboard...

... Aug 31 we are now 2,250 miles out in the sea, the air and winds feel different we are nearing foreign land. Sep 1-2-3 sighted two ships they were big transports making knots for the states. Sept 4 at 4.30 a.m. our lookout sighted six English destroyers of the H 45 type we are just 35 miles from Queenstown, at 6 a.m. the destroyers took charge of the convoy. Two of the English boats circled around us they looked strong and fast.

6.15 a.m. we left the convoy and started for home without seeing land. We hadn't left the convoy ten minutes when we saw three mighty explosions right in the middle of them.

A German sub was in and was trying to sink some ships, we didn't find out if any was sunk or not but I gess [sic] it must of done some damage ... [45]

In August 1918, a total of 169 ships were sunk or captured by U-boats, totalling 301,139 tons of shipping. Eighteen ships were damaged. Without the convoy system and escort ships such as the USS *Minneapolis*, the losses would have been far worse. [46]

September–October 1918

September 1918 brought several important developments in the war. Between 19 and 25 September, Turkish resistance collapsed at Megiddo, with the destruction or capture of most of their forces there. The Battle of Megiddo was the last Allied offensive of the Sinai and Palestine Campaign. The decisive nature of the victory was soon followed by the Ottoman Empire signing the Armistice of Mudros in October, ending the Turkish participation in the conflict.

On the Western Front, German forces were staggering back east under the Allied onslaught. Although the conflict had been locked in a stalemate in the region for several years, the Allies were now able to make substantial progress. The situation deteriorated as the German Army continued to struggle with a lack of supplies and resources due to the Royal Navy blockade, and due to an overall lack of morale and will to continue the fight. Capitalising on this, the Allies launched the Meuse-Argonne Offensive on 26 September. The final Allied offensive of the war, it stretched along the entire Western Front and would last until the armistice was signed in November. It would prove to be the killing blow to the Central Powers' war effort.

At sea, the U-boat war continued to be waged, despite the grim look of things on land. On 5 September, the USS *Mount Vernon* was sailing in a convoy from

WHERE THE TORPEDO STRUCK THE MOUNT VERNON.

The worn bow of USS *Mount Vernon* following the war. Remnants of its dazzle camouflage can be seen below the anchor. (Authors' Collection)

The extensive torpedo damage to the hull of the *Mount Vernon*. (Authors' Collection)

Brest to New York. Formerly known as the passenger liner *Kronprinzessin Cecilie*, the troop ship now sported dazzle camouflage and deck guns. When the ship was approximately 250 miles off the coast of France, a periscope was spotted off its starboard bow. The *Mount Vernon's* gun crew fired on the submarine, which was the *U-82*, but Kapitänleutnant Heinrich Middendorff managed to launch a single torpedo at the ship. The *Mount Vernon's* crew took evasive action, but the torpedo struck the ship amidships, with the resulting detonation taking out half of the boilers, flooding the middle compartments, and killing thirty-six men.

The U-boat was soon driven away by the vessel's gun crews and depth charges, and the destroyer escorts began throwing up a smokescreen to obscure the view of the ship. Damage control teams raced to save the vessel, and soon the *Mount Vernon* was able to proceed under its own power, making it to Brest. Once in port, the ship underwent temporary repairs, before proceeding to Boston to be fully mended.

Captain D.E. Dismukes filed the following report with the United States Navy describing the attack on his vessel, and the efforts to save it:

Destroyer escorts begin throwing up a smokescreen after the *Mt Vernon* (foreground) was struck by a torpedo. (United States Naval History and Heritage Command Collection, NH 89149)

Captain D.E. Dismukes aboard USS *Mount Vernon*. (Authors' Collection)

About 250 miles from the coast of France, on the morning of September 5, 1918, the *Mount Vernon* and *Agamemnon* in convoy, escorted by six destroyers, were proceeding homeward bound from Brest, speed 18 knots … The weather was fine and the sea smooth, making it possible to sight a submarine periscope a long distance … Suddenly a periscope popped above the surface of the water about 500 yards distant. Our starboard gun opened fire at once, but the periscope remained on the surface only a few seconds. Just as it disappeared, the wake of a torpedo coming straight for the ship … immediately afterwards the torpedo struck us, throwing up a huge column of water on our starboard side amidships.

The explosion was so terrific that for an instant it seemed that the ship was lifted clear out of the water and torn to pieces. Men at the after guns and depth-charge stations were thrown to the deck, and one of the 5-inch guns thrown partly out of its mount. Men below in the vicinity of the explosion were stunned into temporary unconsciousness.

… the torpedo had struck the ship fairly amidships, destroying four of the eight boiler rooms and flooding the middle portion of the ship from side to side for a length of 150 feet. The ship instantly settled 10 feet … but stopped there. This indicated that the water-tight bulkheads were holding, and we could still afford to go down 24 feet more before she would lose her floating buoyancy.

The immediate problem was to escape a second torpedo. To do this two things were necessary, to attack the enemy, and to make more speed than he could make submerged. The depth charge crews jumped to their stations and … A barrage of depth charges was dropped, exploding at regular intervals far below the surface of the water. This work was beautifully done. The explosions must have shaken the enemy up, at any rate he never came to the surface again to get a look at us.

The other factor in the problem was to make as much speed as possible, not only in order to escape an immediate attack, but also to prevent the submarine from tracking us and attacking after nightfall.

The men in the firerooms knew that the safety of the ship depended on their bravery and steadfastness to duty. It is difficult to conceive of a more trying ordeal to one's courage … The profound shock of the explosion, followed by instant darkness, falling soot and particles, the knowledge that they were far below the water level enclosed practically in a trap, the imminent danger of the

The deck of the *Mount Vernon*, cluttered with lifeboats and rafts. (Authors' Collection)

ship sinking, the added threat of exploding boilers – all these dangers and more must have been apparent to every man below, and yet not one man wavered in standing by his post of duty …

… In at least two instances in this crisis below men who were actually in the face of death did actually forget or ignore their impulse for self-preservation and endeavored to do what appeared to them to be their duty. C.L. O'Connor, water tender, was in one of the flooded firerooms. He was thrown to the floor and instantly enveloped in flames from the burning gases driven from the furnaces, but instead of rushing to escape he turned and endeavored to shut a water-tight door leading into a large bunker abaft the fireroom, but the hydraulic lever that operated the door had been injured by the shock and failed to function. Three men at work in this bunker were drowned.

If O'Connor had succeeded in shutting the door, the lives of these men would have been saved, as well as considerable buoyancy saved to the ship. The fact that he, though profoundly stunned by the shock and almost fatally burned by the furnace gases, should have had presence of mind and the courage to endeavor to shut the door is as great an example of heroic devotion to duty as it is possible for one to imagine. Immediately after attempting to close the door O'Connor was caught in the swirl of inrushing water and thrust up a ventilator leading to the upper deck. He was pulled up through the ventilator by a rope lowered to him from the upper deck.

The torpedo exploded on a bulkhead separating two firerooms, the explosive effect being apparently about equal in both firerooms, yet in one fireroom not a man was saved, while in the other fireroom two of the men escaped. The explosion blasted through the outer and inner skin of the ship and through an intervening coal bunker and bulkhead, hurling overboard 750 tons of coal. The two men saved were working the fires within 30 feet of the explosion and just below the level where the torpedo struck.

It is difficult to see how it was possible for these men to have escaped the shower of debris, coal, and water that must instantly have followed the explosion. However, the two men were not only saved but seem to have retained full possession of their faculties. Both of them were knocked down and blown across the fireroom. Their sensations were first a shower of flying coal, followed by an overwhelming inrush of water that swirled them round and round and finally thrust them up against the gratings above the top of the firerooms. Both of them fortunately struck exit openings in the gratings and escaped.

One of the men, P. Fitzgerald, after landing on the lower grating and while groping his way through the darkness trying to find the ladder leading above, stumbled over the body of a man lying on the grating. He at first thought the man dead but on second impulse he turned and aroused him and led him to safety. The man had been stunned into semi-unconsciousness and would undoubtedly have been lost if Fitzgerald had not aroused him. As a matter of fact, the water rose at once 10 feet above this grating as the ship settled … draft.

Another interesting instance of presence of mind and the effect of training may be cited. The attack occurred when all the men not on watch were at breakfast … Naturally, when the shock of the explosion came the men at the tables made a rush for the exit hatch. One of the men, Thomas F. Buckley by name, at first thrown to the deck by the force of the explosion, jumped upon one of the steps, turned and yelled, 'Remember, boys, we are all Americans and its only one hit' … This warning from Buckley was electrifying. All men immediately calmed themselves and went, not to their boats to abandon ship, but to their collision stations to save her.

From what has been outlined above, the following inference may be safely drawn. That however grave the danger, a well-trained and intelligent body of Americans do not lose their heads. The whole mental mechanism of the ship was instantly directed toward the work in hand …

This account would not be complete without the mention of the part played by the ship's hospital corps and the 150 helpless, wounded, and crippled soldiers who had done their part so nobly on the battle fields of France and were on their way home and deserved to get there. Within a very few minutes after the explosion all of these poor fellows were safely stowed in their boats, wrapped in warm blankets, and served with hot soup and other refreshments. They were made so comfortable in the boats that they preferred to remain in them all the way back to Brest for a period of about 18 hours.

Thirty-five men were killed by the explosion and 13 injured, one of them later dying from his injuries, the large number of casualties being due to the fact that the torpedo struck just at the time the watch was being relieved.

Victims from the attack on the *Mount Vernon*. (Authors' Collection)

The saving of the ship is attributed to the following circumstances: The fact that the water-tight doors were closed, that the bulkheads were tight and held, that additional strength was gained by blanking off all air-port lenses with steel plate, and that there was an organization well conceived and well carried out to meet the emergency.

The practice of keeping all water-tight doors closed at all times while at sea had been strictly adhered to on this vessel, with the result that the crew learned to give it enthusiastic support.

That a second and third torpedo were not fired was undoubtedly due largely to the fact that a shot from No. 1 gun, fired almost immediately after the explosion, struck the water near the periscope, and the barrage of depth charges was completed in 1 minute and 20 seconds after the torpedoing.[47]

On 9 September, the former Canadian Pacific Ocean liner *Missanabie*, which was serving as a troop transport, was travelling from Liverpool to New York in a convoy. It was attacked by *UB-87* and sank in seven minutes with the loss of forty-five lives. An unidentified witness who had been aboard another ship in the convoy described the sinking as follows:

We were in convoy, and the *Missanabie* was the only ship in the fleet carrying passengers and mails. We proceeded, in fairly choppy weather, at about eight knots, with the *Missanabie* the last ship in line. She had engine trouble, and had been forced to drop behind the main body of the convoy.

On Monday morning, however, she caught up. At 11.15 o'clock that morning she was hit by a torpedo. The missile struck aft and a few seconds later another torpedo hit the vessel. For some reason it was impossible to stop *Missanabie*'s engines. A few moments passed and then the ship's magazine exploded and the vessel immediately began to sink by the stern. The crew began to lower the boats and within four minutes the stern was well underwater.

This made it impossible to launch the forward boats, owing to the slant of the steamship. Some of the aft boats got away, but I saw at least one boat overturned. Because of the choppiness of the sea I am sure that it would take wonderful seamanship to keep any of the small boats afloat very long.

From a ship next to the *Missanabie* I could see some of the passengers jumping into the water from the stern. Destroyers and patrol boats immediately the ship was observed in distress and rushed to the scene and commenced to drop depth charges in the area from whence the torpedo had apparently been discharged. No one saw a submarine nor was a periscope visible at any time. I am unable to say, from my knowledge, whether the depth charges proved effective.

The *Missanabie* by this time had sunk well down by the stern, and the water going through her funnels caused her to stand almost perpendicular. The bow disappeared from view within a short time, and the life of the steamship from the time she was struck to the time she sank was about seven minutes.

As we came away I saw seven lifeboats in the water and apparently having a hard time of it. There were also many people in lifebelts afloat. The rescue vessels were near at hand, however. Shortly after the *Missanabie* was hit a torpedo was fired at another ship in the convoy, but this missed, going astern. When the stricken steamship was almost perpendicular, with her bow pointing skyward, her engines, anchors, and other heavy material crashed toward the stern, and this and the blowing up of the magazine undoubtedly caused her to sink so rapidly.[48]

A total of 109 ships were sunk or captured by U-boats in September, amounting to 192,900 tons. Fourteen ships were damaged. This was the final month in the war in which the number of ships lost to submarines reached triple digits.[49]

By October 1918, Germany's military situation was utterly hopeless, with its forces surrendering or retreating at a rapid pace, often abandoning vital equipment and guns in the process. Both the Allies and Central Powers began posturing for the inevitable peace talks. The German General Staff pressed Kaiser Wilhelm II to request an immediate ceasefire and begin making democratic reforms, in order to win a more favourable peace agreement. Following this and statements by President Wilson that the Kaiser could no longer be a party to peace negotiations, the entire German Empire erupted in turmoil and chaos. Riots and uprisings began to break out within Berlin and other cities in Germany, and suddenly the Kaiser found himself fighting battles abroad and with his own people. On 4 October, Germany formally asked the Allies for an armistice, although there was much negotiating that would need to be accomplished before peace could take hold. By 12 October, Wilhelm II was reported to have 'declared his willingness to abdicate in order that he may not stand in the way of peace', although he still hoped to retain the kingship of Prussia.[50]

Meanwhile, Red Cross Nurse Mary E. Maxwell had just completed a transatlantic crossing from America, and was assigned to US Base Hospital No. 40, formerly Sarisbury Court, in Hampshire, England. The 186 acre estate could house up to 8,000 wounded soldiers from the Western Front, and was lavishly appointed.[51] On 16 October, Maxwell wrote a letter to a friend in the United States named Kitzie, stating that 'This has been a wonderful experience', and that they 'have kept real well – have a comfortable place and plenty to eat – Everything agrees with me'.

She described the hospital as a 'beautiful place – the walks and gardens, are lovely and the old manor house has almost fifty or sixty rooms … we are so comfortable, it is hard to believe a war is going on – if it were not for the poor sick boys'. While Maxwell was enjoying her service in England, her transatlantic crossing was anything but smooth, although this had nothing to do with U-boats or enemy action:

> We came over on a White Star Liner – had every comfort, and everything was done for our pleasure – Had a lovely stateroom, hot and cold water – right there all the convenience of home – The ocean was wonderful, and we glided along so smoothly – could scarcely tell we were moving – I got along beautifully until about the fourth day – then I was sea sick – My! it certainly was the sickest-sick feeling I ever had in all my life – It seemed to me I never could feel well again.[52]

Another American, a Sergeant John E. Hertz, wrote a letter home to a friend named Bertha in October, telling of his own struggles with seasickness when he had crossed the Atlantic several months prior. He downplayed the seasickness, saying 'we arrived here on the boat. It sure was a fine trip across with only two days of rough weather and even then that was not so bad'.[53] Most of the Americans being shipped out to the war had never been far from their home towns, much less crossed the ocean on a liner, so seasickness was a very common occurrence.

On 19 October, Art White wrote to his mother, describing another transatlantic crossing aboard the cruiser USS *Minneapolis*. Even at this late stage, U-boats were still operating just off the coast of the United States. Describing the incident, White seemed disappointed that his ship did not get a chance to exact revenge on the undersea predators that had plagued the Atlantic for so long:

> Our trip up to Sidney Nova Scotia was a fair one. The only excitement we had was on are [sic] way back. It was off Long Island Sound, four U boats were operating there, we got a wireless they were just ahead of us but just our bad luck we either missed them or they wanted to miss us, because our ship looks like an over grown destroyer that is the only way I can figure it out …
>
> … We had quite many men sick just before we left so we dropped them off at a hospital ship. I am feeling pretty good just at present so I am thankful.

The sickness that White mentions in his letter refers to the 'Spanish Flu' outbreak, which had begun in January 1918. Before the pandemic burned itself out in 1920, over 500 million would be infected, and estimates of the number killed range between 50 and 100 million.[54] During the last year of the war, fear of the flu was a constant worry, particularly on troop transports and hospital ships, where people were often crowded aboard and below decks, in close proximity to others. White's reassurances to his mother that he was feeling well make sense when read in this context.

Meanwhile, John Metzger, who was still serving aboard the troop transport USS *Rijndam*, received disturbing news from home that his brother Dewey had fallen ill, quite possibly from the 'Spanish Flu'. He sent the following letter home, reassuring his family and brother that he would be okay:

ON BOARD SHIP
Oct. 26, 1918

Dear Folks at home:-

I just received your letter and was very glad to get it out very sorry to hear Dewey is sick … I don't think Dewey has got the Spanish influenza and don't think he has. We had that on board and I did not get it. Well if he has got it give him good care and I am sure he will soon be over it. It is only a bad cold and has to be taken care of. I had a very pleasant voyage returning. I sent you a long letter upon arrival which you should have received by now … I have been very busy this last trip … Love to all and trusting in God to guide us always.
Your SON, BRO, and uncle John E. Metzger

Well Dewey hurry up and get well and you will get a chance yet to help whip the Kaiser. You are not very sick and don't let them tell you that you are. I will write and tell Mildred to come out and see you. That is if you want her to. Well Dewey I will close hoping you are well when I return. Your Bro: J.E. Metzger[55]

As October came to a close, the threat of being torpedoed was superseded by the threat of Spanish Flu and concerns relating to seasickness and the comfort of accommodations. U-boats no longer seemed to be as substantial a threat as they had throughout the war. However, the weather and conditions on the North Atlantic still remained a hazard, as was the case in peacetime. Tragically, with the end of the conflict just weeks away, a horrific accident occurred, claiming the lives of many American soldiers before they ever had a chance to set foot in Europe.

On the morning of 6 October, the HMS *Otranto* was transporting American soldiers from the United States to Glasgow and Liverpool. The *Otranto*, an Orient Steam Navigation Company liner, had been requisitioned and fitted out as an armed auxiliary cruiser in August 1914. The vessel encountered a heavy storm, strong winds and poor visibility off the north coast of Islay, Scotland, and collided with the HMS *Kashmir*. The vessel took on a heavy list, and the flooding quickly disabled the engines and the generators, putting out the lights.

The destroyer HMS *Mounsey* came alongside and began taking men off the ship, but the rough conditions caused the two ships to knock together, crushing people struggling in the water in between the vessels, or who had tried unsuccessfully to jump across the gap. The *Otranto* soon grounded itself on rocks, and broke up and sank. Due to the conditions, 431 men were killed, the majority American troops. The ship's captain, Ernest W. Davidson, went down with his ship, saluting his men one last time before being dragged under.[56]

The *Otranto*. (Authors' Collection)

One of the American survivors was Eugene Turro, a soldier from New York. He escaped with minor injuries to his head and face, and gave the following account of the sinking:

> There were about one thousand of us on board the *Otranto*, and on Sunday morning about twenty minutes to nine I was between decks when the disaster occurred. We were very near the Irish coast, and could not see the hills plainly, so we did not think of any danger.
>
> There was a bunch of us playing cards when the crash came, but we didn't think much of it, and only went up on deck when we were called. But when I reached deck I found another vessel had smashed into our bows and done a lot of damage. Still there was no panic or scramble. We got standing around the deck, and when a British destroyer came along the order was given, 'Every man for himself', and I jumped overboard our vessel into the deck of the destroyer.
>
> It was in the fall that I got my head and face hurt. There 250 of us got away on that destroyer, but I could not tell if any others were saved or if any other destroyers were on the scene.
>
> But the captain of the British destroyer knew his work. It was a terribly rough sea at the time and a gale was blowing, but he managed to come alongside of us and stop there, rising and falling in the waves until we jumped into her, and then he moved away. It was as dangerous for him as for us, but he managed great.[57]

Another survivor who gave an account of the sinking was Lieutenant Cantwell, from Denver, Colorado. However, the *Otranto* sinking was overshadowed in the newspapers by headlines such as 'Kaiser Prepares to Quell Riots', 'Foe's Whole Champagne Front Collapses and Germans Flee', etc:

> The crash occurred within a stone's throw of the grave of the *Tuscany* [*Tuscania*] … Buffeted by the seas which were running mountain high when the *Kashmir* coming out of the mist, crashed into us and ripped a jagged hole in the *Otranto's* side.
>
> Everyone rushed up to the deck as the shrieking whistles of the two vessels followed the resounding echoes of the crash. The first two lifeboats lowered were smashed against the side of the *Otranto*.
>
> I saw the head of one soldier crushed and all the occupants of both boats disappeared beneath the waves. The British destroyer *Maunsey* [sic] gamely tried to reach us in spite of the storm. As she came as close as possible alongside, many American soldiers and British seamen threw off their heavy clothing and leaped for the destroyer's deck … below. Some of them were thrown back between the destroyer and the *Otranto* and were ground to death. One soldier was cut half in two by twin wire cables.
>
> The *Kashmir* backed immediately after the collision apparently unharmed. I remained on the *Otranto* for four minutes and then jumped for the destroyer's deck with a dozen others. We were washed off the deck by a huge wave, which wrecked the destroyer's bridge. But we fought back to the deck with the next wave.
>
> The *Otranto* was finally abandoned by the destroyer after more than 300 of us had been saved.[58]

Many of the American survivors of the sinking ended up spending significant time in hospitals recovering, so it seems likely that few of them ever ended up setting foot on the battlefields of Europe.

While the U-boat war was gasping its last breath, there were still some ships being torpedoed. One of these was the City of Dublin Steam Packet Company liner, RMS *Leinster*. On 10 October, the mail vessel, painted in dazzle camouflage and armed with a 12-pounder and two signal guns, was sailing through the Irish Sea, carrying passengers from Dublin to Holyhead, Wales. The majority of the passengers were English, Irish, Canadian, Anzac or American troops coming home from leave, or going on leave.

Around 10.00 a.m., the *Leinster* was sailing through a heavy swell when *UB-123* fired two torpedoes at it, missing with the first, and scoring a hit with the second. The *Leinster*, damaged but still underway, made a 180° turn in an attempt to return to port. However, the ship was soon struck by another torpedo, and the ship 'exploded into a mass of debris and smoke'. It sank by the bow in minutes. The official number killed in the sinking was 501 men, although research suggests that the number was actually higher. The survivors managed to cling to the lifeboats, remained afloat in their lifebelts, or clung to debris in heavy seas until rescued.[59]

One of the lucky survivors was a British soldier with the last name Dane, who was serving in the West Kent Yeomanry. He wrote the following account of the sinking to his father:

Just a few lines to you to let you know that I am still alive and quite well, with the exception of a few bruises, and I think I am very lucky to get off so lightly after the terrible time I went through. I suppose you have heard by now that the I was on board the ill-fated *Leinster* coming home for fourteen days' leave. Well, we left Kingstown at 8.55. All went well for about forty minutes, when all of a sudden I saw a very small torpedo coming towards the bow. At first I thought it would miss us, but we were unlucky, and the explosion was enough to stop us. The ship now started to go down by the head, but not far, and I think that she would have kept up all right until help arrived. Anyway, I was not leaving anything to chance, so I got ready for a swim. I first took off my overcoat by the way, these drowned a good many men, and then put my lifebelt on. Then I started to take my puttees and boots off, and had one boot undone when the next explosion came, and I can tell you it was a terrible one. It seemed to lift the whole ship out of the water, and when she dropped back again she simply went to pieces. I might mention people were blown sky high by this second explosion. No sooner had this occurred than she began to sink at once. I was, all this time, in the stern of the ship. The stern came clean out of the water, and I should imagine from the top of the deck where I stood to the water was quite sixty feet. There was nothing else to do but go down with the ship or slide down the side into the water, so I got over the rail and slid down the side into the water, and I can tell you it was a slide that I shall never forget. When I reached the water I swam for all I was worth, as I did not want to get caught in the suction and dragged down. I made straight for a lot of wreckage that was floating, and I succeeded in getting hold of a couple of planks, which kept me up quite well for a time, but the sea was so rough at the time it was very hard work to hang on to them. Then a boat got mixed up with this lot of wreckage, and I thought to myself 'I'm making for that to see if I can manage to get into it'. Well, when I go to it I found she was over loaded so I had to hang on to the life-lines that run round the sides. This I succeeded in doing, but every now and again the sea would almost knock you off, but I hung on. There were quite twenty hanging on to her. Some of the men who were hanging on became exhausted and dropped off (poor devils). I then having more room to move, I managed to get my left leg over the top of the rope which runs round the sides of the boat. That got me out of the water a bit, but I was getting very weak when one of the chaps in the bow of the boat put a bit of rope around my shoulders, and hung on to me for a time. Then after about an hour and a half in this awful position, there came four destroyers to our assistance. I remember seeing one of them come up alongside. The next I remember was getting down in the bottom of the boat, which by this time was swamped. When I fell down I came to my senses and all there was in the boat was myself and a sailor. He came and got hold of me and put a rope round my shoulders, and I was dragged on board the destroyer. I believe I was more dead than alive, as I could not walk. I was taken down below, and they stripped me and knocked a bit of life into me. We were then taken back to Kingston, and I was sent straight into hospital, where I have been in bed ever since, but I am feeling all right in myself, only for my legs, which are terribly bruised by my hanging on to the planks and then the boat, but never mind, I am alive, and that's worth something. I cannot described the awful scenes that I saw, and the screaming of the people who were drowning, so I will say no more about it, as it does not bear thinking about.[60]

The *Leinster* sinking was described by author Roy Stokes as 'the greatest disaster to befall Irish citizens travelling in Irish waters'.[61] The sinking served as a swansong of sorts for the U-boat war, as Germany had already asked the Allies for a peace agreement. Following the *Leinster* tragedy, President Woodrow Wilson responded, stating on 14 October that as long as U-boats continued attacking passenger liners, there could be no peace. Not wanting to jeopardise peace talks, Commander-in-Chief of Germany's High Seas Fleet Scheer issued the following orders on 21 October:

> To all U-boats: Commence return from patrol at once. Because of ongoing negotiations any hostile actions against merchant vessels prohibited. Returning U-boats are allowed to attack warships only in daylight. End of message. Admiral[62]

Tragically, many of the bodies of victims of the *Leinster* sinking were never recovered, which prevented families from having closure. One example of this is Private Harry S. Barlow, a British soldier in the 2/1st Duke of Yorks Own Loyal Suffolk Hussars who died in the sinking. With his body missing, his widow Mary desperately wrote to everyone and anyone she could think of, hoping that her late husband's body could be returned to her for a proper burial. Sadly, he was never found, a difficult fact which a records officer had to relay to her after she mistakenly received news that Harry's body had been discovered:

11/2/19

Madam,

In reply to your letter attached, I beg to inform you that the body of your husband has not been recovered. I have just received a communication from the War Office to the effect that the body which has been buried was that of a female passenger of the same name as that of your husband.

 Will you please complete the enclosed memo. + return at your early convenience.

      I am, Madam,
Your obedient Servant,
          J. Clark Lt. for btl. [sic]
          i/c Cavalry Records, Hussars[63]

Mary carried a telegram from her husband with her for many years afterward, and it may have been one of his last messages home. It is dated the third of an indistinguishable month, possibly October. It was written after his leave had been cancelled, and read as follows:

    Cannot come will write later keep smiling
        Harry[64]

The U-boat that sank the *Leinster* met a tragic end as well. Just nine or ten days after the sinking, *UB-123*, which had a very young crew, made an attempt to cross the Northern Barrage. Nobody ever heard from the submarine again, and it was presumed to have struck a mine, all thirty-six aboard being lost at sea.[65]

 Shortly after Germany's U-boat fleet was ordered to return from their patrols, the Naval Order of 24 October 1918 was issued. Commander-in-Chief of Germany's High Seas Fleet Scheer had ordered Admiral von Hipper to come up with plans for provoking one final battle between the Royal Navy's Grand Fleet and Germany's High Seas Fleet in the southern portion of the North Sea. The High Seas Fleet had largely remained in

Mary Barlow. (Authors' Collection)

port since the Battle of Jutland. Their intention was to inflict substantial damage on the Royal Navy, no matter what the cost, in order to position Germany for a more favourable peace agreement. The newly freed-up U-boats would be tasked with ambushing the British fleet. Even at this late hour, Scheer remained a true believer in the potential of U-boats to propel Germany to victory.

While planning for the final attack was underway, the crew of *UB-116*, commanded by Oberleutnant zur See Hans Joachim Emsmann, were preparing for a desperate final mission to preserve the honour of the German Navy. The crew had received orders on 25 October to attack the Grand Fleet at Scapa Flow to 'weaken the enemy as much as possible before the decisive battle'. Passing through Hoxa Sound on 28 October, the U-boat was detected by shore-based hydrophones, and unbeknownst to the crew, was heading into a minefield. Once the submarine had penetrated the sound, an Allied operator flipped a switch, detonating a row of mines, destroying the submarine with all hands. *UB-116* was the final U-boat destroyed during the war.[66]

Meanwhile, mutiny broke out aboard two of the German battleships in Wilhelmshaven on 29 October when orders to prepare for the attack on the Royal Navy were given. The German sailors had no intention of being treated as sacrificial lambs in the closing days of the war, and felt that the suicidal attack would undermine the peace talks rather than improve their lot. Even though the crewmembers responsible were rounded up and arrested, the uprising and doubt about the loyalty of their sailors forced the attack to be cancelled. However, the anger of the war-weary military and population in Germany continued to smoulder, and would explode once more just days later.

For the month of October, a total of eighty-four ships were lost, equalling 127,453 tons. The heaviest losses were around the British Isles and in the Mediterranean, with lighter losses off the North American coast, reflective of most months later in the war. Ten additional ships were damaged.[67] While more ships would be sunk before the war's end, the heavy losses were finished. The long nightmare that transatlantic crossings had become was about to end.

November–December 1918

By November 1918, the naval protests in Germany continued. Sailors and workers in Kiel held a large meeting on 2 November 'at which inflammatory speeches were made demanding the abolition of the monarchy and the officer class, and the release of the imprisoned mutineers … '. The uprising spread to industrial workers, and soon only the loyalty of U-boat crews could be relied upon. On 3 November, the protestors made additional demands, including an end to the war and an increase in food rations. The protestors marched on the military prison, eventually being fired on after refusing to halt, with multiple people being killed or injured. The crowd was dispersed.

On 4 November, the protests turned into an actual mutiny, with the sailors and worker representatives taking over Kiel and establishing a council. They soon issued a series of demands for peace and government reforms. Reports of, and outrage regarding, the protestors being fired upon rapidly spread, and soon additional revolts were breaking out across the empire, including in Berlin. By 9 November, a full-blown revolution was underway, and Kaiser Wilhelm II, having lost the support of his military, had no choice but to abdicate his throne. A republic was declared, and the following day, the Kaiser fled into exile in the neutral Netherlands.[68] This would lead to the German Revolution and eventual establishment of the Weimar Republic.

Two days later, the Armistice of Compiègne was signed. The agreement officially went into effect at 11.00 a.m. on 11 November 1918. For the first time since 1914, the Western Front fell silent, no longer inundated with the sound of artillery, machine-gun fire, and the cries of the wounded or dying. While not technically a surrender, the Germans had agreed to remove their troops from the Western Front and back beyond their own borders, and there was a promise to pay reparations. As part of the terms, they had to surrender their navy to Britain, and the High Seas Fleet was soon interned in Scapa Flow. Germany also had to hand over all of their submarines.

British and American minelayer crewmembers celebrate the announcement of the armistice. (Authors' Collection)

By 20 November, a group of twenty U-boats arrived at Harwich flying a white flag, and were handed over to the British. Others would be surrendered in the coming days. While some U-boat commanders thought of scuttling their vessels or fleeing to neutral nations to be interned there, Britain threatened to occupy their island base in Heligoland if they did. Still, seven U-boats 'foundered' during their passage to England, either a great coincidence, or an attempt by their crewmembers to retain some of their dignity by not having to turn over their vessels. Stephen King-Hall, one of the Royal Navy officers supervising the transfer of the submarines, told a poignant tale. When Kapitänleutnant Oelricher handed over *U-98*, the British officer asked him if the binoculars Oelricher had

Members of the public tour surrendered U-boats in Southampton. (*Southampton Pictorial,* 1919/Authors' Collection)

around his neck were owned by him, or his government. Oelricher replied that they were his government's. King-Hall described the scene that followed:

> [He] solemnly placed them round my neck. He then held out his hand rather shyly. We were strictly enjoined to have no intercourse with the German captains but I shook him by the hand; he looked so miserable with the White Ensign flying over the German ensign. He brushed aside a tear and muttered a 'thank you' as he stepped off his ship on his way back to Germany.[69]

Although the conflict was over, it would take six long months of negotiations before the official peace agreement, the Treaty of Versailles, would be signed. However, the U-boats' reign of terror was officially over when the armistice was signed in November. During the four years of the bloody conflict, U-boats sank over 5,000 ships, equalling more than 12,000,000 tons of shipping. Around 15,000 people died in the sinkings. The U-boat crews managed to accomplish this despite losing 178 U-boats and 5,000 crewmen. This was nearly one-third of all the men who served aboard U-boats.[70]

During the peak of unrestricted submarine warfare in the spring of 1917, there were very real concerns that Britain might be starved into submission, being down to only six weeks' reserve of food.[71] However, the German Government had wavered in their support of unrestricted submarine warfare for too long, and their late reversal was not enough to turn the tide of the war. If the conflict had dragged on longer, the U-boat war may have reignited, as there were no fewer than 226 new U-boats under construction when the armistice was signed.[72] Like the decision to wage unrestricted submarine warfare, this full-scale production of new submarines came too late. However, the world saw the potential of submarine warfare, and Germany would implement what they learned a few decades later to deadly effect during the Second World War, nearly bringing Britain to its knees once again. German U-boats were so technologically advanced by the end of the First World War that they differed little from the U-boats Germany utilised at the beginning of the next war.

With the ending of the Great War, people around the world could take a deep breath, say prayers, bury the dead, and begin the long and painful task of rebuilding and trying to move on with their lives. For some, things would never be the same, but from the destruction and mayhem, hope that this war would prove to be the one to end all wars sprung eternal.

6

Epilogue, 1919

New Year 1919 was described by the *Boston Globe* as more 'joyous, noisy and fervent than for many years, and at midnight compared in some measure with the demonstration that marked the reception here of the news of the signing of the armistice between the warring nations. The gaiety and clamor were greater because of the birth of the peace year, the general thanksgiving that thousands of soldiers and sailors have returned safely from posts of duty in their country's service'. Wryly, the paper went on to say celebration was greater due to the fact national prohibition was about to take effect.[1]

One of the vessels heading overseas to bring American troops back home was the USS *Louisville*, formerly the SS *St Louis* until it was requisitioned as a

Canadian troops heading home after the war crowd the forecastle of the *Olympic* as it departs Southampton. (*Southampton Pictorial*, 1919/Authors' Collection)

troop transport by the US Navy in April 1918. The following account tells of the voyage, which began on 19 January:

Louisville, Lieutenant-Commander Hartley commanding, began her sixth voyage under the ... Navy ... on Sunday, January 19 ... She left Pier No. 61, North River, bound for Liverpool and thence to Brest, France ... Only three fourths boiler power ... was used on this trip, to enable the boilers being kept in good shape and cleaned at sea, as well as to save coal consumption. The weather continued satisfactory until ... January 24, when ... a heavy north-northwest sea was encountered in which the ship rolled heavily.

Fastnet Light was passed shortly following noon of Monday, January 27. The sea was still running heavily, but moderated when the ship reached the protection of the Irish coast.

Bar Light Vessel, outside of Liverpool, was passed ... Tuesday morning in the Mersey River opposite the city. Going through Sandon Basin, the ship was finally moored a little after 10 o'clock that night in West Canada Docks. The first of the naval passengers for transportation to the United States came aboard on Wednesday. Coal barges drew alongside, and the work of coaling was started. Several nurses for transportation to Brest also came aboard. More naval passengers came on the ship on Friday, as well as some army officers and army enlisted personnel. It was on Friday, January 31, that the first of the wives of army and naval personnel, who had been married in England, came aboard for passage to America. They traveled under orders entitling them to stateroom accommodations free of cost, provided they were equipped with sufficient funds with which to defray the expenses of their mess aboard, and railroad transportation upon reaching the United States, from New York to the points of their respective destinations. The run to Brest was started on Sunday, February 2, the ship shoving off from Canada Docks at 9 o'clock in the morning ... First Lieutenant Merrell reported to the commanding officer that the port propeller had touched the dock while passing from Sandon Basin to the river. Consequently a request was prepared for a diver to make an examination of the propeller at Brest. At 6.45 o'clock Sunday evening, Lieutenant (junior grade) W.B. McCarthy, U.S.N.R.F., found a stowaway in the fire-room. He gave his name as Fred James Richmond and his address as the British Y.M.C.A., Church Street, Liverpool. Mechanics who were repairing No. 4 hatch had apprentice boys carrying their tools and Richmond said that he had passed onto the ship as an apprentice boy. He was placed under guard to be transferred from the ship at Brest. The boy had an honorable discharge, No. 161,718, from the British Navy.

... Brest was reached ... Monday evening. As there was no pilot present or available, the commanding officer and navigating officer conned the ship to anchorage. While going into the harbor the U.S.S. *Leviathan* was passed coming out. The boy stowaway was taken ashore Tuesday morning. He left the ship in the custody of the master-at-arms, F. Wurth, chief gunner's mate, U.S.N. All passengers for Brest were disembarked and cargo unloaded onto lighters that had come out from the shore.

The troops for passage to America started coming aboard at noon, Wednesday, February 5, from a lighter ... A diver from the U.S.S. *Bridgeport* descended, at the stern, examined the port propeller and reported that four inches of one end of one blade had been bent. This did not prevent use of the propeller. The return trip to New York was started at nine minutes after 1 o'clock Thursday morning, February 6, the westward passage, just the same as the eastward, being made on three-fourths boiler power. Heavy seas were encountered for several days, none even moderate being had until just before a landfall had been made. On Monday, February 10, two women stowaways were found in room No. 45 on D deck. They were Miss Bowie Bell and Miss Margaret Smith, of Liverpool. A board of investigation of which Lieutenant-Commander Meek was senior officer, took up the investigation into the case of the presence of the two women stowaways on board the ship.

A very exciting situation was created ... Tuesday evening, February 11, when, as the result of an especially heavy sea which produced on the port bow a wave resembling tidal proportions, the ship rolled to starboard thirty-five degrees,

Jubilant American troops celebrate their return home aboard USS *Leviathan*. (Authors' Collection)

went to port thirty-seven degrees, then rolled once more to starboard thirty-nine degrees and finished with a roll back to port of forty-one degrees, the last two rolls having taken the *Louisville* entirely through an even eighty degrees ... The soldiers being taken back to the United States were mostly negroes, and many of them were in the mess-hall at the time. They instinctively grabbed hold of the mess-table for support, because the deck was tilted at an unstable angle. The tables, however, would not stand up under the weight placed upon them, and with the successive rolls were ripped loose from the deck. Troops, mess-gear, sailors, tables and food were piled indiscriminately together on the deck. A noteworthy fact of the situation was the coolness of the sailors ... Only five men with nothing more than bruises, but one with a dislocated shoulder, were taken to sick-bay for treatment. A disconnection of one of the electric light lines added acuteness to the situation ... but lighting was quickly restored. In the ward-room, two of the women passengers fainted but were soon revived. To add to the apprehensions of the passengers, the general alarm switch was closed by the heaviest of the rolls. The impression was gained at once that it had become necessary to abandon the ship. The possible tragedy of such a necessity can be imagined only by those who have gone through the raging storm of an Atlantic Ocean winter. Intense excitement permeated the atmosphere, but the officers and crew of the ship ... intervened and quieted the women and soldiers ... The *Louisville* continued to roll and pitch during the night, but nothing like the series of rolls experienced at 6 o'clock was again encountered. The mess-hall deck had to be used for the next two days in lieu of tables, while the latter were being repaired ... Ambrose Channel Light Vessel was reached ... Saturday night, February 15, and anchorage at quarantine was made at 10.30 o'clock. The ship was berthed ... at noon of the next day. This round voyage was made in twenty-seven days. All troops carried on the westward passage were off the vessel by the middle of the afternoon. On Monday, February 17, immigration officials came on board and took charge of the two stowaways from Liverpool, Miss Bell and Miss Smith, and they were taken to Ellis Island, where a special board of investigation was convened ... It took the board only five minutes to decide that the two women should be returned to Liverpool ... at 12.15 o'clock Tuesday afternoon, February 18, Charles Dunham, gunnery sergeant, United States Marine Corps, a passenger on the *Louisville* on the westward passage, died from lobar-pneumonia. The first three of the heavy guns of the ship, two four-inch and one five-inch pieces, were removed on Tuesday, and taken to the navy yard. The two forward four inch guns had been taken off the ship during the previous stay in New York. On Friday, February 21 ... A number of the ship's company were released from active duty under the Bureau of Navigation order providing for a gradual reduction of the Cruiser and Transport Force ships' personnel.[2]

Thousands upon thousands of letters like the following one from US troop Hank Deckert, who was returning home on the former Hamburg America liner USS *Pretoria*, were sent to relieved relatives and friends. No doubt, it was written with an equal amount of joy and relief:

April 30, 1919

My dear old folks at home,

To relieve the stress on your minds probably you have of our voyage across the deep, briny blue. It was a very pleasant one for me. I received your telegram this morning about 8 o'clock and try and do if possible as you said but conditions are so now that we are here one day and morning the same day or next. So do not come or write any letters or send anything for probably I will have to go to Jersey for being discharged and will let you know when I am coming.

Now will try and tell you a little about our homeward voyage ... They got us up at 3.30 in the morning to prepare to embark. Marched about the same distance back. Stood around with our packs on our back and embarked aboard the U.S.S. *Pretoria* at 11 o'clock. We pulled out of Brest at 4 p.m. for our journey across the sea ... The first day I felt a little dizzy, but after that I felt good. On the ship could buy sweets and cakes and on Easter Sunday had church service at sea an there was a very fine sermon. On the other days there was singing and talent pulled off by the boys on board ship. The last Sunday there was also a church service. The last two days at sea were cold and rough. Monday morning about 6 a.m. there came a Boston pilot on board to take us into Boston harbor at 7 pulled into the harbor and I wish you could have seen the welcome we got. Whistles blowing, ships coming out to meet us. On one ship was a band and the Welcome Board. The band playing cheery songs, throwing chocolates and cigars to the boys and at 11 got off the boat. The different societies sure did use us fine. The Red Cross gave us coffee and cinnamon rolls. The Y.M.C.A. and Salvation Army gave us a box of candy, matches, smokes, and newspaper and a telegram. So that is how you came to get that telegram. They sure did use us fine. About 11.30 we pulled for Camp Devens about 50 miles from Boston. Along the route, factory whistles and everyone waving hands and flags. When the train would stop people would come up and especially the girls would come up and shake our hands and welcome us. So that was our journey ... Now we are awaiting our orders to go and beat it for home ... Will close with my best wishes and hope to meet you all face to face.

As ever from your anxious son,
Hank[3]

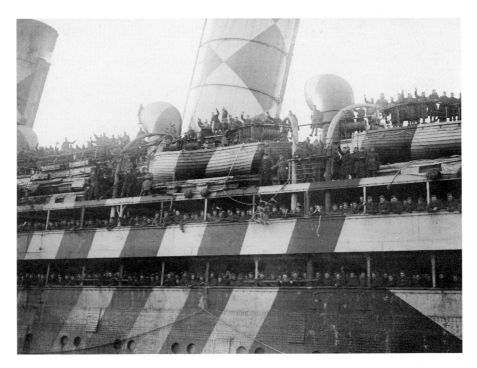

American troops aboard the *Mauretania* celebrate as they return from the battlefields of Europe. (Authors' Collection)

Meanwhile, the *Imperator* was one of the German vessels that had been laid up in Hamburg Harbour during the war. The vessel became so immersed in mud after sitting during the conflict that a channel had to be dredged in order to bring it out. As part of the post-war agreement, Germany turned over the ship to the United States Government to be used as a transport on May 5, 1919. It was commissioned as the USS *Imperator* that same day with Captain J.K. Robison, United States Navy, in command. Besides German vessels such as the *Leviathan* which had been seized by the US upon joining the war, Germany ceded other vessels to the Allies after the armistice. An example of this is the North German Lloyd vessel *Berlin*, given as compensation for the *Arabic* sinking. Subsequently purchased by the White Star Line, the vessel was renamed *Arabic*, becoming the third vessel of that name.[4] A description of the *Imperator's* impressive medical facilities was given in the following article. They were apparently very well equipped and ready to transport home sick or convalescent troops. Even with the war over, this would remain a large area of need for some time to come:

> The sick bay ... consisted of fifty bunks on 'G' deck forward and was formerly used for sick steerage passengers. There were also three rooms on 'A' deck

USS *Imperator*. (Authors' Collection)

amidships formerly intended for first-class passengers – but no use was made of them. To get an idea of the decks it should be remembered that on the *Imperator* the uppermost deck is 'A' and the lowest deck 'K'.

Upon the ship's arrival in New York, on May 2, 1919, she was fitted with standees for troops, new mess halls, latrines, and bath rooms and a sick bay was constructed by navy yard workmen.

The sick bay was built on 'D' deck aft and was formerly the social hall and smoking room for second-class passengers. There were two wards provided, a medical and a surgical. Six nurses were assigned to the *Imperator* for duty and hospital corpsmen but only 33 were desired by the senior medical officer. This number has proved to be entirely adequate.

The medical ward consists of 80 bunks, has ample ventilation with 7 windows and a large skylight, which renders artificial light unnecessary during the day.

The color scheme of the medical ward is Nile green on the bulkheads and beaded white paneling on the ceiling … On the edge of the skylight are placed ferns, trailing ivy and other potted plants, so that … you are greeted by a veritable bower of potted flowers in full bloom …

Directly forward of the medical ward are the examining room and dispensary. With a crew of 2,300 men it is necessary to obtain rapidity in holding sick call and to this end four medical officers hold morning sick call at the same time …

When 10,000 troops are taken aboard at Brest the problem of their care becomes more complicated. For their sick call 12 substations are established in the troop compartments all over the ship. Twelve Army medical officers are assigned to these stations and treat all mild cases there. Hospital cases are transferred to the ship's hospital and thus pass under the care of the naval medical officers ...

Three isolation wards are arranged in a row on the port side of the medical ward, each containing eight bunks. They have the same color scheme as the medical ward as well as the same lighting and concrete deck.

The surgical ward consists of 80 bunks. The color scheme here is mahogany and white and the ventilation is the same as that of the medical ward. Electric candelabras furnish the artificial lighting. The surgical ward has a dressing table which can be readily moved about the ward ...

The operating room on the starboard side of the surgical ward is equipped with a standard United States Navy sterilizing outfit and operating room cabinet. It has a tile deck and is equipped with operating table and ample light and water.

The dressing room for pus cases is located forward on 'F' deck, has a tile deck and plenty of light and fresh water. The equipment consists of an operating table, electric sterilizer, and a full set of instruments.

The eye, ear, nose, and throat room is situated on 'E" deck below the main sick bay and has all modern equipment ...

The genito-urinary room, located on 'G' deck just below the dressing room, is outfitted with a cystoscope, urethrescope, and operating table and is also used for the administration of salvarsan.

The venereal treatment room is just aft of the genito-urinary room and all venereal prophylactics and venereal treatments are given there.

The diet kitchen is located on the port side of the surgical ward and is glass-enclosed. It is equipped with electric ovens and stoves and has a refrigerated ice box which is cooled by coils from the ice plant on board. Here the special diets are prepared. All patients' diets are placed on trays and served in the ward by the hospital corpsmen ...

Any diet can be readily prepared upon an order from the medical officer in charge of the ward. A nurse is in charge of the diet kitchen, assisted by two hospital corpsmen.

The outstanding feature of the *Imperator*'s sick wards is the effective combination of artistic surroundings with an atmosphere of comfort. To obtain this the existing decorations of the two spaces allotted were disturbed as little as possible. The beautiful Nile green paneling on the bulkheads, the beaded white paneling overhead, and all gilt moldings, bronze medallions, etc., were left in their original state. Three-pronged bronze candelabras are spaced generously on all sides of the wards, each holding an imitation electric candle of frosted glass.

The standee bunks when erected were finished in white enamel and this with the snowy white linen presents a pleasing contrast to the other colors.

The light Nile green and white naturally suggest something of outdoors and to enhance this effect potted plants are utilized at every opportunity.

The surgical ward presents a marked contrast to the medical ward in its arrangement of colors. Here the room was originally finished in mahogany the wood being used in panels with a natural finish. The deck was covered with a heavy black-and-white-squared linoleum. In general appearance there is more solidity in this room than in the medical ward. Again all existing ornamentation and decoration was carefully left undisturbed and utilized to produce a peaceful and pleasing air. All bunks were finished in white enamel.

In addition to the decorations there was much beautiful furniture left that could be used for the various offices separated from the wards by colonial glass partitions. In the passageway between the two wards leather sofas were allowed to remain. The Red Cross supplied mission writing desks such as are used in hotels, enabling convalescent patients to enjoy the luxury of a modern club. This space is used as a lounging room.

What has been the result of this effort to produce something almost ultra-beautiful in the way of sick accommodations? Has it been of practical value? The members of the Hospital Corps of the *Imperator* think that it has. They saw a very poorly ventilated, poorly lighted, depressing sick bay abolished and a beautiful, airy space take its place through which the ocean breezes circulated almost as freely as though it were a garden by the sea. They witnessed trays being served from a diet kitchen equipped with electric stoves and coilcooled ice boxes.

… the Army officers traveling on board the *Imperator* have better rooms than on any other transport …

'Do you treat officers the same as enlisted men?' was a question asked the senior medical officer of the ship. 'Most certainly not … we try to treat enlisted men the same as officers'. In that phrase is expressed the standard of the medical department of the *Imperator* which the Hospital Corps has tried hard and successfully to attain. When a man is sick he is a patient, a human being in distress, whether he be officer or enlisted man. In medical work there can be no other ideal.[5]

A final bit of excitement occurred as the Treaty of Versailles was about to be signed. German Rear Admiral Ludwig von Reuter skillfully orchestrated for the German High Seas Fleet to be scuttled in Scapa Flow where they remained interned, over worries that the ships would be seized and divided up amongst the Allies after the armistice expired, and perhaps in an attempt to preserve some of their honour. At noon, on 21 June, the hoisting of a red flag was the signal to begin their destruction. The seacocks were opened, explosives strategically placed and the destruction began. The skeleton crews began abandoning their ships.

Within an hour, ships such as the *Derfflinger, Hindenburg, Von der Tann, Moltke* and *Seydlitz* were side-by-side as they sank. The *Seydlitz* turned over with just her keel showing.[6]

The crewmembers in the lifeboats were ordered to cheer by their superiors as they came alongside the HMS *Victorious*. One German officer came aboard with his sword to be handed over to the British officer who had been in command of the interned ships. 'Peace was signed today … We had our orders and have carried them out'. They had not been aware that the armistice had been extended. Slowly they came aboard with large bundles, banjoes and their dogs. An officer wearing the Iron Cross gestured towards the sea dotted with sinking vessels and said, 'See how the German Navy goes down with its flags flying'. A few, such as the *Baden* and *Emden*, remained afloat and were beached.[7]

Finally, on 28 June, following six months of negotiations at the Paris Peace Conference, the Treaty of Versailles was ready to be signed. The key signers, using one gold-plated bronze pen, two white quill pens and three amber-handled gold pens, were US President Woodrow Wilson, British Prime Minister David Lloyd George, German Colonial Minister Dr Johannes Bell, German Foreign Minister Dr Hermann Müeller, and French Premier Georges Clemenceau.[8] Sir Harold Nicholson wrote down his impressions of the day:

> Clemenceau at once breaks the silence. 'Messieurs', he rasps, 'la seance est ouverte'. He adds a few ill-chosen words. 'We are here to sign a Treaty of Peace'. The Germans leap up anxiously when he has finished, since they know that they are the first to sign. William Martin, as if a theatre manager, motions them petulantly to sit down again. Mantoux translates Clemenceau's words into English. Then St. Quentin advances towards the Germans and with the utmost dignity leads them to the little table on which the Treaty is expanded. There is general tension. They sign. There is a general relaxation. Conversation hums again in an undertone.
>
> The delegates stand up one by one and pass onwards to the queue which waits by the signature table. Meanwhile people buzz round the main table getting autographs. The single file of plenipotentiaries waiting to approach the table gets thicker. It goes quickly. The Officials of the Quai d'Orsay stand round, indicating places to sign, indicating procedure, blotting with neat little pads.
>
> Suddenly from outside comes the crash of guns thundering a salute; It announces to Paris that the second Treaty of Versailles has been signed by Dr. Muller and Dr. Bell.[9]

Some declared that the conditions of the treaty were too lenient while others decried them as too harsh. Modern historians still debate this very subject. There were penalties including enormous war reparations (claims for loss of life

Allen (left) and Catherine (right) Loney, *Lusitania* victims. (Kit Abbott Mead Collection/ Patricia Abbott Michl Collection)

Virginia Loney. (Authors' Collection)

and possessions for sinkings like the *Lusitania*, *Sussex* and *Laconia* went on for years), territorial changes and losses, and also Germany was to disarm and 'strictly ... observe the military, naval and air clauses'. Arguably, resentment and anger over the treaty conditions and their economic impact were a significant factor that allowed Adolf Hitler and the Nazi Party to rise to power in the coming decades.

A sample claim for reparations is as follows:

Allen D. Loney, an American national, 43 years of age, with his wife, Catherine [sic] Wolfe Loney, 38 years of age, and only child, Virginia Loney (now Virginia Loney Gamble, by marriage with Robert Gamble ...), then lacking a few days of being 16 years of age, took passage at New York May 1, 1915, on the *Lusitania* for Liverpool. When the *Lusitania* was torpedoed Mr. and Mrs. Loney were lost but their daughter, a claimant herein, was rescued.

Mr. Loney was an experienced broker and bond salesman with an earning capacity of more than $10,000 per annum. For several years prior to his death Mr. Loney had devoted most of his time to assisting his wife in the management of her estate and to the attention and training of their daughter and only child. At the inception of the World War Mr. Loney was in England and shortly thereafter gave up all business activities and joined the Norton-Harjes Ambulance Corps in France. In April 1915, he returned to the United States for his wife and daughter. Mrs. Loney had arranged to take charge of and manage a hospital for convalescent soldiers in England.

As they planned to remain abroad for a considerable time, each member of the family had on the *Lusitania* personal effects of considerable value. The property belonging to Mr. Loney was of the value of $1,235, Mrs. Loney's property was of the value of $11,650, and that of her daughter ... was of the value of $1,700. Claim is also made for expenses incurred by the executors of Mrs. Loney's estate directly resulting from the torpedoing of the *Lusitania*. Some of these items, including legal expenses and disbursements in preparing and presenting this claim, are rejected, but items of expense totaling $3,800 are allowed.

Mr. Loney died intestate, but his daughter ... has inherited his entire estate, which does not appear to have been large. The claimant ... was the sole legatee of her mother's large estate and came into possession of it upon attaining the age of 21 years on May 19, 1920. Both Mr. and Mrs. Loney were physically strong, active socially and in civic affairs, and devoted to the rearing and education of their daughter and only child. This claimant has sustained substantial pecuniary loss in being deprived, at the tender age of 16 years, of the care and supervision of both parents.

Applying the rules announced in the *Lusitania* Opinion and in other decisions of this Commission to the facts as disclosed by the record, the Commission decrees that under the Treaty of Berlin of August 25, 1921, and in accordance with its terms the Government of Germany is obligated to pay to the Government of the United States on behalf of (1) Mrs. Virginia Loney Gamble the sum of twenty-five thousand dollars ($25,000.00) with interest thereon at the rate of five per cent per annum from November 1, 1923, and the further sum of one thousand seven hundred dollars ($1,700.00) with interest thereon at the rate of five per cent per annum from May 7, 1915; (2) the United States Trust Company and George McKesson Brown, Executors of the Estate of Catherine Wolfe Loney, the sum of fifteen thousand four hundred fifty dollars ($15,450.00) with interest thereon at the rate of five per cent per annum from May 7, 1915; and (3) Mary B. Chamberlaine, Executrix of the Estate of Allen D. Loney, the sum of one thousand two hundred thirty-five dollars ($1,235.00) with interest thereon at the rate of five per cent per annum from May 7, 1915.

Done at Washington February 21, 1924.
Edwin B. Parker[10]

With the war over, commendations and praise were being heaped on those that contributed to the Allied victory. Amongst the many veterans, women in the nursing service were nearly unanimously praised by those they tended to. A good example of this is one of the commendations given to American nurses by France:

> Dear Editor: On July 6, tired, hot and thirsty, we all stood in line on board the ship *Imperator*, waiting assignment to our cabins. Our tug had not been able to get to the gang-plank, as they were coaling on one side and taking on troops on the other. After much heated discussion between the tug's captain and the ship's officers, it was decided to raise the gang-way stairs and pull us up to the open door. The difficulty being thus overcome and we had quite safely landed in the hold. Going up several flights of stairs, we were finally brought to a standstill in a crowded hallway and told to wait. A little later we were told that the nurses were wanted in the Recreation Room on B deck. Upon our arrival there, we found the officer in charge of the Army Personnel who, in a few words of introduction, informed us that the French Military Headquarters at Brest had sent out a representative to decorate the nurses of the A.E.F. He then introduced a French General (I am sorry I did not get his name) who made a very pleasing address, in English, in which he said the French military organization and the civilian population of France had looked on with interest at the large number of American women nurses that were brought to France to care for the sick and wounded. To-day he took this opportunity of telling these nurses and through them, all nurses of the A.E.F., that France was very grateful to them for their services in helping to carry the war to a successful issue, that France considered it a privilege to have had these women throughout the length and breadth of her land and honored them for their great help to humanity everywhere. He then introduced some six or eight ladies who came forward, followed by a dozen young girls dressed in white, carrying large bouquets of lilies and roses, which they presented to the chief nurses. Eleanor Keely, with a few appropriate remarks, accepted the decoration for all A.E.F. nurses. All were then formally introduced to the visitors and had a pleasant half-hour trying to converse in French.

> U.S.A. General Hospital No. 2, Laura A. Bekcroft.
> Fort McHenry, Md. Chief Nurse, A.N.C.[11]

Praise was heaped equally on the brave crewmen of former ocean liners that had been pressed into military service and who were demobilising and heading home, as the following letter to the crew of the USS *Louisville* illustrates:

July 31, 1919
Commander H. Hartley, USNRF,
U.S.S. *Louisville*
(Through the Secretary of the Navy).

My dear Commander:

The joint operations of the Army and Navy in connection with our overseas force is rapidly drawing to a close. Before the Navy forces engaged in the Army Transport Service are demobilized, I desire to extend to you and the officers and men under your command, the thanks and appreciation of the War Department for the splendid service you have rendered in connection with the transportation overseas of the American forces.

I know of no one thing that stands out more prominently than the close co-operation which has existed between the services during the past emergency and I am sure it is equally gratifying to you to know that we are near the end of a successful operation of transporting overseas and returning to the American shores, a force of over two million men.

Cordially yours,

Newton D. Baker,
Secretary of War[12]

With peace established and the world recovering from its wounds, people gradually began to resume their pre-war routines. However, it would take years before some travellers were able to cross the ocean without being on the lookout for U-boats on the prowl, or some other threat. Wartime experiences would remain vivid in the minds of many for the rest of their lives, whether they experienced the horrors of it on land or sea, or as a soldier or civilian. Looking back on the First World War was Cunard Purser Charles Spedding, who served on the *Aquitania*, and had survived the sinking of the *Laconia*. Rightly or wrongly, he claimed, 'So after all we did not suffer in vain, for what the sinking of the *Lusitania* started, the sinking of the *Laconia* finished'.[13]

Captain Herbert Hartley (right) shakes hands with US Secretary of Labor James J. Davis (left) during a post-war crossing on the *Leviathan*. (*Camden Courier-Post*, 1923/Authors' Collection)

Bibliography

Abbatiello, John, *Anti-submarine Warfare in World War I: British Naval Aviation and the Defeat of the U-boats*, Oxford: Routledge, 2011.

Amerine, William H., *Alabama's Own in France*, New York: Eaton and Gettinger, 1919.

Anderson, Isabel, *Zigzagging*, Boston: Houghton Mifflin Company, 1918.

Austin, Walter, *A War Zone Gadabout*, Boston: R.H. Hinkley Company, 1917.

Benedict, Clare, *Six Months, March–August 1914*, Cooperstown: Arthur H. Christ Co., 1914.

Bird, Will R., *Ghosts Have Warm Hands, A Memoir of the Great War, 1916–1919*, Ottawa: CEF Books, 1997.

Bridgland, Tony, *Sea Killers in Disguise: Q Ships & Decoy Raiders of WWI*, Annapolis: Naval Institute Press, 1999.

Byrne, William J., Editor, *The Deck School Log of the Navy Auxiliary Reserve*, New York: Wynkoop Hallenbeck Crawford Co., 1920.

Chirnside, Mark, *The Olympic Class Ships: Olympic, Titanic, Britannic*, Stroud: The History Press, 2011.

Davis, Richard Harding, *Adventures and Letters of Richard Harding Davis*, New York: Charles Scribner's Sons, 1917.

Davis, Richard Harding, *With the Allies*, New York: Charles Scribner's Sons, 1919.

Erickson, Edward J., *Ordered to Die: a History of the Ottoman Army in the First World War*, Westport: Greenwood Press, 2001.

Gibson, R.H. and Prendergast, Maurice, *The German Submarine War, 1914–1918*, Maryland: US Naval Institute Press, 2003.

Gilbert, Martin, *The First World War: A Complete History*, New York: Henry Holt, 1994.

Gray, Edwyn A., *The U-Boat War, 1914–1918*, London: Leo Cooper, 1994.

Gray, Randal, *Kaiserlacht 1918: The Final German Offensive*, Oxford: Osprey Publishing, 1991.

Grey, Jeffrey, *A Military History of Australia*, New York: Cambridge University Press, 2008.

Halpern, Paul G., *A Naval History of World War I*, Oxford: Routledge, 2003.

Hawk, George J., *A History of the SS St. Louis, Also Known as the USS Louisville, 1895–1919*, publisher not listed, 1919.

Heckscher, August, *The Politics of Woodrow Wilson*, New York: Harper & Brothers Publishers, 1956.

Hesperidas, Annual Register, 'A Review of Pubic Events at Home and Abroad for the Year 1916', London: Longmans, Green, and Company, 1917.

Hinman, James Rolen, *Ranging in France with Flash and Sound*, Portland: Press of Dunham Printing Company, 1919.

House, Edward Mandell, *The Intimate Papers of Colonel House*, vol. 2, Boston: Houghton Mifflin Company, 1928.

Jessop, Violet, *Titanic Survivor, The Newly Discovered Memoirs of Violet Jessop who Survived both the Titanic and Britannic Disasters*, Introduced, Edited and Annotated by John Maxtone-Graham, New York: Sheridan House, 1997.

Joel, Arthur H., *Under the Lorraine Cross*, Charlotte: Charlotte Tribune, 1921.

Keegan, John, *An Illustrated History of the First World War*, London: Random House, 2001.

Kramer, Harold Morton, *With Seeing Eyes, the Unusual Story of an Observant Thinker at the Front*, Boston: Lothrop, Lee & Shepard Co., 1919.

Lawrence, Jack, *When the Ships Came In*, New York: Farrar & Rinehart, Inc., 1940.

Layton, J. Kent, *The Edwardian Superliners, A Trio of Trios*, Stroud: Amberley, 2013.

Layton, J. Kent, *Lusitania, An Illustrated Biography*, Stroud: Amberley Publishing, 2010.

Masefield, John, *Gallipoli*, London: William Heinemann, 1916.

Massie, Robert K., *Castles of Steel, Britain, Germany, and the Winning of the Great War at Sea*, New York: Random House, 2003.

May, Ernest R., *The World War & American Isolation, 1914–1917*, Chicago: Quadrangle Books, 1966.

Messimer, Dwight R., *Verschollen, World War I U-Boat Losses*, Annapolis: Naval Institute Press, 2002.

Millholland, Ray, *The Splinter Fleet*, New York: The Bobbs-Merrill Co., 1936.

Moorehead, Alan, *Gallipoli*, New York: HarperCollins Publishers, 1956.

Niezychowski, Alfred von, *The Cruise of the Kronprinz Wilhelm: The True Story of a German Cruiser in WWI*, Garden City: Sun Dial Press, Inc., 1938.

Philadelphia War History Committee, *Philadelphia in the World War, 1914–1919*, New York: Wynkoop Hallenbeck Crawford Co., 1922.

Preston, Diana, *Lusitania: An Epic Tragedy*, New York: Walker & Company, 2002.

Purdom, C.B., *Everyman at War: Sixty Personal Narratives of the War*, London: J.M. Dent & Sons, 1930.

Simpson, Colin, *Lusitania*, New York: Penguin Books, 1990.

Simpson, Colin, *The Ship that Hunted Itself*, New York: Stein & Day, 1977.

Spedding, Charles T., *Reminisces of Transatlantic Travellers*, Philadelphia: J.B. Lippincott Company, 1926.

Stenson, Patrick, *The Odyssey of C.H. Lightoller*, New York: Norton & Company, Inc., 1984.

Stevenson, William Yorke, *At the Front in a Flivver*, Boston and New York: Houghton Mifflin Company, 1917.

Stokes, Roy, *Death in the Irish Sea, The Sinking of the RMS Leinster*, West Link Park: The Collins Press, 1998.

Tarrant, V.E., *Jutland, the German Perspective, A New View of the Great Battle*, 31 May 1916, Annapolis: Naval Institute Press, 1995.

Tarrant, V.E., *The U-Boat Offensive 1914–1945*, New York: Sterling Publishing, 2000.

Tennent, A.J., *British Merchant Ships sunk by U-Boats in the 1914–1918 War*, Rogerstone: The Starling Press Limited, 1990.

United States Army Corp of Engineers, *The Three Hundred and First Engineers, A History*, Boston and New York: Houghton Mifflin, 1920.

United States Army AEF 1917–1920, *The Battle of 'Chatillon': A Graphic History of the Second Corps Aeronautical School*, Michigan: The Dean-Hicks Company, 1919.

Wheeler-Bennett, John W., *Brest-Litovsk, The Forgotten Peace, March 1918*, New York: Macmillan and Company, 1938.

Williams, David, *Naval Camouflage 1914–1945: A Complete Visual Reference*, Annapolis: The US Naval Institute Press, 2001.

Williams, David, *Wartime Disasters at Sea*, Somerset: Haynes Publishing, 1997.

Williamson, Gordon, *U-boats of the Kaiser's Navy*, Oxford: Osprey Publishing, 2011.

Willmott, H.P., *World War 1*, New York: Dorling Kindersley, 2003.

Wilson, Bryant & Tooze, Lamar, *With the 364th Infantry in America, France, and Belgium*, New York: The Knickerbocker Press, 1920.

Wyllie, W.L. and Wren, M.F., *Sea Fights of the Great War*, London: Cassell and Company, 1918.

Notes

1 THE DAWNING OF THE GREAT WAR, 1914

1 Willmott, H.P., *World War 1*, New York: Dorling Kindersley, 2003.
2 'How War Came About Between Great Britain and Germany' by H.E. Legge, *Dollar Magazine*, March 1915.
3 *Lawrence Journal-World*, 28/07/1924.
4 Private letter on *Aquitania* letterhead, 4 July 1914. Mike Poirier Collection.
5 Diary entries of an unidentified female passenger who had travelled aboard *Oceanic*, 4 July–4 August 1914. Mike Poirier Collection.
6 *Grand Forks Herald* (henceforth cited as *GFH*) 12/08/1914.
7 Private letters from an identified passenger on *Mauretania* letterhead, dated 1 August–6 August 1914. Mike Poirier Collection.
8 *The Hartford Courant* (henceforth cited as *THC*), 10/08/1914.
9 *Dallas Morning News* (henceforth cited as *DMN*), 18/08/1914.
10 *THC*, 10/08/1914.
11 *DMN*, 18/08/1914.
12 *GFH*, 14/04/1914.
13 *THC*, 10/08/1914; *DMN*, 18/08/1914.
14 *THC*, 10/08/1914.
15 *GFH*, 12/08/1914.
16 Private letters on *Mauretania* letterhead, dated 1 August–6 August 1914. Mike Poirier Collection. The writer's name is unknown.
17 *THC*, 10/08/1914.
18 *DMN*, 18/08/1914.
19 *THC*, 10/08/1914
20 Ibid.
21 Ibid.
22 'RMS *Mauretania* War Service', http://www.tyneandweararchives.org.uk/mauretania/story-warservice.html; Layton, J. Kent, *The Edwardian Superliners, A Trio of Trios*, Stroud: Amberley, 2013 (henceforth cited as *ESL*, 2013).
23 *ESL*, 2013.
24 Layton, J. Kent, *Lusitania, An Illustrated Biography*, Stroud: Amberley Publishing, 2010. (Henceforth cited as *Lusitania*, 2010.)

25 Wyllie, W.L. and Wren, M.F., *Sea Fights of the Great War*, London: Cassell and Company, 1918 (henceforth cited as *Sea Fights*, 1918); Barnes, Eleanor C., *Alfred Yarrow, His Life and Work*, London: Edward Arnold & Co., 1923.

26 *Sea Fights*, 1918; 'Loss of HMS *Amphion* in World War I', http://www.perthone.com/ pampww1.html; List of casualties from the sinking of the *Amphion*, http://www.naval-history.net/xDKCas1914-08Aug.htm. Some sources list the number of crewmembers killed in the *Amphion* sinking as 150 or 151. However, the official casualty list contains the names of 148 crewmembers. There is a discrepancy as to whether eighteen or nineteen of the German survivors from the *Königin Luise* were killed aboard the *Amphion*, and whether twenty or twenty-one were aboard to begin with. Part of this confusion may come from the fact that flying debris from the explosion killed at least one German survivor being held on a nearby ship, muddling the count.

27 *Lusitania*, 2010.

28 *Lusitania*, 2010; Simpson, Colin, *The Ship that Hunted Itself*, New York: Stein & Day, 1977.

29 Niezychowski, Alfred von, *The Cruise of the Kronprinz Wilhelm: The True Story of a German Cruiser in WWI*, Garden City: Sun Dial Press, Inc., 1938 (henceforth cited as *Kronprinz*, 1938).

30 *Cleveland Plain Dealer*, 12/04/1915.

31 Olch, Lt. Isaiah, 'A Breach of Neutrality', *US Naval Institute Proceedings*, vol. 62, July–December 1936.

32 Article on the *Kronprinzessin Cecilie*, http://www.greatships.net/kronprinzessincecilie.html.

33 *The Salt Lake Tribune* (henceforth cited as *SLT*), 05/08/1914.

34 *SLT*, 05/08/1914.

35 Ibid.

36 *GFH*, 12/08/1914.

37 *SLT*, 05/08/1914.

38 *The Illustrated London News* (henceforth cited as *ILN*), 22/08/1914; *Lusitania*, 2010.

39 *ILN*, 22/08/1914. The passenger who gave this account is unnamed.

40 Davis, Richard Harding, *Adventures and Letters of Richard Harding Davis*, Charles Scribner's Sons, 1917 (henceforth cited as *Adventures and Letters*, 1917).

41 *Winnipeg Free Press* (henceforth cited as *WFP*) 29/08/1914. Corey's account was written on 12/08/1914.

42 *WFP*, 29/08/1914.

43 *ILN*, 22/08/1914. The passenger who gave this account is unnamed.

44 *WFP*, 29/08/1914.

45 *Adventures and Letters*, 1917.

46 Davis, Richard Harding, *With the Allies*, New York: Charles Scribner's Sons, 1919.

47 *WFP*, 29/08/1914.

48 Ibid. Guy Standing was a British stage actor, and eventual film actor, who served in the Royal Navy Volunteer Reserve throughout the First World War.

49 Ibid.

50 *ESL*, 2013.

51 *Lusitania*, 2010.

52 Williamson, Gordon, *U-boats of the Kaiser's Navy*, Oxford: Osprey Publishing, 2011.

53   Messimer, Dwight R., *Verschollen, World War I U-Boat Losses*, Annapolis: Naval Institute Press, 2002 (henceforth cited as *Verschollen*, 2002).

54   Gibson, R.H. and Prendergast, Maurice, *The German Submarine War, 1914–1918*, Maryland: US Naval Institute Press, 2003 (henceforth cited as *German Submarine War*, 2003); Tarrant, V.E., *The U-Boat Offensive 1914–1945*, New York, Sterling Publishing, 2000 (henceforth cited as *U-Boat Offensive*, 2000).

55   Kristiania is the modern day Oslo.

56   *GFH*, 26/08/1914.

57   Bainbridge, Sister Carrie, '(US) A Trip Abroad', *Locomotive Engineers Journal*, vol. 49, 1915.

58   Chirnside, Mark, *The Olympic Class Ships: Olympic, Titanic, Britannic*, Stroud: The History Press, 2011 (henceforth cited as *TOCS*, 2011).

59   Ibid.

60   Benedict, Clare, *Six months, March–August 1914*, Cooperstown, Arthur H. Christ Co., 1914.

61   *The Times-Picayune*, 30/08/1914.

62   *TOCS*, 2011.

63   Ibid.

64   Massie, Robert K., *Castles of Steel, Britain, Germany, and the Winning of the Great War at Sea*, New York, Random House, 2003 (henceforth cited as *Castles*, 2003).

65   There is some disagreement as to the number of crewmembers who were aboard the *Pathfinder* when it was sunk, with most contemporary sources indicating that there were between 267 and 277 individuals aboard. The best information, including a list of casualties compiled by the Admiralty (ADM 116/1356 List of Casualties), and a list of the known survivors, indicate that there were 277 individuals aboard, comprised of 275 crewmembers and two civilian canteen assistants. Only eighteen individuals have been documented as having survived the sinking. The actual numbers were confused by newspaper reports, such as that in the 06/09/1914 issue of *The Times*, which incorrectly suggested there were as many as fifty-eight survivors and eighteen wounded, when in fact just eighteen survived.

66   'The Destruction of HMS *Pathfinder*', by Bob Baird and the Clio Collection, http://www.wrecksite.eu/docBrowser.aspx?557?1?1.

67   Log of Kapitänleutnant Otto Hersing.

68   Stenson, Patrick, *The Odyssey of C.H. Lightoller*, New York: Norton & Company, Inc., 1984 (henceforth cited as *Odyssey*, 1984). The details of the *Oceanic*'s loss are drawn from this source.

69   *Castles*, 2003; Weddigen, Lieutenant Otto, 'The First Submarine Blow is Struck', 22/09/1914.

70   Information courtesy of uboat.net/wwi.

71   Not to be confused with the island nation of Trinidad and Tobago, located off the north-eastern coast of Venezuela.

72   *Sea Fights*, 1918.

73   *The Illustrated War News*, 18/11/1914.

74   *Kronprinz*, 1938.

75   Martyn, Frederic, 'Adventures of a Newspaper-Man', *The World Wide*, vol. 43, 1919.

76   *Odyssey*, 1984.

77   'Scotland's designated wreck sites (Protection of Wrecks Act 1973)', http://www.
      historic-scotland.gov.uk/campaniasitedescription.pdf.
78   Austin, Walter, *A War Zone Gadabout*, Boston: R.H. Hinkley Company, 1917.
79   Tennent, A.J., *British Merchant Ships Sunk by U-Boats in the 1914–1918 War*, Rogerstone:
      The Starling Press Limited, 1990 (henceforth cited as *British Merchant Ships*, 1990).
80   House, Edward Mandell, *The Intimate Papers of Colonel House*, vol. 2, Boston: Houghton
      Mifflin Company, 1928.
81   *Lusitania*, 2010.
82   May, Ernest R., *The World War & American Isolation, 1914–1917*, Chicago: Quadrangle
      Books, 1966 (henceforth cited as *Isolation*, 1966).
83   Gray, Edwyn A., *The U-Boat War, 1914–1918*, London: Leo Cooper, 1994 (henceforth
      cited as *U-Boat War*, 1994).
84   *Notts Local News*, 31/10/1914.
85   *The New York Times* (henceforth cited as *NYT*), 26/11/1914; *Auckland Star*, 15/02/1915.
86   *The Daily Mirror* (henceforth cited as *TDM*), 02/11/1914; *Daily Express* (henceforth
      cited as *DE*), 02/11/1914; BBC *Coast*, Series 7, Episode 4, 'Peril from the Seas', aired 3
      June 2012, available online at: http://www.bbc.co.uk/iplayer/episode/b01jrv9l/Coast_
      Series_7_Peril_from_the_Seas/.
87   *DE*, 06/11/1914.
88   List of losses by month, available online at: http://www.uboat.net/wwi/ships_hit/
      losses_year.html. (Henceforth cited as *Monthly Losses*.) This list provides the name,
      nationality, details and tonnage of ships lost per month to U-boats during the war. Also,
      the list available on naval-history.net at the following URL lists the losses of ships by
      month during the war, both from U-boats and other causes: http://www.naval-history.
      net/WW1LossesBrMS1914-16.htm.
89   List of U-boat construction by year, available online at http://www.uboat.net/wwi/
      types/shipyards.html (henceforth cited as *U-boat Construction*).
90   *U-Boat War*, 1994.

2   ESCALATION, 1915

1   *Monthly Losses*.
2   *Isolation*, 1966.
3   Ibid.
4   Ibid.
5   *Schenectady Gazette*, 09/02/1915.
6   *Los Angeles Times*, 28/02/1915; The 'Seton-Thompson' mentioned in Irwin's account was
     actually Ernest Thompson Seton, the famed writer and wildlife artist.
7   *Lusitania*, 2010.
8   *NYT*, 03/02/1915.
9   *Duluth News-Tribune* (henceforth cited as *DNT*), 28/02/1915.
10   *Lusitania*, 2010.
11   *Monthly Losses*.
12   'The Dover Barrage', by Michael Duffy, http://www.firstworldwar.com/atoz/
     doverbarrage.htm; *Verschollen*, 2002.

13 *Lusitania*, 2010.

14 Private letter written by Jack Bolar on *Lusitania* letterhead, dated 24/03/1915. Mike Poirier Collection.

15 Private letter written by Len Sloane on *Lusitania* letterhead, dated 26/03/1915. Mike Poirier Collection. 'Lehar Op' appears to be a reference to the operas of Franz Lehár, an Austro-Hungarian composer who was popular at the time.

16 Stringer, Craig, 'Falaba's sinking begins march to war', *Voyage*, vol. 53, Fall 2005. Details on the sinking of *Falaba* are drawn from this article.

17 *Grey River Argus*, 03/05/1915.

18 Ibid.

19 *The Liverpool Echo*, 30/03/1915.

20 Ibid.

21 *Isolation*, 1966.

22 *Isolation*, 1966; Simpson, Colin, *Lusitania*, New York, Penguin Books, 1990.

23 *Isolation*, 1966.

24 *Monthly Losses*.

25 *Lusitania*, 2010

26 *The Lima Sunday News*, 30/05/1915.

27 *Cleveland Press*, 30/04/1915.

28 *The Brooklyn Daily Eagle*, 30/05/1915.

29 *Lusitania*, 2010.

30 Erickson, Edward J., *Ordered to Die: a History of the Ottoman Army in the First World War*, Westport, Greenwood Press, 2001.

31 Moorehead, Alan, *Gallipoli*, New York: HarperCollins Publishers, 1956; Masefield, John, *Gallipoli*, London: William Heinemann, 1916. Details of the Gallipoli Campaign are drawn from these sources.

32 *The American Journal of International Law*, vol. 15, January 1921.

33 *Monthly Losses*.

34 *ESL*, 2013.

35 Preston, Diana, *Lusitania: An Epic Tragedy*, New York: Walker & Company, 2002.

36 *The Times History of the War*, vol. 5, 1915.

37 *ESL*, 2013.

38 *NYT*, 8 May 1915.

39 *NYT*, 2 May 1915

40 *NYT*, 8 May 1915

41 *NYT*, 8 May 1915; *NYT*, 2 May 1915.

42 *The Daily Star*, 8 March 1915; *NYT*, 2 May 1915.

43 *ESL*, 2013; *Lusitania*, 2010. Details on the *Lusitania*'s final voyage from the departure until this point are primarily drawn from the above works.

44 War Diary of *U-20* written by Walther Schwieger, translated from German by the American War Archives of the Navy, and held by the National Archives and Records Administration. Courtesy of J. Kent Layton.

45 Ibid.

46 *The Denver Post*, 16/04/12.

47 *New York Tribune*, 30/04/12.

48   Memoirs of Angela Countess Bakeev, dated 04/12/1929. Courtesy of Demetrio Baffa
      Trasci Amalfitani di Crucoli, and translated from Italian by Jill Capaldi. Angela states in
      this account that James Baker was with her and her husband when the torpedo struck.
      However, Baker doesn't mention Angela or her husband in his own 1915 account, saying
      that he was alone when the torpedo struck. Her memory was likely playing tricks on
      her since several years had passed. In fact, she kept naming Baker, when she seems to
      have meant Leonidas Bistis, described as being with her husband and her in some of her
      earlier accounts, and as having boarded the lifeboat with them. Additionally, Bakeev's
      mention of where Sir Hugh Lane's paintings were located during the voyage is the first
      mention of this in ninety-nine years. The paintings appear to have been in his portside
      cabin, D-26, which was an outside cabin.

49   Private letter written by Angela Countess Bakeev to her father, courtesy of Demetrio
      Baffa Trasci Amalfitani di Crucoli, and translated from Italian by Jill Capaldi.

50   Dole, Nathan Haskell, *America in Spitsbergen*, vol. 2, University of Michigan Library, 1922.
      Turner's accounts are drawn from this book.

51   *U-Boat War*, 1994.

52   *NYT*, 9 May 1915.

53   *Isolation*, 1966.

54   Ibid.

55   *U-Boat War*, 1994.

56   Private typed letter written by an American citizen to a British soldier named Val, dated
      23/07/1915. Tad Fitch Collection.

57   Private letter from a girl named Beatie on *Missanabie* letterhead, dated 14/05/1915. Mike
      Poirier Collection.

58   *Trenton Evening Times*, 02/06/1915.

59   'RMS *Mauretania* War Service', http://www.tyneandweararchives.org.uk/mauretania/
      story-warservice.html.

60   *ESL*, 2013.

61   *Monthly Losses*.

62   *NYT*, 22 June 1915.

63   Ibid.

64   *NYT*, 23 June 1915.

65   *Monthly Losses*.

66   List of U-boat losses between 1914 and 1918, available online at: http://www.uboat.net/
      wwi/fates/losses.html. (Henceforth cited as *U-boat Losses*.)

67   *U-Boat War*, 1994.

68   *The Survey*, 31/07/1915.

69   *NYT*, 18/07/1915. The details and accounts pertaining to *Orduna* prior to this point are
      drawn from this source.

70   *DMN*, 18/07/1915; *New York Times*, 18/07/1915.

71   *Monthly Losses*.

72   *Verschollen*, 2002. Graeff's account is quoted from this source.

73   Article on Q-ships, 'British Special Service or Q-Ships', http://www.naval-history.net/
      WW1NavyBritishQships.htm. It is noted in this article that because of problems with
      definition, duplication and the highly secretive nature of Q-ship operations, the figures
      of the number of U-boats sunk and the number of Q-ships lost are approximate. It is also

clarified that not all of the Q-ships lost were while on Secret Service, but some may have been sunk after reverting to other duties.

74 The number of men listed as having died in this sinking varies widely depending on the source. A.J. Tennent reports in *British Merchant Ships*, 1990, that 132 were lost, which is the lowest number given, and seems to account for crewmembers only. Uboat.net lists the number as 866. On the high end, Martin Gilbert, in his book *The First World War: A Complete History*, New York: Henry Holt, 1994, gives the number as 1,865. Other researchers seem to settle on every number in between.

75 *Western Daily Press*, 11/09/1915.

76 *Isolation*, 1966.

77 *Oakland Tribune*, 09/09/1915.

78 Affidavit of Frederick Steele, filed at the United States Consulate in Liverpool on 17/08/1915.

79 Affidavit of William Cummins, filed at the United States Consulate in Liverpool on 21/08/1915.

80 Affidavit of Claude M. Roode, filed at the United States Consulate in Liverpool on 21/08/1915.

81 Affidavit of William Finch, filed at the United States Consulate in Liverpool on 23/08/1915.

82 *Verschollen*, 2002; Halpern, Paul G., *A Naval History of World War I*, Oxford: Routledge, 2003; Bridgland, Tony, *Sea Killers in Disguise: Q Ships & Decoy Raiders of WWI*, Annapolis: Naval Institute Press, 1999. The details of the '*Baralong* Incident' are drawn from the above listed sources.

83 Doenecke, Justus D., *Nothing Less than War, A New History of America's Entry into WWI*, Lexington: The University Press of Kentucky, 2011 (henceforth cited as *Less than War*, 2011).

84 Hesperidas, *Annual Register, A Review of Pubic Events at Home and Abroad for the Year 1916*, London: Longmans, Green, and Company, 1917.

85 *NYT*, 06/01/1916.

86 'Scandal of the Baralong Incident was Hidden in Veil of Secrecy', by Gary O'Neill, *Iris na Mara*, vol. 1, Spring 2006.

87 *Isolation*, 1966. The political manoeuvrings following the *Arabic* sinking are pulled from the above source.

88 *Isolation*, 1966; *U-Boat War*, 1994; Article on the U-boat war, 'Für Kaiser und Reich, His Imperial German Majesty's U-Boats in WWI', by Clemens Brechtelsbauer, http://www.uboat.net/history/wwi/ (henceforth cited as *Für Kaiser*). The description of the resolution to the diplomatic crisis following the *Arabic* sinking is drawn from the above listed sources.

89 *Less than War*, 2011.

90 *Isolation*, 1966; *Für Kaiser*; *U-Boat War*, 1994.

91 *The Morning Oregonian*, 18/09/1915.

92 *ESL*, 2013.

93 *Monthly Losses*.

94 Article on the Battle of Loos, http://www.webmatters.net/france/ww1_loos.htm.

95 *TDM*, 06/09/1915.

96 Affidavit signed by *Hesperian's* senior officers, cabled to the State Department on 07/09/1915 by Consul Frost in Queenstown.

97 *DE*, 09/09/1915.

98 *Isolation*, 1966.

99 *The Singapore Free Press and Mercantile Advertiser*, 01/11/1915.

100 *TOCS*, 2011.

101 *Monthly Losses*.

102 *The Sydney Morning Herald*, 11/12/1928.

103 *The Ballarat Courier*, 08/12/1915.

104 Private letter written by Harold Beechey, dated 05/10/1915. This letter is quoted with the permission of the Lincolnshire Archives.

105 *Monthly Losses*.

106 *The Indianapolis Sunday Star*, 21/11/1915

107 Deposition of Cecile Greil, filed at the United States Consulate in Tunisia, 18/11/1915.

108 *The New York Times Current History: The European War* (henceforth cited as *NYT Current History*), vol. VI, January–March 1916.

109 *Isolation*, 1966.

110 *NYT*, 11/11/1915.

111 Private letter written by James MacKinnon to Marion Howard, undated. Tad Fitch Collection.

112 *Monthly Losses*.

113 Grey, Jeffrey, *A Military History of Australia*, New York: Cambridge University Press, 2008.

114 Correspondence from Consul Keblinger to Secretary of State Lansing, 08/01/1916.

115 Rolls-Royce recently produced a short film discussing the origins of the 'Spirit of Ecstasy', which is titled the 'The Graceful Little Goddess', and that is available at the following URL: http://www.rolls-roycemotorcars.com/stories/21st-century-legends/.

116 Affidavit of John W.E. Douglas-Scott-Montagu, filed at the United States Consulate in Alexandria on 09/01/1916.

117 Affidavit of Charles L. Martin, filed at the United States Consulate in Alexandria on 09/01/1916.

118 Affidavit of Harold G.S. Wood, filed at the Foreign Office on 20/01/1916.

119 *Isolation*, 1966; BBC *Timewatch* series, episode 'The Lost Liner & the Empire's Gold', aired 21/01/2004. The information regarding Valentiner's log book is drawn from the latter source.

120 BBC *Timewatch* series, episode 'The Lost Liner & the Empire's Gold', aired 21/01/2004.

121 *Monthly Losses*.

122 U-boat Losses.

123 *U-boat Construction*.

3 THE WANING AND RESURGENT U-BOAT OFFENSIVE, 1916

1 Tarrant, V.E., *Jutland, the German Perspective, A New View of the Great Battle*, 31 May 1916, Annapolis: Naval Institute Press, 1995.

2 *ESL*, 2013.

3   *Kai Tiaki: The Journal of the Nurses of New Zealand*, vol. X, Issue 1, January 1917.

4   *Monthly Losses*.

5   Article on the battle, 'The Battle of Verdun', http://www.historylearningsite.co.uk/battle_of_verdun.htm.

6   The History Channel article, 'This Day in History: Battle of Verdun Begins', http://www.history.com/this-day-in-history/battle-of-verdun-begins.

7   *ESL*, 2013.

8   *U-Boat War*, 1994.

9   *The Journal-Tribune*, 02/03/1916.

10 'The End of *Empress of Fort William*', by W.D. Shepherd, *The Marine Review*, vol. 46, November 1916.

11 *Monthly Losses*.

12 *ESL*, 2013.

13 Stevenson, William Yorke, *At the Front in a Flivver*, Boston and New York, Houghton Mifflin Company, 1917.

14 *U-Boat War*, 1994.

15 *U-Boat Offensive*, 2000.

16 *Verschollen*, 2002.

17 *ESL*, 2013.

18 *Monthly Losses*.

19 *NYT*, 15/04/1916.

20 *Philadelphia Inquirer*, 16/05/1916.

21 *Isolation*, 1966.

22 *U-Boat War*, 1994; *Isolation*, 1966.

23 *Monthly Losses*.

24 *German Submarine War*, 2003.

25 *The Missionary Review of the World*, vol. 39, January–December 1916.

26 Private letter from Wilfred Satchell to his mother, 06/04/1916. Quoted with permission of the letter's owner, who wishes to remain anonymous.

27 *The Horsham Times*, 02/10/1914.

28 *Monthly Losses*.

29 Ibid.

30 Detailed and interactive description of the actions at the Battle of Jutland, available online at: http://www.battle-of-jutland.com/; Article on the Battle of Jutland, 'The Battle of Jutland, 1916', by Michael Duffy, http://www.firstworldwar.com/battles/jutland.htm; *U-Boat War*, 1994. The description of the Battle of Jutland is drawn from the above sources.

31 Details on the sinking of the *Hampshire*, available online at: http://www.uboat.net/wwi/ships_hit/2691.html.

32 Some sources indicate that there were fourteen survivors, and there is disagreement in contemporary reports.

33 *The Press*, 17/06/1916.

34 *U-Boat War*, 1994.

35 'Steamrollered in Galicia: The Austro-Hungarian Army and the Brusilov Offensive, 1916', by John. R. Schindler, *War in History*, vol. 10, number 1, January 2003; Keegan, John, *An Illustrated History of the First World War*, London, Random House, 2001

(henceforth cited as *Illustrated History*, 2001). Details of the Brusilov Offensive are drawn from these sources.

36   *Monthly Losses.*

37   *ESL,* 2013.

38   *U-Boat War,* 1994; *NYT Current History,* vol. IX, October–December 1916.

39   *Illustrated History,* 2001; Article on the Battle of the Somme, http://www. historylearningsite.co.uk/somme.htm. Details of the Battle of the Somme are drawn from these sources.

40   Article on Fryatt's capture and execution, 'World War I History: Germans Execute Captain Fryatt of the British Mercantile Marine', http://unnamedharald.hubpages. com/hub/World-War-1-History-Germans-Execute-Captain-Fryatt-of-the-British-Merchant-Marine; Additional details pulled from a real photo postcard commemorating the death of Captain Fryatt that was printed in 1918.

41   *Monthly Losses.*

42   *ESL,* 2013.

43   Abbatiello, John, *Anti-submarine Warfare in World War I: British Naval Aviation and the Defeat of the U-boats,* Oxford: Routledge, 2011.

44   Message on the back of a postcard featuring *UC-5,* dated 30/06/1916. Tad Fitch Collection.

45   *Monthly Losses.*

46   *U-Boat War,* 1994.

47   Entry written in the log book of *U-57* by Kapitänleutnant von Georg.

48   *U-Boat War,* 1994.

49   *Monthly Losses.*

50   *ESL,* 2013; 'RMS *Mauretania* War Service', http://www.tyneandweararchives.org.uk/ mauretania/story-warservice.html.

51   *NYT Current History,* vol. IX, October–December 1916.

52   *THC,* 26/10/1924.

53   *NYT Current History,* vol. IX, October–December 1916.

54   *THC,* 20/10/1916.

55   *Idaho Statesman,* 17 October 1916.

56   *NYT Current History,* vol. IX, October–December 1916.

57   *U-Boat War,* 1994.

58   Information on the sinking of the *Rappahannock*: http://www.wrecksite.eu/wreck. aspx?12551#130740.

59   *Monthly Losses.*

60   *ESL,* 2013.

61   Jessop, Violet, *Titanic Survivor, The Newly Discovered Memoirs of Violet Jessop who Survived both the Titanic and Britannic Disasters,* Introduced, Edited and Annotated by John Maxtone-Graham, New York, Sheridan House, 1997 (henceforth cited as *Titanic Survivor,* 1997).

62   *Titanic Survivor,* 1997. All quotes and references to Jessop throughout this section are drawn from this source.

63   *TOCS,* 2011; *ESL,* 2013. The details and events of the *Britannic*'s sinking throughout this portion of the text are drawn from these sources.

64   *The Queenslander,* 17/03/1917.

65   *NYT*, 24/11/1916.

66   *The Sydney Morning Herald*, 25/11/1916.

67   *The Scotsman*, 21/11/2008. Jewell's letters about the *Titanic* and *Britannic* were recently auctioned off.

68   http://www.divernet.com/Wrecks/159163/the_truth_about_britannic.html. Sadly, Spencer died while filming the *Britannic* wreck in 2009.

69   Private letter dated 02/01/1917, Trevor Powell Collection.

70   *Monthly Losses*.

71   *U-Boat War*, 1994; *Isolation*, 1966.

72   The text of the peace note is available online: http://germanhistorydocs.ghi-dc.org/ sub_document.cfm?document_id=985.

73   *The Kansas City Star*, (henceforth cited as *TKCS*) 04/01/1916.

74   Details on Holtzendorff's case as well as the complete text of his memorandum are available online at the following URL: http://www.gwpda.org/naval/ holtzendorffmemo.htm.

75   *Monthly Losses*.

76   *U-boat Losses*.

77   *U-boat Construction*

4   UNRESTRICTED, 1917

1   *Western Perth Mail*, 23/02/1917.

2   *The Advertiser*, 24/02/1917.

3   *Isolation*, 1966.

4   *The Lowell Sun*, 01/02/1917.

5   Williams, David, *Wartime Disasters at Sea*, Somerset, Haynes Publishing, 1997.

6   *Illinois State Journal Springfield*, 01/01/1918.

7   *Monthly Losses*.

8   *U-Boat War*, 1994.

9   Issue of *Cunard Daily Bulletin* printed aboard *Laconia* and saved by survivor Arthur Kirby. 22/02/1917. Mike Poirier Collection.

10   *Supplement to the American Journal of International Law*, vol. 11, No. 4, October 1917. All the *Laconia* affidavits are from this source.

11   Private account written by Jacob Fotheringham, courtesy of Neil Fotheringham.

12   *The Syndney Morning Herald*, 24/06/1924.

13   *THC*, 26/10/1924.

14   *Philadelphia Inquirer*, 18/03/1917.

15   *Isolation*, 1966.

16   The text of the Zimmerman Telegram is available online: http://wwi.lib.byu.edu/index. php/The_Zimmerman_Note.

17   Read more at the American Presidency Project: Woodrow Wilson: Address to a Joint Session of Congress, 'Request for Authority': http://www.presidency.ucsb.edu/ ws/?pid=65398#ixzz2gKhtjPyX.

18   *Isolation*, 1966.

19   *Monthly Losses*.

20 *The Atlantic Monthly*, vol. 121, January–June 1918.
21 *Monthly Losses*.
22 Heckscher, August, *The Politics of Woodrow Wilson*, New York: Harper & Brothers Publishers, 1956.
23 Ibid.
24 http://www.worthpoint.com/worthopedia/hmt-arcadian-1891-royal-mail-306503693.
25 Purdom, C.B., *Everyman at War: Sixty Personal Narratives of the War*, London: J.M. Dent & Sons, 1930.
26 *The Aberdeen Daily Journal*, 16/05/1917. Threlfall is correct about the date of the sinking being the anniversary of the *Titanic* disaster, but it was a Monday when it sank, and a Sunday when the *Arcadian* did.
27 *The Red Cross Magazine*, vol. 13, no. 7, July 1918.
28 *Monthly Losses*.
29 http://www.clydesite.co.uk/clydebuilt/viewship.asp?id=19107.
30 *The Argus*, 17/08/1917.
31 Hinman, James Rolen, *Ranging in France with Flash and Sound*, Portland: Press of Dunham Printing Company, 1919.
32 *Bay City Times*, 08/06/1917.
33 *Monthly Losses*
34 Ibid.
35 *The Evening Star*, 01/07/1917.
36 *Monthly Losses*.
37 *U-Boat War*, 1994.
38 *Monthly Losses*.
39 http://www.cityofart.net/bship/u_boat.html.
40 Lawrence, Jack, *When the Ships Came In*, New York, Farrar & Rinehart, Inc., 1940; Williams, David, *Naval Camouflage 1914–1945: A Complete Visual Reference*, Annapolis: The US Naval Institute Press, 2001; Raven, Alan, *The Development of Naval Camouflage, 1914–1945*, http://www.shipcamouflage.com/1_1.htm. The information about early camouflage efforts and the development of dazzle camouflage is drawn from the above sources.
41 Private letter written by John E. Metzger on board the *Rijndam*, dated 01/09/1918. Tad Fitch Collection.
42 *Being the Narrative of Battery A of the 101st Field Artillery*, Boston: Loomis & Company, 1919.
43 *Monthly Losses*.
44 Biographical details of Walther Schwieger: http://www.uboat.net/wwi/men/commanders/322.html.
45 *Boston Herald*, 22/09/1917.
46 Anderson, Isabel, *Zigzagging*, Boston: Houghton Mifflin Company, 1918.
47 *Monthly Losses*.
48 Amerine, William H., *Alabama's Own in France*, New York: Eaton and Gettinger, 1919.
49 *Monthly Losses*.
50 Kramer, Harold Morton, *With Seeing Eyes, The Unusual Story of an Observant Thinker at the Front*, Boston: Lothrop, Lee & Shepard Co., 1919.
51 *The Nursing Mirror and Midwives' Journal*, 09/02/1918.

52 Ibid.
53 *Daily Chronicle*, 10/02/1918; http://www.warpoetry.co.uk/Maureen_Jones.html.
54 *U-boat Losses*.
55 *U-boat Construction*

5   OVER THERE, 1918

1   The complete text of the 'Fourteen Points' address is available at the following link: http://www.ourdocuments.gov/doc.php?flash=true&doc=62.
2   *ESL*, 2013.
3   Philadelphia War History Committee, *Philadelphia in the World War, 1914–1919*, New York: Wynkoop Hallenbeck Crawford Co., 1922.
4   *Monthly Losses*.
5   Wheeler-Bennett, John W., *Brest-Litovsk, The Forgotten Peace, March 1918*, New York: Macmillan and Company, 1938.
6   *THC*, 8/02/1918.
7   *THC*, 26/10/1924.
8   Article on the *Tuscania* sinking, 'The Loss of the Troopship *Tuscania*', http://www.islayinfo.com/loss-troopship-tuscania-islay.html.
9   Acacia Fraternity, *The Triad*, vol. 12–14, 1918.
10 *Darlington Democrat*, 11/07/1918.
11 *Ohio State University Monthly*, vol. 9–10, Ohio: Ohio State University Alumni Association, 1918.
12 United States Army AEF 1917–1920, *The Battle of 'Chatillon': A Graphic History of the Second Corps Aeronautical School*, Michigan: The Dean-Hicks Company, 1919.
13 *Monthly Losses*.
14 Gray, Randal, *Kaiserlacht 1918: The Final German Offensive*, Oxford, Osprey Publishing, 1991; *Illustrated History*, 2001. Details of the Spring Offensive are as described in these sources.
15 *ESL*, 2013.
16 *Monthly Losses*.
17 Article on the *Leviathan*, http://www.ocean-liners.com/ships/vat.asp; *ESL*, 2013.
18 *The History of the 306th Field Artillery*, New York: The Knickerbocker Press, 1920.
19 *Monthly Losses*.
20 *The Fort Wayne Journal-Gazette*, 06/07/1919.
21 *Monthly Losses*.
22 Millholland, Ray, *The Splinter Fleet*, New York: The Bobbs-Merrill Co., 1936.
23 *The New Orleans Item*, 08/06/1918.
24 *The Northern Barrage, Mine Force, United States Atlantic Fleet*, Annapolis: The US Naval Institute Press, 1919. This yearbook contains a record of the activities of the Mine Force; 'The Northern Barrage', by Albert Therberge Jr., *Hydro International*, vol.17, no.2, March 2013.
25 Private letter written by an American sailor named Frank, 30/11/1918. Tad Fitch Collection.
26 United States Army Corp of Engineers, *The Three Hundred and First Engineers, A History*, Boston and New York: Houghton Mifflin, 1920.

27 *DNT*, 08/07/1918.

28 *The Independent*, 18/12/2006.

29 'German War Trials: Judgment in Case of Lieutenants Dithmar and Boldt', *The American Journal of International Law*, vol. 16, October 1922.

30 Information available online at http://www.uboat.net/wwi/men/commanders/237.html.

31 *Monthly Losses*.

32 Articles on the battle, 'Second Battle of the Marne', http://www.worldwar1.com/dbc/2marne.htm; 'The Second Battle of the Marne, 1918'; http://www.firstworldwar.com/battles/marne2.htm; *Illustrated History*, 2001. Details of the battle are drawn from these sources.

33 Byrne, William J., Editor, *The Deck School Log of the Navy Auxiliary Reserve*, New York: Wynkoop Hallenbeck Crawford Co., 1920.

34 Private letter written by John E. Metzger on board the *Rijndam*, dated 06/07/1918. Tad Fitch Collection.

35 Private letter written by John E. Metzger on board the *Rijndam*, dated 14/07/1918. Tad Fitch Collection.

36 Joel, Arthur H., *Under the Lorraine Cross*, Charlotte: Charlotte Tribune, 1921.

37 *ESL*, 2013.

38 Wilson, Bryant & Tooze, Lamar, *With the 364th Infantry in America, France, and Belgium*, New York: The Knickerbocker Press, 1920.

39 Bird, Will R., *Ghosts Have Warm Hands, A Memoir of the Great War, 1916–1919*, Ottawa: CEF Books, 1997.

40 *NYT*, 20/07/1918.

41 Affidavit of William Prothero, filed at the United States Consulate in Liverpool on 19/07/1918.

42 *The Boston Globe* (henceforth cited as *TBG*) 29/07/1918.

43 *Monthly Losses*.

44 Private letter written by Art White, dated 17/08/1918. Tad Fitch Collection.

45 Private letter written by Art White, dated 20/09/1918. Tad Fitch Collection.

46 *Monthly Losses*.

47 Annual Report of the Secretary of the Navy, For the Fiscal Year of 1918, Washington: Government Printing Office, 1918.

48 *NYT*, 20/09/1918.

49 *Monthly Losses*.

50 *Utica Herald Dispatch* (henceforth cited as *UHD*), 12/10/1918.

51 *NYT*, 18/08/1918.

52 Private letter written by Mary Maxwell, dated 16/10/1918. Tad Fitch Collection.

53 Private letter written by John E. Hertz, dated 23/10/1918. Tad Fitch Collection.

54 Private letter written by Art White, dated 19/09/1918. Tad Fitch Collection; Center for Disease Control article on the 'Spanish Flu', http://wwwnc.cdc.gov/eid/article/12/1/05-0979_article.htm.

55 Private letter written by John E. Metzger, dated 26/10/1918. Tad Fitch Collection.

56 Article on the *Otranto* sinking: http://freepages.military.rootsweb.ancestry.com/~cacunithistories/HMS_Otranto.html.

57 *The Courier*, 12/10/1918.

58 *UHD*, 12/10/1918.

59 Stokes, Roy, *Death in the Irish Sea, The sinking of the RMS Leinster*, West Link Park: The
    Collins Press, 1998 (henceforth cited as *Irish Sea*, 1998).

60 *The Dover Express and East Kent News*, 18/10/1918.

61 *Irish Sea*, 1998.

62 *Für Kaiser.*

63 Private letter written by J. Clark, dated 11/01/1919. Tad Fitch Collection.

64 Telegram sent to Mary Barlow. Tad Fitch Collection.

65 *Verschollen*, 2002.

66 Ibid.

67 *Monthly Losses.*

68 *U-Boat War*, 1994.

69 Ibid.

70 *Für Kaiser.*

71 Article on the U-boat war by Dr. Gary Sheffield, 'The First Battle of the Atlantic',
    http://www.bbc.co.uk/history/worldwars/wwone/battle_atlantic_ww1_01.shtml.

72 *Für Kaiser.*

6 EPILOGUE, 1919

1   *TBG*, 01/01/1919.

2   Hawk, George J., *A History of the SS St Louis, Also Known as the USS Louisville, 1895–
    1919,* publisher not listed, 1919 (henceforth cited as *St Louis,* 1919)

3   Private letter written by Hank Deckert, dated 30/04/1919. Tad Fitch Collection.

4   http://www.greatships.net/arabic3.html.

5   'A Sick Bay Deluxe', *Hospital Corps Quarterly*, Issues 8–11, 1919.

6   *Macon Telegraph*, 22/06/1919.

7   *TKCS*, 23/06/1919.

8   *Wilkes-Barre Times-Leader*, 28/06/1919.

9   http://www.eyewitnesstohistory.com/versailles.htm.

10 US Mixed Claims Commission, 1925.

11 *The American Journal of Nursing*, vol. 20, number 12, 1920.

12 *St Louis*, 1919.

13 Spedding, Charles T., *Reminisces of Transatlantic Travellers*, Philadelphia: J.B. Lippincott
    Company, 1926.

Index